Economic Evaluation in Education

Third Edition

Sara Miller McCune founded SAGE Publishing in 1965 to support the dissemination of usable knowledge and educate a global community. SAGE publishes more than 1000 journals and over 800 new books each year, spanning a wide range of subject areas. Our growing selection of library products includes archives, data, case studies and video. SAGE remains majority owned by our founder and after her lifetime will become owned by a charitable trust that secures the company's continued independence.

Los Angeles | London | New Delhi | Singapore | Washington DC | Melbourne

Economic Evaluation in Education

Cost-Effectiveness and Benefit-Cost Analysis

Third Edition

Henry M. Levin
Teachers College, Columbia University

Patrick J. McEwan
Wellesley College

Clive Belfield
Queens College, City University of New York

A. Brooks Bowden
North Carolina State University

Robert Shand
Ohio State University

Los Angeles | London | New Delhi
Singapore | Washington DC | Melbourne

SAGE

FOR INFORMATION:

SAGE Publications, Inc.
2455 Teller Road
Thousand Oaks, California 91320
E-mail: order@sagepub.com

SAGE Publications Ltd.
1 Oliver's Yard
55 City Road
London EC1Y 1SP
United Kingdom

SAGE Publications India Pvt. Ltd.
B 1/I 1 Mohan Cooperative Industrial Area
Mathura Road, New Delhi 110 044
India

SAGE Publications Asia-Pacific Pte. Ltd.
3 Church Street
#10-04 Samsung Hub
Singapore 049483

Copyright © 2018 by SAGE Publications, Inc.

Printed in the United States of America

ISBN 978-1-4833-8180-0

This book is printed on acid-free paper.

Acquisitions Editor: Helen Salmon
Editorial Assistant: Chelsea Neve
Production Editor: Olivia Weber-Stenis
Copy Editor: Megan Markanich
Typesetter: C&M Digitals (P) Ltd.
Proofreader: Scott Oney
Indexer: Scott Smiley
Cover Designer: Glenn Vogel
Marketing Manager: Susannah Goldes

MIX
Paper from
responsible sources
FSC® C014174

17 18 19 20 21 10 9 8 7 6 5 4 3 2 1

Brief Contents

Detailed Contents

List of Tables, Figures, and Examples

Tables

Figures

Examples

Preface

The first edition of this volume was published in 1983 and the second edition in 2001. Unfortunately, over this long period, there was mostly a lot of talk about cost-effectiveness (CE) analysis, but there was not very much action.

In the past decade, there has been a lot more investigation of CE and benefit-cost (BC) analysis. At every level of government, education decisionmakers are being asked to accomplish more with the same or even fewer resources. There is great hope that new educational technologies will improve education and reduce cost, but decades of promises have resulted in few studies incorporating effectiveness and cost and even less conclusive evidence. Philanthropies are more eager to calculate their "return on investment" in social programs. And, in an era of greater accountability, the general public is increasingly scrutinizing how resources are allocated to schools and colleges. Even academic journals have become more accepting of articles applying CE and BC analyses. These pressures and interests have fostered more research and inquiry into the efficiency of educational spending.

With this new attention, it is especially important that cost evaluation be performed to a rigorous standard and that it be expressed in such a way that it can be widely understood by policymakers, education professionals, and the general citizenry. To meet this imperative, these audiences need a thorough and detailed explication of what cost evaluation is and how it should be performed.

To our knowledge, this book remains the only full-length treatment of the subject for education researchers. Some general textbooks for evaluators devote a section to the topic (notably Boardman, Greenberg, Vining, & Weimer, 2011), and two recent books have set out general standards and principles (for health, see Neumann, Sanders, Russell, Siegel, & Ganiat, 2016; for general methodology, see Farrow & Zerbe, 2013). By contrast, this book is focused completely on the rationale and methods of economic evaluation in the field of education. Its primary distinction from other texts is its extensive treatment of how to perform cost analyses.

Since the second edition of this book, there has been considerable methodological development in the evaluation literature. This development in part reflects the intensive use of CE analysis by health researchers, but it also reflects the greater empiricism practiced by education researchers. We hope this new edition clearly expresses these methodological developments so that researchers can apply more advanced methods. As well, we hope this new edition adequately includes this new empirical research so that more is known about what investments are socially efficient.

The volume has undergone substantial modification from earlier editions. As in the second edition, we continued to replace and update many of the examples with recent cost studies from education. We further updated the text with references to methodological and applied research.

We have also added several new chapters. There is a new chapter (Chapter 2) on how to structure an economic analysis so that it is properly integrated with an impact evaluation. Often, getting the right structure for an economic evaluation is one of the most difficult challenges; in Chapter 2, we describe how such an evaluation should be articulated to a theory of change. To more clearly explain cost evaluation, we have expanded to four chapters (Chapters 3–6), with an explicit separation between identifying ingredients (in Chapter 4) and pricing them out (in Chapter 5). This edition includes a separate chapter (Chapter 7) on how to measure effectiveness; perhaps surprisingly, how effectiveness is measured is often the most contentious part of CE analysis. This new Chapter 7 sets out the preferred qualities of an effectiveness measure for the purposes of performing a CE analysis, the reporting that is formally set out in Chapter 8. Following on, this edition has an additional chapter—and much more detail—on estimating benefits (Chapter 9); this makes it easier to explain BC analysis (Chapter 10). The final new chapter (Chapter 11) is on uncertainty and how to perform sensitivity testing. The last two chapters—on checklists and policy issues—are carried over from the second edition, although the policy discussion is newly updated to address current debates and controversies. Each chapter includes a set of discussion questions and exercises. Answers to selected exercises are given in Appendix A. Finally, Appendix B includes a discussion of a new tool—*CostOut*—for aiding researchers in performing harmonized and rigorous CE studies.

As we look across the past three-plus decades, we hope this new edition reaffirms our fundamental claim: Economic evaluation of education is important and should be taken seriously.

Acknowledgments
to the Second Edition

This book benefited greatly from discussions and suggestions over the years about how we might update, expand, and improve the first edition of this book. Over the span of 17 years and 13 printings, we received considerable feedback from scholars, policy analysts, and students that surely improved the content and presentation of the revision. Many researchers, too numerous to mention, have generously shared their work. We want to express our thanks to all of them. We also thank Darrell R. Lewis and Jon S. Eberling for their review of the final manuscript.

Henry M. Levin wishes to dedicate this edition to the memory of his close friend, Professor Jose Luis Moreno Becerra. Moreno was a professor of applied economics at the University of La Laguna in the Canary Islands, Spain. He was a graduate student in the Economics of Education at Stanford some two decades ago and returned to Spain, receiving the highest score in the nation in a competition for a prestigious professorship in applied economics. Such a performance gave him the first choice of positions at any Spanish university. He returned to his home in the Canary Islands, and over the years, he became a leading voice of the economics of education throughout Spain. He was a founder and the first president of the Economics of Education Society of Spain, a group with a dynamic agenda and an annual meeting of very high quality. His sudden death in 1999 saddened a wide circle of colleagues and friends, and we cherish our associations with him, both academic and personal. We wish to present this as an homage to Jose Luis for his wife, Tere, and his two children, Ernesto and Elena.

Finally, Patrick J. McEwan wishes to dedicate this edition to the memory of his father. Richard T. McEwan always harbored aspirations of being an academic, but his family was not wealthy and many educational opportunities were unavailable. By working many years at a job that was less than fulfilling, he ensured that both his children would be sufficiently privileged to choose careers that were denied to him. Unfortunately, he did not live long enough to share in their accomplishments. If this book succeeds in its goals, then it is partly due to his curiosity, his intellect, and his encouragement.

Acknowledgments
to the Third Edition

Since the second edition of this book, much has changed: Methods of economic evaluation have become more sophisticated and detailed, and the attention paid to questions of efficiency and cost-effectiveness (CE) has increased greatly. We hope this new edition clearly expresses these methodological developments. But we especially hope that it captures the sense that economic evaluation of education should be taken seriously.

In revising this book, we have benefited greatly from discussions and interactions with many researchers, policymakers, and professionals. Most recently, with support from the Institute of Education Sciences, we have been privileged to teach economic evaluation to education researchers; their perspectives and contributions have made this a better book. Also, we appreciate the contributions of Meridith Friedman for assembling the references, Viviana Rodriguez Andrade for formatting the book, and all our colleagues at the Center for Benefit-Cost Studies of Education (CBCSE) at Teachers College, Columbia University. We want to express our thanks to all these persons. Collectively, they are working to make education systems more effective and more efficient and to provide a better future for new generations of students. As, we hope, are we.

ACKNOWLEDGMENTS FROM HENRY M. LEVIN ●

In the early 1970s, as a young academic with a few publications on cost-effectiveness (CE) analysis, I was asked by Marcia Guttentag to write a chapter for the forthcoming *Handbook of Evaluation Research*, which SAGE published in 1975. Although I surveyed the field in the old way of searching for library sources and reports and writing to contributors to the field, there was little application to social endeavors. Rather, the literature focused primarily on infrastructural projects; defense; and a few attempts to incorporate regression-focused models on crime, health, and education. To say the least, the field was underdeveloped, and few had attempted to apply it to evaluation. What struck me most was that the measurement of costs was chaotic. Most CE or benefit-cost (BC) studies were vague or silent about methods and sources of costs or even definitions of what was meant by costs. Others simply reported budgetary expenditures without explaining how they had analysed budgets designed for accounting purposes into cost evaluations of specific projects or interventions. Thus, the 1975 effort focused on establishing a general method for determining cost based upon economic concepts and the integration of that model with how costs were financed, two separate analyses. Less attempt was made to elaborate on how to measure effectiveness (experiments were favored) or how benefits were measured.

Although a few evaluators took interest in the topic, many asked for more detail on procedures. So, in 1983, I published the first edition of this book, attempting to assist evaluators to undertake cost analysis, using the ingredients approach. Although the book sold well, we found few new studies in the literature. In the middle 1990s at Stanford, I encountered a wonderful student, Patrick McEwan, who took great interest in the subject. He agreed to be the coauthor of a second edition, which would expand the analysis with special attention to the measurement of effectiveness and benefits. The second edition was published in 2000 (copyright 2001), some 17 years after the first edition, and it received increased attention.

In 1999, I moved to Teachers College, Columbia University, and continued to undertake research on CE and BC analysis in education. In 2000, I was joined by Clive Belfield in our National Center for the Study of Privatization in Education, and we decided that with the additional focus we had on CE and BC, we would start the Center for Benefit-Cost Studies of Education (CBCSE) in 2007. Although Clive accepted a position in the Department of Economics of Queens College, City University of New York, we continued to collaborate on cost analysis in educational evaluation. At this time, we were also joined by Brooks Bowden and later by Rob Shand, both PhD students in educational policy and economics of education. Since 2001, there was a flowering of developments in economics and other disciplines on the estimation of effectiveness in education, particularly the use of randomized controlled trials and quasi-experimental studies. At the same time, our second edition was approaching the 17-year length of publication of the first edition.

Given the flow of new ideas and applications and the steady increase in new applications of CE and BC studies in education, we decided as a group to prepare a third edition of the book, which would encompass progress in cost estimation and both measurement and estimation of effectiveness and benefits. We have attempted that in this new edition.

It is my pleasure to thank Clive for coordinating this effort as Patrick took the lead on the second edition. To a large degree, this is a thankless task of process, particularly with multiple authors. But, in both cases, the key coauthors made substantive improvements in presentation and content. In addition, our new additions, Brooks Bowden and Rob Shand, shared insights and content from their own studies and polish that was missing from earlier editions. For an older author, it is nice to know that such competent and strong colleagues will carry on the tradition, perhaps to a fourth edition in 2034.

I also wish to thank Fiona Hollands, who took the lead in enabling us to bring forth our computer platform to assist evaluators in doing their own cost analysis. Although Clive and I began this project with others, the ability to move it along to a user stage and procedures is due to Fiona's leadership and care. We hope that readers of the third edition will use *CostOut* to do their own cost analyses. We also appreciate the constant support of Emma Garcia, Yilin Pan, Barbara Hanisch Cerda, Meridith Friedman, Henan Cheng, Viviana Rodriguez Andrade, Atsuko Muroga, Anyi Wang, Amra Sabic-El-Rayess, Maya Escueta, and many others who have contributed to the work conducted by CBCSE.

Finally, as in all my work, I must thank my wife, Pilar Soler, for tolerating my preoccupation with this project and encouraging me. And I am grateful to my son, Jesse Levin, for his support and professional insight and suggestions derived from so many projects that he undertook in both the Tinbergen Institute and University of Amsterdam and at the American Institutes for Research.

FROM A. BROOKS BOWDEN   ●

Alyshia Brooks Bowden wishes to dedicate this edition to her mentor, former professor, and friend, Professor Rebecca Maynard. In her roles as an expert in rigorous evaluation, an economist, a professor, a scholar, a mother, and a person, Professor Maynard is an exemplary human being. Her instruction, feedback, support, and encouragement have been invaluable.

● FROM ROBERT SHAND

Robert Shand would like to dedicate this edition to his teachers, from whom he learned the potent combination of boundless curiosity and logical empiricism. He hopes this book contributes in some small way to employing those values in the service of educating future generations.

About the Authors

Henry M. Levin is the director of the Center for Benefit-Cost Studies of Education (CBCSE), the William H. Kilpatrick Professor of Economics and Education at Teachers College, Columbia University, and the David Jacks Professor of Higher Education and Economics, Emeritus, at Stanford University. He has been engaged in cost-effectiveness (CE) and benefit-cost (BC) studies in education and other fields since 1970. He is the author of 22 books and about 300 scholarly articles on these topics as well as others in the economics of education and educational policy.

Patrick J. McEwan is a professor of economics at Wellesley College and the director of Latin American Studies at Wellesley College. His research interests include the impact and cost evaluation of education and social policy in Latin America, especially Chile and Honduras. His work has been published in the *American Economic Review*, the *Journal of Public Economics*, *Educational Evaluation and Policy Analysis*, and other journals of economics and education policy. For more information on his research, visit www.patrickmcewan.net.

Clive Belfield is a professor in the Department of Economics at Queens College, City University of New York. He is also principal economist at the Center for Benefit-Cost Studies of Education (CBCSE) at Teachers College, Columbia University, faculty member for The Evaluators' Institute at Claremont Graduate University, and a research affiliate at the Community College Research Center, Teachers College, Columbia University. He received his PhD in economics from the University of Exeter, England. His research interests are economic evaluation of education programs. He has authored three books and more than 75 articles in the field of the economics of education.

A. Brooks Bowden is an assistant professor of methods and policy in the Educational Leadership, Policy, and Human Development department at North Carolina State University. She is the director of Training and associate director at the Center for Benefit-Cost Studies of Education (CBCSE) at Teachers College, Columbia University. She received her PhD in education policy with a specialization in economics from Columbia University. She specializes in program evaluation and economic analysis, focusing on applications and methodology of the ingredients method of cost analysis. She recently coauthored publications for the *American Journal of Evaluation*, the *Journal of Research on Educational Effectiveness*, the *Journal of Benefit-Cost Analysis*, and *Educational Evaluation and Policy Analysis*.

Robert Shand is the Novice G. Fawcett postdoctoral researcher in educational studies at The Ohio State University. He completed his PhD in economics and education at Teachers College, Columbia University. As a former K–12 teacher, his research focuses on how educational practitioners use evidence on effectiveness and costs to improve decision-making and how teachers improve over time through formal training and learning from colleagues.

1

Introduction to Economic Evaluation

Objectives

1. Describe the objectives of this book.

2. Define economic evaluations of educational interventions.

3. Identify and describe the types of analysis.

4. Provide motivation for economic evaluation.

A book should begin by tempting the reader with the importance of the subject or the excitement of the story that follows. In our case, this might appear to be a tall order. Yet, consider the size of the education industry in the United States—over $1 trillion in 2015—and across the world—approximately 5% of gross domestic product (Organisation for Economic Co-operation and Development [OECD], 2014). Despite this enormous resource base, educational institutions are constantly engaged in a quest for more resources to meet new aspirations or unfulfilled needs. If efficiency in the United States were to improve by only 2%, then $22 billion would be available for other purposes. At the level of a school district, an improvement of that magnitude would provide an additional $180 per student or about $4,500 per classroom in the K–12 system. However, these gains can be accomplished only by identifying ways to use existing resources more efficiently. Can we identify these ways? We can imagine spending $1 trillion each year and wondering the following: Is this the right amount? Is it too much or too little? Are we getting the biggest payoff we can from this investment? Should we move resources from colleges to schools? From administrators to teachers?

The purpose of economic evaluations is to answer these efficiency questions. Performed as cost-effectiveness (CE) analysis, it is a method for choosing among alternatives in order to select those that are able to accomplish a given result most parsimoniously. Performed as benefit-cost (BC) analysis, it is a method for determining whether the society is investing efficiently in education and whether the returns on education justify the costs.

Some might say that we ought to be less concerned with the quest for efficiency and more concerned with simply finding more resources, although this is hardly an either–or proposition. For example, imagine that a new state lottery is expected to yield hundreds of millions of dollars in new revenues for public education. Legislators and school administrators have proposed a number of alternative uses, including class size reduction, teacher training, and renovation of aging school facilities. How should the funds be apportioned among these alternatives if our goal is to maximize student learning? Or, on a smaller scale, imagine that each teacher in a school has been given $500 in discretionary funds. How should these funds be invested in the classroom so as to contribute to the greatest improvements in learning? Conversely, the education revenues of a large urban district might have declined sharply such that programs must be eliminated to stay within budget: If the goal is to minimize the declines that might occur in student learning, which programs should be eliminated? In fact, across the United States this cost-cutting question is becoming more salient: Within the K–12 sector, 31 states provided less funding per student in real terms in 2014 than they did in 2008; similarly, community college revenues fell every year from 2008 to 2013 (Desrochers & Hurlburt, 2016; Leachman, Albares, Masterson, & Wallace, 2016).

In all of these cases, and within this economic context, we are understandably concerned with obtaining the most "bang" for the "bucks" that are spent on education. Instead of relying upon guesswork or politics to make these hard decisions about education programs or interventions, we could undertake a systematic economic evaluation. This would first require estimation of costs. Then these costs would be linked to effects to establish cost-effectiveness or with benefits to establish the value of the program or intervention. We believe these evaluation methods can make an important contribution to education policy. Indeed, this is our motive for writing this book.

In this introductory chapter, we first set out the purposes of this book and what we hope to provide for the reader. Next, we explain why economic evaluation may be useful in many educational contexts as a way to understand and interpret research findings. We then give an overview of the best way to calculate costs—the ingredients method—and three methods of economic evaluation: (1) cost analysis, (2) CE analysis, and (3) BC analysis. Lastly, we explain how we see economic evaluations working in the policy context. As an overview, this material serves as preparation for the greater detail provided in the subsequent chapters.

1.1. PURPOSE AND GOALS OF THE BOOK   ●

The purpose of this volume is to provide a diverse audience—evaluators, researchers, educational administrators, and graduate students—with a systematic introduction to the use of cost analysis in educational evaluation. Accordingly, the volume has been written with the intention of familiarizing this audience with the ingredients method, a systematic approach to examining costs, and the nature and use of cost-analytic tools, as well as showing how to plan and implement a research study. Economic evaluation refers to a broad set of techniques for evaluation and decisionmaking, including CE, BC, cost-utility (CU), and cost-feasibility (CF). Each type of analysis will be developed separately for consideration, but we will refer to the group of methods taken together as central components of economic evaluation.

The term *economic evaluation* is deliberately broad. Fundamentally, economics is the study of the allocation of scarce resources, with emphasis on the term *scarce*. It is not sufficient to investigate how effective an intervention is—or whether one intervention causes a particular outcome. Although these are important and in many cases necessary investigations, they are not fully economic investigations: They do not incorporate the idea of scarcity and in particular do not weigh effects against the opportunity costs incurred to obtain the effects. There are many such examples in education. For example, there is much attention to teacher value added models and how important teacher quality is for learning outcomes. Unquestionably, this is an important area of social science inquiry. But it is isolated from the ultimate question: Is it worth giving up scarce resources to improve teacher quality? What is the opportunity cost of professional development programs to increase teacher quality? By economic evaluation, we mean the class of evaluations that explicitly address the cost of implementing a policy, reform, or intervention or that explicitly compare costs with benefits. In our specific case, these evaluations all relate to education.

The general goal of this volume is to provide the reader with an understanding of how to design and construct an economic evaluation that is valid for educational policy. To meet this overall goal, the intent is to provide the reader with an understanding of how to identify and measure costs using a standard, rigorous approach that is based on the economic principle of opportunity costs, the ingredients method. For CE analysis, the goal is to provide the reader with an understanding of how to specify impacts and effects for the purposes of economic evaluation and combine this evidence on effects with information on costs. For BC analysis, the goal is to assist the reader in how to specify benefits and their monetary values for the purposes of economic evaluation and combine the benefits with costs to produce BC analysis. The final two goals span all types of economic evaluation: One is to emphasize the need for sensitivity analysis; the other is to establish how economic evaluations must link with the requirements of decisionmakers, stakeholders, and policy professionals.

In addition, it is expected that the volume can serve a different need, which will vary among members of our audience. Some educational administrators and evaluators will wish to go beyond learning about the method and its uses to understanding how to actually apply the method to evaluation and administration within their own work settings. For example, an educational administrator may wish to ascertain how to do studies of CE among various alternatives for providing reading instruction or school lunches, or for designing budget cuts. An educational evaluator may wish to learn how to augment a standard evaluation of alternatives with information on costs. While this volume is not designed to prepare such persons to do these tasks in the absence of other training or assistance, it should be considered a necessary step in that direction. By mastering this introduction, an evaluator or administrator should be able to work effectively with a technical specialist on CE or BC analysis or should be able to undertake additional study in mastering the techniques that will be presented.

We have attempted to design the volume so that an individual can utilize it as part of an informal course of self-study or in a formal course on the subject. At various stages, the learner will be introduced to concepts and their applications. These are accompanied by numerous examples drawn from the applied literature, focusing almost entirely on educational examples. Exercises are provided at the end of the chapters to enable the reader to test his or her understanding of the topic that is being covered. Sample answers to selected exercises are provided in Appendix A.

As a point of clarification, we should emphasize one purpose for which this volume—and economic analysis in general—is not intended. This book is not meant to train individuals to "audit the books" of programs or organizations, or gauge compliance with expenditure requirements and the like. The set of concepts and methods that we describe are meant to assist individuals in weighing the costs of interventions against their outcomes and then in choosing the best intervention.

Accordingly, a final word on the purpose of the presentation is important. In these days of do-it-yourself instruction, it is appealing to provide a set of mechanical steps that one can simply follow verbatim in order to learn a new skill. Unfortunately, this approach is not appropriate for training in cost analysis and economic evaluation. Although one can provide a set of principles that can be used for carrying out the analysis, the actual application in any particular setting will require judgments on the part of the administrator or evaluator. Thus, this volume will not be a substitute for a sensitive and judicious effort by the evaluator in applying his or her craft. Rather, it will provide a new set of concepts and analytic tools that can be incorporated into that activity. Although the guidelines for incorporating these new dimensions will be presented and illustrated, the applications will require careful guidance for the analyst or user.

1.2. THE IMPORTANCE OF ECONOMIC EVALUATIONS   ●

Why should educational evaluators or school personnel be concerned with economic evaluation? The most superficial answer to this question is that reference to such analysis is often an important source of persuasion as a rhetorical claim. By saying that one has compared the CE of different approaches and found a particular one to be most cost-effective, one can often disarm opponents. Unfortunately, this is the principal way in which the terminology is used in the educational sector. This volume will go beyond such banality. CE analysis should be a topic of concern because it can lead to a more efficient use of educational resources—it can reduce the costs of reaching particular objectives, and it can expand what can be accomplished for any particular budget or other resource constraint. Similarly, BC analysis can identify which investments make the most sense and how much society should invest in education. But these results must be derived from application of rigorous methods.

This book emphasizes that a proper assessment of costs and effectiveness or benefits is a necessary element of a serious evaluation. All too often, either costs or effects are considered separately, and any combined inferences may be misleading. For the most part, educational evaluators attempt to establish whether an intervention is effective in attaining some goal, such as raising academic achievement. Business managers and administrators are often concerned with lowering educational costs in order to fit school or district expenditures within a fixed budget. Nevertheless, both parties should share a common goal: They wish to attain maximal school effectiveness for a given budget, or conversely, they wish to attain a given level of effectiveness at a minimal cost. They are unlikely to accomplish this goal if higher effectiveness and lower costs are pursued as independent goals. To illustrate this point, it is useful to consider three examples in sequence.

First, there is the peril of ignoring costs. This peril is nicely illustrated by looking at the development of policies related to smaller classes. During the 1990s, reducing class size was among the most popular and intuitively appealing options for improving schools; it seemed to provide a rare instance of agreement among parents, teachers, administrators, and even politicians. It led to a number of initiatives to reduce class size, especially in the primary grades, with the largest being in California's effort in 1996 to reduce class size in the early primary grades to 20 students (Brewer, Krop, Gill, & Reichardt, 1999).

Much of the support for class size reduction was based on the promising results of the Project STAR experiment in Tennessee (Krueger, 1999; Mosteller, 1995). This experiment compared the achievement of students who were randomly assigned to three kinds of classes: students in regular classes (22 to 25 students) without teacher aides, students in regular classes with teacher aides, and students in small classes (13 to 17 students). Performance on standardized tests increased by 4 percentile points during the first year in which students were assigned to smaller classes (Krueger, 1999). Each subsequent year of participation in a smaller class further increased achievement by about 1 percentile point. (Teacher aides were found to have little effect on student achievement.) Overall, the results provided strong evidence that reducing primary class size has important effects on student achievement (Chingos, 2012). Looked at in isolation, these results might justify policies to reduce class size.

But reducing class size is very expensive—often prohibitively so (Brewer et al., 1999). To get the expected improvements in achievement would require a sizable number of new teachers—presumably trained to the same standard as the evaluated cohort—and it would involve much sorting and job changing as junior teachers moved across schools. New classrooms would have to be built and furnished, and changes to the school organization would also be substantial. When these resource issues were examined, the case for class size reduction diminished (Grissmer, 1999). Moreover, when the resource commitment was evaluated against what needed to be reallocated and lost from other school practices or potential interventions, the call for smaller class sizes further weakened.

Second, there is the peril of ignoring effectiveness. Declining enrollment in schools often forces administrators to make difficult decisions about school closure. Should numerous smaller schools be maintained, or should their enrollments be consolidated into a single larger school? On the surface, the decision might seem to be related exclusively to costs. The accountant or business manager should merely calculate the cost of each alternative and implement the least costly.

Indeed, average costs may be lower in larger schools due to economies of scale (Colegrave & Giles, 2008; Lee & Smith, 1997). Larger schools may benefit from lower prices on bulk purchases of school supplies or furnishings. Perhaps most important is that the fixed costs of operating a school can be spread over a larger number of pupils. For example, a larger school needs to maintain only one playground and cafeteria, pay one electricity bill, support one library, and so forth. Numerous smaller schools would be forced to duplicate these fixed expenditures, and per-pupil costs could rise. In rural areas of developing countries, isolated schools may not enroll enough students to fill even a standard classroom. Since even five students require a teacher, per-pupil costs may turn out to be quite high. Of course it is not a foregone conclusion that larger schools are less costly: excessively large schools may have higher management costs, there may be extra transport costs, and small schools that are physically close to their communities may be better poised to generate donated resources from local parents and citizens.

Let us presume, however, that the overall cost per student declines in larger school units. Does school size alter the effectiveness of schools? There is some evidence that larger schools have lower educational effectiveness across many different outcomes, although not in all specifications (Barrow, Schanzenbach, & Claessens, 2015; Leithwood & Jantzi, 2009). Precisely why this is so is unclear. It may be that larger schools are more depersonalized and provide both students and educational professionals with less of a feeling of individual importance and involvement. Or it might be traced to the presence of a core curriculum in smaller high schools that emphasizes academic excellence for all students, regardless of their abilities or aspirations (Lee & Smith, 1997). In areas of low population density, students may be forced to travel long distances to reach a larger school. Their resulting fatigue could reduce their learning once they arrive or even deter attendance in the first place (Bray, 1987).

Despite the cost savings of larger, consolidated schools, they may entail sacrifices in effectiveness, though this obviously needs to be analyzed on a case-by-case basis. Thus, larger schools that are less costly may ultimately prove to be less cost-effective. Administrators might consider other means of cutting educational costs that will not undermine effectiveness. For example, smaller schools can reduce costs by sharing teachers and administrators and, in the case of secondary schools, by drawing on such community resources as courses offered by community colleges. They can also lease unused classroom space for child care, senior citizen centers, and private educational endeavors such as computer schools or tutoring centers. The key point is that each of these alternatives should be clearly established, so that the relative costs *and* effects of each alternative can be evaluated.

The third peril arises when we ignore benefits. Over the period from 2003 to 2013, the amount of public subsidies for community college fell in real terms by 6% (Desrochers & Hurlburt, 2016). Despite rapidly growing enrollments at community colleges, the inflation-adjusted amount of public funding per student has fallen. As public funding has fallen, student tuition and fees have increased to make up the difference. Some might see this as a smart efficiency gain: The students who directly gain from college have to pay for it.

But this policy change neglects the fact that college produces a substantial benefit to the local taxpayer—for example, in terms of higher tax revenues (because of higher income and spending) and lower government spending (on welfare and the criminal justice system). In fact, according to estimates from Trostel (2010), each new community college graduate contributes more than $140,000 more in fiscal benefits (higher taxes and lower public spending on other services). In other words, the public sector, by deliberately reducing the resources available to community college students, is directly reducing its own economic well-being.

Each example illustrates the pitfalls of concentrating exclusively on either outcomes or costs. If evaluators intend the results of their studies to be used for decisionmaking, the information on effects of alternatives (such as class size reduction) is not adequate in itself to make a choice. If educational administrators wish to provide suggestions for cutting expenditures, the cost consequences of the alternatives (such as school consolidation) are not adequate in themselves for making an informed decision. And if taxpayers want to maximize revenue and minimize spending, they should consider educational investments that do this (such as investments in college subsidies). In short, information on costs, effects, and benefits is necessary to adequately inform the decision.

1.3. ECONOMIC EVALUATION FOR DECISIONMAKING IN EDUCATION

One of the more confusing aspects of incorporating cost analysis into evaluation and decisionmaking is that a number of different, but related, terms are often used interchangeably. These include cost (along with cost-feasibility), cost-effectiveness (along with cost-utility) analysis, and benefit-cost analysis. Although each is related to and can be considered to be a member in good standing of the cost-analysis family, each has important differences that make it appropriate to specific applications (Levin, 1975). Here we provide an overview of each approach and the main differences among them; a full explanation is given in the relevant chapters. We demonstrate the key ideas and practice with concrete examples from the educational literature. These examples are not intended to inform readers of which interventions are actually most efficient; rather, they are illustrative of what is involved in an economic evaluation.

1.3.1. Cost Analysis

All the types of analyses discussed in this volume involve calculation of costs. This calculation is an essential part of economics—that implementing any program or intervention requires resources that have value. The ingredients method, as described in detail next, requires a descriptive itemization of all resources. Thus, the first type of analysis is simply to calculate the costs of these resources by applying the ingredients method. In itself, these calculations are useful: They can reveal a great deal of information about each educational intervention. Such information includes the extent of dosages, who delivers them, what types of professional staff are needed, and what resources are used instead of the intervention. Perhaps surprisingly, many education reforms proceed with only a terse description of the resources being applied.

Moreover, estimates of costs alone are important for another reason: They are a guide to affordability. CF analysis refers to the method of estimating only the costs of an alternative in order to ascertain whether or not it can even be afforded. If the cost of any alternative exceeds resources that are available, there is no point in doing any further analysis. As a concrete illustration, one might view the situation of compensatory education, in which a specified amount is available for augmenting the education of each disadvantaged child. If this amount is $400 per child, then any alternative that violates this constraint would not be feasible. Nevertheless, even this limited scope is helpful for policymaking. CF represents a limited form of analysis that determines whether or not alternatives are within the boundaries of consideration. It cannot be used to determine which affordable options should actually be selected. As another example, we can imagine a community that believes it is equitable to spend the same amount on each grade; early interventions in first grade, even if they are found to be highly effective, might be rejected on equity grounds because they involve giving disproportionate resources to a single grade. See Example 1.1 for CF analysis of class size reduction.

Example 1.1   Cost-Feasibility Analysis of National Class Size Reduction

Class size reduction has been a popular policy for improving educational outcomes, and the evidence that it increases achievement in the early elementary school grades is compelling (Krueger, 1999). A school district—faced with accountability pressures to improve performance—might consider reducing class size. But even before considering whether class size reduction will boost test scores, a much simpler and more basic question is whether such a sweeping plan could be feasibly implemented in light of current and future budget constraints. Would the costs associated with a national class size reduction be prohibitive?

Dominic Brewer and his colleagues (1999) estimated the expected costs of different approaches to national class size reduction in Grades 1 through 3. To yield a baseline cost, this estimation required a number of assumptions about the scope and design of the policy. Their baseline assumptions were as follows. First, there are three possible targets for class size reduction: 20, 18, and 15. Second, class size reduction is implemented districtwide (such that class size reduction is an average per district, with flexibility per classroom and per school). Third, the policy applies uniformly to all students such that there is no targeting of the policy toward specific groups such as high-poverty schools or districts. Finally, and most importantly, only operational costs are considered, such as salaries and benefits of teachers, aides, and administrators, as well as instructional materials and supplies. No consideration is given to the costs of facilities and infrastructure and no cost is given to the process of transitioning from larger to smaller classes. If these costs were included, the overall cost of class size reduction—the actual cost—would be considerably higher. Upon arriving at their baseline estimates, they varied several key assumptions in order to observe the sensitivity of cost estimates. Their baseline estimates are given in the following table.

Maximum Class Size	Additional Operating Costs	
	Total ($ billions)	Per-Pupil
20	$3.19	$280
18	$7.57	$670
15	$16.57	$1,470

Source: Brewer et al. (1999, Table 2).

Note: Adjusted to 2015 dollars.

In 2015 dollars, the cost of operating the education system with class sizes of 20 in Grades 1 through 3 would be an additional $3.19 billion each year (or $280 extra per pupil). Lowering class size to 15 would result in substantially higher total and per-pupil operational costs of $16.57 billion and $1,470, respectively. Leaving aside transition costs and the resources required for facilities, these cost amounts raise questions as to whether reducing class size meaningfully is affordable.

With sensitivity analysis, the authors can tell us what makes the biggest difference to costs. For example, class size reduction is less costly if the targeted levels of class size must only be met on average across the entire state, rather than across districts. On the other hand, it is more costly if average class sizes in each school must meet targeted levels. Moreover, the policy is much less costly if it is targeted only at schools with large numbers of high-poverty students.

(Continued)

(Continued)

Cost-feasibility (CF) estimates cannot inform decisionmakers as to whether class size reduction is a socially desirable investment in absolute terms or whether it is relatively more desirable than another investment. This can only be accomplished by weighing the costs of class size reduction against its benefits or effectiveness. Nevertheless, the cost estimates can tell decisionmakers whether national class size reduction is feasible within the current set of budget constraints. This information is especially useful in situations where the resource requirements are not easily observable (e.g., when the school might not know how many new teachers to hire or how much it will cost to reorganize the school schedule).

Source: Adapted from Brewer et al. (1999).

1.3.2. Cost-Effectiveness Analysis

CE analysis is an evaluative technique that compares policies or programs based on their ratios of costs to educational results on a quantifiable (but not monetized) effectiveness measure (Boardman, Greenberg, Vining, & Weimer, 2011, Chapter 18; Levin, 1975). This analysis allows us to take account of both the costs and effects of selecting alternatives, making it possible to choose those alternatives that provide the best results for any given resource outlay or that minimize the resource utilization for any given outcome. For example, we can compare alternative interventions for improving academic performance in mathematics or reading to consider the interventions that show the largest achievement gain relative to their costs.

Standard approaches to evaluation are more limited because they primarily focus on the effectiveness of alternatives, such as impacts on test scores, socioemotional skills, high school graduation, and so on. Presumably one need just choose those interventions that show large effect sizes over those that show small effect sizes. However, the absence of cost information means that such results should never be used for decisionmaking in isolation. For example, if one of the interventions is associated with an effect size on achievement of 0.6 and another of 0.4, it does not necessarily follow that the first of the interventions is the superior one. What if the cost of the first intervention is $400 per student and the cost of the second is $200 per student? For any given budget, the overall effect of spending it entirely on the second intervention may improve achievement far more than spending it on the first alternative. By combining cost information with appropriate measures of effectiveness, we are able to use resources more productively and improve educational outcomes with given resources. Policy decisions in the public sector must be based increasingly upon a demonstrated consideration of both costs and effects.

Effectiveness can be measured in various ways, depending on the needs of the decisionmaker. For example, alternative interventions can be evaluated on the basis of their cost for raising student test scores by a given amount, or the cost for each potential dropout averted, or the cost per instance of conduct disorder. Moreover, the education system can serve to effect broader societal change: the installation of water fountains in schools can reduce obesity, for example, by reducing the consumption of sugary beverages (Muckelbauer et al., 2009; Schwartz, Leardo, Aneja, & Elbel, 2016). From a decision-oriented perspective, the most preferable alternatives would be those that show the lowest cost for any given increase in the selected effect. By choosing the most cost-effective alternative, we free up resources that can be invested in other aspects of education (or in another endeavor). However, CE requires that (a) only programs with similar or identical goals can be compared and (b) a common measure of effectiveness can be used to assess them. These effectiveness data can be combined with costs in order to provide a CE evaluation that will enable the selection of those approaches that provide the maximum effectiveness per level of cost or that require the least cost per level of effectiveness. For an illustration of this, see Example 1.2.

Example 1.2   Cost-Effectiveness Analysis of Primary School Investments in Northeast Brazil

The states that form northeast Brazil are among the poorest areas in the world. In the 1980s, many children did not even attend primary school. Of those children who did, schools were often attempting to provide education without many basic resources, including infrastructure, classroom materials such as textbooks, and well-trained teachers. In an environment of low student achievement and resource scarcity, determining the cost-effectiveness (CE) of school investments becomes particularly important. How can the limited funds available to the school system be spent in order to maximize the academic achievement of students?

The following table shows the results from a CE analysis by Harbison and Hanushek (1992). First, the range of possible educational interventions are specified; these are shown in the first column. The first category is infrastructure: the provision of potable water, of basic school furniture (e.g., desks),

(Continued)

(Continued)

and additional school facilities (e.g., school offices), and then a combination of all these ("hardware"). The second category, material inputs, includes two interventions: (1) student textbooks and writing materials and (2) the combination ("software"). The teacher category includes two separate in-service teacher training programs (*curso de qualificação* and *Logos II*), either 4 or 3 years of additional formal schooling, and an increase in teacher salaries.

Costs, Effects, and Cost-Effectiveness Ratios for Primary School Investments

Intervention	C Cost per Student per Year	E Effect on Portuguese Test Score (Points)	C/E Cost- Effectiveness Ratio
Infrastructure:			
Water	$4.31	3.51	$1.24
School furniture	$12.97	NE	NA
School facilities	$20.94	7.23	$2.90
"Hardware"	$38.22	8.97	$4.26
Material inputs:			
Textbook usage	$3.93	6.4	$0.62
Writing material	$4.19	4.7	$0.88
"Software"	$8.12	4.86	$1.67
Teachers:			
Training: *Curso de qualificação*	$5.95	NE	NA
Training: *Logos II*	$4.38	3.59	$1.21
4 years primary school	$5.26	3.18	$1.67
3 years secondary school	$13.21	2.38	$5.55
Increasing teacher salary	$0.93	0.06	$15.47

Source: Adapted from Harbison and Hanushek (1992, Table C6-1).

Notes: The original table presents effectiveness-cost ratios, rather than the CE ratios presented in this table. For an explanation of the difference, see Chapter 8 of this volume. NE: no evidence of positive effect. NA: not applicable. Adjusted to 2015 dollars.

The second step is to determine the costs of each intervention. To derive these costs as an annual per student amount, the authors used the "ingredients" method. The ingredients of each intervention, such as materials and personnel time, were exhaustively listed and priced out; the costs of durable inputs, such as infrastructure, were annualized. As shown in the second column of the table, the cost per student varied across the interventions, with more intensive investments (e.g., hardware and software) being progressively more costly within their category. The cost per student is low because this is a poor area, the interventions are from the 1980s, and the exchange rate was low when translated into dollars.

The third step is to estimate the effectiveness of each intervention. Here, the measure of effectiveness is a test of Portuguese language achievement among second graders. To estimate incremental effectiveness per intervention, the authors use nonexperimental regression analyses. Notably, the interventions vary significantly in effectiveness: hardware, school facilities, and textbooks are the most effective at increasing test scores; and some interventions have no statistically significant impact on achievement.

The final step is to combine the data on costs and effectiveness by calculating a CE ratio. The ratio indicates the cost required to attain a 1-point increase in achievement. The final column of the table shows which interventions are the most cost-effective—that is, yield achievement for the least amount of resources. Clearly, we should be most interested in investing in those interventions that exhibit the lowest cost per unit of effect.

A simple examination of the CE ratios shows that material inputs have the lowest CE ratios. By providing more textbooks and writing materials, policymakers can attain 1 point of effectiveness at a cost of $0.62 and $0.88 per student. In contrast, increasing teacher salaries costs $15.47 per unit of effect; it requires more than 20 times as much resource to obtain the same gain in learning as textbooks.

How would our decisions have been different if costs had been excluded from the analysis? We might have been tempted to invest heavily in school facilities and hardware, which exhibit the highest effectiveness. But they are also among the most costly inputs and, consequently, somewhat less cost-effective. Unsurprisingly, the most effective interventions may be too costly to justify their use.

Source: Adapted from Harbison and Hanushek (1992).

There is no presumption that the most effective intervention is also the most cost-effective. There may certainly be either cases where highly effective interventions are so costly to implement that they no longer appear to be viable or justifiable or cases where interventions with very modest effects are worthwhile because of their low cost. Yet, without an analysis of costs, which is then linked to effects, it would be impossible to know this.

The CE approach has a number of strengths. Most important is that it merely requires combining cost data with the effectiveness data that are observed from an educational evaluation to create a CE comparison. Further, it lends itself well to an evaluation of alternatives that are being considered for accomplishing a particular educational goal. Its one major disadvantage is that one can compare the CE ratios only among alternatives with a similar goal. One cannot compare alternatives with different goals (e.g., reading vs. mathematics or high school completion vs. health), nor can one make an overall determination of whether a program is worthwhile in an absolute sense. That is, we can state whether a given alternative is *relatively* more cost-effective than other alternatives, but we cannot state whether its total benefits exceed its total costs. That can be ascertained only through BC analysis.

1.3.3. Cost-Utility Analysis

CU analysis is a close cousin of CE analysis. It refers to the evaluation of alternatives according to a comparison of their costs and their *utility* (a term that is often interpreted as value or satisfaction to an individual or group). Unlike CE analysis, which relies upon a single measure of effectiveness (e.g., a test score, the number of dropouts averted), CU analysis uses information on a range of outcomes to assess overall satisfaction. These outcomes are then weighted based on the decisionmaker's preferences—that is, how much each outcome contributes to total utility. Data on preferences can be derived in many ways, either through highly subjective estimates by the researcher or through more rigorous methods designed to carefully elicit opinions as to the value of each outcome. Once overall measures of utility have been obtained, however, we proceed in the same way as CE analysis. We choose the interventions that provide a given level of utility at the lowest cost or those that provide the greatest amount of utility for a given cost. This CU analysis is like CE analysis except the outcome is weighted based on stakeholders' perceptions or preferences.

We can apply CU analysis to a simple example of alternative reading programs that have outcomes that are not valued equally by the decisionmaker. One reading intervention raises test scores by 0.6 standard deviations, and another reading intervention raises test scores by 0.4 standard deviations. With a statewide achievement policy that a test score gain of 0.2 meets accountability standards for the school, then, although incremental test score gains are desirable, they are not valued in the same way as gains up to an effect size of 0.2. So, if we assume gains beyond 0.2 are worth half as much as gains below 0.2, then the utility of intervention one is 0.4 (= 0.2 + (0.6 − 0.2)/2) and of intervention two is 0.3 (= 0.2 + (0.4 − 0.2)/2). Now, with respective costs of $400 and $200, the second intervention is preferred from a CU basis: The first intervention is twice as costly but only one-third more valuable. Of course, we could imagine utility weights that would overturn this conclusion.

CU analysis is in one sense an extension of CE analysis. That is, CU analysis requires that the preferences of the decisionmakers be explicitly incorporated into the research. The classic example of a utility-based measure is the quality-adjusted life year (QALY) used by health sciences researchers (Drummond et al., 2009; Neumann, Thorat, Shi, Saret, & Cohen, 2015). Unfortunately, the challenge of CU analysis is that of finding valid ways to determine the values of outcomes in order to weight these preferences relative to costs. This quest requires separate modeling exercises often of substantial complexity. The simple reading example in the previous paragraph was made easier because there was only one outcome—test scores; when there are multiple outcomes that need to be combined, the utility calculations become more difficult and subjective.

1.3.4. Benefit-Cost Analysis

BC analysis is an analytical tool that compares policies or interventions based on the difference between their costs and a monetized measure of their effects (Boardman et al., 2011, Chapters 3–5). This tool allows us to see if we should invest in educational programs and how much we should invest. Since each alternative is assessed in terms of its monetary costs and the monetary values of its benefits, each alternative can be examined on its own merits to see if it is worthwhile. In order to be considered for selection, any alternative must show benefits in excess of costs. In selecting from among several alternatives, one would choose that particular one that had the highest BC ratio (or, conversely, the lowest ratio of costs to benefits).

Because BC analysis assesses all alternatives in terms of the monetary values of costs and benefits, one can ascertain (a) if any particular alternative has benefits exceeding its costs; (b) which of a set of educational alternatives with different objectives has the highest ratio of benefits to costs; and (c) which of a set of alternatives among different program areas (e.g., health, education, transportation, police) shows the highest BC ratios for an overall social analysis of where the public should invest. The latter is a particularly attractive feature of BC analysis because we can compare many programs with widely disparate objectives (e.g., endeavors within and among education, health, transportation, environment, and others), as long as their costs and benefits can be expressed in monetary terms.

We can adapt the previous example examining alternative programs for reading to illustrate BC analysis. Imagine if the first educational intervention generates effect size achievement gains of 0.6, which leads to an increase in wages after high school of $600 in total. Given that the intervention costs only $400, the community should be motivated to invest in this intervention as it will be gaining $200. Indeed, the community might consider whether to invest even more in this intervention to see if it can get a benefit surplus in excess of $400 by expanding to more students. By contrast, in a labor market where the association between effect size gains and earnings is not linear, the second intervention with its effect size gain of 0.4 increases wages by only $100. In this case, the community should not be motivated to invest: At a cost of $200, the increase in wages is not worth it (by –$100). Of course, this is a simplified example—the main point is that the value of education depends on the relationship between learning outcomes and changes in economic well-being relative to the costs of getting those changes. That relationship could take a variety of forms, and changes in the value of economic well-being might be multiple, including wages, health status, or civic engagement. BC analysis helps us decide which investments will produce the greatest educational returns to society. See Example 1.3.

Example 1.3   Benefit-Cost Analysis of Dropout Prevention in California

The problem of high school dropouts is of substantial concern to educators, policymakers, and society at large (Rumberger, 2011). It is well known that dropouts tend to earn lower wages than high school graduates, and this gap is widening (Autor, 2014; Belfield & Levin, 2007). This suggests that benefits for reducing dropouts, as measured by their additional wages over a lifetime, may be extensive. Of course, programs or reforms that encourage students to remain in school are also costly. We can determine whether it is worthwhile to undertake these programs only by carefully weighing the costs against the benefits.

In the early 1980s, the state of California instituted a dropout prevention program in the San Francisco peninsula. A number of "Peninsula Academies" were created as small schools within existing public high schools. Academy students in Grades 10 through 12 took classes together that were coordinated by academy teachers. Each academy, in concert with local employers, provided vocational training. As an evaluation, the state wanted to know whether the costs of the academies were justified in terms of the economic value generated from having fewer dropouts.

The results of the evaluation are summarized in the following table.

Costs, Benefits, and Benefit-Cost Analysis of a Dropout Prevention Strategy

Academy	Costs (C)	Dropouts Saved (D)	Benefits per Dropout Averted (B)	Benefits (D × B)	Net Present Value (B − C)	Benefit-Cost Ratio (B/C)
A	$178,850	−3.4	$172,000	−$584,800	−$763,650	—
C	$349,200	21.5	$172,000	$3,698,000	$3,348,800	10.6
D	$214,000	1.8	$172,000	$309,600	$95,600	1.5
E	$70,560	2	$172,000	$344,000	$273,440	4.9
F	$765,660	5.8	$172,000	$997,600	$231,940	1.3
G	$115,070	−2	$172,000	−$344,000	−$459,070	—
H	$273,140	0.2	$172,000	$34,400	−$238,740	0.1
K	$436,450	3.4	$172,000	$584,800	$148,350	1.3
All	$2,402,930	29.3	$172,000	$5,039,600	$2,636,670	2.1

Source: Adapted from Stern, Dayton, Paik, and Weisberg (1989, Table 6).

Notes: Adjusted to 2015 dollars. Rounded to nearest ten.

The first step of the evaluation is to estimate the additional costs of each academy, beyond what would have been spent on a traditional high school education. The second column gives the total costs for the 3-year (Grades 10 through 12) program delivered to the 1985–1986 cohort. The cost ingredients included personnel (teachers, aides, and administrators), facilities and equipment, and the cost of time donated by local employers. Academy costs tended to be higher because of their relatively smaller class sizes and extra preparation periods that were given to some teachers.

The evaluators then estimated the benefits produced by lowering the number of high school dropouts. To do so, the authors employed a quasi-experimental design. Prior to initiating the program, a comparison group of observationally equivalent students attending the traditional high school was

(Continued)

(Continued)

selected. After 3 years, the academy dropout rates were compared with those of the comparison group. In most schools, the academies reduced dropouts (indicated by a positive number of "dropouts averted" in the table), although in a few schools, the dropout rate was higher in academy schools (indicated by a negative number). To monetize these changes—that is, to transform them into benefits—the authors calculated the lifetime income gain for a high school graduate over a dropout. Their estimate of $172,000 is a present value, discounted to reflect for the differential timing of the benefits received (a complete discussion of discounting is given in Chapters 3–6). The number of dropouts averted is multiplied by this value to derive each academy's total benefit.

The final step is to subtract costs from benefits. The net benefits column suggests that the program is worthwhile in academies C, D, E, F, and K (i.e., the benefits are greater than the costs). In academies A, G, and H, however, the costs outweigh the benefits. Across all eight academies, the overall benefits of the program exceed the costs. Another metric for comparing benefits and costs is the benefit-cost (BC) ratio. Ratios greater than 1 suggest that benefits are greater than costs. Despite the favorable results, the final results are heavily influenced by a single academy (C).

This analysis assumes we have exhaustively catalogued the relevant costs and benefits. However, we may have excluded important benefits—for example, the savings incurred because more-educated adults are less likely to become incarcerated. The authors also present evidence that academy schools are effective at producing other outcomes such as higher grades. Some measures of effectiveness may be difficult to monetize and so to include in BC analysis (although they might be usefully included in a cost-effectiveness [CE] analysis).

Source: Adapted from Stern et al. (1989).

BC analysis can be a useful way to gauge the overall worth of a program or policy. If the program costs are greater than its benefits, it should not be implemented. Also, we can judge a project by the overall size of the net benefits—that is, by how much benefits exceed costs. Further, to the degree that other educational endeavors and those in other areas of public expenditure (such as health, transportation, environmental improvement, or criminal justice) are evaluated by the BC method, it is possible to compare any particular educational alternative with projects in other areas that compete for resources.

The disadvantage of this method is that benefits and costs must be assessed in pecuniary terms. It is not often possible to do this in a systematic and rigorous manner. For example, while the gains in earnings attributed to increased graduation rates might be assessed according to their pecuniary worth, how does one assess benefits such as improvement in citizen functioning of the educated adults or their enhanced appreciation of reading materials? This shortcoming suggests that only under certain circumstances would one wish to use BC analysis. Those situations would occur when the preponderance of benefits could be readily converted into pecuniary values or when those that cannot be converted tend to be unimportant or can be shown to be similar among the alternatives that are being considered. That is, if the decision alternatives differ only on the basis of those benefit factors that can be converted to pecuniary values, the other aspects can be ignored in the BC calculations. Or, if those dimensions of benefits that cannot be assessed in pecuniary terms are considered to be trivial, one can limit the BC comparison to the factors that can be evaluated with monetary measures. However, in those cases in which the major benefits are difficult to assess in pecuniary terms, some other mechanism for assessment must be found.

1.4. SUMMARY OF APPROACHES TO ECONOMIC EVALUATION

Having defined and illustrated the approaches to economic evaluation, we provide a summary that allows them to be compared. As shown in Table 1.1, the approaches are similar but have key distinctions. Each has strengths and weaknesses. Although BC analysis is the most comprehensive, it requires the most analytical effort and may not be required to respond to a particular decisionmaker's needs. After reading the subsequent chapters, you may find it helpful to return to Table 1.1 in order to solidify your understanding.

Most economic evaluations use either CE or BC analysis (CF is often incorporated as a preliminary endeavor, and CU analysis is a derivative of CE analysis). The bulk of our attention is therefore directed to these two methods.

Although they seem similar, CE and BC analyses are different in one very important way. We distinguish between the two in simple terms. The CE analyst would ask, What is the lowest cost alternative to get outcome X? The BC analyst would ask, Should we invest in program Y that produces outcome X? So, one might investigate with CE analysis whether the Wilson Reading System is more cost-effective than Corrective Reading. Instead, one might investigate with BC analysis if investing in reading is more valuable than investing in math (remembering that doing one implies less of the other because of resource constraints). Formally, both questions can be described as

Table 1.1 Summary of Approaches to Economic Evaluation in Education

Type of Analysis	Analytical Question(s)	Measure of Cost	Measure of Outcomes	Strengths of Approach	Weaknesses of Approach
Cost analysis	• What is the full resource cost of each alternative?	Total social value of all resources	None	• Describes all resources used for each alternative, regardless of who pays for them	• Cannot establish if each alternative is worth that resource use or which alternative is most efficient
Cost-feasibility	• Can a single alternative be carried out within the existing budget?	Monetary value of resources	None	• Permits alternatives that are not feasible to be immediately ruled out, before evaluating outcomes	• Cannot judge overall worth of project, because it does not incorporate outcome measures
Cost-effectiveness	• Which alternative yields a given level of effectiveness for a given educational goal for the lowest cost (or highest level of effectiveness for a given cost)?	Monetary value of resources	Units of effectiveness	• Easy to incorporate standard evaluations of effectiveness • Useful for alternatives with a single objective or a small number of objectives	• Difficult to interpret results when there are multiple measures of effectiveness • Cannot judge overall worth of a single alternative; only useful for comparing two or more alternatives

Type of Analysis	Analytical Question(s)	Measure of Cost	Measure of Outcomes	Strengths of Approach	Weaknesses of Approach
Cost-utility	• Which alternative yields a given level of utility at the lowest cost (or the highest level of utility at a given cost)?	Monetary value of resources	Units of utility	• Incorporates individual preferences of stakeholders with units of effectiveness • Can incorporate multiple measures of effectiveness into a single measure of utility • Promotes stakeholder participation in decisionmaking	• Sometimes difficult to arrive at consistent and accurate measures of individual or group preferences • Cannot judge overall worth of a single alternative; only useful for comparing two or more alternatives
Benefit-cost	• Which alternative yields a given level of benefits for the lowest cost (or the highest level of benefits for a given cost)? • Are the benefits of a single alternative larger than its costs?	Monetary value of resources	Monetary value of outcomes	• Can be used to judge absolute worth of a project • Can compare BC results across a wide variety of projects in education or other areas (e.g., health, infrastructure)	• Often difficult to place monetary values on all relevant educational benefits

efficiency questions: CE refers to productive efficiency, and BC refers to allocative efficiency. However, to avoid confusion we describe results from CE analyses based on whether they are cost-effective relative to alternatives; BC analyses have tended to use the term *efficiency*, so we use that term here.

The consistency that carries throughout economic evaluation is the measurement and reporting of the intervention's cost. This textbook describes and discusses the application of the ingredients method. The ingredients method utilizes the economic principle of opportunity cost to include all resources that were utilized during implementation to generate an outcome. The approach is transparent and easy to interpret by following common procedures in cost accounting. The resulting research on costs provides the audience with information about the resources uses, including their qualities and quantities, as well as the price value of each resource. The resulting estimate of total social cost and average cost per student are consistent for any of the economic evaluations discussed here.

1.5. ECONOMIC EVALUATIONS AND POLICYMAKING

We suspect that some education professionals and researchers may question the use of economic evaluation methods. With CE, they may argue that an education intervention with complex and multifaceted outcomes cannot be evaluated using a single measure. With BC, researchers may reject the idea of turning education processes and student growth into dollars based upon monetary values that can then be moved around to generate efficiency gains.

We believe the case for economic evaluations is strong. Fundamentally, there is the essential idea of scarcity and opportunity cost. Resources are required to implement preschool programs; those same resources cannot then be used to provide youth support programs. By using economic resources to implement preschool programs, we are therefore implicitly saying that these have a priority over using similar resources for youth support programs. Using economic evaluation gives this decision a scientific basis rather than relying solely on preferences without consideration of other alternatives.

Moreover, the issue is not whether every educational program or policy should be evaluated closely using economic concepts. Rather, the issue is whether too much or too little economic evaluation is being performed (Belfield, 2015). Based on a very general review of education research, we believe that more educational evaluation should be performed. Although the application of these methods is expanding in education, large subfields of education include little or no CE or BC analysis—school choice, teacher value-added modeling, and special education are notable examples. Also, despite an exhaustive focus on test score accountability, few studies look at how to increase test scores for the lowest cost or even how valuable it would be to increase test scores. As already noted, it would have been very helpful to know the costs of class size reduction (or vouchers or small schools) before embarking on research to determine the effects on achievement.

More generally, economic evaluations can function as a framework for many of the factors that might influence a decision about education provision. Reform of the education system or the introduction of new programs raises a whole array of policy issues. Not all of these are about efficiency. For instance, more school choice may help students who seek alternative educational opportunities, but it may hinder those who are left behind in failing schools. The efficiency of school choice should be traded off against the potential increase in inequities for students in low-quality schools. Teacher accountability mechanisms may raise the quality of instruction but may reduce teacher job satisfaction and undermine a culture of professionalism. The gain in instructional quality may be offset by the extra risk to teachers that they will lose their jobs. Investing in science programs may increase the earnings of science graduates at the expense of funding for graduates in the humanities; similarly, investing in preschoolers means fewer resources for disadvantaged youth. All policies entail trade-offs, and most educational changes have political and social repercussions. However, by performing an economic evaluation we can identify some of these issues and distinguish between efficiency and equity. For instance, if we know that preschool is actually an investment that saves money—with fewer students later retained in grade such that the savings outweigh or offset the costs of preschool—this means more resources are available for disadvantaged youth (and perhaps they lead to a reduction in disadvantaged youth). Similarly, if accountability systems better demonstrate high-quality instruction, then parents might be more willing to pay for quality; teacher salaries might increase to compensate for the riskier work environment. Economic evaluation can clarify some issues and frame other key issues, allowing the decisionmaker to make better informed judgments and decisions.

It is important to clarify the purpose of economic evaluation: It is to help decisionmakers make better decisions. If it does not help with decisionmaking and thereby improve the policymaking process, it is not necessary (Posner, 2000). Critically, however, there is a logical step between providing an economic evaluation and making a decision. This step is clearly explained in U.S. government Executive Order 13563 issued in January 2011 (a supplement to Executive Order 12866 issued in September 1993). This order establishes that U.S. government agencies must "propose or adopt a regulation only upon a reasoned determination that its benefits justify its costs (recognizing that some benefits and costs are difficult to quantify)." BC analysis will yield an economic metric that has implications for investment of public funds. But that does not mean that these funds must be invested. As Executive Order 13563 states, there may be some benefits and costs that were not quantified; these may be sufficiently important to override the economic imperative. Moreover, the decisionmaker must still make a "reasoned determination"—that is, explicitly justify the decision. Economic evaluations should help make that decision, but they do not determine it. Just because an intervention does not pass a formal BC test does not mean it should not be supported. If society believes that open-access college is an important commitment that a community should make to its future, then this belief need not be automatically negated by an economic evaluation that finds that the costs exceed the measured benefits. Throughout this book, we encourage the reader to examine how economic evaluations help improve education policy cognizant of the difference between an economic result and a reasoned determination.

● 1.6. OUTLINE OF THE BOOK

This volume attempts to offer an up-to-date and broad discussion of economic evaluation of education programs. It is a significantly revised and expanded version of two earlier editions addressing the same topics by Levin (1975, 1983) and Levin and McEwan (2001). In some respects, the basics of the method have not changed since the first edition in 1983. The ingredients method is the same, as are the metrics that are intended to represent efficiency. However, there has been a broad expansion of applications for CE and BC. In addition, new methodological developments—in effectiveness and benefits measurement, approaches to cost data collection and analysis, and sensitivity testing—all represent rich topics for improving the use of the tools. These topics are included in this revision. Also, the evidence base on results has grown, and we offer a general review of this evidence. Most importantly, there is now a much greater recognition that economic evaluations can play an important role in both education research and policy formation. New material in this book reinforces the theme that economic evaluations are valuable methods for social scientists to apply.

The remainder of the book will be devoted to a presentation and discussion of the use of economic evaluations in education as well as a description of the principles and techniques for developing such analyses. The next chapter will discuss the decision context, audience, and particular issues that are pertinent to the choice of analysis, its implementation, and its presentation. Chapters 3 through 6 will address the nature of costs and their identification, measurement, and distribution. The reader should be aware that the discussion in these chapters applies equally well to all modes of cost analysis. That is, the differences among the modes are primarily on the outcomes side rather than the cost side. Chapters 7 and 8 focus on how to measure effects and how to perform CE analysis. In a parallel form, Chapters 9 and 10 focus on how to specify benefits and how to perform BC analysis. An essential element of economic evaluation is sensitivity testing and dealing with uncertainty. This topic is covered in Chapter 11. As a review, Chapter 12 provides a checklist for appraising the quality of economic evaluations. Finally, Chapter 13 considers how to link the evidence from economic evaluations to policy and decisionmaking. Each chapter includes exercises and discussion questions. Appendix A gives sample answers to even-numbered exercises at the end of each chapter.

Discussion Questions

1. Typically, educational evaluations look at the effects of alternative interventions on student outcomes without considering the cost consequences. Under what circumstances would adopting the "most effective" alternative actually increase overall costs to the school district for any specific educational result relative to choosing a "less effective" alternative?

2. There have been many studies of the relation between enrollment levels in schools and school districts and the cost per student. These studies purport to show how cost varies with school size, and they attempt to determine the enrollment ranges in which costs are lowest. Do these studies meet the criteria for CE analysis?

3. Imagine a state introduces a new tax on soft drinks, and the tax revenues are earmarked for spending on education. Which level of

education—preschool, elementary school, secondary school, college, or vocational training—should receive priority for public funding from these additional tax revenues?

4. What are the fundamental differences between CE and BC analyses? Provide examples of educational interventions where CE analysis is preferred. Provide examples of educational interventions where BC analysis is preferred.

2

Establishing an Analytic Framework

Objectives

1. Identify the evaluation problem.

2. Determine the audience and perspective for the evaluation.

3. Select the appropriate type of economic analysis and research design in relation to the theory of change.

4. Establish the need for chosen economic evaluation.

Before beginning an economic evaluation, it is important to establish the analytical framework that will be utilized. This framework consists of identifying the nature of the problem and the theory of change, clarifying the specific alternatives that should be considered in the analysis, establishing the identity of the audiences—and the perspective—for the analysis, and selecting the type of cost analysis to use. These tasks are all preparatory to the actual research inquiry, data collection, and analysis, which are addressed in subsequent chapters. At the initial stage, it is important to consider the extent and scope of the inquiry to ensure that the economic evaluation is appropriate and justifiable.

In this chapter, we discuss these issues in turn. Although they might seem outside the scope of a direct economic evaluation, establishing the appropriate structure for the research inquiry is critical. It is going to be very difficult to rederive new estimates of costs and benefits if the research questions change. Importantly, the research findings will depend on how the research is framed. Hence, we describe key issues in establishing the analytic framework for economic evaluation.

● 2.1. IDENTIFYING THE PROBLEM

One of the critical, but sometimes neglected, areas of evaluation design is proper identification of the problem. By proper identification, we mean that the nature and scope of the problem should be posed to justify the intervention and to determine which alternatives for reform appropriately address the issue. To accomplish this, aspects of the problem must be documented to understand who is affected and how (for an overview of evaluation methods and practice, see Rossi, Lipsey, & Freeman, 2004).

For example, it is widely accepted as important that children acquire reading skills progressively through school based on age or grade level. If it is found that children are not reading at the appropriate level, it is important to know how many children are behind in reading, at the age or grade level, how severe the gap is between the skills children have and the skills needed to be on target, and where the children are located who need the most assistance. Based on this information, one should ascertain potential reasons to explain the deficiency. The origins may be community or family based and related to insufficient skills upon school entry, reading deficiencies among the population, or lack of books for children outside of school. Another possibility is that the teaching strategies or materials may not be conducive to the variety of skill in the classroom consistent with up-to-date research on pedagogy for teaching reading. A third possibility could be related to attendance. A fourth could be that the children with lagging reading skills are English-language e-learners. Each of these causes would require a different intervention to sufficiently impact the outcome of interest.

We can also review another example where the problem is one at the system level rather than with student skill development. As noted in Chapter 1, the question that is often posed by school districts facing financial exigencies because of declining enrollments is this: Which school or schools do we close? The real problem that must be faced, however, is how to address a shrinkage in resources that does the least damage to the education system. The alternatives to consider include the possibilities of school closure, but they also include the options of reducing personnel, cutting specific offerings, increasing class size, leasing excess space in existing schools, and taking a variety of other potential routes to cutting the budget or raising school revenues. Narrowing the question to which schools are to be closed is to rule out options that may be more appropriate when economic criteria are used. That is, there can obviously be no economic analysis among alternatives that are not considered.

To select the most efficient program or intervention, all relevant alternatives should be identified and considered. The alternatives for addressing particular problems are those potential interventions that might respond to the problem and improve the situation being addressed. It is important to ask whether all the pertinent alternatives have been placed on the agenda for consideration. Obviously, the classes of alternatives that ought to be considered are those that are most responsive to the problem. Again, this will require a sensitive search for ways of meeting the challenge that has been posed. Although one may wish to draw upon traditional responses as well as those that other entities have used in facing similar problematic situations, one should not be limited to these. In fact, sometimes they may not be the most responsive approaches.

In conducting an economic evaluation of alternative interventions, one must ask not only whether the alternatives that will be considered are responsive to the problem but also whether the "responsive" ones have been included. Often, both administrators and evaluators will rule out alternatives before analyzing them when such options are politically sensitive. That is, the pragmatic aspects of daily life suggest that one avoid pitched political battles by keeping politically sensitive issues off the agenda if at all possible. While one can appreciate the pressures on both evaluators and administrators in this regard, there are two reasons that all of the relevant alternatives should be analyzed.

First, it is a matter of professional integrity to provide information on all of the pertinent alternatives, while letting the decisionmaking and political processes eventually determine the choice among them (Ross, Barkaoui, & Scott, 2007). If those processes are not adequately informed about possible responses, they can never consider the costs and impacts of many of the pertinent alternatives. There is an appropriate place for analysis and one for decisionmaking. If certain alternatives are precluded from consideration by their political sensitivity, then the political and decisionmaking processes have taken place before the information and analyses have been derived. Clearly, the two stages are interrelated, but good decisionmaking should be based upon informed choices rather than ones that eliminate potential options before they are ever analyzed and considered.

A second reason for considering even those alternatives that are politically sensitive is that such sensitivity or opposition may be dependent upon circumstances. That is, while some alternatives are indeed "untouchable" in the normal course of events, they may become salient for consideration under more dire circumstances. If a school district is facing serious budgetary problems, it must consider all possibilities that would reduce the budget. If student proficiencies in certain academic areas are woefully inadequate, then a wide range of programs for improvement begin to enter the realm of consideration. It is important to consider the strengths and weaknesses or the costs and effects of selecting from all of the pertinent alternatives. It should also be borne in mind that the retention of existing practices is always an alternative.

Indeed, this leads to a final comment on alternatives. Cost analysis is premised on the view that decisionmakers have choices. The objective is to make the best selection from competing alternatives. Economic evaluation is done in order to aid in the selection among alternatives. If there are no alternatives, there is no point in doing an analysis. That is, no matter how competent the evaluation, it will simply lack usefulness if one cannot do anything with what is learned. Equally importantly, the analyst should evaluate a given intervention against a reasonable alternative that might otherwise be implemented. The evaluation should not compare the intervention against "nothing" if there is a reasonable expectation that students would receive "something"; the intervention should be compared against the other "something." (The analogy here is with drug trials where a new drug is compared against a placebo rather than a generic version of the drug.) In fact, in order to properly perform an incremental analysis, an economic evaluation should focus as much inquiry on the comparison group as it does on the treatment group.

Ultimately, the goal of an economic evaluation is to help policymakers decide on an alternative. It is to help them choose among alternatives. Of necessity, it can only help them choose among alternatives that have been the subject of the analysis and the type of analysis chosen. Cost-effectiveness (CE) analysis of six school-based reading programs can only provide information as to which reading program is the most efficient; it cannot determine whether school-based programs are more efficient than parental engagement reading programs. Also, it cannot determine whether a district would get higher benefits from investing in math programs instead of reading programs. All research is bounded by the questions included in the analysis, but not all research is so directly intended to influence decisions. The goal of the economic evaluation of reading programs is to help decisionmakers choose one.

2.2. TAKING ACCOUNT OF THE AUDIENCE AND PERSPECTIVE

When identifying the problem and the alternatives that might address the problem, it is important to be clear about the audience or audiences for whom the analysis will be done. The audiences include one or more groups of stakeholders—that is, individuals or institutions with an interest in the outcomes of the evaluation process. It is helpful to think of a primary audience and a secondary audience. The primary audience is generally the decisionmaker (and the clientele whom he or she represents) who has requested the analysis. The secondary audience consists of those persons and groups who will also draw upon the analysis.

Since the analysis is being prepared explicitly for the primary audience, it is important that it meet the specifications of that audience. For example, if one is requested to do a cost-feasibility (CF) study of using educational television in the school curriculum, it is important to ascertain exactly what is behind the request. Is there a specific technological or curriculum approach that the decisionmaker has in mind, or is the charge to be concerned with the costs of a wide variety of approaches, from selected courses to full curriculum coverage? These details can be worked out through dialogue and specification of the issues, and the analysis and report should be written with the needs of the primary audience in mind. Nevertheless, there may be tension if the decisionmaker places certain alternatives beyond consideration even though the alternatives may be in the best interests of the constituents represented by that decisionmaker. For economic analysis, there is an extra tension: With an impact evaluation, there is a risk that the intervention will not be effective; with an economic evaluation, there is an added risk that, even if it is effective, the intervention will not be found to be efficient (Levin, 2001). Hence, it is important to structure the analysis so that all reasonable alternatives are evaluated in the same way and so that the research conclusions are not predetermined.

Often, however, economic reports are read by secondary audiences who wish to use the information to inform decisions regarding replication or scale-up in another setting. If a study will be restricted to its primary audience, one need not be concerned about secondary audiences. However, if a secondary audience is likely to utilize the study, it is important to be clear about what is possibly generalizable to other settings and what is not. For example, in reviewing the costs of instructional programs, a school district may generate cost analyses that exclude resources contributed by the state or other levels of government or by volunteers. For purposes of decisionmaking in the district under scrutiny, this omission may be understandable. But if other school districts attempt to apply those cost analyses, they may discover that they have allocated far too few resources to support such instructional programs. Not every other school district in that secondary audience will have equal access to governmental or volunteer resources. In general, it is preferable to report all costs such that any audience can identify the resources appropriate to their situation no matter who is providing them.

Potentially, there are many audiences. For example, a district may be interested in improvements in teaching English and reading to students from non-English-speaking backgrounds. Among the alternative policies are English as a second language (ESL), bilingual instruction, and total immersion in English. Before performing CE analysis to determine which policy to recommend, the analyst might identify several primary and secondary audiences. The primary audiences—that is, those who must use the results directly for their own decisionmaking—might include the school board, the district administrators, the state education agency, and the pertinent curriculum specialists and teachers. Given the many audiences, it may be useful to interview representatives to ascertain the types of information that they would like to obtain from the evaluation. The secondary audiences—that is, those with an interest in the results—might include non-English-speaking local residents, employers and residents of the district, and other school districts. These audiences may have different needs from the primary audiences. Again, setting priorities is important, since no evaluation endeavor is likely to meet all the needs of every potential primary and secondary audience.

Once the basic outlines of a cost study are agreed upon, the essential next step is to decide whether to perform CE or benefit-cost (BC) analysis. Either analysis may be appropriate. It depends on what decisions will be made as a result of the analysis. For example, imagine a nonprofit agency whose mandate is to improve literacy in kindergarten.

Given the agency's objectives are already established, it would seem that CE analysis would be most appropriate; this would inform the agency which literacy programs are the best value. By contrast, BC analysis helps establish whether it is worth investing in literacy programs at all. Presumably, the agency—in deciding its mandate—had already determined that literacy programs are worth investing in. However, BC analysis may be useful: It can clarify how valuable literacy programs are and so justify—both within the agency and to its donors or funders—further investments in literacy programs. As emphasized previously, the motivating question is this: What decisions will the audience make when presented with the information from economic analysis?

Audiences may be more or less willing to accept certain kinds of analyses that nonetheless yield similar conclusions. For example, BC analysis is less palatable to some audiences because it requires placing a monetary value on certain kinds of outcomes, effectively modeling child learning in terms of its monetary benefits. Although they are different, there is scope to substitute between CE analysis and BC analysis. One could imagine a program that is aimed at reducing high school dropouts. Since the program is designed to reduce the number of high school dropouts, an obvious measure of effectiveness is the number of dropouts averted. Eventually, of course, staying in high school might yield monetary benefits in the form of additional wages. We can conduct either CE or BC analysis, depending on the outcome measure that is chosen (dropouts averted or increased wages). It is conceivable that the CE analysis will be more warmly received by some audiences, because it does not attempt to describe the outcomes of the program in pecuniary terms. If CE and BC analyses do produce similar conclusions for decisionmaking purposes, it seems prudent to choose the analytical technique that is most likely to be well received by the primary audience. However, choosing to conduct CE analysis rather than a more comprehensive BC analysis might entail sacrifices in terms of the depth of analysis. In these cases, the researcher is best advised to allow the demands of the analytical task to guide the choice of analytical technique rather than the demands of the audience.

Thus far, we have described the audience simply as if they are readers of the research evaluation. However, their role is much more influential because they can shape the perspective of the analysis. The perspective is the framework within which costs and effects or benefits should be examined. Thus, the perspective dictates which items should be included in the analysis.

For educational evaluations, we can distinguish three important perspectives. Depending on which perspective is adopted, the analyst will have to calculate the costs, effects, and benefits that correspond to that perspective.

The primary perspective is the social perspective: This requires that all costs should be counted, regardless of who pays for them or even if they are provided in kind, and all benefits should be included, regardless of who accrues them. This social perspective is therefore all-encompassing, and other perspectives can be understood in relation to the social one. Indeed, it makes sense to start with a social perspective and then specify alternative perspectives within this general one. As discussed previously, the audience for the analysis may prefer a perspective that only helps with their decisionmaking and so excludes some costs (or even some benefits). However, this preference may be narrow-minded: If the goal is to maximize social welfare, the decisionmaker should be interested in all the resources used. This holds even when the decisionmaker uses contributed resources; these contributed resources might be used in an alternative way if their current use yields low benefits. Importantly, volunteers who contribute their time should want to know if their contribution—as part of an educational investment—is socially valuable. Volunteers for mentoring programs such as Big Brothers Big Sisters of America, for example, would presumably switch to an alternative activity if they learned that this program generated only small social benefits (or invest more if they had evidence on the social value they were creating). Finally, in order to compare interventions, it is helpful if all evaluators adopt the same perspective, and the social perspective can be adopted for all interventions.

The next perspective is the private individual perspective: This requires calculation of all the costs and consequences for the student (or the student's household) or participant in the education program. Given that many education programs are subsidized by government and other entities, private individuals may reap substantial benefits but pay little of the costs. As such, from a private perspective many educational interventions should appear to be good value. As students are likely to choose the intervention with the highest private returns, this perspective will help explain why students participate in particular programs.

Finally, the analyst may adopt a fiscal perspective—that is, looking only at the costs and consequences from the perspective of the taxpayers or a particular government agency. This perspective is important as a way of justifying public investments in education programs. Government agencies may—by statute—be bound to consider only the implications for their agency. The challenge with using this perspective is that many educational interventions are funded from several sources, have diverse effects, or convey benefits to many individuals and in many domains. Adopting a fiscal perspective would provide a very partial picture for each agency. Nevertheless, some agencies might justify educational investments purely on these narrow grounds: Given the evidence on the effect of education on health, for example, it might be reasonable to label the high dropout rate in the United States as a "public health issue" (Freudenberg & Ruglis, 2007).

2.3. RELATING ECONOMIC EVALUATION ●
TO THE THEORY OF CHANGE

Once one has established the problem, the alternatives to be considered in addressing it, and the audiences, it is necessary to select the type of analytic framework that will be used. In the previous chapter, we identified these approaches as cost and CF analysis; CE and cost-utility (CU) analysis; and BC analysis. Here, we discuss which is appropriate across the range of educational interventions.

As noted in Chapter 1, CE and BC analyses are strictly intended to answer different questions about CE and efficiency respectively. However, the analyst may need to discover which form of analysis is appropriate for each intervention.

The best way to make this discovery is to make sure that the economic evaluation corresponds to the theory of change for each intervention. For our purposes, we can think of the theory of change in terms of (a) an educational intervention that is implemented (b) within a general context or set of existing conditions and that via a (c) connecting outcome or mechanism meets or is intended to meet (d) a set of longer-term goals (Weiss, Bloom, & Brock, 2014). Each of these elements (a–d) is relevant for deciding on the appropriate economic evaluation and how that evaluation is structured (Ludwig, Kling, & Mullainathan, 2011).

The intermediate or longer-term outcomes of some interventions explicitly can be measured in monetary values. For example, a training program may be intended to increase earnings for participants or a social emotional learning intervention may have savings to the school system from reduced conduct disorder as its goal. Given that BC analysis requires all amounts to be measured in monetary terms, this would be the most appropriate evaluative method. While the value of additional earnings and employment from an educational investment might be measured in dollars, some measures—such as positive feelings toward learning—cannot easily be converted into monetary units. Indeed, for many potential educational interventions, the use of BC analysis will be challenging. By contrast, CE and CU analyses can be applied under a wide variety of situations—most notably any intervention with achievement goals. However, if there are many outcomes— and especially if the longer-term goals are far into the future—then BC analysis will be more appropriate. Finally, if no outcomes or longer-term goals can be specified in quantitative terms, it may nonetheless be helpful to consider CF analysis to yield some indication of how much an intervention actually costs in relation to budgets.

The theory of change, as well as the economic method selected, will also affect how that method is applied. The cost analysis must clearly correspond to the scale, scope, duration, and intensity of the intervention that is being implemented. For instance, we can think of a high school support program such as Talent Search that is intended to boost high school completion and college enrollment (Bowden & Belfield, 2015). If the mechanism by which Talent Search is effective is that students successfully apply for college, then the analyst should cost out that application process. Alternatively, if the mechanism is continuous mentoring support through high school, then the costing exercise will have to follow students through their mentoring experiences, perhaps over multiple years. In turn, this means that the comparison group will have to be followed over the same time period. As another example, we can think of socioemotional learning interventions that are intended to change the climate across the school. The cost analysis must measure all changes in resources at the school level (see Long, Brown, Jones, Aber, & Yates, 2015). Cost per student may not be an accurate guide: In order to influence school climate, all (or most) of the students must receive services collectively, not individually, and it is the total cost that is salient.

Similarly, the economic analysis must be responsive to the context in which the intervention is delivered. On the cost side, the availability and prices of ingredients may vary across school districts: In low-income countries, some inputs (e.g., online computing systems) may not be available; in areas of high poverty, the analyst must take into account the opportunity cost of time for schoolchildren who may need to work to support their families. Context also matters on the benefit side. For example, a preschool program might reduce future youth crime—in fact, this effect is one of the main reasons why the HighScope Perry Preschool Program has such a high payoff. But this impact may only be salient for preschools in localities where the crime rate is high (a distinction noted in Barnett & Masse, 2007).

Finally, the analyst may have to infer longer-term outcomes from intermediate ones. In the case of preschool, for example, the researcher cannot wait 15 years for information on earnings; even freshman college programs can have very delayed impacts on future earnings. In these cases, it is important that the BC analyst choose to measure intermediate outcomes (e.g., high school graduation or first-semester credits) that are well correlated with longer-term outcomes. It is also important that any changes in behavior be measured when they occur and for how long they occur. Interventions where change is "fast-acting" and persistent are of higher value because of their immediacy, and the BC analysis should reflect this.

At this stage, we can cover only the main issues. As the theory of change for each intervention becomes more detailed, the economic evaluator should respond accordingly. Fundamentally, each economic analysis should adapt to fit with the theory of change for each specific intervention.

2.4. DETERMINING IF ECONOMIC EVALUATION IS NECESSARY

As a final consideration before beginning the research, it is worth asking whether an economic analysis is needed. Thus far, it has been assumed that in most cases cost analysis should be done and that a lot of valuable information will be obtained from such analysis. However, this reasoning is not definitive. We have already suggested that if there are no alternatives or if a decision is already predetermined, the entire evaluative situation—including economic analysis—becomes moot. Further, if sufficient time or other resources are lacking or if CE types of data will not alter decisions, there is probably not a strong case for doing cost analysis. Even when all the prerequisites for implementing and using cost analysis are present, it is important that such an evaluation be worth doing in the first place.

Moreover, economic evaluation techniques might themselves be interrogated using efficiency criteria: What is the economic payoff to performing CE analysis? Do the benefits of performing BC analysis outweigh the costs? In response, we refer to Scriven's (1974, pp. 85–93) notion of cost-free evaluation. In considering the choice of an analytic approach and supportive design for implementation, one must ask what will be gained by finding a better alternative. If the gains will be relatively small, only a small investment in evaluation would be merited. Indeed, if the potential gains of a good decision are minuscule, it is possible that no formal analytic study should be undertaken. That is, intuition and present knowledge should suffice, given that little will be gained from a more formal and extended evaluation. However, when the value of selecting a new alternative can be very great, it may be worth making a large investment in evaluation and analysis. Scriven would say that this situation meets the cost-free evaluation criterion if the probable gains from the evaluation will be in excess of the costs of the evaluation. It is cost-free in that more is saved by a good and appropriate evaluation than is expended in resources on that evaluation. Put simply, the more costly the intervention is to implement, the more likely it is that an economic evaluation will pay for itself by changing the allocation of resources. Prima facie, the economic case for economic evaluation appears reasonable: Society devotes a substantial amount of resources to education programs, and the information obtained from an economic evaluation is probably substantial and salient.

Nevertheless, in order to know how much economic evaluation to do, one needs a sense of what research effort is involved. We describe the research tasks in detail in the following chapters, so here we offer very general comments. First, it is important to recognize that costs are estimated, just in the same way that impacts are estimated. Cost estimation is therefore a substantial research activity, just as identification of impacts is. When estimating impacts, the researcher is immediately concerned with potential sampling error—that is, the likelihood that the sample chosen reflects the population. Sampling error is ameliorated by properly designing the sampling frame and drawing a sample of sufficient power. This logic also holds when estimating costs: The researcher should draw from the population of sites (e.g., schools or classrooms or students) to ensure that the sample reflects the population. A priori, it is difficult to say if the sample for estimating costs should be larger or smaller than the sample for estimating impacts; it depends on the variation of costs within the population. Overall, whatever research tasks are important for impact evaluations are likely to be required of economic evaluators.

Second, in most BC or CE evaluations, some expertise will be needed from persons who are specialists in these kinds of analyses. Although BC analysis is a standard component of the economics of public finance, many academic economists have not had practical training in either cost analysis or shadow pricing techniques. Also, one should not confuse expertise in accounting with expertise in BC or CE analysis. While BC and CE analysts must have a good understanding of cost accounting, cost accountants need have no understanding of BC and CE analysis. Often, the correct approaches for cost accounting for business firms are inappropriate for estimating the costs of social projects. In fact, one of the rationales of public economics is that, frequently, social costs and benefits differ considerably from private ones. Cost accountants are not usually trained to address social costs and benefits.

That said, economic evaluations do not just rely on economic principles. In order to perform CE analysis, one has to determine what effectiveness means in each educational context. For instance, for reading programs it might be comprehension or vocabulary or fluency; for dropout prevention programs it might be keeping students in school each year, getting them to finish 12 grades, or getting them to complete a high school diploma. The answers to these questions cannot be found in economic theory. Experts in the respective fields are needed to determine which specific outcomes are most valid.

Overall, there is no presumption that an economic evaluation is necessary nor is there a fixed amount of effort that an expert might contribute to perform such an evaluation. Resources would need to cover three discrete research tasks: (1) calculating costs, (2) identifying effects or estimating benefits, and (3) combining the two to report an economic metric. Potentially, such studies might require resources equivalent to those needed for an impact evaluation. The main guiding principle is the proportionality principle—that is, the idea that the amount of effort required should correspond to the value of the knowledge acquired and how that knowledge influences the results of the analysis. Suffice it to say, we hope to establish in this book that the knowledge gained from most economic evaluations is unlikely to be trivial and that more, rather than fewer, such evaluations are worthwhile.

2.5. CONCLUSIONS   ●

Before undertaking an economic evaluation, it is important to understand the research question in detail. This understanding should start with the formal identification and understanding of the problem and the theory of change that each educational intervention adverts to. It should include explicit consideration and selection of alternatives to be evaluated; once these alternatives are set, the economic evaluation will be directed to determining which alternative is the most cost-effective or efficient. The analyst must recognize which audiences will use the evidence. Cognizant of this audience, the analyst must determine the perspective. We propose that each economic evaluation should begin with the presumption that a social perspective should be considered as the first priority even as other perspectives—fiscal, private, or per agency—are valid and important. Next, the analyst must choose the appropriate mode of analysis; the more detailed the investigation of the research question, the easier this choice will be. Finally, the analyst should perform an appraisal as to whether an economic evaluation is worthwhile.

This process requires a substantial research commitment: Each item needs to be decided in tandem, and these decisions will significantly shape the research inquiry. However, once these decisions are made, it is possible to proceed to the next stage of the analysis—how to undertake cost analysis.

Discussion Questions

1. A nonprofit agency wishes to introduce a mentoring program for at-risk youth and wants to perform BC analysis. What are some of the important issues to decide before beginning any data collection?

2. What types of assistance would you need in doing an economic evaluation, and what types of expert could contribute to the activity?

3. Describe potential audiences for different types of cost analyses. What would be the purpose of cost analysis for each audience? What type of analysis would be appropriate for each audience and why?

4. Federal policy in the United States constrains the use of BC analysis to only "economically significant" federal regulations. How should the term *economically significant* be defined?

Exercises

1. For the following interventions, describe how you would determine whether formal cost analysis is worthwhile.

   a. The education department in a particular state has mandated that school districts implement a specific math curriculum, including textbooks, teacher training, computer software, and other materials.

   b. A team of second-grade teachers approached their principal with a proposal to spend 10 minutes each morning performing mindfulness exercises with the students to help reduce stress, increase focus, and increase learning throughout the day.

   c. A community college is considering expanding its online education program to offer a wider range of courses and possibly even full degree programs.

2. For each of the following situations, determine which types of analysis (CE, BC, CU, cost, or CF) are most appropriate:

   a. A school district wishes to increase the employability of students who terminate their formal education at high school graduation. Accordingly, it seeks an answer to the question of whether it should expand vocational educational offerings for students who are presently in the general education program.

   b. The school board wishes to accommodate budget cuts by reducing some of the elective course offerings in the high school. A reduction in the budget of $60,000 has been targeted.

   c. A university must decide if it is desirable to establish a new online degree program.

   d. The state legislature wishes to consider the introduction of tablet computers into every high school in the state. However, it is not clear that the school budget is adequate.

   e. A school district is seeking approaches to improve students' writing skills. Proposed solutions include (a) having smaller class sizes with more stress on writing and more writing assignments, (b) hiring college students with excellent writing skills to assist teachers in grading writing assignments, and (c) developing special writing courses for students in addition to their regular English classes.

   f. A community college must reduce its course offerings in the next academic year to accommodate a dismal budgetary situation. The college offers more than 1,400 courses in some 38 departments and programs. Enough courses must be cut to achieve savings of $500,000.

   g. Both computer-assisted instruction and smaller class sizes are being discussed as ways to improve the mathematics competencies of youngsters in a particular school district. The administration wishes to ascertain which alternative is preferable.

3. Identify a potential problem associated with each of the following five situations. Describe at least two alternatives that might be considered for addressing each problem. Suggest the hypothetical primary and secondary audiences for the evaluations that would follow in each of the five cases. What types of analysis would seem appropriate for each?

   a. Student test scores at the high school level have been declining for the past 5 years.

   b. The physics department of a college is having little success in placing its graduates.

   c. A school district faces an anticipated budget deficit for the next year of $200,000.

   d. A university wishes to consider replacing its computer servers and data management system.

   e. Local residents are unhappy that there is no college in their town.

3

Cost Concepts

Objectives

1. Specify the concept of costs in terms of opportunity costs.

2. Define cost terms for educational interventions.

3. Relate costs to the theory of change.

4. Distinguish between cost information and budgetary data.

5. Provide motivation for performing cost analysis.

To most of us, the notion of cost is something that is both as obvious as the price of a good or service and as mysterious as the columns of data on an accounting statement or budget. In this chapter, we will introduce a concept of costs that will differ somewhat from both of these, and we will discuss in detail how an education analyst might think about costs. Any social intervention or program has both an outcome and a cost. The outcome refers to the result of the intervention. Outcomes of educational interventions include such common indicators as higher student achievement, fewer dropouts, improved attitudes, greater employability, and so on. But why are all interventions associated with costs, and what is meant by costs?

For an economist, understanding the costs of an educational program is a way of understanding how the program works in relation to its theory of change (Hummel-Rossi & Ashdown, 2002). For example, if we know that one of the costs of a new instructional program is the wages paid to a highly trained teacher, we would expect the effects of the program to be mediated through the teacher's competence. As an even easier example, if a new curriculum intervention requires no extra teacher training and no new facilities but simply the substitution of the old textbook by a new textbook, the extra cost will be very low; consequently, we might not expect a very significant effect on academic outcomes (and little effect on teacher performance and probably zero effect on student behaviors). Put simply, the analyst needs to think about costs in conjunction with program implementation. Educational interventions can be implemented in various ways—both by design and inadvertently—and so the resources required for the intervention will vary accordingly.

In this chapter, we describe the key concept that economists use to think about costs—the idea of opportunity cost. We then define cost terms that apply to educational interventions and describe the components of a cost estimate. As a final contribution, we make an important distinction between cost information and budgetary data, emphasizing that budgets do not accurately represent costs.

A critical aspect of assessing costs is the correct use of the terminology of economic evaluation. When terms are used loosely, it is very difficult to explain and interpret costs. Thus, this chapter focuses on defining and clarifying terms. This discussion will provide a foundation upon which to design and apply the ingredients method as described throughout the remaining chapters of the book.

● 3.1. THE CONCEPT OF COSTS

Costs refer to the value of all the resources used to implement the program in question. Every intervention uses resources that could be utilized for other valued alternatives. For example, a program for raising student achievement will require personnel, facilities, and materials that can be applied to other educational and noneducational endeavors. If these resources are used in one way, they cannot be used in some other way that may also provide useful outcomes. The human time and energy as well as the buildings, materials, and other resources used in one endeavor have other valuable uses. By devoting them to a particular activity, we are sacrificing the gains that could be obtained from using them for some other purpose.

If we assume that a specific intervention will have an effect that is found in a good effectiveness study, we want to know what it costs to replicate that intervention to compare its effectiveness. The cost is represented by all of the resources or ingredients required to replicate the program, no matter how they were financed or provided. Virtually all resources have a cost, even if they were provided in kind.

Accordingly, the "cost" of pursuing the intervention is what we must give up by not using these resources in some other way. Technically, then, the cost of a specific intervention will be defined as the value of all the resources that it utilizes had they been assigned to their most valuable alternative use. In this sense, all costs represent the sacrifice of an opportunity that has been forgone. It is this notion of opportunity cost that lies at the base of cost analysis in evaluation. By using resources in one way, we are giving up the ability to use them in another way, so a cost has been incurred.

Although this may appear to be a peculiar way to view costs, it is probably more familiar to each of us than it appears at first glance. It is usually true that when we refer to costs, we refer to the expenditure that we must make to purchase a particular good or service, as reflected in the statement, "The cost of college was $5,000." Here, the statement refers to expenditure on fees and tuition the college charges students who enroll. In cases in which the only cost is the expenditure of funds that could have been used for other goods and services, the sacrifice or cost can be stated in terms of expenditure. However, in daily usage, we also make statements such as these: "It would cost me a full year without working to attend college," or "The time cost of being in class is too high."

In each of these cases, a loss was incurred, which is viewed as the value of opportunities that were sacrificed. Thus, the cost of a particular activity is viewed as its "opportunity cost" and should include all lost options. Of course, this does not mean that we can always easily place a dollar value on that cost. In the case of losing a year of work, one can probably say that the sacrifice or opportunity cost was equal to what could have been earned; a similar logic applies to missing class, even as the actual money value of time for learning might be harder to estimate. These costs should be added to the extra money the student has to pay in fees.

The most common method for placing monetary values on resources is that of using their market prices. According to economic theory, when a market for a particular good or service is perfectly competitive, the equilibrium price established by that market will represent the value of that good (Mankiw, 2011, Chapter 7). The market price reflects the point at which the demands of purchasers and the supplies of providers lead to transactions that clear the market. This is known as market value. These participants are basing their willingness to buy or sell on their own opportunity costs, so the market price should directly reflect opportunity cost.

However, market prices are not a very accurate reflection of opportunity cost in distorted markets. There are many reasons why markets might be distorted. These include highly concentrated markets with less competition, information failures, and externalities. In education systems, monopoly features are common. For example, the cost of hiring a teacher is often based on district salary scales or statewide certification requirements on the demand side and based on collective bargaining contracts on the supply side. These supply and demand distortions may move teacher pay away from what might be considered as a competitive market price for teaching services (see Eberts, 2007; Jacob, 2007). However, teachers can select alternative occupations, and districts/schools must pay competitive wages or their teachers will leave for other districts or schools or for other employment. Generally, the distortion in teacher labor markets might be small such that the market wage is appropriate. Nevertheless, for each input, it is important to consider if there are distortions away from market prices, how large these distortions might be, and if they apply to the decisionmakers' context.

For some resources, market prices may not be available. When attempts are made to ascertain the value of a resource that does not have a competitive market price, the estimated value is called a shadow price (see Boardman, Greenberg, Vining, & Weimer, 2011, Chapters 16–17). Shadow prices should be based directly on opportunity cost. For example, a school district may decide to lend an old facility to a new program. There is no financial transaction, because the building was purchased and paid for a long time ago. Moreover, no market exists for this type of facility; there is no direct market price, so we must impute a shadow price valuation although the facility may have some lease value to nonschool users. This resource must therefore be valued based on what is would cost to maintain the facility in its current state, or to demolish the facility, or to refurbish it for alternative use. Another more common example is volunteer time: By definition, volunteers are unpaid, so there is no direct market price. Volunteer time must therefore be based on the opportunity cost of the volunteers' time.

Both market and shadow pricing approaches may be used for purposes of cost estimation. Both approaches are derived from the idea of opportunity cost, although we recognize that opportunity cost is a subtle concept that requires careful interpretation. Imagine a school with a gym that is typically unused in the summer. A nonprofit agency proposes a summer school basketball program for high school dropouts. Claiming that the gym is empty, the school might think that the opportunity cost is zero. However, a zero opportunity cost is rarely appropriate because the facility has other uses that represent an opportunity cost if not exploited. It is unlikely that there really is no other alternative use of the gym (e.g., for a different program or leasing for nonschool activities). Also, using the gym in the summer will likely necessitate maintenance costs later. Finally, the assumption of zero opportunity cost might be invoked in an ad hoc way for any resource (e.g., for example, the assumption that the cost of parental time contributions are zero because the parents would otherwise be relaxing at home). Potentially, the analyst could claim that a lot of resources had no alternative use and hence assert that the costs of the program are almost nothing. The conventional—and correct—assumption is that all resources have a positive opportunity cost, as all are needed to replicate the program regardless of financing.

3.2. COST PER UNIT ●

It is important to be clear about what we mean by costs of education (for a parallel exercise for costing out prevention programs, see Foster, Porter, Ayers, Kaplan, & Sandler, 2007). Strictly speaking, in economics the term *cost* refers to "cost per unit of output," for example, cost per car manufactured, cost per 1,000 computers produced, or cost per medical consultation. With this definition, an enterprise that has a lower cost per unit of output is more cost-effective (efficient) than one with a higher cost. This definition corresponds directly to the terminology of a standard economics textbook: Total cost is the cost to produce a given quantity of output, average cost is the cost per individual unit of output, and marginal cost is the cost per additional unit of output. These definitions work well for production decisions.

For educational services, the term *cost* is slightly different. It refers to the value of all the resources needed to deliver the intervention to the intended population. The *cost* term is therefore cost per participant, per cohort, or per class. It is helpful to always think about adding the word *per* after *cost* to clarify what is meant. This definition is more apt because we typically do not know how effective the intervention is (strictly speaking, the intervention's output). Number of students served—the cost per student—is unlikely to be a satisfactory measure of effectiveness. Lower cost per student is likely to be associated with lower quality and hence lower effectiveness. Indeed, effectiveness is what the analyst is often seeking to identify in relation to costs as an explicit cost-effectiveness (CE) analysis. Importantly, in the cost analysis framework, total cost is the cost for the entire population served by the program or education (e.g., a school of 1,000 students), average cost is the cost per unit of education provided (e.g., each student within the school), and marginal cost is the cost per extra unit provided (e.g., from the 999th to the 1,000th student). When referring to costs of education, it is typically cost of provision that is intended.

The terms *costs* and *expenditures* should be distinguished: They are not interchangeable. Expenditures typically refer only to dollar outlays by a specific group. For example, commentators often refer to increases in the "cost of college" when they actually mean the "price of college paid by enrollees" or "what students spent on college." Tuition prices paid by students are not the cost of college. The cost includes all the resources used to provide college and, because of public subsidies and charitable support, student tuition fees do not pay for all these resources (Desrochers & Hurlburt, 2016). In cost analysis, we are explicitly interested in all resources, regardless of where the dollars come from or if any money was transacted. In fact, cost analysis explicitly distinguishes between costs and financing—that is, between resources used and who pays for them.

An important cost concept for educational evaluation is incremental cost. As discussed in Chapter 2, CE and benefit-cost (BC) analyses evaluate programs relative to baseline, counterfactual, or business-as-usual conditions. Incremental cost refers to the relative difference in costs (Gray, Clarke, Wolstenholme, & Wordsworth, 2011, p. 13). (Incremental cost is not the same as marginal cost because we do not know how output has expanded.) In many cases, an intervention might be a supplement or add-on to regular schooling or college programs; incremental costs are then the costs of the program. But there are other cases. One is where the intervention involves a redistribution of resources such that intervention students get extra lessons in writing but fewer lessons in math; incremental costs might be very low in this case or even negative (if writing classes cost less than math classes). Another case is where students receive progressively more intensive interventions. So, if the analyst estimates the cost of a mentoring program at $1,000 per student and an after-school program with a similar objective at $1,500 per student, the incremental cost of the after-school program is $500. Note that in each case, we assume that each student receives some regular schooling, so the cost is genuinely incremental over regular schooling. Later on, we compare incremental costs with effects to derive an incremental cost-effectiveness ratio (ICER).

Sometimes, the term *cost* is used to describe economic losses or burdens. For example, a policy discussion might draw attention to the "cost of school failure" or the "cost of juvenile delinquency." This usage may be confusing. These are not costs in the sense of resources expended to provide an educational intervention. Instead, they are burdens or losses caused by not implementing effective educational interventions. The so-called cost of juvenile delinquency is what is spent on the juvenile justice system, not what is spent on educational programs to reduce delinquency. As such, this "cost" is better understood as the economic benefits from overcoming school failure or reducing juvenile delinquency. (Even then, it is sometimes an inaccurate measure of benefits because it includes both preventive and remedial expenditures; see the discussion of defensive expenditures in Chapter 9.)

3.3. COSTS AND THE THEORY OF CHANGE   ●

The analyst must identify, and then calculate, all resources involved in "making the intervention work." In practice, identifying all resources requires detective work and a thorough understanding of the intervention. To help acquire this understanding, it is helpful to think about the costs of an intervention in relation to its theory of change (for an example with a resilience program for youth, see Crowley, Jones, Greenberg, Feinberg, & Spoth, 2012).

The primary cost will be the actual delivery or implementation of the program within its educational setting. For example, a school might purchase a new math curriculum, so the costs will be all the resources required to teach children using this new curriculum. It should include all the preparatory resources needed to ensure that the program can be implemented, such as training of teachers in the new curriculum and changes to the school schedule.

This implementation cost must be related to the resources required for the alternative or counterfactual program. The alternative might entail no resources, but this must be established by the researcher. For example, a pull-out reading program for struggling third-grade students will require resources, but the students remaining in class are now in a smaller group and may receive more personalized instruction. Also, many struggling readers do already receive additional learning supports, and these may not be available if the student is pulled out of the classroom. The researcher must measure the resource use that is additive, beyond what would have otherwise been received.

Strictly, we think of costs as the costs to provide the program or implement the policy and to make sure it works. We do this so that a policymaker can understand what resources are actually needed for implementation. However, there are often other costs associated with educational interventions.

Induced costs are those arising from behavioral change after an intervention has been implemented. These induced costs should be examined in relation to the theory of change: They are the changes in resource use associated with the mediators of an intervention (Bowden, Shand, Belfield, Wang, & Levin, 2016; Chandra, Jena, & Skinner, 2011; Weiss, Bloom, & Brock, 2014). For instance, career academies are intended to help students get better jobs (Maxwell & Rubin, 2000). We can estimate the incremental cost of a career academy over an alternative youth training program; this would be the direct implementation cost. However, career academies often encourage students to stay in school longer, after which they get even better jobs. Whereas the delivery cost is the amount of resources needed to implement a career academy education, the induced cost is the cost of staying in school longer. If we are interested in the full cost of career academies, we should account for these induced costs. (These induced costs are sometimes referred to as indirect or mediated costs; for BC analysis, they are better thought of as negative benefits; see Chapter 9.)

In fact, when viewed in the context of their theory of change, many interventions explicitly anticipate these induced costs. Often, interventions begin with a diagnosis of educational need or a foundational treatment, which then leads to further services. These additional services are the mediator through which the program is effective.

For example, interventions to change remedial education lead to new college pathways; a new placement test might reassign students to fewer remedial classes, saving on resources as well as boosting college completion rates (see Scott-Clayton, Crosta, & Belfield, 2014). One prominent example is simplification of the FAFSA college aid application process (Bettinger, Long, Oreopoulos, & Sanbonmatsu, 2012); this simplification helped students apply for college and so induced them to attend and make progress in college. Student counseling and informational interventions work in the same way (Castleman, Page, & Schooley, 2014), and financial incentives in the first semester boost credit-taking in later semesters (Barrow, Richburg-Hayes, Rouse, & Brock, 2014).

Also, much of the research literature on school choice should be appraised in light of its induced costs: giving families a choice of school is likely to mean they will choose a school with a different—increased—level of school resources (Hsieh & Urquiola, 2006). These interventions affect students directly, but they also place students on a different educational or developmental pathway—and this new pathway has resource consequences. Finally, we can think of interventions that induce new resources outside the school. For example, the federal early childhood program Head Start has been found to influence parental time: Head Start children receive more help from their parents at home (Gelber & Isen, 2013; for a similar family-mediated effect with the Chicago Child-Parent Center program, see Reynolds, Ou, & Topitzes, 2004). These family resources mediate the effect of Head Start on longer-term outcomes. From a social perspective, these family resources are a cost.

For many interventions, therefore, it is important to estimate these induced costs and distinguish them from the costs of the intervention. In fact, these costs might be larger than the cost of delivering the intervention. Nevertheless, if the theory of change is clearly specified, these induced resources will be an explicit part of how the intervention is expected to work.

Another cost that is often neglected is raising funds to pay for a program. The ingredients might include the "deadweight loss" associated with raising funds to support the program (Haveman & Weimer, 2015). The deadweight loss is the distortion in other markets. For example, a city may wish to implement a new public school program in a city funded through a local sales tax. This tax will distort consumption decisions away from the taxed goods, leading to a deadweight loss or marginal excess tax burden (METB). Estimates of the METB for the United States are approximately 13% (Allgood & Snow, 1998)—that is, to generate $100 in funds for a program imposes a distortion of $13. Other countries may have larger METBs. If every public program imposes a deadweight loss, then the incremental effect may be very small. However, the size of the loss depends on how the tax is levied and at what level of government. It is important to check that the necessary funding for a given education program does not impose large distortions.

One other cost that is often ignored is that of reallocation of resources from one program to another. Often, school personnel assume that there is no cost because the shifts came from inside the school. But there is an opportunity cost if the shifted resources were producing valued outcomes in the previous program—that is, the cost is the value of the resources in their previous use, which is likely to be nonzero.

3.4. COSTS DATA AND BUDGETARY INFORMATION

A very common question often arises: Why should we go to all this trouble to estimate costs? Almost all social programs have budgets and expenditure statements, which presumably contain expenditure data that can be used to address the cost issues. However, there are many reasons why budgetary information is inadequate for cost analysis.

First, although the existence of budgets is universal, the assumption that they will contain all the cost information that is needed is usually erroneous. First, budgets often do not include cost information on all the resources used in the intervention. Contributed resources such as volunteers, donated equipment and services, and other "unpaid" inputs are not included in budgets.

Second, when resources have already been paid for or are included in some other agency's budget, they will not be easily observed. For example, a building that is provided to a school district by some other unit of government or one that is fully paid for will not be found in the budget of a school district. Many education interventions receive ingredients from multiple levels. For example, Reading Partners, a reading program coordinated through a national office, operates through reading centers within schools and utilizes resources from AmeriCorps, the national community service organization, as well as relying on volunteers (Jacob, Armstrong, Bowden, & Pan, 2016). To accurately estimate costs, all resources used to implement Reading Partners should be calculated.

Third, the standard budget practices may distort the true costs of an ingredient. Typical public budgets and expenditure statements charge the cost of major repairs or facility reconstruction only to the year in which the cost was incurred. Thus, when the roof or heating system of a school is replaced, the expenditures are found in the budget for the year in which the repairs were financed—typically the year in which the reconstruction was done rather than being amortized properly. Yet, a new roof or heating system may have a 30-year life so that only about one-thirtieth of it should be charged to the cost of programs in any given year. Budgetary conventions would typically charge the costs of such capital investments to a single budgetary year, overstating the true costs for that year and understating the costs of operating the program for the 29 subsequent years.

Fourth, the costs of any particular intervention are often embedded in a budget or expenditure statement that covers a much larger unit of operation. Therefore, it may be difficult to isolate the unique costs of a new reading program in a school district budget, since the budget is not constructed according to the costs of particular interventions or activities. In fact, most educational budgets are "line item" classifications of expenditures according to functions and objects. Examples of functions include administration, instruction, and maintenance. Examples of objects include teachers, supplies, clericals, and administrators. It is not only difficult to tie such budget listings to particular activities or interventions but also often impossible even to ascertain what the costs are for a given school or broad instructional program such as a language program, since no such breakdowns are usually provided.

Finally, most budgetary documents represent plans for how resources will be allocated rather than classifying expenditures after they have taken place. This means that, at best, they refer to planned disbursements rather than actual ones. Accordingly, beyond all their other limitations for cost analysis, budgets may not provide precise figures for actual resource use. Actual statements of expenditures may be more accurate, but they are still subject to the shortcomings mentioned before.

Finally, budgets rarely help elucidate how a program is implemented—or at least not in a way that is related to the theory of change or the counterfactual. This point is illustrated in the cost analysis of Read 180 by Levin, Catlin, and Olson (2007). Using the ingredients method, the researchers calculated program costs at three selected sites where Read 180 was being delivered; they also calculated the program costs based on the developer's recommended version of Read 180 from interviews and documents. Given that Read 180 is a reasonably formulaic reading intervention, we might anticipate that the actual costs at the three sites would be close to the recommended cost. The developer's recommended version of Read 180 required changes in both personnel and materials. However, as implemented, some sites relied on adding more personnel than others while others yet varied in materials. The result was a significant difference in average costs for each site.

For these reasons, cost analysis cannot place primary reliance on budgetary or expenditure documents to ascertain the costs of interventions. Of course, these documents may still provide supplementary data that will be very useful. However, they cannot serve as a principal source for constructing cost estimates.

● 3.5. MOTIVATION FOR COST ANALYSIS

Understanding the costs of an intervention is of course a prerequisite for performing CE and BC analyses. In itself, cost analysis is also valuable. It allows us to perform a cost study and a cost feasibility analysis (we provide examples of these in subsequent chapters). Even before that, however, cost analysis helps the analyst learn about the intervention in two key respects. These are the main motives for performing a cost analysis per se.

First, cost analysis is a way of describing an intervention. Many educational interventions are complex or multifaceted; by providing details on the resources, we are explaining what is required for the intervention. Information on costs can indicate the quality or intensity of a program. For example, the number of counselors per student may indicate the quality of counseling programs, as would data on the number of days of training required for counselors before the program begins operation. As well, the cost per student for a program will reflect the dosage of the treatment each student receives. For example, the annual cost of a mentoring program might be $500, but the cost per student will depend on how many years each student participates.

Information on costs sheds light on the types of resources needed to implement a given program. Some interventions may require a substantial commitment of in-kind resources; these include volunteer-intensive youth supports such as Big Brothers Big Sisters of America and elementary school literacy programs such as Time to Read (Grossman & Tierney, 1998; Miller & Connolly, 2012). Other interventions may require significant capital investments; for example, massive open online courses (MOOCs) may necessitate investment in an expensive technology infrastructure before any students have enrolled (Bowen, Chingos, Lack, & Nygren, 2014). For some interventions, there may be reorganizational costs that are not obvious. For example, implementation of Success for All requires cross-grade grouping—that is, putting students from different grades in the same classroom; this grouping may have implications for how the school day is organized (Quint, Zhu, Balu, Rappaport, & DeLaurentis, 2015). Finally, some programs may have substantial induced costs such that the biggest cost item is not the intervention itself but the extra resources that flow from implementing the program. A series of examples, showing how costs change as students progress through community college at different rates, is modeled by Belfield, Crosta, and Jenkins (2014).

Relatedly, cost analysis can be applied to check for fidelity of implementation of an intervention. For example, high-quality preschool programs are expected to have a trained lead teacher; the cost analyst can verify if sufficient funds were allocated to ensure that this is affordable. Subject to the caveats just noted, the analyst can compare actual resource use with an *ex ante* budget to see whether the program resources match the intended design.

The second intrinsic value of cost analysis is that it helps the researcher with prediction and modeling. It is important to recognize that costs are estimated, just as effects are in an impact evaluation. The researcher is estimating an expectation based on the sample units of the intervention. In some cases, the analyst will want to estimate the actual costs of the program as it was delivered in a particular setting for a specific group of students. It is more likely that the analyst will prefer to estimate expected costs—that is, the best prediction of what the program will cost if implemented again. These two estimates will be different: For expected costs, the analyst will use actual ingredients but general prices; for actual costs, the analyst will apply the actual (or as close as possible) prices each site paid for a particular ingredient. This latter approach is similar to a budget approach and so must be applied cautiously.

The use of expected costs allows the analyst to more accurately model costs. One concern for education research is how to take a successful small or pilot intervention and implement it at scale with the same level of success (Quint, Bloom, Black, Stephens, & Akey, 2005). For instance, the policymaker might mandate a class size reduction policy such that all classes must be 10% smaller. What resources would be required to implement such a mandate? It may require proportionately (10% extra) teachers and classroom space but only a smaller proportion (less than 10% extra) of administrative faculty and school facilities. With information on the costs of reducing class size by various proportions, it is possible to predict average cost as the intervention expands (i.e., economies of scale). For example, in their analysis of a schoolwide positive behavioral support intervention, Blonigen and colleagues (2008) estimated significantly lower costs for districts with 10 schools relative to districts with just one school. Deming, Goldin, Katz, and Yuchtman (2016) showed the use of online learning in higher education can shift the average cost function downward—that is, lower the cost per student.

Cost information can also be used to model different versions of the intervention. With data on how programs vary in their resource use, the analyst can see if there are alternative mixes that yield a similar cost per participant. For example, a preschool program might be able to hire four different levels of instructor (e.g., master teacher, lead teacher, adjunct, or teacher aide). Cost analysis can help determine how these instructor types can be combined in a way that would yield a given cost per preschooler. For a thorough example using cost functions for child care, see Blau and Mocan (2006).

Finally, information on the distribution of financing of resources across stakeholder groups is useful for policy modeling. Typically, costs are distributed among various social stakeholders: These might include the federal government, school districts, schools, parents, local businesses, philanthropic agencies, and so on. By understanding the distribution of the financing of costs, we are in a better position to analyze how stakeholders might support or oppose an educational program. For example, the economic value of college is typically found to be very high, prompting questions as to why students do not invest more (Avery & Turner, 2012). But if this value is shared across the student and society, then the student may not have an incentive to stay in college for longer (Trostel, 2010). Alternatively, an intervention may make economic sense to a school district because it does not have to fully fund the intervention: With matched federal funding, a program need only be modestly effective to be worthwhile to the school district.

• 3.6. CONCLUSIONS

This chapter examines costs conceptually. We do so to make several key points for cost analysis.

The first point is that resources should be valued in terms of their opportunity cost. This simple idea is very powerful in two ways. First, it forces us to always think about the scarcity of resources: No teacher's time is free, nor is any student's time free. Second, it forces us to think about valuation in two steps: One is identifying each ingredient; the next is putting a value on that ingredient that reflects its opportunity cost. Thus, opportunity cost is the foundation of the ingredients method discussed in the next three chapters.

The second point is that the costs of an educational intervention are "all the resources needed to make the intervention work." We emphasize all resources because educational programs typically draw on contributions from various sources: different levels of government; different tiers within a school system; a range of community resources; and, of course, changes in how students spend their time. A systematic and comprehensive way of thinking about costs—related to the theory of change—is needed to accurately value each program.

Third, we want to dispel the notion that cost analysis is a simple exercise using budgetary information. A cost analysis is an actual research endeavor in the same way that an impact evaluation is. As we illustrate in upcoming chapters, this necessitates a research design for data collection and analysis that is methodologically valid.

Finally, we hope we have encouraged the reader to devote more attention to cost analysis within the field of education research (see Chandra et al., 2011). A rigorous cost analysis generates a lot of information about each intervention, and this information can be useful in many different ways for educational decisionmakers.

In the next set of chapters (Chapters 4–6), we apply these concepts to cost analysis using the ingredients method.

Discussion Questions

1. What is meant by the term *cost* when used in *cost analysis*? What is meant by "incremental" cost? Provide a hypothetical example.

2. When might it be inappropriate to use a market price for employing a particular ingredient in future replications of an educational evaluation?

3. In what ways can understanding a program's logic model or theory of change help you design a cost study of the program?

4. What characteristics of budgets make them inappropriate sources for estimating costs?

Exercises

1. What are the "costs" associated with the following situations?

   a. The school your children attends is temporarily closed because of building violations.

   b. The district decides to reduce the number of schools a family can apply to for high school.

   c. The school sponsors an outdoor party for the student body that destroys a major portion of the lawns and shrubbery.

   d. A rise in school crime and vandalism requires that some teachers be used to patrol the campus rather than teach.

   e. The birth of a child places heavy demands on your family schedule so that you must defer the completion of courses for a master's degree.

2. You observe a mentoring program over several years and across several sites. The program is 1 year long, and you observe very little year-over-year and site-by-site variation in implementation and costs. You are therefore able to estimate that programs that serve few to no students (e.g., during start-up years) cost about $10,000, sites that serve 25 students in a year cost $12,500, and sites that serve 100 students in a year cost $20,000. Therefore, you use linear regression methods to estimate the cost function as $C = 10,000 + 100q$, where C represents total cost and q represents the number of students served by a site in a year.

   a. What is the fixed cost of the program?

   b. What is the variable cost?

   c. What is the average cost per participant?

   d. What is the marginal cost?

   e. Under what circumstances would you use each of the estimates in a through d?

3. A school district has asked you to evaluate a reading tutoring program targeting struggling readers in upper elementary grades. Students take regular reading classes with their peers and also receive tutoring by trained college student volunteers in groups of four on a pull-out basis, meaning that the tutors bring students to a small classroom for 45 minutes of class time daily for more individualized instruction. Tutors are trained by university literacy faculty for 20 hours and use an instructor guidebook, student workbooks, and works of children's literature for each student in their instruction. Students use their own notebooks and pencils from reading class to complete assignments and take notes.

   a. Which costs of the program are incremental? Which are not? Why?

   b. Under what circumstances would you want to consider the incremental cost versus the total cost of the program?

4

The Ingredients Method

Objectives

1. Present the ingredients method for measuring costs.

2. Identify ingredients in educational interventions.

3. Specify ingredients by category.

4. Describe data sources and needs for various types of ingredients.

5. Provide examples of ingredients and descriptive data.

The ingredients method is a straightforward approach to estimating costs of educational interventions. The method is designed to assist in economic evaluations by providing policy-relevant information on resource use, which may then be linked to effectiveness or economic benefits. The method is founded on the economic principle of opportunity costs and cost accounting (Levin 1975, 2001). As described in Chapter 3, the idea of opportunity cost is that every resource utilized in implementing an intervention has a value or cost. If the ingredients are identified and costs ascertained based on their opportunity cost, we can calculate the total cost of the intervention.

The ingredients method involves a set of steps: (1) identifying and specifying ingredients, (2) valuing and pricing ingredients, and (3) calculating total cost and analyzing costs in such a way that the cost results relate to the theory of change for the relevant intervention. As an extension, the calculations of costs from the ingredients method can be paired with impacts to perform cost-effectiveness (CE) or benefit-cost (BC) analysis.

This chapter presents the first of these steps—the method for identifying and specifying ingredients. Once we have specified all the ingredients required, we begin the separate task of placing prices on these ingredients. The next two chapters will show how to place a value on ingredients to calculate their costs and how to ensure that the cost estimates correspond to the delivery of the intervention and its intended outcomes.

● 4.1. IDENTIFYING INGREDIENTS

The first step in applying the ingredients method is to identify and specify the ingredients of the intervention, program, or reform needed to replicate the implementation (and hence the impact). Accordingly, the ingredients method starts with a simple question: What resources are required to obtain the observed impacts? The list of resources must be comprehensive to include all required resources identified by the program for implementation and any subsequent induced resource requirements. At this stage, it does not matter who finances these resources or if anyone contributes without being directly paid for their contribution; all required resources should be counted.

To begin this process, it is important to be knowledgeable about the problem being addressed, the theory of change, and the components of the intervention as designed and as implemented. This was discussed in Chapter 3, but the importance of obtaining familiarity with the intervention being studied—and its counterfactual—cannot be overstated. Prior to compiling a list of ingredients, one must know well the intervention under consideration and how it is proposed to impact the outcome of interest. This understanding is necessary in order to provide the considerable detail needed on the resources that are required to achieve an impact. Educational interventions differ tremendously, even within a grade level: The policy options might include an add-on to the traditional school day, a pull-out program during the school day but not replacing instructional time, or replacement for the standard curriculum being used during class time. In each of these different options, it is important to be clear about the purpose and content of the intervention in comparison with the counterfactual.

Three overriding considerations should be recognized in identifying and specifying ingredients. First, the ingredients should be specified in sufficient detail so that their value can be ascertained in the next stage of the analysis. Thus, it is important that the qualifications of staff, characteristics of physical facilities, types of equipment, and other inputs be specified with enough precision that it is possible to place reasonably accurate price values on them.

Second, the categories into which ingredients are placed should be consistent, but there is no single approach to categorization that will be suitable in all cases. The categorization proposed in this book—personnel, materials, facilities, and other inputs—is a general classification scheme that is rather typical. It is possible, however, that there need be no "other inputs" category if all ingredients can be assigned to existing classifications. For example, insurance coverage can be included with facilities and equipment to the degree that it is associated with the costs of those categories. Likewise, if parents are required to provide volunteer time, that ingredient can be placed under client inputs rather than under personnel. The categories are designed to be functionally useful rather than orthodox distinctions that should never be violated.

Third, the degree of specificity and accuracy in listing ingredients should depend upon their overall contribution to the total cost of the intervention. Most educational interventions are labor-intensive such that the worker (teacher or other instructor) time will clearly be important. For interventions that involve computerized learning or distance learning, capital may also be important. In contrast, learning supplies can often be estimated with much less attention to detail, since they do not weigh heavily in overall costs. The important point is that an eventual error of 10% in estimating teacher time will have a relatively large impact on the total cost estimate because of its relative importance in the overall picture. However, a 100% error in office supplies may create an imperceptible distortion, because office supplies are usually an inconsequential contributor to overall costs. In general, the most effort in identifying and specifying ingredients should be devoted to those ingredients that are likely to dominate the cost picture.

4.2. SPECIFYING INGREDIENTS   ●

The identification and specification of ingredients is often facilitated by organizing ingredients into five or six main categories that have common properties. A typical breakdown would include (1) personnel, (2) training, (3) facilities, (4) equipment and materials, (5) other program inputs, and (6) required client inputs. Examples of ingredients are discussed next. It is important to describe the full set of ingredients, especially including ingredients that do not have direct market prices or are not paid for with money outlays. Example 4.1 illustrates the importance of volunteer resources. Example 4.2 illustrates how a full set of ingredients should be reported.

4.2.1. Personnel

Personnel ingredients include all the human resources required to implement the program. This category includes not only full-time personnel but also part-time employees, consultants, efforts of other school staff, volunteers, and parents. All personnel should be listed according to their roles, qualifications, and time commitments.

One way to ensure that all personnel are included is to begin by listing all individuals involved for each task. Personnel roles refer to responsibilities, such as administration, coordination, assessment, teaching or tutoring, receiving or providing training, curriculum design, record keeping or data collection, and so on.

Qualifications refer to the nature of training, experience, and specialized skills required for the positions. A description of a teacher's qualifications may include degree, certification status, total number of years of experience, special talents, and number of years of experience in this position.

Time inputs refer to the amount of time that each person devotes to the intervention in terms of percentage of a full-time position or the number of hours or days spent. In the latter case, there may be certain employees, consultants, and volunteers who allocate only a portion of a full workweek or work year to the intervention.

Typically, as programs rely on teachers to carry out the main components of the intervention, it is important to understand thoroughly the responsibilities, time commitment, and characteristics of the teachers themselves. For personnel, while roles and qualifications are more qualitative and descriptive, the data on time must be able to be quantified into units used (such as 15 days per year). Also, if the treatment is expected to vary among teachers or across sites, rich data on the individuals providing the intervention are important in understanding how resources varied during implementation. If, however, a teacher's role in a program's delivery is small, say for recruitment and occasional updates on student progress, then extensive qualitative information may not be required because it will have a limited impact on costs.

Also, labor time is often the most common example of in-kind resources. (See Example 4.1.) Parents may contribute time to help the school (e.g., by tutoring students, chaperoning class trips, or renovating facilities). As well, student time may be considered as an in-kind resource. A direct example is peer tutoring, where students help each other. A more general issue is how to value student time in the classroom relative to student time outside the classroom. For example, an after-school program may increase achievement. However, some students would have been employed during this period after school; the opportunity cost of the after-school program is therefore their lost wages. For college students, the opportunity cost of time is especially important. Also, the "consumption value" or experiential value of being in class is important: Some students may enjoy participating in class; others may not. This consumption value influences the opportunity cost.

Example 4.1   Why Should Volunteers Be Considered as Ingredients?

There are many instances in which schools are the recipients of volunteer services. To illustrate this point, let us compare two hypothetical public school districts: Springfield and Middletown. They are similar in most every respect (e.g., per-pupil spending and the socioeconomic mix of their students).

Springfield has proven quite adept at marshaling the services of a broad array of volunteers in ways that Middletown has not. The Springfield district is near a large college, where a group of motivated students have organized a homework tutoring program to assist low-achieving school students. The Parent-Teacher Association (PTA) in Springfield is quite dynamic; it has assisted the district in locating regular classroom volunteers among parents and other community members. Also, the Springfield district is located next to a large biotechnology firm whose chief executive is concerned about the quality of science education in public schools; she has arranged for several research scientists to take off work time to assist high school teachers in designing new curricular units and to participate in class presentations.

Given this state of affairs, how should we compare the average cost of public education in the two districts? Our immediate instinct might be to simply compare per-pupil expenditures in each district. At first glance, their costs might appear to be quite similar. After all, Springfield may have

(Continued)

(Continued)

more volunteers, but these individuals do not receive salaries, so where is the cost incurred? The notion of including the donated time of volunteers as a program "cost" could strike many as counterintuitive.

However, we need to remember how we are conceptualizing costs. Whenever a resource (or ingredient) is employed in an educational program, it can no longer be employed in alternative ways. This represents a clear sacrifice to some members of society. For example, the college students who volunteer to be tutors are sacrificing valuable time that could be devoted to their own studies or part-time work or leisure activities. Similarly, the parents, community members, and scientists who participate in classroom activities may be less productive at work or enjoy less free time. The cost of volunteerism is what society must give up by not using the time of volunteers in its most valuable alternative use. Of course, this presents knotty problems of what money value to assign to the time of volunteers. Fundamentally, volunteers in the Springfield community are making sacrifices of other valued alternatives that should be weighed as costs.

Employing this definition of costs enriches the potential of cost analysis in many ways. First, we can analyze how costs are distributed among various groups: Springfield district officials might be more likely to support the program if they know it relies heavily on resources it does not pay for. Second, knowing about volunteer costs should provide a better guide to program implementation. If another school district is planning implementation of the program, it will need to establish that volunteer resources equivalent to those in Springfield are available or need to pay for additional personnel. If the cost analysis did not include the value of services provided by volunteers, this would be misleading as to the costs of replicating the Springfield program. Finally, including all costs helps inform social decisions. District officials might compare this program with one that uses other in-kind resources. Also, the volunteers must decide whether the program is efficient and so whether or not they should, in fact, volunteer (rather than pursue alternative ways to improve educational outcomes).

4.2.2. Training

Often, educational interventions require teachers or other personnel to learn new ways of delivering instructional or student support services. It is thus important to include training ingredients, such as coaches, professional development, or other formal training programs. The analyst should be careful to specify how much training is involved compared with trainer time that is actually program design; how much preparation time the trainer needs in order to help the trainees; and how much time is needed before the personnel need retraining. Teachers may also use the training for more than one year, so it is important to know if the intervention will be used for a longer period and if the teachers are likely to stay over that longer period. In this case, cost burdens may be distributed over more than 1 year.

4.2.3. Facilities

Facilities refer to the physical space required for the intervention. This may include space for program delivery or training or meetings or storage for materials. Space in educational interventions often includes classrooms, offices, storage areas, play or recreational facilities, and other building requirements. Given that the space is required to implement the program, all space should be documented and described whether paid for by the project or not. All such requirements must be listed according to their dimensions and characteristics, along with other information that is important for identifying their value. For example, facilities that are equipped with whiteboards and laptops for student use are different from a standard classroom with desks or tables. Any facilities that are jointly used with other programs should be identified according to the portion of use that is allocated to the intervention.

Information about facilities can be difficult to obtain when the space utilized by the program is contributed in kind by the school or college for the program to operate. Obtaining this information can also be challenging as people tend to struggle in estimating square footage and in estimating how much space is actually being used. It can be helpful to know the size of a standard classroom or any regulations surrounding a required amount of square feet per student. In addition to the amount of space used and the types of accommodations required within the space for the program, it is also important to consider overhead or maintenance that is related to the nature of the facility.

4.2.4. Equipment and Materials

Many educational interventions are focused on changing instructional strategies of schools, and others seek changes in curriculum content. These interventions may require new books, manuals, computers, and software. Broadly, this category also refers to furnishings, instructional equipment, and materials that are used for the intervention. Additional examples include computers and their peripheral devices, software, audiovisual equipment, scientific apparatuses, printers, phones, Internet access, printed materials, office machines, paper, commercial tests, and other supplies. Both the specific equipment and materials specifically allocated to the intervention and those that are shared with other activities should be noted.

Depending on the design of the intervention, computers are ingredients that may be important (costly) or not in the estimate of the total cost of a program. If the program requires dedicated computers or a specific processor or screen size, these characteristics must be accounted for in pricing. In the instance where standard computers are used in a computer lab, it is important during data collection to note the number of computers and the amount of time the computers were used for the program.

Some materials, such as books, software, or instructional aids, are used for more than one year. Thus, it is necessary to understand the typical life or time of use for the object as well as the length of time the object will be or is expected to be used during the implementation under study. This information is important in calculating the annual value of the object, which is discussed in the following chapter.

4.2.5. Other Program Inputs

Some educational programs provide transportation, prizes, food, or scholarships to participating students. Increasingly, educational programs involve imaginative approaches to changing student behavior; so ingredients might include financial incentives or motivational bonuses conditional on attendance or completion (Barrow, Richburg-Hayes, Rouse, & Brock, 2014). Analogously, interventions might involve changing teacher behavior through bonuses or other incentives (Fryer, 2013; Jackson, 2014). Because these types of additional ingredients vary widely from one intervention to another, this category is designed to be flexible in order to capture all other ingredients that do not fit readily into the categories set out previously. Other examples might include any extra liability insurance that is required beyond that provided by the sponsoring agency, or it might include the cost of training sessions at a local college or university. Any ingredients that are included in this category should be specified clearly with a statement of their purpose.

Often, some inputs are necessary to ensure that an intervention can be implemented and is being implemented appropriately. These may include personnel, facilities, or materials to design the program, monitor its delivery, and ensure that all students comply with the intervention. These inputs may also include the resources required to evaluate the program. As a general rule, these inputs should be included in the analysis if they are required for replication of the measured effects. Therefore, ingredients needed for initial program design may be omitted if they are not required for replication and research. Similarly, ingredients for evaluation may be omitted if they do not contribute to program implementation and effects (in some cases, the evaluation may involve data collection that generates reactive behavior in either the treatment or control group). However, if evaluation activities, such as assurance of implementation fidelity, monitoring may have affected program delivery and thus contributed to measured effects, these ingredients should be included in the analysis.

4.2.6. Required Client Inputs

This category of ingredients includes any contributions that are required of the clients or their families. Clients are those persons being served by the intervention. For example, if an educational alternative requires the family to provide transportation, books, uniforms, equipment, food, or other student services, these should be included under this classification. The purpose of including such inputs is that the success of some interventions will depend crucially on such resources, whereas the success of others will not. Most college programs require students to pay for textbooks and other learning resources, for example, and these contribute to the positive outcomes from college. To provide an accurate picture of the resources required to replicate any intervention that requires client inputs, it is important to include these inputs in the analysis.

Student time is an ingredient that may require consideration if the student is likely to be giving up another activity. For example, youth who attend a summer school or after-school program may be giving up the opportunity to earn wages. Typically, if an intervention serves individuals over age 18, participant time is valued at the forgone wage to attend the program.

Example 4.2 Ingredients of the HighScope Perry Preschool Program

In the 1960s, a well-known experiment was conducted among a small group of at-risk children in Ypsilanti, Michigan. Some children were randomly assigned to participate in the Perry Preschool Program, while others were designated as the control group. The program was designed to provide a high-quality preschool environment for at-risk children, including 2-hour classes on weekday

(Continued)

(Continued)

mornings and weekly 90-minute home visits by teachers. A series of benefit-cost (BC) analyses by Steven Barnett have sought to weigh the costs of the program against its benefits (later on, in Example 7.1, we discuss the full results of these evaluations).

The cost analysis was based upon the ingredients method. The list of ingredients was derived from a thorough examination of program publications and from interviews with former teachers and administrators. The main categories of cost ingredients include the following:

- *Instructional staff.* Four teachers were employed in each year of the program; in addition to their salaries, it is important to consider the fringe benefits that they received (e.g., retirement contributions) and employer contributions to the Social Security tax.
- *Administrative and support staff.* Teachers were not the only personnel involved in the program. Other program staff managed the special education program, including a special services director.
- *Facilities.* The program was held in the facilities of the Ypsilanti Public School District. Thus, an important cost ingredient is the existing physical plant of the school district that was utilized by the program, including classroom space.
- *Equipment.* To set up and furnish the preschool classroom, some equipment was purchased especially for the program.
- *Classroom supplies.* These include several subcategories of ingredients, including the food that was used for the children's daily snacks and other nondurable educational materials that were used by the children.
- *Developmental screening.* Prior to initiating the program, a large number of children were tested and interviewed. The screening process was used to decide which children were eligible to participate in the program, based upon family incomes and risk of educational failure.
- *School district overhead.* The program was operated within the Ypsilanti Public School District. As might be expected, the district assumed many program expenses. These include maintenance, utilities, and the costs of providing the support of general administrative and nonteaching staff.
- *Client inputs.* The client inputs used in the program were judged to be negligible. No fees were charged to parents, and all supplies were given to parents (and thus accounted for by previous ingredient categories). Parents lived within walking distance of the school, so there were no additional transportation costs borne by them. The only possible ingredient supplied by clients is the time that parents spent with teachers in occasional home visits. However, these visits were strictly voluntary and some parents chose not to participate.

The prior list provides an essential starting point, but it is important to specify in greater detail the exact nature and quantity of each ingredient (of course, Barnett followed this procedure in carrying out his cost study). For example, what are the qualifications of the teaching staff (e.g., experience, formal education, and training)? What kinds of equipment were used to furnish the classroom (e.g., desks)? How many of each kind were used to furnish the classroom? When conducting cost analysis, we can generally save ourselves a great deal of trouble by exhaustively detailing the ingredients. As we will see in Chapter 5, it is difficult to place a reliable value on an ingredient that is only vaguely specified. One should also keep in mind the admonitions of the last section and focus the greatest attention on the ingredients that are likely to occupy the greatest weight in the final cost estimates—instructional staff being the most obvious.

Source: Adapted from Barnett (1996, pp. 19–25).

4.3. SOURCES OF INGREDIENTS INFORMATION   ●

The first step in collecting ingredients data is to identify the sample of sites for which information will be collected. It may be valid to follow the same sampling frame as would be used for an effectiveness study. Indeed, a general rule might be to collect ingredients data from all the sites for which effectiveness data would need to be collected. If the sampling frame for an impact evaluation is designed to be representative of the population of possible treatment effects, then it should also be representative of the costs of those possible treatments. Certainly, information on ingredients should not be collected from only a few sites, particularly if the intervention can be implemented in very different ways across sites.

Ingredients information can be derived from multiple sources. These sources include reports and descriptions of the interventions, interviews with informants such as personnel and participants, and direct observations. An initial ingredients list can be drafted from information available from the program developers and administrators, previous evaluations, and other implementations. These documents may include general descriptions of the program prepared by program staff or outsiders, budgets and expenditure statements, websites, reports by previous evaluators of the program, internal memos or e-mails, and countless other sources of information. The evaluator must approach this task as a good detective might, attempting to turn up every bit of potentially useful documentary evidence. In some cases, this initial search might produce a veritable mountain of paper that is rather daunting to the cost analyst; in others, the evaluator might be stymied by an unfortunate lack of documentation or perhaps even a failure to obtain cooperation from program staff. In sifting through the available information, one should not view it as necessarily encapsulating the entirety of actual ingredients used in the program. Indeed, a program description may sometimes ignore significant categories of ingredients (such as client inputs or volunteers) or provide an overly optimistic discussion of how some ingredients are used (such as teacher training sessions). However, a thorough review will provide the evaluator with sufficient background to establish the overall purpose of the study.

In addition to aiding in study design, having an understanding of what the program will include in advance of the study allows the research team to design data collection instruments and to integrate data collection into the evaluation, rather than being a separate piece or component. In doing so, the evaluation can incorporate differences based on context. For example, if it is expected that the program will vary among sites, then the data collection strategy should be designed to capture variation in ingredients, in number, description, and quantity.

The most comprehensive and detailed source of information on ingredients is accessible from those who are involved in implementing the intervention. These individuals might include the program designers; program directors and administrative staff; school personnel such as principals, teachers, and aides; and parents. In some cases, particularly when adults or older children are participants, it may be helpful to interview the program recipients directly. In conducting interviews, the evaluator should seek to confirm or contradict the impressions left by documentary evidence. For example, does the program actually use three full-time teachers or are some part-time? Do training sessions occur every week as stated on the program website, or do they occur less frequently? In every case, we should be concerned with identifying the ingredients that are *actually* used in the intervention, rather than the ingredients that were supposed to have been used in the ideal case.

Interviews can also provide rich data on the context, the ways in which ingredients were used, and important qualitative data, especially regarding personnel. Having a discussion via a semistructured interview allows the researcher to explore what might make a particular site distinct from other sites, if any staff members hold special responsibilities, and to learn about other activities and aspects of the program that may not be prescribed for implementation. While interview data is rich, it may require a considerable amount of time from staff to provide the data and time from researchers to collect and analyze qualitative data. Also, it is unlikely that a preexisting interview protocol can be adapted to every study: Each intervention is different in terms of ingredients used, duration of usage, and scale of operations. Nevertheless, there are some interview protocols that may be adapted to each case (see Hollands et al., 2013; Levin et al., 2012; Rodriguez, Bowden, Belfield, & Scott-Clayton, 2014).

If the primary data source is interviews, it is very important to conduct these interviews contemporaneously with the delivery of the intervention. If sources are consulted long after the program has ended, they are unlikely to remember all the salient information. It is also unlikely that all key personnel will be available or contactable after the program has ended.

Another source of ingredients data from individuals involved in implementation is a survey. Surveys might be best for easily obtainable or quantifiable ingredients. This might include the amount of time spent on a task, the number of students served, or the number of books provided. If the time available for interviews is limited, it may be best to begin by collecting as much data as possible via survey and then following up with interviews as needed for more detail.

Another form of data collection is observation. Observations of programs allow the researchers to document ingredient use without requiring personnel to divert attention away from the program or to devote additional time to the study. During observation, the research team may also learn of ingredients to add to the list that may not have been described elsewhere. This might include bulletin boards, displays, book challenges, or prizes offered to students. The physical space may be important to note as well, especially if the qualities of the space are notably pleasant or in serious need of repair. In a reading program, for example, the evaluator might sit in on several classes. Again, the purpose of doing so is to ascertain the ingredients that are actually being used. If the program designer mentioned that students should have individual workbooks, is it the case that all students in the class have workbooks? If program documents state that 50 minutes of classroom time is devoted to instruction, is this revealed during classroom observations?

In reading, interviewing, and observing, it is important to search for agreement and disagreement across sources. Ultimately, we hope that various sources of information will aid in triangulating upon a reasonable set of cost ingredients. (Such triangulation is especially important when the research protocols vary across studies; whenever multiple sources of information can be used to confirm a result, it strengthens our confidence in the findings.) Where there are significant disagreements, we might be inspired to probe more carefully.

Often, however, disagreements cannot be easily resolved. For example, it may be that a particular intervention was implemented in two substantially different ways across a series of program sites; each version of the program used a different set of cost ingredients. In cases such as these, we should be candid about the uncertainty. A helpful procedure is to present results from several variants of cost analysis, using different sets of assumptions about the specific cost ingredients that are employed.

Whenever the intervention is a subject of effectiveness evaluation, it is possible and desirable to document the ingredients as a component of the evaluation. That is, just as the "treatment" that constitutes the intervention can be observed and documented during the evaluation, it is also possible to identify the ingredients that are being used in the intervention. This must be done systematically rather than casually. Qualitative observers who document the intervention can also identify and specify the ingredients following the ingredients method. We believe that this is the preferred approach because it does not entail a time lag in data gathering, which jeopardizes accuracy in identifying ingredients. Whenever a systematic evaluation of an educational intervention is undertaken, it is desirable to gather ingredients information that can be used later to estimate costs.

● 4.4. CONCLUSIONS

The intention of economic evaluation is to identify and analyze the costs of an intervention required to achieve a particular outcome or to generate economic benefits for the purpose of aiding decisionmaking. To successfully estimate the cost of producing an effect, we must carefully identify all ingredients utilized in implementation. The ingredients method provides a standardized approach to identifying and describing resources so that the total social cost of the intervention can be estimated. Key to this process is allowing implementation, through fidelity, variation, or improvisation, to guide the specification of ingredients. Thus, data collection is best when planned to occur at the time of implementation. In doing so, data collection is more likely to be efficient, the data obtained are more likely to be precise, and the analyses are less likely to be bound by data limitations.

In the next chapters, the method is further explained to describe how qualitative and quantitative data are used to place monetary values on ingredients and how the estimates of costs are calculated and analyzed.

Discussion Questions

1. What are the main distinctive elements of the ingredients approach to estimating costs versus other approaches?

2. How should the costs of facilities be ascertained?

3. When might it be appropriate to omit ingredients from the analysis?

4. What information about ingredients would be most challenging to ascertain? Describe what data collection tools you would use, including specific survey and/or interview questions, to obtain the necessary details about ingredients.

Exercises

1. A principal is dissatisfied with the quality of mathematics instruction in her school. She has discussed the matter with the teachers, and they believe that a combination of a new curriculum and in-service training for teachers will improve matters.

   a. What ingredients would likely be required to implement the proposed change?

   b. What questions would you ask the principal and teachers to gather additional information about the ingredients?

2. Indicate the types of ingredients that are likely to be required for the following programs. Provide as much detail as you are able.

   a. A peer tutoring program will be established in which sixth graders will spend 2 hours a week tutoring third graders who are not making adequate progress in reading or mathematics. The school will set aside a special room for this purpose and will use parent volunteers to coordinate the tutors and set a tutoring schedule. Tutors will be trained in a 10-hour course that will take place over the first two weeks of school. A teacher with experience in peer tutoring will do the training.

   b. A high school is considering the establishment of a soccer team for both males and females that will undertake a full schedule of interscholastic competition.

   c. A school district is considering the establishment of its own program for the education of children with speech and hearing impairments. Previously, such students were sent to classes sponsored by the county.

d. A dedicated early education center is being built for 100 children who were previously in preschool classrooms inside elementary schools.

3. A university dean proposes replacing all permanent faculty in the economics department with adjunct faculty while maintaining the same amount of activities of instruction, teaching, and service. How would this change the ingredients required by the economics department?

5

Placing Values on Ingredients

Objectives

1. Present methods for placing values on specific types of ingredients.

2. Specify sources of information on prices of ingredients.

3. Adjust for inflation by expressing prices in constant dollars.

4. Set out the method for expressing money flows as present values.

The previous chapters described the ingredients approach to constructing cost estimates and set out the principles and procedures for identifying and specifying ingredients. In this chapter, we wish to assign prices to each of the ingredients in order to obtain an estimate for total costs and for cost components of interventions.

At this point, we presumably know the resources, or ingredients, that are required for each educational program or intervention. However, the fact that we know which ingredients are required does not yet enable us to estimate costs. We need to determine the prices of these ingredients, where prices reflect the value of the lost opportunity when using these ingredients to provide educational programs. This chapter provides details on the methods and primary sources for pricing ingredients. When prices have been derived for each ingredient, we can then calculate costs as the product of ingredients times their respective prices. Before completing this calculation, however, it is important that all money values be expressed in constant dollars and in the same time period. Hence, we describe adjustments with respect to inflation and the need for discounting.

● 5.1. METHODS FOR VALUING INGREDIENTS

The most common method for placing monetary values on ingredients is that of using their market prices. According to economic theory, when markets for a particular good or service are perfectly competitive, the equilibrium price established by that market will represent the value of that good (Dorfman, 1967). Using market prices has two additional attractive features: (1) availability and (2) simplicity. Since there are reasonably competitive markets for many goods and services used in educational interventions (including workers, facilities, and equipment), there will be a set of prices readily available that can be used to determine the costs of those inputs.

As discussed in Chapter 3, competitive markets are not always the only source of ingredients. In some cases, there is a market for a particular ingredient, but the market does not meet the criteria for perfect competition. There are relatively few buyers or sellers, or other market imperfections exist. In these cases the existing market price may be an inaccurate reflection of the cost of obtaining additional units of an ingredient, and adjustments must be made to provide a more appropriate cost measure. For example, assume that a talented program director is presently receiving salary and other benefits valued at $80,000 a year, but there are very few persons who possess such talents. If one wished to ascertain the cost of using such talent to replicate an intervention at many new sites, one would have to take account of the fact that the scarcity of such talent may generate a considerably higher cost for additional qualified persons as demand for such talent increases.

Alternatively, there may be no obvious market for a particular ingredient. For example, a school district may decide to lend an old facility to a new program. There is no financial transaction, because the building was purchased and paid for a long time ago. Moreover, no obvious market exists for this type of facility. In these cases, it is necessary to ascertain what the value of the ingredient would be if there were a market or to identify the closest relevant market. When attempts are made to ascertain the value of a good that does not have a clear competitive market price, the estimated value is called a shadow price (Boardman, Greenberg, Vining, & Weimer, 2011, Chapter 11). Both market and shadow prices can be used to ascertain the values of the ingredients for purposes of cost estimation.

In those cases in which market prices are inaccurate reflections of the true cost, one must adjust the market price appropriately. In the case of scarce talent or indeed any input that is not perfectly elastic in supply, an increase in demand will result in a higher price. Accordingly, some effort must be made to ascertain how demand will increase for such ingredients as a result of the intervention as well as what the consequences such a shift in demand will have on the market price. Most cost analysis in education will not require this adjustment if one is dealing with a single intervention rather than an attempt to replicate it numerous times. In the single intervention case, the use of an ingredient will generally not affect the market; however, in the case of numerous duplications of the intervention, demand for the ingredient may increase enough to raise its price.

When market prices are not available, one must use some estimate of what those prices would be, or shadow prices. For example, there may be no specific market for an old school building, but there are various ways that we could ascertain what the market price would be if there were a market. There may be no market for the services of sixth graders who are asked to tutor first graders. But there may be a way of measuring the social sacrifice or cost of using the time of sixth graders to tutor first graders by asking, "What is the value of the sixth graders' time in other uses, such as learning?" For example, what if it were found that sixth graders who spend their time tutoring learn less than similar sixth graders who do not tutor? One way of ascertaining the shadow price of their time in tutoring is to estimate what it would cost to maintain their learning achievements at the level of their nontutoring peers. Each case in which shadow prices must be estimated presents a different, idiosyncratic challenge. Fortunately, the problem is rare enough in educational cost analysis that one will not encounter it very frequently.

Given these overall principles, it is possible to set out methods for ascertaining the value of ingredients for each of the categories stipulated in the previous chapters.

5.1.1. Site-Specific and Expected Prices

Before specifying the prices of ingredients, the analyst must make an important decision regarding how to derive prices. There are two options, which we can differentiate as *site-specific* versus *expected* or *local* versus *national*. Site-specific prices are the actual prices that the education program faces in its local context, such as the wage rates that apply within the school district or salary schedules of professors at the college site. By contrast, expected prices are those prices that we would expect someone to face if they were to implement this program, on average, across the nation. Potentially, site-specific and expected prices might be quite different.

One might think that the analyst would obviously decide to collect local prices. After all, these were the prices that the school or college faced when it was implementing the program or intervention. However, the choice between the pricing options depends on the purpose of and audience for the analysis.

Indeed, there are strong grounds for collecting prices that are national or expected prices. Analyses that compare the costs of several programs in different jurisdictions or that aim to generalize the costs of a single program in one location to other settings should employ national average prices. The use of national average prices focuses the analysis on differences in costs due to differences in resource utilization, as opposed to those that are due to differences in the conditions of local markets. If local prices were used, every intervention in a high-price urban setting would appear less cost-effective than each intervention in a low-price suburban setting, for example. Further, the actual price of a particular good or service, or the wages or salary of a particular individual involved in an intervention, is subject to random noise that will wash out with the use of averages. Conceptually, the analyst usually considers impacts to be "estimated" or drawn from an expected distribution, and it may be helpful to regard prices in the same way.

There are, however, disadvantages in using national prices. First, while a national average generalizes to the entire country under study, it does not represent actual costs for any individual jurisdiction and may therefore be less meaningful to policymakers. Second, national average prices may not be available for all ingredients. For many personnel ingredients, commonly the largest category of costs in educational interventions, government agencies such as the Bureau of Labor Statistics and other large institutions such as labor unions conduct large-scale surveys that estimate average salaries for a wide range of occupations, conditional on varying qualifications such as education level and experience. Nonetheless, these surveys may not include all personnel ingredients for a particular intervention and may not fully account for differences in qualifications or working conditions, requiring the analyst to make assumptions regarding which prices are most similar to the ingredients required for an intervention or to make adjustments to prices for education, experience, working conditions, and other factors. Finally, prices for some ingredients such as equipment, materials, and supplies may not have "national average" prices that can be obtained from large surveys. This concern is minor under many circumstances because these ingredients typically comprise a small share of the costs of educational interventions so that even large pricing errors will lead to small errors in the final results and because the prices of these ingredients typically vary less by geographic area than the prices of land and labor. Therefore, prices from national and Internet providers may serve as reasonable proxies for national average prices for many consumer goods.

The alternative option is to use site-specific or local prices—that is, prices that are specific to the intervention under study or prices from the local market of a particular intervention. In essence, the advantages and disadvantages of this approach are the converse of those of using national average prices: The final cost estimates are more closely linked with the actual intervention in a particular context and may be more informative to local decisionmakers when planning to replicate or expand an intervention. When available, individual salaries and prices of other ingredients used for an intervention can be used, necessitating fewer assumptions than using national prices that may not map precisely onto the respective ingredients. However, as noted previously, such prices may be difficult to obtain for privacy reasons, may be subject to random noise that is not relevant to the implementation of the intervention, and may not generalize well to other settings.

To make the choice between the options, it may be helpful for the analyst to consider the audience for the study and to determine whether national or local prices are most informative for that audience. Ultimately, it is most important for the analyst to be explicit and transparent as to whether the prices are national or local.

5.1.2. Adjusting National Prices for Geographic Location

The case may arise whereby an analyst elects to use national average prices for generalizability and the other reasons outlined previously but then would like to estimate how much it would cost to replicate a program in a particular locality. In that case, geographic price indices, constructed for consumer price indices (CPIs) used for inflation adjustment, can be used to approximate how national average prices would adapt to a specific setting. Note that this only provides an estimate, as using an index will adjust all prices by the same amount, while there is likely within-project variation in how much prices vary by geographic location—rent, for instance, will vary greatly between metropolitan and nonmetropolitan areas, while computers will likely cost the same. Further, it abstracts from substitution effects—in locations where gas prices are relatively high, for instance, parents may choose to drive less and use public transportation more, changing the mix of ingredients and bringing their total costs closer to the national average. Nonetheless, geographic indices can provide a reasonable first approximation as to how costs will change in a local context.

Among the several geographic price indices that exist, one that is particularly relevant to the field of K–12 education is the Comparable Wage Index (CWI), constructed by Lori Taylor, Mark Glander, and William Fowler for the National Center for Education Statistics. The official index has not been updated since 2005, but Lori Taylor continues to update the index unofficially (https://nces.ed.gov/edfin/adjustments.asp). The CWI uses salaries for college graduates outside education to estimate approximately how much teachers would need to be paid, compared with the national average, based on differences in cost of living and amenities in a geographic area in order for wages to be comparable between two areas (Taylor & Fowler, 2006). An alternative set of indices, the regional price parities computed by the Bureau of Economic Analysis, compares the cost of living between states and between metropolitan and nonmetropolitan areas within states using the prices of consumer goods (Atten, Figueroa, & Martin, 2012).

5.2. PLACING DOLLAR VALUES ON INGREDIENTS

In order to accurately assess the value of each ingredient, the data gathered via interviews, surveys, observations, analysis of program documentation, and other methods (as described in the previous chapter on the ingredients method) need to include descriptive information on the characteristics of ingredients, in addition to the quantities of ingredients a program used. The greater the detail the analyst has on the ingredients, the more accurately these ingredients can be priced. Next, we discuss data requirements and how these data inform the selection of either a national average or local price for each category of ingredients.

The analyst may need to search for each price individually. An alternative is to use an existing database of prices. One example is the *CostOut* tool, developed by the Center for Benefit-Cost Studies of Education (CBCSE; see Appendix B). This web-based tool helps the analyst distinguish ingredients and prices and place the total cost estimate into a decisionmaking framework. In addition, the tool includes a database of educational prices, grouped according to personnel, facilities, materials, and other and with particular detail on wages for instructional personnel at U.S. schools and colleges. The tool can also be used to adjust for inflation and for discounting of prices (as discussed next).

There are several advantages to using such a tool or compendium of existing prices. First, independent sources for prices are preferred: Their independence reduces the likelihood of researcher bias in the choice of prices. Second, by drawing on lists of prices, the analyst can more readily examine how prices might vary (especially hourly wages versus salaries) and apply sensitivity tests using different prices. Third, existing databases may be useful either for hard-to-specify prices (e.g., rental rates for school spaces) or for assumptions (e.g., the expected life of a capital asset such as a college building). Finally, building on other studies allows for greater comparability across possible policy options.

5.2.1. Personnel

Since personnel typically account for most of the total costs of educational interventions, it is important to devote considerable effort to obtaining accurate estimates of their costs. The services of most personnel are purchased in the marketplace, so it is data derived from such market transactions that we should consider first. When a personnel position can be filled by attracting persons with the appropriate education, experience, and other characteristics at the prevailing salary and fringe benefits generally paid for such talent in the marketplace, the cost of such a person is considered to be the monetary value of the salary and fringe benefits.

This determination presumes that a market exists in that there are many employers seeking such personnel, and there are many people seeking such positions. At any one time, these dynamics will result in a prevailing salary and fringe benefits that must be paid to obtain persons for any given position and that these prevailing salaries and fringe benefits represent their costs. Therefore, ingredients data on the nature of a position and required qualifications and training can be used to estimate a national average salary for a position using available databases, such as the National Compensation Survey by the Bureau of Labor Statistics, various surveys by the National Center for Education Statistics of the United States Department of Education such as the Schools and Staffing Survey, and other sources (see Appendix B). It is important to point out that the price of obtaining personnel in different school districts or teaching situations is also affected by working conditions and other factors (Chambers, 1980). Thus, even though there may exist a general market for particular types of personnel, any specific analysis should take account of observed differences in the employment situation, such as particularly difficult working conditions that may require higher salaries to attract workers with the necessary qualifications. Further, point estimates of salary and fringe benefits reported in national surveys are often mean or median salaries; particular circumstances may call for using salary estimates from other points along the distribution, such as the 10th or 90th percentile, or to incorporate the full distribution into an analysis of uncertainty, discussed further in Chapter 11.

In assuming that the prices of personnel are established in markets, it is important that these prices reflect market conditions. In metropolitan areas of the United States, there are usually many independent school districts competing for the same pools of personnel. In some metropolitan areas, the numbers of school districts competing for teachers, for example, approaches 100 or so, and in larger regions, the number may approach a multiple of these. But in rural areas, there may be little competition, and in many nations, there is a set national price for teacher remuneration that varies only with qualifications. Thus, the degree of competition must be ascertained in order to verify that prices of personnel are market-determined rather than being set by other processes.

If the analysis employs local or idiosyncratic prices, the salary and fringe benefits for each person can usually be obtained from normal payroll or expenditure data. It is important to add to each salary all the fringe benefits, including employer contributions to Social Security, other pension plans, health and life insurance, and perquisites that benefit the employee, such as the use of a car for private purposes. In many cases, fringe benefits packages are expressed as an overall percentage of salaries, since some fixed percentage of salaries is allocated to these benefits. Often these benefits are not included directly in salaries but are part of "employer costs of compensation" (see the Bureau of Labor Statistics Employer Costs for Employee Compensation at www.bls.gov). A typical estimate is that

30% of salaries might be allocated to fringe benefits. In such a case, one need only obtain salary data and add the fringe benefits based upon the percentage allocation for that purpose.

Education interventions often require or motivate participation by volunteers. These volunteers may include family members or persons who believe that the intervention will have beneficial outcomes. All volunteer time has an opportunity cost (see Chapter 4) and should be priced accordingly—that is, the value of a volunteer corresponds to the market value of the services that the volunteer will provide. Thus, if the volunteer has the qualifications for and will serve as a teacher's aide, one can use the salary and fringe benefits of a teacher's aide to set the value of the volunteer to the program. This approach is preferred over estimating volunteer prices based on the private earnings of the volunteer (e.g., a volunteer parent whose occupation is as a high-paid surgeon is assumed to cost the same per hour as a parent who is not working). Salary and fringe benefit data for pricing out the contributions of volunteers can be obtained from the Bureau of Labor Statistics; in some cases, a flat wage rate might be used for all volunteers (as recommended by www.independentsector.org).

In situations in which one has data on actual expenditures for particular categories of personnel, personnel costs can be readily ascertained. In other cases, such as new interventions that are being proposed, expenditure data that can be used to assess costs are not as obvious. In these cases, it is necessary to estimate the market value of the personnel services that are provided. For example, in the case of estimating the costs of a proposed program, one can use data from other existing interventions or the marketplace to calculate the expected costs for each type of personnel.

5.2.2. Training

Some programs require personnel to undergo program-specific training to prepare for program delivery. This may be brief, such as a half-day workshop delivered to teachers on a new reading curriculum or software package, or intensive, such as the yearlong training required for teachers delivering Reading Recovery (see Hollands et al., 2013). We include training as a specialized subset of personnel ingredients because it requires careful consideration of three factors: One is that if the training is sufficiently general, it may increase the productivity of the personnel delivering the intervention such that their salaries for outside opportunities on the labor market would increase or that the salary required to attract a similarly qualified replacement would increase. Many trainings for educational interventions are sufficiently tailored to the particular intervention that this is a relatively minor concern. A second consideration is the need to avoid double counting. For instance, if a training requires personnel to participate for 1 week, but the analysis already accounts for full-time personnel for the period in question, the training time should not be counted again. Similarly, if a training requires teachers to reallocate their time from instruction, that time should be counted as an opportunity cost to the school represented by the teachers' wages and benefits for that time, or the cost to hire substitute teachers for the day should be included but not both costs. Finally, many trainings may be seen as a longer-term investment in human capital whose results pay out over multiple years, both in the case of a multiyear intervention (discussed at the end of this chapter) and for an intervention that lasts for only one year or less but may be repeated in the future. In these cases, attributing the full cost of the training to the first year of the intervention overstates costs for that year and understates costs in subsequent years. To accurately account for costs, they should be annualized over the length of time for which the training will be useful (which may need to be projected based on how long the program will likely last) or the time until which the training is "used up" such that it will need to be repeated due to attrition of personnel or the need for a refresher course. The procedure for annualizing facilities costs, discussed later in this section, can also be applied to annualizing training costs.

5.2.3. Facilities

In the case of facilities, there are two possibilities. The first is that the intervention will utilize rented or leased space so that its market value is evident—either from direct expenditures if using local or idiosyncratic prices or from national average prices for leasing similar facilities if using expected prices. When a portion of a leased facility is used for the intervention, the cost value can be determined by ascertaining the portion of the lease cost that should be allocated to the intervention. For example, if 25% of a building is being used for the intervention, then about one quarter of the annual cost of that space should be allocated to the intervention.

In many cases, however, the facilities are owned rather than leased by the sponsoring agency. That is, they were purchased or constructed in the past by the school district or university that is sponsoring the intervention. Since there is no financial transaction, how can one determine what the value of the facility is for a given year? The simplest way to estimate that cost is to ask what the cost would be for similar space. That is, although a market for leased school facilities does not necessarily exist, it is possible to ascertain what space in similar types of buildings might cost to lease. When gathering data on facilities ingredients, it is important to note any special features of the facilities, in addition to square footage and the amount of time utilized, that may impact the construction costs or rental rates of the facilities. This might include specialized space, such as gymnasiums, auditoriums, or science labs, or particular construction requirements. The costs of leasing space in a school for an educational program, for instance, may be higher than the general price of commercial real estate because of heightened safety requirements and other regulations affecting educational institutions.

If using local prices, one will need the assistance of a local real estate agent to make this estimate. In that case, one needs to have an overall picture of the amount of space that is being used for the intervention and of such features as its age, construction, improvements, and amenities. These can be conveyed to a person who is knowledgeable about the local real estate market to get an estimate of the lease cost for such space.

An alternative way of estimating the value of a facility is to compute its annual cost by taking account of depreciation and the interest on the remaining, or undepreciated, value. This procedure requires knowledge of three factors: the replacement cost of the facility, the life span of the facility, and the rate of interest that is forgone by investing in a building rather than in an alternative investment.

The replacement cost of the building represents the amount that it would take to construct a similar facility. If only a part of the facility is being used for the intervention, one should estimate that portion of the overall facility and its cost that should be allocated to the intervention. Alternatively, one can get estimates of facility costs on the basis of the cost per square foot and multiply this amount by the square footage used for the intervention. National average estimates of replacement costs of educational facilities, including land acquisition and new construction, can be obtained from trade organizations' relevant publications in the field of school construction.

Depreciation refers to the amount of the facility that is "consumed" in a year. Essentially, depreciation costs are estimated by determining the life of the facility and dividing the total replacement cost by the number of years of use. For example, if a building has a useful life of 30 years, about one thirtieth of the facility is "used up" each year. Thus, the depreciation cost would be equal to one thirtieth of the replacement value of the building.

However, depreciation is not the only cost involved. The undepreciated portion of the facility represents an investment in resources that could have been used in some other way. By using those resources to construct the facility, alternative investment possibilities and their potential income and services have been forgone. These forgone income opportunities can be reflected by asking, "What interest rate could have been earned had the investment been made in the best alternative project?" That is, alternative ways of using those resources would have yielded a financial return that is approximated by multiplying an interest rate by the undepreciated portion of the facility investment.

This is the second component of costs: the forgone income on an investment that could have been realized if the resources had been used for some other alternative. For example, consider that had an amount equal to the undepreciated portion of the facility been invested in a bank account and lent out by the bank for some other purpose, a rate of interest would have been paid on this investment. Because of the forgone opportunities represented by the sunken investment in the undepreciated portion of the facility, we calculate the cost to us of that investment. Accordingly, the second part of the annual cost of a facility is determined by applying a rate of interest to the undepreciated portion of the facility—that is, the value of the facility that remains after taking account of its past depreciation.

In sum, the method of determining the annual value of an "owned" facility is to take the following steps. First, determine the replacement value of the facility and its operating life. Next, divide the replacement value by the number of years of life to obtain the cost of depreciation for each year of use. Then, multiply the undepreciated portion by an appropriate interest rate to obtain the opportunity cost of having resources invested in the undepreciated portion of the facility. Finally, add the annual cost of depreciation and the annual interest forgone on the remaining investment to obtain an annual cost.

Although this procedure is a valid one and is used by businesses to estimate the annual cost of facilities and equipment, it suffers from a serious problem with respect to social investments. Clearly, such a cost estimate will depend crucially upon the age of the facilities in that the greater the undepreciated portion, the higher the opportunity costs. Yet, the value of the services received in any one year may not differ substantially from that of other years, regardless of the age of the building. For this reason, attempts have been made to "annualize" costs by estimating an average of the combination of depreciation and interest on the undepreciated portion over the life of the facility.

Although there is a formula for annualizing the cost of a facility, Table 5.1 provides a much simpler method that can be used by the analyst. Table 5.1 shows annualization factors for facilities with different lifetimes at a variety of interest rates. For example, if a facility has a 20-year life and the appropriate interest rate is 5%, the annualization factor is 0.0802. One need only multiply this factor by the replacement cost of the facility to obtain an annual cost. For instance, if the replacement cost of the facility is $100,000, the annual cost

Table 5.1   Annualization Factors for Determining Annual Costs of Facilities and Equipment for Different Periods of Depreciation and Interest Rates

Lifetime of Assets (n)	Interest Rate					
	1%	3%	5%	7%	10%	15%
1						
2	0.5075	0.5226	0.5378	0.5531	0.5762	0.6151
3	0.3400	0.3535	0.3672	0.3811	0.4021	0.4380
4	0.2563	0.2690	0.2820	0.2952	0.3155	0.3503
5	0.2060	0.2184	0.2310	0.2439	0.2638	0.2983
6	0.1725	0.1846	0.1970	0.2098	0.2296	0.2642
7	0.1486	0.1605	0.1728	0.1856	0.2054	0.2404
8	0.1307	0.1425	0.1547	0.1675	0.1874	0.2229
9	0.1167	0.1284	0.1407	0.1535	0.1736	0.2096
10	0.1056	0.1172	0.1295	0.1424	0.1627	0.1993
15	0.0721	0.0838	0.0963	0.1098	0.1315	0.1710
20	0.0554	0.0672	0.0802	0.0944	0.1175	0.1598
25	0.0454	0.0574	0.0710	0.0858	0.1102	0.1547
30	0.0387	0.0510	0.0651	0.0806	0.1061	0.1523
40	0.0305	0.0433	0.0583	0.0750	0.1023	0.1506
50	0.0255	0.0389	0.0548	0.0725	0.1009	0.1501

Note: The annualization formula is $a(r,n) = \dfrac{(r(1+r)^n)}{((1+r)^n - 1)}$ where r = interest rate and n = lifetime of asset for depreciation.

would be about $8,020. This table can also be applied to a portion of the facility by determining what proportion of the total facility is used for the intervention. It is that proportion of the replacement cost that would subsequently be used for the calculation.

Assuming that the replacement cost and life of the facility can be estimated, it is only necessary to choose the interest rate. The basic problem in choosing this rate is that economists themselves are not able to agree upon an exact number. Economists have made strong arguments that interest rates should range between 0% and 11%, with a range of 3% to 7% as perhaps the most plausible (Barnett, 1996; Moore, Boardman, & Vining, 2013). The selection of an appropriate rate also relates to the choice of a discount rate, discussed later in this chapter in the section on multiyear programs. Note that, while interest rates for depreciation and the discount rate are often the same within a single project for consistency and comparability, the logic governing the selection of each differs and they need not be identical.

In summary, the annual cost of facilities can be estimated from using their annual leasing cost or rental value or estimating their annual value by considering depreciation and opportunity costs of the undepreciated investment. Table 5.1 can be of great assistance in making the latter calculation.

5.2.4. Equipment

The rules for estimating the costs of equipment are quite similar to those for estimating the costs of facilities. The annual cost of all leased equipment can be easily established. As noted previously, local and national prices are unlikely to differ substantially for many categories of equipment so that actual local expenditures or prices from national markets such as Internet retailers can be used as market prices. One can also use the rental or lease value to obtain estimates of the cost value of equipment that is donated or borrowed. In the absence of such information, one can use the replacement cost of a piece of equipment to estimate the annual cost by applying the annualization factors in Table 5.1. For example, if a piece of equipment has a replacement cost of $10,000 and a 10-year life, the annualization factor for a 5% interest rate is 0.1295 and the annual cost is about $1,295. This figure reflects both the cost of equipment depreciation and the cost of income that was forgone because funds were unavailable for alternative uses. In general, these principles can be used quite readily to set annual values on equipment.

5.2.5. Supplies

The costs of supplies are often difficult to estimate using the ingredients method because it is too arduous to set out their composition and price in detail. For example, office supplies may consist of paper, pens, pencils, toner cartridges, paper clips, calendars, and so on. It would take enormous resources to list each of these and determine market prices. Also, such supplies typically account for less than 5% of the total cost of educational interventions, so errors in estimating their costs do not create very much distortion in the total cost figure. For example, a 20% error in the cost of a category that makes up only 5% of the total cost estimate will result in only a 1% distortion. But a 20% error in the cost of a category that makes up 75% of total costs, such as personnel, will create a 15% distortion, or a distortion that is 15 times as great as for supplies.

Accordingly, one might estimate the cost of supplies by simply adding the total expenditures on supplies to the estimated value of those that are contributed. Only in the case in which supplies are a large part of the intervention would one wish to devote greater effort to the details of this category.

5.2.6. Required Client Inputs

The method for determining the cost of client inputs will depend upon the types of inputs under consideration. Here, we are referring only to ingredients that must be provided by clients, such as transportation. We are not referring to fees that are charged to clients, since these represent a financing mechanism that will be addressed in Chapter 6. Some educational programs may provide their own transportation, and it is important to take account of the value of this ingredient regardless of who is supplying it.

The usual approach to ascertaining the costs of transportation is to include the total expense. For example, if parents must purchase bicycles, protective headgear, and other equipment for their children for getting to school, this can be assessed according to the method for costing out equipment. The replacement value for the equipment can be converted into an annualized cost through the use of Table 5.1. If the bicycle (or other equipment) will be used only 10% of the time for going to school, then we might estimate the cost as 10% of the annualized value.

Example 5.1   Pricing the Ingredients
of the HighScope Perry Preschool Program

In the last chapter, Example 4.2 described several categories of cost ingredients in the Perry Preschool Program. Once ingredients are identified, values need to be attached to each of these ingredients. The values for this analysis were represented by local prices in Ypsilanti, Michigan. The cost analysis of the program incorporated a variety of methods and data in order to calculate the program costs in 5 separate academic years (1962–1963 to 1966–1967). The overall cost estimates for a single year (1962–1963) are briefly described here:

- *Instructional staff.* The salaries of teachers were obtained directly from the accounting files of the Ypsilanti School District. At the time, contributions to social security and retirement accounts were an administratively determined percentage of salaries. Thus, the appropriate percentages were applied in order to obtain the cost of fringe benefits.
- *Administrative and support staff.* The costs of administrative and support staff were obtained from the annual audit reports and budgets of the Ypsilanti Public School District. These costs could be obtained for only a single year (1968–1969). Thus, these figures were applied to each of the previous years for which a cost estimate was needed after making adjustments for inflation.
- *Facilities.* The facilities belonged to the school district and were in use before (and after) the Perry Preschool Program. Therefore, it would be misleading to use their overall value to calculate an annual facilities cost. Instead, the evaluator calculated the annualized cost of interest and depreciation, following the methods that were described earlier in the chapter. The interest rate was set at 3.5%, and the facilities were assumed to lose 3% of their total value in each year due to depreciation. (The study author also obtained cost estimates using several other interest rates; in the next section, we address the issue of how to choose an interest rate.)
- *Equipment.* The program used a variety of equipment. Like facilities, this equipment lasts for more than 1 year, and it is necessary to calculate an annualized cost. Again, the interest rate was set at 3.5%; equipment was assumed to lose 10% of its total value in each year due to depreciation.
- *Classroom supplies.* In each year of the program, $480 was allocated to classroom supplies; this figure was used as the annual cost of classroom supplies.
- *Developmental screening.* Children who participated in the program received developmental screening prior to their entry. The ingredients of this screening were estimated at $234 in 1962–1963.
- *School district overhead.* The Ypsilanti Public School District provided services that benefited the preschool students, including maintenance, utilities, and general administrative support. To calculate the costs of overhead, the evaluator divided the total annual expenditures

of the district on these services—obtained from annual audit reports—by the total number of students enrolled in district schools. This produced a per-student overhead cost that was multiplied by the number of students participating in the Perry Preschool Program.

This pricing information can be used to calculate the average and total costs of the HighScope Perry Preschool Program.

Source: Adapted from Barnett (1996, pp. 19–25).

If the parents transport their children to school in a car pool, it is possible to calculate the annual cost based upon estimated mileage and the value of parental time. The major car rental companies make estimates of the cost per mile for operating a car. Since the car is not likely to be purchased solely for this purpose, one should probably consider only the operating cost of the additional mileage (gas, oil, tires, maintenance) rather than a part of the "fixed" cost (depreciation, interest, insurance). One might check with local businesses to determine the amount that is reimbursed for each mile of auto travel (e.g., 50 cents per mile), or for a national average, one might use the Internal Revenue Service standard mileage rates, which are 54 cents per mile as of 2016 (https://www.irs.gov). The value of parental time can be estimated by considering what it would cost to hire someone (such as a school bus driver) to provide this service. That cost in wages and fringe benefits can be applied to the number of hours a year required for parental driving.

If the child takes public transportation, it is the average cost per passenger of the transportation system that can provide the most reasonable cost estimate. Each public transportation system has an estimate of such a cost. Of course, the rider pays only a portion of that cost, and taxpayers pay the remainder. However, it is the overall cost that is required for cost estimation, and the allocation of cost can be made at a subsequent stage.

5.3. COSTS OVER MULTIPLE YEARS

All cost analyses must be referenced to a time period. That is, we are concerned with what the costs (and benefits, effects, or utility) of an intervention are for a particular period of time. Since educational programs are typically planned on an annual basis, a period of a year is often used as the basis for estimating costs. In many cases, however, educational programs occur over a period of 2 or more years. When costs extend over 2 or more years, the analysis should consider two separate issues: (1) inflation and (2) discounting. We shall discuss each of these in turn.

5.3.1. Adjusting Costs for Inflation

For each year of a multiyear project, it is possible to undertake an ingredients analysis and to estimate the costs of each ingredient. However, this analysis will not reflect the fact that costs may be higher in future years because of price inflation. To account for inflation, the costs from each year should be adjusted to the price level of a single year. The choice of this year is arbitrary, although once chosen it should be used consistently. Note that even for a single year program, if the prices used for ingredient valuation come from different sources, they may also need to be adjusted so that all prices are expressed in terms of the same year. When costs are not adjusted for inflation, they are said to be expressed in "nominal" or "current" terms. After adjustments are made, they are said to be expressed in "real" terms. If, for example, the nominal costs in 1996 are adjusted to the prevailing level of prices in 2015, the costs are expressed in "real 2015" terms.

Information on the overall rate of inflation can generally be derived from a price index that reflects the changing prices of a standard "basket" of goods and services. To illustrate how to account for inflation, Table 5.2 provides a small example. A hypothetical CPI is presented over a period of years. It is equal to 100 in 2010, which is designated as the base year. The CPI is 105.8 in 2012; this indicates that a typical basket of consumer goods and services rose in price between 2010 and 2012 from $100 to $105.80.

Table 5.2   Using a Hypothetical Consumer Price Index to Adjust Costs

	2008	2010	2012	2014
CPI	91.8	100.0	105.8	112.5
Nominal dollars	$85.00	$100.00	$110.00	$120.00
Real 2010 dollars	$92.59	$100.00	$103.97	$106.67
Real 2014 dollars	$104.17	$112.50	$116.97	$120.00

In the next row, there is a stream of nominal costs that are not adjusted for inflation. Let's say that we wish to adjust the nominal cost of $85 in 2008 to the price levels of 2010 (i.e., real 2010 dollars). The CPI for 2010 is divided by the CPI for 2008, which is then multiplied by the nominal cost of $85:

$$\$85 \times \frac{100.0}{91.8} = \$92.59$$

What if we wanted to convert the nominal cost of $85 in 2008 to real 2014 dollars? This is accomplished by the following:

$$\$85 \times \frac{112.5}{91.8} = \$104.17$$

A more detailed way of adjusting costs for inflation is to use different price indexes for different ingredients, rather than using a single index. For example, although personnel and facilities costs may rise over time, they often rise at different rates. Some prices, such as those in service-heavy industries like education and health care, tend to rise faster than the general rate of inflation, while others, such as technology, tend to rise more slowly than the general rate of inflation or even fall over time. There are separate price indexes published for different categories of goods and services.

For higher education in the United States, there are several indices. In general, the Bureau of Labor Statistics CPI is probably sufficient for obtaining a good approximation to changes in prices. However, given the particular technology and provision of higher education, the choice of a price index may sometimes matter (Gillen & Robe, 2011). Three indices are commonly used: (1) the Higher Education Price Index (HEPI), (2) the Higher Education Cost Adjustment (HECA), and (3) the Consumer Price Index for All Urban Consumers (CPI-U; for details on each of the inflation measures, see State Higher Education Executive Officers Association [SHEEO], 2009, Appendix A). The HECA may be preferred over the privately developed HEPI, which is heavily weighted toward faculty salaries, and the CPI-U, which has oil prices as a large component. Inflation trends using the CPI-U, HECA, and HEPI are somewhat different. For instance, inflation over the period 1993 to 2008 was 49% according to the CPI-U but 60% using the HECA and 71% using the HEPI (SHEEO, 2009, Appendix Table 11). Therefore, real spending grew 20% less using HEPI than CPI-U. However, annual differences are much smaller, such that the path of inflation is consistent across the indices.

5.3.2. Discounting Costs

We must also adjust costs for their time value, a procedure that is referred to as "discounting." The basic idea is that costs occurring in the future are less of a burden than costs occurring in the present. Thus, we need to discount future costs to properly compare them with present costs. Unfortunately, discounting is frequently confused with adjusting for inflation, even though the two are completely distinct. Even in the absence of inflation, there is still a need to discount costs for their distribution across time.

Let us imagine two different projects. The first incurs a cost of $1,000 in the first year, while the second project incurs a cost of $1,000 in the second year. Which project is less costly? Our immediate instinct might be to assume that both have the same opportunity cost, but this would be a mistake. Since the costs of the second project are deferred by a year, we could invest the $1,000 elsewhere, perhaps placing it in a bank account that earns interest. Thus, the second project is less costly because it does not tie up funds that can be profitably employed elsewhere. It is also less costly because we are impatient—that is, we have a positive marginal rate of time preference. Fundamentally, incurring costs in the future is preferable to incurring them now, and getting benefits in the present is preferable to getting benefits later. To reflect this in our analysis, we should discount all money flows that occur in the future.

There is a simple procedure for discounting any money value. The underlying issues can be seen more clearly if we take a simple example of three expenditure patterns over a 5-year period. As shown in Table 5.3, where these patterns are illustrated, the total expenditure in all three cases is $1,000. However, in the case of Program A, the entire amount is spent in the first year, whereas in the case of Program B, the amount is divided into equal annual payments of $200. In the case of Program C, the entire amount is spent in the last year. From the perspective of the sacrifice principle of costs, Program B has incurred a lower cost than Program A, because Program B allows for some of the money to earn interest for almost all of the 5-year period. Program C has the lowest cost of all, since this expenditure pattern permits use of the entire amount in the first four years—perhaps held in an interest-bearing savings account—sacrificing it only in the final year of the period. In contrast, Program A must give up all $1,000 in the first year and therefore has the highest opportunity cost. The result is that Program A sacrifices more value in alternative opportunities than do Programs B or C, even though the total outlay of each over a 5-year period is $1,000.

Table 5.3   Three Alternative Expenditure Patterns

Year	Program A	Program B	Program C
1	$1,000	$ 200	0
2	0	$ 200	0
3	0	$ 200	0
4	0	$ 200	0
5	0	$ 200	$1,000
Total (undiscounted)	$1,000	$ 1,000	$1,000
Present value (discount rate of 5%)	$1,000	$909	$823

This can be seen more clearly if we look at Year 2. Program A has already relinquished $1,000 and must sacrifice $1,000 in alternatives. However, Program B has relinquished only $200 and can use the other $800. For example, if Program B were to put the $800 into a 1-year investment at an interest rate of 5%, it would realize an additional $40 in income for that year. Clearly, the expenditure pattern represented for Program B would leave the investor better off than Program A. In the case of C, the investor could earn the 5% for each of the first 4 years and receive additional income each year. Thus, even though each program requires an outlay of $1,000 over the 5-year period, the value of the outlay is most costly for A and least costly for C.

The principle embedded in this example also holds when we ascertain the costs of multiyear projects for social entities. In general, the more that we are able to defer costs until the latter part of the investment period, the lower the sacrifice, or opportunity costs, to the entity. The method for doing this is to compare alternative investment patterns by calculating their present values in a way that reduces the impact of future expenditures relative to current ones. This procedure takes account of the fact that deferring costs enables one to have access to resources for a longer period. Thus, the present value tends to neutralize differences in the time pattern of allocations when adding up the cost outlays for a multiyear project.

The calculation of present value uses an interest rate (or "discount" rate) to discount future costs relative to current ones. The formula for estimating the present value of a future cost outlay is as follows:

$$PV = \frac{C_t}{(1+r)^t}$$

In this formulation, *PV* stands for present value; *C* denotes the cost; *r* denotes the discount rate; and *t* is the year in which the cost outlay will be made, where *t* is equal to 1 for this year, 2 for next year, 3 for the following year, and so on. To show how to use the formula, we can take as an example the outlay of $1,000 in Year 5, as reflected in the expenditure pattern of Program C in Table 5.3, and use a discount rate of 5%:

$$PV = \frac{\$1,000}{(1+0.05)^4} = \frac{\$1,000}{1.216} = \$823$$

On the basis of this calculation, it appears that the present value of a $1,000 disbursement made 5 years hence at a discount rate of 5% is about $823. If a higher discount rate were used, such as 10%, the present value would be $683, reflecting the higher opportunity cost attached to using the resources. Later on, we provide a discussion of the criteria for choosing a discount rate. More generally, the present value of any time pattern of expenditure can be found by using this expression:

$$PV = \sum_{t=1}^{n} \frac{C_t}{(1+r)^{t-1}}$$

When this expression is applied to the 5-year expenditure patterns of Programs A, B, and C with a 5% discount rate, one finds that the present value of the cost for A is $1,000, for B it is $909, and for C it is $823. That is, C has the lowest sacrifice in costs, even though it, too, requires expenditures of $1,000 over the 5-year period.

There is a consensus that discounting should be applied in this manner to reflect the preference by individuals and society for having resources sooner rather than later. Most textbooks on benefit-cost (BC) analysis provide a thorough discussion of the procedures for discounting (e.g., Boardman et al., 2011, pp. 133–166). Note that the concepts and methods of discounting are also applicable to patterns of benefits, effects, and utility over time. In subsequent chapters, we return to a discussion of discounting in these specific contexts.

5.3.3. Choosing a Discount Rate

Although there is widespread agreement on the need to discount future costs, there is less agreement on the specific discount rate that should be used in the analysis. Part of the controversy stems from the fact that there are a number of conceptual approaches to determining the discount rate. In one approach, the discount rate is reflected by the returns on consumer savings options (e.g., the interest rate on treasury bills). That is, what returns are being sacrificed by consumers in order to consume resources now instead of saving them? Another approach suggests that the discount rate should reflect the average returns on investments that are made by entrepreneurs in the private sector. That is, what are entrepreneurs sacrificing by investing resources in a particular project instead of using them for other profitable endeavors? Also, we should recognize that education is often a social, not a private investment, and so we should use a social discount rate; this rate will reflect social valuations, not private valuations of the future. (As society has a longer time horizon than private individuals, this social discount rate will be lower than the private discount rate.) Yet another approach advocates using a weighted average of the two preceding private rates. For an excellent discussion of these and other views, see Boardman and colleagues (2011, Chapter 6). Fundamentally, the analyst should look at where the funds for the project are coming from and ask this: What is the opportunity cost of capital for that agency?

In practice, analysts have utilized a variety of discount rates, ranging between 0% and 11% (Barnett, 1996). The ambiguity is perhaps encouraged by the different standards that are often set by government offices. The Office of Management and Budget, the Congressional Budget Office, and the Government Accountability Office have all set different standards for the discount rates that should be used in project evaluations (Boardman et al., 2011, Chapter 10). At least one author feels that the most credible range of estimates of the discount rate varies between 3% and 7%, with the true discount rate probably at the lower end of that range (Barnett, 1996). In health, a recent set of national guidelines suggests that a discount rate of 3% is probably most reasonable, although good arguments can be made for a somewhat larger range (Lipscomb, Weinstein, & Torrance, 1996; Neumann, Sanders, Russell, Siegel, & Ganiat, 2016).

The disagreement in the literature suggests that evaluators should choose an initial discount rate of 3% to 5%. But as verification, the analyst should then calculate their estimates of money flow using a wider range of discount rates, perhaps from 0% to 10%. By following this procedure—referred to as a sensitivity analysis—one can assess whether the key findings about costs are substantially altered by employing different assumptions. Chapter 11 provides a more detailed discussion of sensitivity analysis.

5.4. CONCLUSIONS

The valuation of ingredients requires taking each category of ingredient and using appropriate methods to ascertain their prices. This includes all ingredients, even those that do not have obvious prices (such as volunteer time or temporarily leased school facilities). Ideally, all the ingredients will have clear market prices, and these are the best approximation of society's willingness to pay. The quantity of ingredients should then be multiplied by their prices. We emphasize that these steps should deliberately be separated; ingredients should be specified and then prices and then their product is the estimate of costs. Ingredients and prices should be separated for three reasons. First, this approach stands in distinction to budgetary data, where prices and ingredients are combined in a single number. As discussed previously, budgetary data should be treated very cautiously. Second, this approach—by explicitly documenting each price—makes clear what option the analyst has chosen with regard to using national or local prices. Finally, for an independent reader, it is very difficult to understand and appraise cost information when there is no information on ingredients or prices but there is only information on their product. A lot of the information on how the education program is implemented is lost if ingredients are not itemized, and a lot of information on how costs are derived is lost if prices are not itemized.

With information on ingredients and prices, the calculation of costs becomes straightforward. However, costs must still be reported in a clear way such that they can be used either directly by policymakers for cost-feasibility (CF) analysis or as part of cost-effectiveness (CE) or BC analysis. We show how to report costs for analysis purposes in the next chapter.

Discussion Questions

1. What are shadow prices, and when should they be used to estimate the costs of ingredients? Give examples of each.

2. Under what circumstances would you use program-specific or regional prices, and under what circumstances would you use national average prices for ingredients?

3. What specific details about labor ingredients are needed in order to appropriately match an ingredient to a price?

4. What is the difference between inflation and discounting?

Exercises

1. Assume that a piece of equipment has a replacement cost of $10,000 and an 8-year life. What is its annualized cost at an interest rate of 15%?

2. Assume that you are asked to review the costs of a 5-year project. After a careful identification and specification of ingredients and their prices, you obtain the following costs:

   Year 1: $11,000

   Year 2: $13,000

   Year 3: $18,500

   Year 4: $10,800

   Year 5: $27,000

   Derive the present value of this stream of costs for both a 3% and a 7% discount rate. Is the average of these present values equal to the present value for the average of these two discount rates? What are the implications of your answer?

3. For each of the following ingredients of a youth development program, describe how you would obtain an estimate of the ingredient's price. Based on your knowledge of educational programs and research, what sources of data would you use to obtain estimates of market value? For each, is it a market price or a shadow price? What more would you want to know in order to be more confident in your selection of a price?

   a. The social worker who runs the program at the school level

   b. Teachers

   c. Parental time

   d. Donated winter coats and backpacks through one community partner agency

6

Analyzing and Reporting Costs

Objectives

1. Apply the ingredients method using a cost worksheet.

2. Report total costs and average cost per participant for decisionmaking purposes.

3. Analyze costs and account for context.

4. Illustrate the range of types and uses of cost analyses.

The previous three chapters explored the definition of costs and the ingredients method for estimating them. We also discussed the identification and specification of ingredients and methods for determining the prices attached to each of them. Chapter 4 provided guidelines to identify ingredients and collect data, and Chapter 5 described the procedure for matching each ingredient to a valid price. The purpose of this chapter is to bring ingredients and prices together to report costs and to analyze costs. This analysis is intended to convey to decisionmakers what resources are required for educational interventions.

Ingredients data and costs can be stored and analyzed in a range of formats. The format discussed here, and in previous editions of this textbook, involves a worksheet where data are provided for each ingredient utilized by the intervention. The worksheet is designed to store qualitative and quantitative ingredients data in an easily accessible format and to calculate the total cost and average cost per student. The specific columns of the worksheet and ordering of ingredients are adaptable based on different types of programs, audience requirements, or perspective adopted. In this chapter, we provide a basic example of a worksheet and offer some general discussion and guidelines in data management and organization.

● 6.1. TABULATING TOTAL COST USING A COST WORKSHEET

6.1.1. Worksheet Basics

A worksheet format enables you to list ingredients with associated descriptive data, quantities, units, prices, and the cost of each ingredient. The worksheet can also incorporate data on the evaluation, demographic data for each site, and data on how each ingredient was financed. Additionally, the worksheet can also include sheets for analyses and tables for reporting. Because a worksheet is very flexible, the file can be expanded and can utilize multiple sheets as needed.

Table 6.1 shows a straightforward format for a cost worksheet that can be used to set out and analyze costs using the ingredients method. The spreadsheet houses information on ingredients and their prices together so that the analyst can estimate the cost of the program.

The first column lists the ingredients, sorted by category. The second column allows the analyst to document any important notes about the ingredient. These notes might include special qualifications of personnel that may be relevant in selecting a price, characteristics of the room utilized for the program, or assumptions that may be varied in sensitivity analysis. For multiyear programs, the third column documents the year in which each ingredient was used; ingredients can then be "stacked" by year. Alternatively, the quantity can be documented by year, such as number of teacher hours in Year 1, Year 2, etc. A third option for multiyear interventions is to construct separate sheets for each year to obtain annual program costs that are summed for the total cost. Column 4 includes the quantity and unit for the ingredient. To simplify, an additional column can be added for the unit so that the

Table 6.1   Sample Cost Worksheet

Column 1	Column 2	Column 3	Column 4	Column 5	Column 6
Ingredient Name	Description, notes, and assumptions	Year used	Quantity	Price	Cost
Personnel					
...					
Facilities					
...					
Materials and equipment					
...					
Required client inputs					
...					
Other inputs					
...					
Total Cost					
Number of participants					
Average Cost per Participant					

quantity can easily be multiplied by the price. The shadow or market price is listed in Column 5. To avoid errors and to simplify sensitivity analyses, the price listed should be derived directly from the method of pricing and be appropriately adjusted for inflation and expressed in present values (see Chapter 5). Essentially, the worksheet price should be reported so that there is price compatibility within the evaluation of one intervention or among alternatives being compared.

Some adjustment to ingredient prices or quantities may be necessary in order for their units to align appropriately to be able to multiply them together. For instance, ingredient quantities may be expressed as a number of hours, but the price may be an annual salary plus fringe benefits. In this case, the analyst could convert the number of hours into a percentage of time for a year in the manner of full-time equivalents [FTEs], which is expressed as a fraction of time for a number of employees, or could be used to convert the annual salary into an hourly wage.

Finally, Column 6 tabulates the cost of each ingredient, which is simply the product of price and quantity. This column is summed to calculate the total cost of the intervention.

6.1.2. Total Cost

The tabulation of ingredient quantities and prices to obtain a total cost is a straightforward arithmetic exercise: Simply multiply the quantity needed of each ingredient by its market or shadow price and then sum across all ingredients to obtain a total cost estimate for an intervention. These calculations, however, can be deconstructed further in useful analyses on the dimensions along which costs vary. This section discusses these analyses, along with the important choices and assumptions that must be made about the measure of participation used and the units of quantities and prices used in order to complete the calculations. See Example 6.1 for the costs of the HighScope Perry Preschool Program (and earlier examples in prior chapters on the program's ingredients and prices).

Example 6.1   Reporting the Costs of the HighScope Perry Preschool Program

We can now complete the cost analysis of the HighScope Perry Preschool Program, building on the ingredients listing and pricing of these ingredients (see Examples 4.2 and 5.1). The cost tabulation is given here.

Ingredient Costs of the Perry Preschool Program

	Annual Cost (in 1962–1963)	Annual Cost (in 2015 dollars)
Instructional staff	$28,853	$226,496
Administrative and support staff	$1,134	$8,902
Facilities and equipment (annualized depreciation and interest)	$2,337	$18,345
Classroom supplies	$480	$3,768
Developmental screening	$234	$1,837
School district overhead	$1,722	$13,518

	Annual Cost (in 1962–1963)	Annual Cost (in 2015 dollars)
Total per year	$31,760	$249,316
Number of children	21	21
Cost per child per year	$1,512	$11,869

Source: Adapted from Barnett (1996, Table 4).

Note: Adjusted to 2015 dollars using the Consumer Wage Index for Urban Wage Earners and Clerical Workers (CPI-W).

For one year of the program, delivered to 21 children, the total cost was $249,316 in 2015 dollars. Expressed per child participant, the average cost is $11,869 annually; notably, this amount is not substantially different from current expenditures per low-income child in high-quality preschool at the present time (Barnett, Carolan, Squires, Clarke Brown, & Horowitz, 2015). With this cost information, along with duration of time in the program, the analyst can now look at how cost-effective or socially efficient the program is.

Another interesting feature of the estimates in the table is that instructional staff accounted for 91% of costs in 1962–1963. This is often the case in educational programs that rely heavily on the services of teachers. When identifying and valuing ingredients, the evaluator is often pressed for time and money. Thus, it would be wise to follow the advice of Chapter 4 and focus one's efforts on the categories of ingredients that are likely to weigh most heavily in the final estimates, such as personnel.

Total costs are defined as the total social value of all the resources required for any particular intervention. Given our definition of cost, this can be thought of as the value of the sacrifices made by society—the value of what must be given up—to undertake the intervention. Thus, the total cost is the opportunity cost to society of undertaking the intervention rather than using the ingredients for their most productive alternative use.

It is necessary to emphasize the importance of the total cost estimate as a product of prices and quantities. An estimate of total costs provides an overall summary that includes specification and costs of all ingredients, regardless of how they are obtained or financed. When a cost-effectiveness (CE) study is disseminated beyond the initial site of the evaluation, it is crucial that all of the required ingredients, irrespective of their source, be included to inform decisionmakers of the resources required to implement the program as it was evaluated.

If the study were to be limited to only those costs that were paid for by the initial sponsor, the results would provide a misleading picture of the true overall costs for replication. It is the total costs that should be reported for explaining the effectiveness of an intervention, although any adoption can also specify the costs that will be provided by a specific entity such as the sponsoring school. Since researchers cannot foresee all potential financing options for future implementation in new locations, analyses should include a complete accounting in the overall statement of costs. For example, some local school districts have no difficulties in finding volunteers, while others have to pay all personnel (for a discussion of this scenario, see Example 4.1). If a district in the former category were to leave out of its cost analysis all volunteer staff on the grounds that volunteers do not require a financial outlay by the district, it would not be apparent to a second district what the true ingredients requirements and costs would be in a situation in which all personnel must be paid. Accordingly, it should be left to the secondary user of the data to ascertain which of the total ingredients must be paid for and which can be obtained through contributions and volunteers.

6.1.3. Average Cost per Student

Average cost is simply the total cost of the program or intervention divided by the number of participants. (As we noted previously, average cost in this context means average cost per participant, not average cost per unit of output). Hence, in order to calculate average cost, the analyst must select the number of participants to use in the denominator. For interventions for which there is no attrition, or for projecting costs for a planned intervention for a specified number of participants, the choice is straightforwardly the observed or planned number of participants.

In most educational settings, however, students frequently enter and exit interventions. This complicates the measurement of dosage (how much of the treatment is received) and participation—some students may start but not complete an intervention, and depending on the intervention design, students may enter partway through. This is even more likely in multiyear interventions, when students are most likely to move or change schools entirely between school years. The choice of the appropriate number of participants for the denominator, then, will depend upon the relevant question for decisionmakers along with design features of the intervention.

This discussion is related to the selection of intent-to-treat (ITT) versus treatment-on-the-treated (TOT) estimates of program effectiveness. Not all students selected for an intervention, whether by lottery or by another method, actually participate. Therefore, the number who actually receive the treatment may differ considerably from those who were selected. As discussed in Chapters 2 and 3, cost analysis requires calculation of all the resources needed to implement the program. This includes resources that are allocated to those whom the program intended to treat but did not treat. Therefore, the analyst should report total cost for the entire ITT sample; average cost is then derived as total cost divided by those the program intended to treat. (However, when performing CE, the analyst should not divide average cost by the TOT estimate; this will overstate the CE. Instead, the analyst should divide total cost by the product of the ITT estimate and the ITT sample size. If only the TOT estimate is available, this estimate should be weighted by the proportion treated. If it is unclear whether TOT or ITT estimates are available, a conservative principle would be to report whichever calculation makes the proposed program look less cost-effective.)

6.2. REPORTING COSTS

While the total cost provides an overall picture of the resources utilized by a program, it may be useful to unpack that estimate to better understand how the costs varied. It may be that program sites within the evaluation used resources differently, program alternatives do not require the same investment at the start of the intervention, or some types of students were targeted for different resources than others. In the following subsections, we discuss some ways of reporting costs at a more disaggregated level. Several of these ways are illustrated in our cost analysis of Talent Search, given as Example 6.2 (see later in this section).

6.2.1. By Site

Unlike interventions in other fields of economic evaluation, particularly in health, educational interventions are often "bundled" at the level of a school, classroom, or small instructional grouping. The notion of what constitutes a "site" can vary and in the context of a randomized controlled trial often refers to the unit of analysis at which randomization occurs, such as a school or a classroom. Seldom are interventions delivered on an individual level without clustering or blocking at a higher level. This limits the ability to analyze variation in resource use at the individual level, with the possible exception of differences in dosage for highly individualized interventions such as tutoring and mentoring. Decisionmakers may be interested in straightforward reports of costs for each site, particularly if the number of sites is low. Also, the analyst might be interested in how resource utilization varies when an intervention is delivered at multiple sites.

Reporting site-level variability in resources can be useful as a supplemental analysis for many types of programs. If a program is designed to adapt to the context and local needs, it is important to document how the treatment differed across sites in terms of resources allocated. Alternatively, if the program is highly prescribed, sites where costs are far from the mean might not have implemented the program with fidelity. In both cases, the results inform the audience regarding implementation, continued development of the program, and the possibility of replication or scale-up.

In fact, resource use may vary substantially between sites even when an intervention is clearly defined and highly prescriptive. Looking at home-visiting services to enhance child development, Burwick and colleagues (2014) illustrated how unit and total costs can vary across agencies. Looking across 23 agencies, they estimate an average cost per week of family participation at between $70 and $520 and average duration of participation by families of between 17 and 61 weeks (Burwick et al., 2014, Table A3, adjusted to 2015 dollars). Consequently, the average cost per family in the home-visiting program varied significantly, from $2,210 to $25,970 (2012 dollars), and the cost of each visit delivered varied from $230 to $3,080 across the 25 sites. Given this variation, it seems very unlikely that the low-cost and high-cost sites were delivering a program that could be considered equivalent.

Another example is Read 180, a literacy intervention that aims to improve skills in decoding, fluency, and comprehension among struggling older readers. The program comprises curricular and instructional materials for whole-group; small-group; and individualized, computer-based instruction. Scholastic, the program developer and publisher, provides clear guidance to school districts using the program on details of implementation such as time commitment and class size. In spite of the clear direction from program developers, an investigation of costs at three sites found that on-the-ground implementation varied significantly with regard to class size, personnel, and technology utilization. As shown in Table 6.2, average and total costs varied significantly by site (Levin, Catlin, & Elson, 2007).

If the study includes a very large number of sites, reporting the costs for every site may become unwieldy and difficult to interpret. In these cases, the analyst may be interested in constructing a distribution

Table 6.2   Average and Total Costs of Read 180

	Site 1	Site 2	Site 3
Cost per student:			
Personnel (teachers)	$420	$1,250	$90
Personnel (administrators, technicians, coordinators)	$70	$530	$80
Equipment/materials (computers, licenses)	$330	$200	$180
Other (prof. dev., sub teachers, other)	$0	$10	$10
Average Cost	$810	$1,990	$370
Students	6,701	1,080	2,400
Total Cost ($m)	$5.428	$2.149	$0.888

Source: Adapted from Levin et al. (2007).

Note: Adjusted to 2015 dollars.

of costs across sites, testing whether the differences in costs between sites are statistically significant, and examining how meaningful summary statistics such as the pooled average cost across sites may be for a decisionmaker. These analyses are further discussed in Chapter 11 on analysis of uncertainty.

With enough sites and sufficiently provided and detailed information about ingredients, implementation, and sample characteristics, the analyst can use statistical techniques such as multiple regression to determine what factors best "explain" differences in implementation and costs across sites—for instance, different samples, different mixes of ingredient categories, different contextual factors. (A discussion of stochastic cost functions is beyond the scope of this book; readers should consult Kumbhakar and Lovell [2000] and Gronberg, Jansen, and Taylor [2011]; for a cost study of child care centers, see Blau and Mocan [2006].) Higher-cost sites may serve needier students, be more personnel intensive than lower-cost sites, or provide more services. It is important to exercise caution in interpreting and reporting results on cost variability and potential explanatory factors associated with that variability. Even when sites are randomly assigned to treatment status, the details of implementation, context, and sample characteristics are often not random and may be correlated with other unobserved factors that may explain site-level differences.

6.2.2. Over Time

Many multiyear programs will have reasonably consistent annual costs so that their costs can be calculated on an annual basis with the costs in subsequent years discounted to present value at the start of program implementation (as discussed in Chapter 5) to obtain a total cost. However, there are two important issues when thinking about costs over time.

One issue is that programs are often delivered with different amounts of resources over multiple years: Each year of program implementation may involve different ingredients and thus different costs. The Talent Search program in Example 6.2 illustrates this simply: The annual per student cost of the program is only one sixth of the cost of delivery because students stay in the program for 6 years. Another example is the National Guard Youth ChalleNGe Program (NGYCP), a quasi-military training program offering at-risk youth disciplinary training as well as academic and personal supports. The first phase of the 18-month program is at a residential camp; the second phase involves academic and personal supports as follow-up. Per student, the residential phase was significantly more costly than the follow-up (Perez-Arce, Constant, Loughran, & Karoly, 2012).

Example 6.2   Reporting the Costs of Talent Search

An example of a program that is designed to target the needs of the local context is Talent Search. One of the original federal TRIO programs, Talent Search provides a range of services to students with the goal of increasing financial literacy, applications for postsecondary financial aid, high school completion, and postsecondary enrollment. The program is adaptable to which grade levels are served, to the materials used or provided, and in other areas such as SAT prep or overnight visits to college campuses.

	Cost of Talent Search (for One Academic Year)
Personnel	
Talent Search staff: Directors	$850,870
Talent Search staff: Counselors (Level A)	$1,051,390
Talent Search staff: Counselors (Level B)	$932,690

	Cost of Talent Search (for One Academic Year)
Talent Search staff: Other	$572,910
Talent Search work study	$42,480
Talent Search staff: Professional development	$23,110
School staff: Principals/teachers	$44,690
School staff: Guidance counselors	$121,350
School staff: Other	$35,520
In-kind personnel	$14,100
Facilities	
Host college	$189,250
School sites	$71,970
Overhead charged to Talent Search	$247,670
Materials/Equipment	
Talent Search site	$118,450
Contributed	$19,750
Other Inputs	
Transportation	$162,570
Other Talent Search inputs	$101,430
Other in-kind inputs	$358,620
Total annual cost	**$4,958,760**
Number of students	7,084
Average annual cost	**$700**

Source: Adapted from Bowden (2014).

Notes: Cost pooled across nine sites; costs reported in 2015 dollars rounded to nearest 10.

Using the ingredients method, Bowden (2014) calculated the costs of Talent Search at nine sites. A full tabulation of the average cost pooled across the nine sites is given above. Talent Search is labor-intensive: It requires a significant commitment of personnel across different job classifications and

(Continued)

(Continued)

prices (wages). In addition, there are other inputs of facilities, materials, and other inputs (transportation and in-kind contributions). The total cost of the program at the nine sites for one year was $4,958,760; across the 7,084 students, the average cost is therefore $700.

Analysis of these cost data yields several interesting results. One observation is that $700 is significantly above the per-student federal funding that is allocated to Talent Search (Bowden, 2014); schools and colleges are subsidizing the program by a nontrivial amount. More importantly, this average cost is far below the cost per Talent Search "treatment." Students typically attend the program for 6 years, and so reporting costs over time becomes salient. Bowden (2014) estimated the treatment total cost per student at $3,630 (defined as the expected program delivery costs per site-specific complete-dosage student expressed as a present value with a 3% discount rate at age 18 in 2015 dollars). This higher figure is the relevant cost for a decisionmaker who wants to support an additional student through the Talent Search program (as well as for cost-effectiveness [CE] and benefit-cost [BC] analysis).

Also, the pattern of costs differed significantly across Talent Search sites. Whereas one site used only $470 of resources per year for Talent Search, another site applied $790 of resources (i.e., two thirds more). At one site, the personnel costs were 56% of total costs; at another site, these were 81% of all costs. Finally, sites drew on in-kind resources to varying extents. On average, the sites obtained 17% of their resources from in-kind sources; however, this proportion varied from 7% to 39% across the sites. Possibly, some of these differences may be explained by scale—the nine Talent Search sites varied from 610 to 1,100 participants per year.

The other issue is that of changes in costs from learning by doing. As a program is delivered, providers learn how to deliver it at a lower cost (the learning curve). This may be due to implementing changes over time; scaling up or down to provide the treatment to different samples; learning through experience, leading to improvements in efficiency; and taking other actions as a program may evolve. For this reason, analysis of how costs evolve over time can be an informative way to disaggregate total costs. One example of a program whose costs declined over time is 4Rs, a program that infuses social and emotional learning into literacy instruction so that students are provided with lessons in specific literary texts that are relevant to their social and emotional development. Long, Brown, Jones, Aber, and Yates (2015) estimated that the costs of delivering the program in nine schools declined in 2015 dollars from $829,020 in Year 1 of the intervention to $687,420 by Year 3. They attributed this 17% decline in part to lessened need for support and oversight as program delivery became more practiced.

6.2.3. By Category of Ingredient

Policymakers are often interested in which ingredients or types of ingredient constitute the bulk of an intervention's cost. This analysis may be performed in conjunction with other analyses to determine whether particular groupings of ingredients are associated with higher or lower costs and combined with CE analysis to determine whether some programs or sites achieve efficiency by obtaining similar results at lower cost. Costs by ingredient category can also be analyzed within a single program across sites, across programs, or across years. While the allocation of resources may not be causal (for instance, a site or intervention that uses relatively more personnel and fewer materials may do so for unobserved reasons that are also related to costs and effects), they can provide descriptive insight into important policy questions. In particular, whether in the form of computer-assisted instruction, massive open online courses (MOOCs), or myriad other forms, the question of whether (and if so, how) technology can be used to enhance efficiency and productivity of educational delivery has been important in policy and research for decades (Levin & Woo, 1981). Careful analysis of costs can determine how the allocation of resources across ingredient categories varies by intervention and, when combined with effectiveness data in CE analysis, can provide insight into whether certain forms of delivery are more efficient.

CE analysis of early literacy programs listed in the What Works Clearinghouse that were found to have positive, statistically significant effects on alphabetics skills among young readers found wide variability in program design, target audience, resource utilization, and effects. This heterogeneity suggests that looking at costs per ingredient category may help in understanding how programs work. While the authors encourage extreme caution in interpreting results, given differences in measures and target populations among seven programs, they were able to compare ingredients and costs between programs that targeted similar populations. Two programs that targeted struggling first grade readers were Fast ForWord and Reading Recovery; despite their similar goals, the programs used substantially different approaches. Fast ForWord focused on technology use, while Reading Recovery focused extensively on teacher training. As a result, 70% of the $310 per student incremental costs of Fast ForWord (in 2015 dollars) went toward materials and equipment, with only 26% devoted to personnel, whereas 93% of the $4,500 per student incremental costs of Reading Recovery went to personnel (Hollands et al., 2013; adjusted to 2015 dollars).

6.2.4. By Scale of Operation

In many cases, stakeholders are interested in the average cost per participant, particularly as that estimate can provide guidance on the costs of replicating an intervention at a given scale (on scale-up of preschool programs, see Temple & Reynolds, 2015). However, stakeholders may be interested in marginal cost—that is, the cost of serving additional participants. Marginal cost provides insight into the costs of program expansion and economies of scale.

In theory, the analyst should be able to calculate the marginal cost of each educational intervention. However, because programs are often delivered at a school site or within a classroom, it may not be obvious what the marginal cost is. Potentially, the marginal cost will be dramatically different from the average cost. In an undersubscribed athletic program in which the primary ingredients are a teacher and a gymnasium, the marginal cost of an additional student approaches zero. Conversely, the marginal cost of a one-on-one tutoring program with highly trained tutors can be quite high. For example, the marginal cost of an additional student in Kindergarten Peer-Assisted Literacy Strategies (K-PALS), a whole-class instructional strategy designed to promote early literacy skills among beginning readers, is much lower than that of Corrective Reading, a small-group tutoring program for older readers still struggling with beginning literacy skills (Hollands et al., 2013). Finally, the marginal cost function may be non-linear or have sharp discontinuities. If a program is being delivered to 25 students in a single classroom, marginal cost may be close to average cost. However, if 5 or 10 more students arrive, it may be necessary to divide the students into two classrooms in which case, marginal cost will be significantly above average cost.

6.2.5. By Subgroup

Stakeholders may also be interested in how costs vary by demographic subgroup. For instance, students who enter an intervention with lower academic skills on a pretest used for placement may require more intensive treatment involving smaller group sizes or higher dosage. A treatment may also vary by design in how it targets students who come from higher- or lower-income families, or boys and girls. Finely grained data on costs for individual students, or students by subgroup, are seldom available unless there are many sites with differing demographic characteristics or treatments are sufficiently disaggregated so student or subgroup level variation can be analyzed. In cases when such data are available, however, these analyses may be informative.

6.3. ALLOCATING COSTS AMONG CONSTITUENCIES ●

In many cases, all the ingredients will not be provided by a single agency such as the school district or the university. Some alternatives may be eligible for support from federal and state agencies. It may be possible to obtain volunteers to staff some interventions, and various costs might be met through contributions of services. It is important to know not only the total cost of each alternative but how the costs were financed among such constituencies as the school district, parents, the state government, the federal government, private agencies, and so on. If the school district will be making the decision, it is likely to consider only its share of the cost burden rather than the overall costs in ranking alternatives. In contrast, the other constituencies that are sharing the costs will be most concerned about the costs to them. Indeed, both costs and effects should be viewed from the perspective of different constituencies or groups that have a stake in the outcome (Bryk, 1983). The ranking of alternatives by each constituency will largely reflect the perceived costs (and, as we discuss later, the perceived effects and benefits) to that constituency rather than the larger societal perspective. For this reason, we must estimate not only the total ingredients cost of an intervention but also the cost of that intervention for each constituency or "stakeholder."

Table 6.3 illustrates the format for a worksheet for reporting costs across stakeholders. This worksheet has been designed to meet two purposes. It can be used to report the total ingredients cost for an intervention, and the first and second columns show the list of ingredients and the total resource cost of providing those ingredients (corresponding to the information in the worksheet in Table 6.1). Importantly, this worksheet can be used to show how the costs of each proposed or actual intervention are distributed among different constituencies or stakeholders.

After reporting the total cost in the second column, worksheet Columns 3 through 6 are used to list the costs that will be borne by each of several different constituencies or stakeholders. Column 3 represents the cost to the sponsor. For example, if the sponsor of the prospective intervention were a school district, we would write in the name of the district. Column 4 provides a listing of costs that will be paid by another government agency, and Column 5 would include costs paid from private sources such as volunteers, charitable foundations, churches, and private contributions. Additional columns can be provided for subgroups such as different levels of government or different government agencies. This should be determined separately for each cost analysis. Column 6 refers to those costs that must be borne by students and their families. For instance, some programs require students and their families to provide books, equipment, and transportation in

Table 6.3   Sample Worksheet for Costs Across Stakeholders

Column 1:	Column 2:	Column 3:	Column 4:	Column 5:	Column 6:
Ingredients	Total Cost	Cost to Program Sponsor	Cost to Other Government Agencies	Cost to Other Private Organizations	Cost to Students and Parents
Personnel ...					
Training ...					
Facilities ...					
Materials and equipment ...					
Other inputs ...					
Required client inputs ...					
Total ingredients cost					
User fees		−			+
Cash subsidies		−	+	+	
Total cost (net)					

order to participate. Finally, this worksheet includes additional rows that capture how user fees and cash subsidies reconcile the total costs in each column.

6.3.1. Distributing Ingredients and Costs

The first step in ascertaining the costs that will be paid by each constituency is to determine which ingredients will be provided by each. In this way, the cost for each ingredient in the first column can be entered in the appropriate column (3 through 6) that represents the entity that will provide that ingredient. Bear in mind that in distributing the estimated costs among constituencies, we are not estimating any additional costs. We are merely allocating the existing costs to the constituencies that financed them. This is analogous to first estimating the cost of a piece of property to an investment partnership and then distributing the cost to the different partners. The questions of what an intervention costs and who pays for it are analytically separate issues. By accounting for the value of all the ingredients, Column 2 already includes the total cost of the intervention.

As an illustration of this procedure, we can refer to personnel costs. Personnel costs that are paid by the school district would be entered in Column 3. Those that would be paid by the state or federal government would be entered in Column 4. The cost of community volunteers would be entered in Column 5 and so on. A similar procedure would be followed for facilities, materials and equipment, and other inputs. A check on the accuracy of these entries can be made by making sure that the sum of the entries for each ingredient in Columns 3 through 6 is equal to the cost entry for that ingredient in Column 2.

6.3.2. Distributing Cash Subsidies

There is one final calculation that we will need in order to ascertain the net cost for each constituency. In addition to providing ingredients, the various constituencies may provide cash contributions and payments that subsidize the purchase of ingredients provided by other constituencies. For example, students and their families may be charged user fees to participate. In addition, various constituencies may provide cash contributions or subsidies to the sponsoring school district. These transactions—shown in the bottom rows of the worksheet as user fees and cash subsidies—serve to create subsidies or cash transfers from some constituencies to the sponsoring school district. Such subsidies will reduce the net costs to the school district and increase the costs to the other constituencies. It is important to emphasize that user fees, subsidies, and other cash transfers are not ingredients or costs, as they do not affect total cost but only who pays the cost.

User fees are any cash charges that must be paid by participants in order to have access to the proposed program. For example, schools may charge fees for participation in some extracurricular activities such as athletics; universities charge an array of fees for many different activities or college options. In this case, we would add the total amount of user charges to the total amount of ingredients costs at the bottom of Column 6. Since these would be transferred to the sponsoring school district, we subtract an identical amount at the bottom of Column 3 to reflect a reduction in the net cost that will be borne by the school district. The total costs represented by their ingredient or resource values have not changed; only the apportionment of those costs among constituencies has changed.

In like manner, we take the cash subsidies, grants, and contributions from other government agencies and add those to the total ingredients costs under Column 4 and do the same for cash contributions from private sources under Column 5. Obviously, since these cash disbursements increase the cost commitments of these constituencies, they will increase the net costs to those groups. Since these are also transferred to the sponsoring school district, they should be deducted from the ingredients cost for the district. That is, they reduce the costs to the school district as reflected in a net total cost for that entity that is lower than the direct ingredients provided by the sponsoring district.

6.3.3. Calculating Net Costs to Each Constituency

After these cash transfers are noted, we can calculate the net cost to the school district and to the other constituencies or stakeholders. These totals are shown at the bottom of Table 6.3 and are literally the "bottom line" in terms of cost burdens for the various constituencies. The net cost for each constituency is the total ingredients cost for that constituency less cash payments received from other constituencies or plus cash payments made to other constituencies. In this way, we can not only derive the total ingredients cost of the intervention, which is the overall social cost, but also divide that into the costs paid by each of several constituencies.

Of course, this worksheet is designed to be general. That is, it is possible to do this analysis for any set of constituencies, such as advantaged and disadvantaged families or different government agencies within a level of government. The most important factor in determining which constituencies to evaluate is to ask which ones have a stake in the decision and will be sharing the costs by providing ingredients or cash subsidies.

In summary, it is important to know not only the total costs of an intervention but also how those costs are distributed among different constituencies or stakeholders. A worksheet like that in Table 6.3 will enable the analyst to specify ingredients and estimate their costs and the total cost of the intervention. It will also enable the analyst to distribute those costs among the major constituencies so that each of the stakeholders can evaluate its own cost burden for each alternative. Of course, this type of cost analysis should be done for each of the alternatives under consideration. When combined with the effectiveness of each alternative, it can be used to ascertain the relative desirability for each stakeholder of the various proposed interventions.

With multiyear programs the cost distribution might change over time. That is, in the early years, the sponsor might receive grants from foundations or government in order to provide an incentive for a new approach. At some future time, however, this assistance might be withdrawn as the contributing agency turns its attention in other directions. For this reason, it is important to review carefully the allocation of ingredients and cash subsidies provided by other constituencies to the sponsoring one to see if they hold for the period of analysis. If it is likely that some of them may be reduced or increased in subsequent years, these changes should be taken into account in considering the costs to each stakeholder or constituency and in using that information to assess priorities among competing alternatives.

In practice, the easiest method of constructing and analyzing a cost worksheet is to use spreadsheet software, such as Microsoft Excel. Each of the ingredients and ingredient costs in both Tables 6.1 and 6.3 can be entered in the corresponding cells of a spreadsheet. Formulas can be entered in each row of Column 2 that sum the costs of each ingredient in Columns 3 through 6. At the bottom of Columns 2 through 6, formulas can be entered that sum the total ingredients costs and the net costs to each constituency. There are many advantages to analyzing costs in a spreadsheet. For example, small features of the analysis can be varied—such as the cost of an ingredient to a particular constituency—and the spreadsheet will use the formulas to automatically calculate the new total costs. This is extremely helpful when conducting a sensitivity analysis. Moreover, the worksheet can be easily expanded to include new categories of ingredients (rows) or new constituencies (columns). A completed worksheet for the Reading Partners program is provided in Example 6.3. *CostOut* (see Appendix B) is designed to undertake many of these functions, and it is licensed by the Center for Benefit-Cost Studies of Education (CBCSE) at no charge to users.

Example 6.3   Determining Who Pays the Costs

To illustrate financing issues and the distribution of costs, we consider Reading Partners, a program that provides trained volunteer tutors to participating schools. Reading Partners aims to assist schools with limited resources to increase reading achievement among their struggling readers. The program is resource intensive: One-on-one tutoring obviously requires a fair amount of

(Continued)

(Continued)

personnel who further require training, oversight, and facilities space. However, it is important to determine how the burden of these resources is spread across different groups.

Determining Who Pays: Reading Partners

		Distribution of Cost			
Ingredients	Cost per Student ($)	Cost to School	Cost to Volunteers	Cost to Reading Partners	Cost to Ameri Corps
Reading Partners staff	$710			$710	
AmeriCorps members	$960			$960	
School staff	$90	$90			
Volunteer time and transportation	$1,570		$1,570		
Facilities	$310	$310			
Materials and equipment	$80			$80	
Cost	$3,730	$400	$1,570	$1,750	$0
Fee for service		$330		−$330	
AmeriCorps grant				−$280	$280
Net cost per student		$730	$1,570	$1,150	$280
Portion of net cost per student (%)		20	42	31	7

Source: Jacob, Armstrong, Bowden, and Pan (2016).

Note: Adjusted to 2015 dollars.

In order to calculate the costs to replicate Reading Partners, Jacob and colleagues (2016) used the ingredients method to estimate all resources required even if these were funded by outside entities or provided voluntarily or in-kind. In fact, Reading Partners has a complex arrangement, with resources being funded from various sources. The program is supported by school resources, is assisted by volunteers, and receives support from the Reading Partners offices and AmeriCorps. Each school pays a fee to Reading Partners to finance a portion of resources provided by the organization, such as staff and materials. Also, AmeriCorps provides a grant to Reading Partners to finance some of the costs of the AmeriCorps fellows employed by the program. There are also fees for services provided by Reading Partners.

These complex arrangements are summarized simply in the table. The cost per student for Reading Partners is $3,730. But this is divided among four sources. When expressed as cost net of fees for service, the largest contribution is from volunteers (valued at $1,570). The Reading Partners office contributes the largest gross amount ($1,750), but this amount includes the payments from schools and AmeriCorps contributions. Notably, schools contribute a relatively small proportion (20%) of the total resources required to implement the program. Therefore, provided that capable volunteers are available to participate in the program and other ingredients are available for program use, Reading Partners may be a low-cost option (at $730) for schools with very limited resources to help their struggling readers achieve greater success. It may also appear economical for schools, given the subsidies (of 80%) obtained from other sources.

6.4. ANALYZING COST DETERMINANTS AND GENERALIZING COSTS

6.4.1. Context

The preceding sections addressed how to report cost estimates so they provide as much information as possible. However, these estimates still have to be interpreted and explained to policymakers.

As with any method of program evaluation, the cost estimate for an intervention depends heavily on the evaluation context. Depending upon the audience for and objective of an analysis, the analysts or decisionmakers may wish to generalize from one instantiation of an intervention to the intervention more broadly, from a site or a sample of sites to the population of current or hypothetical future sites, or even from one specific way of implementing an intervention to other possible variants. Such generalization and out-of-sample extrapolation requires caution and careful consideration of what assumptions may be required to support valid inferences about how findings from a specific evaluation may extend more broadly. It requires a clear understanding of the context in which the initial results were generated and is somewhat parallel to the concept of external validity in evaluation of effectiveness of an intervention.

Of particular interest are contextual factors, similar to moderators in the language of randomized controlled trials, which may affect either program implementation (and so ingredients) or costs. These factors may include demographic characteristics of program participants, the relative level and homogeneity of need for the intervention based on prior academic or nonacademic measures, and the size and competitiveness of local market conditions that may affect the availability of necessary ingredients and their prices. With a large and variable enough sample of sites, the effect of context on costs can be estimated empirically, but if the number of sites is limited or sites are relatively homogeneous on dimensions of interest, extrapolation may be more tentative and speculative.

Several aspects of the evaluation context are worth noting. With cost analysis, either ingredients or prices (or both) might vary across contexts. Variation in prices is probably more likely than variation in ingredients (leaving aside whether the program is implemented with fidelity). Computing and Internet-based educational ingredients may rapidly decrease in price either as they increase in power or because their fixed costs can be spread over more students (as is expected for MOOCs in higher education; see Bowen, Chingos, Lack, & Nygren, 2014). However, where educational interventions are labor-intensive, it is unlikely that there will be much technological change and so there will be little change in ingredients. Peer tutoring, for example, cannot be expanded to more than a few students in each cluster, so the ingredients for peer tutoring are likely to be similar from school to school. But its effectiveness may depend critically on the talent, previous experience, and other measured and unmeasured characteristics of the tutors.

Another contextual feature is the extent to which in-kind and externally funded resources are available. Some school districts may have many parents who are willing to support their school, and these families can contribute both time and direct funding. Districts will also vary in their access to external funds, either state subsidies or philanthropic donations. A completed worksheet as per Table 6.3 should indicate to the decisionmaker what funds might be needed in different contexts.

Finally, educational evaluations often adopt a cohort-based perspective—that is, they focus on just one cohort of students. The cost for one cohort is not necessarily the same as the annual cost of the program. For example, colleges may offer advising supports for students: In the first year, the advising is intensive, but it then attenuates over subsequent years as students need less advising. An annual budget for advising would therefore include services for several cohorts of students (those in their first year of college and those in later years).

The cost for a cohort of students to receive advising throughout their time in college is therefore different from the annual cost of advising; simply extrapolating or multiplying from the costs in the first year to extend across all college years would therefore be inappropriate. The analyst must be very clear which cohorts of students and intensity of services the cost estimate refers to.

6.4.2. Induced Costs

For clarity, we have described cost as all the resources needed to implement a program. Yet, a program may have implications for resource allocation well after the program itself has ended. As noted in Chapter 3, these postprogram costs are called induced costs (or negative benefits in benefit-cost [BC] analysis). Regardless of their exact classification, they should be considered in order to capture the full resource implications of a program over the long term. For instance, a community college program to improve completion rates of introductory courses will lead to higher costs in future semesters according to the continuation rates of successful students. While completion and additional attainment is likely a positive outcome of an educational intervention, there are resource implications that should be considered (for further discussion of these "service media-tion interventions," see Bowden, Shand, Belfield, Wang, & Levin, 2016). The decisionmaker is not helped by having information on the cost of a program but on its induced costs. For example, a mentoring program for at-risk high school students may be affordable if pro-gram costs are considered. But it may be unaffordable if the school realizes that it will have to provide more instruction in later grades. Potentially, successful reforms will be undermined because of future resource constraints (as found in a cost study of a community college, by Belfield, Crosta, & Jenkins, 2014).

We illustrate how to report induced costs using as an example the City Connects program. City Connects aims to help schools more sys-tematically alleviate the out-of-school factors that can impede student learning by assigning one or more full-time, trained coordinators to evaluate the myriad needs of every student; refer them to appropriate follow-up services sponsored by the school and community partner agencies; and monitor student progress, making revisions to the service plan as necessary. Evaluations have found the program to be effective in raising student achievement (Walsh et al., 2014). Clearly, the program has two elements: (1) needs assessment and (2) additional service receipt conditional on need. Both elements need to be costed. Using the

Table 6.4   Average Costs and Induced Costs of City Connects

	(1) Core + No Difference in Service	(2) Core + Full Services	(3) Core + Estimated Service Change
Core cost	$1,570	$1,570	$1,570
Service cost	$0	$7,680	$3,090
Total cost (C)	$1,570	$9,250	$4,660

Source: Adapted from Bowden et al. (2016).

Notes: Adjusted to 2015 dollars. Present value at kindergarten, discount rate 3.5%, Boston average prices.

ingredients method, Bowden and colleagues (2016) calculated the cost per student to receive City Connects needs assessment. The researchers then estimated the costs of additional service receipt mediated through this needs assessment. The costs are shown in Table 6.4.

The core cost of City Connects (needs assessment and some direct services) is calculated at $1,570 per student. However, the extent of induced costs can be difficult to estimate: It is not obvious exactly what services fall under the heading of the program and what services are ancillary but are a consequence of the program (in the context of the evaluation, it was also uncertain what services students would have received in the absence of the program). Therefore, Bowden and colleagues (2016) estimated the service charge based on information on usage of services by students. For comparison, the researchers also estimated the cost if a student was eligible for a comprehensive set of services after school (rather than a set based on student need). A third scenario is that City Connects did not affect the services a student would receive. As given in Table 6.4, these induced costs vary significantly: Obviously, if City Connects did not change service receipt, then the induced cost is zero and the total program cost is $1,570. However, if a student received a comprehensive set of new services, these would cost $7,680; the total cost of City Connects would therefore be 4 times higher (at $9,250) than the core program costs. Finally, the best estimate of induced cost based on service usage was $3,090; the total cost per student was $4,660. These figures are considerably higher than the baseline program cost and represent important information for the decisionmakers (as well as for CE; see Chapters 7 and 8).

6.4.3. Sensitivity Testing

At this stage, the overall method for estimating costs and distributing them to different constituencies or stakeholders has been presented. Thus far, we have assumed that costs—both the ingredients and their prices—can be estimated with certainty. This assumption should be subject to scrutiny: To estimate costs requires data collection from a sample of the population, so it is likely there will be a sampling error. The research analyst should directly consider the precision of the cost estimates.

Sensitivity testing is the general approach for examining the precision of the cost estimates. At this stage, we note that there are two general sources of uncertainty (see Chapter 11 for more detail). The first source of uncertainty is that ingredients were measured incorrectly (or some ingredients were omitted in error from the data collection). Given the challenges involved in data collection and the reliance on interviewees or survey respondents, this is possible. The analyst might check to see what ingredients were used in similar interventions as a comparison. The second source of uncertainty is that the prices are estimated with error. This uncertainty may be easier to test: the analyst may simply select alternative prices for ingredients (e.g., from alternative sources) and recalculate the cost results to see how different they are. These recalculations allow the analyst to create a range of high and low cost estimates and so put boundaries on the estimate of costs. We discuss sensitivity testing in Chapter 11.

6.4.4. Decisionmaking

A final set of issues relating to the use of costs in decisions is how to integrate cost analysis with the decision framework and theory of change. As demonstrated previously, it is possible to determine overall social costs of an intervention as well as the costs to the sponsor and to other constituencies. In general, the type of decision that will be made as well as who will make it will determine which cost figure will be pertinent. For example, if we do a national study to ascertain the most efficient way to raise computer literacy, we may wish to rely on the total ingredients costs of the alternatives as well as their effectiveness. The reason that we would choose the total ingredients costs is that, from a national perspective, we are usually concerned with the most efficient deployment of national resources rather than the cost to particular constituencies. Of course, even at the national level, we might have some concern about how the burden would be shared between the federal government and the states or between the public and private sectors.

As pointed out previously, however, each constituency, or stakeholder, will typically be concerned with the costs to its members (and the benefits or results for its members) rather than the overall ingredients costs. A local school district, a state, or a parent group would normally wish to assess the costs and the benefits, or effectiveness, of each alternative for its constituents. Indeed, each constituency may rank the same alternatives differently if the distribution of costs and effects differs among them. Thus, a major dimension of cost analysis from the decision perspective is to provide information so that a variety of decisionmakers can utilize the results.

When a school or school district is considering alternative programs, they may be interested in examining the feasibility of implementing the different options from their perspective with the local resource context factored into the analysis. This analysis is considered cost-feasibility (CF) analysis and the issue of whether the decisionmaker has adequate resources to consider the alternative. In this case, the potential educational outcomes are not taken into consideration. The only issue is whether the alternative is feasible from the cost perspective. The answer to that question is determined by comparing the total cost requirements and those for each constituency with the resource constraints of each constituency for every alternative. Alternatives that require greater cost outlays than available resources, in total or for the various constituencies, are probably not feasible. Thus, CF analysis simply determines which alternatives are within the boundaries of further consideration by the decisionmaker.

● 6.5. CONCLUSIONS

This chapter has addressed the analysis of cost information by showing how such data can be developed through the use of a worksheet; how cost estimates can be disaggregated; and how the cost burdens can be analyzed among different constituencies, or stakeholders. It also described how cost reporting and analysis—when placed in context—can help decisionmakers better understand the resources required for a program or intervention. This chapter is the culmination of all the research described in Chapters 2 through 5, with the ultimate goal being a dollar value cost estimate that accurately reflects the resources needed to implement an education program or intervention. As may be clear from our lengthy description of cost analysis, this dollar value cannot be approximated simply by looking at the prices of a few of the main components of an intervention.

Cost analysis is important in itself as a way to understand what resources are required and whether a school, district, or college can afford them. Yet, the primary reason for conducting a cost analysis is so that CE and BC analyses can be performed. The next chapters will discuss how to estimate the effects—and hence CE—of interventions. After that, we will combine cost analysis with estimation of benefits to establish the net present value (NPV) of educational interventions. Of course, these economic evaluations are possible only if costs have been estimated accurately.

Discussion Questions

1. It is possible to compare the costs of alternatives by estimating their overall costs over a multiyear period rather than following the more conventional approach of estimating their annual costs. Why is it not acceptable to simply obtain the sum of the annual costs to derive the multiyear costs?

2. Under what circumstances should your cost analysis be based on marginal costs? Provide an example.

3. Why might you be interested in the distribution of costs across constituencies? How would you account for different constituencies providing ingredients versus cash transfers via fees and subsidies?

Exercises

1. You run a program for disadvantaged youth who are soon to be entering the labor market. For Program A, you are able to obtain a subsidy from the federal government of $10,000. For Program B, you are able to obtain volunteers to run the employment registry and to solicit jobs in the community; in addition, you are able to get a private foundation to contribute $5,000 for Program B, but the foundation requires students pay $100 if they are successfully placed in a full-time job. Show how you would use these data to distribute the cost burden among the various constituencies.

2. You are opening a preschool company that is contracted to serve 4,200 children across 10 sites. At each site, the maximum class size

is 15, and children are in class for the full week and 180 days per year. At each site, the staffing will require a principal, a part-time administrative assistant, and a deputy principal; posted full-time salaries per annum for these positions are $60,000, $30,000, and $50,000 respectively. Full-time teachers are paid $40,000. Each facility will be 1,000 square feet; rent is assumed to be the same as for commercial space. Each child receives food services paid directly by the state government of $5 per day and is provided with transport that the centers can claim reimbursement for from the federal government of $10 per day. Materials costs are estimated at $100 per child per year. Finally, parents are expected to volunteer 20 hours each year.

3. Create an ingredients worksheet with columns for costs to the preschool company, government agencies, and other groups. Calculate the total cost of preschool provision and the cost per child. For more accuracy, you may wish to include more ingredients and adjust some of the prices.

4. Evidence indicates that school breakfasts may improve educational outcomes and reduce obesity rates among schoolchildren. To increase their breakfast program take-up, a school district wants to change from a no-charge breakfast available in the school cafeteria to a no-charge breakfast in the classroom. How would you think about differences in costs between these options?

7

Effectiveness

Objectives

1. Define measures of effectiveness.

2. Identify valid measures of effectiveness for cost-effectiveness (CE) analysis.

3. Assess the main identification strategies in relation to CE analysis.

4. Describe multiattribute utility functions to enumerate effectiveness.

Economic evaluation must consider both the costs and results of interventions. By comparing both costs and results among alternatives, one can choose the alternative that provides the best results for any given cost outlay or that minimizes the cost for any given result. In previous chapters, the assessment of costs and their measurement were presented. In this chapter, we discuss the effectiveness of educational interventions. In the subsequent chapter, we combine this information with costs in order to evaluate the overall CE of interventions.

Often, when we propose CE analysis of an educational intervention, the immediate question is this: How will you measure effectiveness? The simple answer is "in the same way that any impact evaluator in the social sciences would measure effectiveness." That is, we would use the same measure as chosen by the impact evaluator and apply the same method to identify effects as the impact evaluator would.

In this sense, this chapter will appear to be a case of déjà vu for evaluators, for the heart of the evaluation exercise is often precisely that of ascertaining the effects of interventions on particular criteria. For example, evaluators often face situations in which they are asked to ascertain the impact of alternative curricula on reading scores or the effects of an in-service teacher training program on teacher performance. In this respect, the evaluation of outcomes is a familiar endeavor, and it is not the purpose of this book to provide an exhaustive description of evaluation designs. For this, the reader is advised to consult one of the excellent manuals on evaluation, research design, and econometric identification strategies that already exist (e.g., Angrist & Pischke, 2009; Murnane & Willett, 2010; Newcomer, Hatry, & Wholey, 2015; Rossi, Lipsey, & Freeman, 2004).

Here, our purpose is more specific: It is to consider effectiveness measures that can be used for CE analysis. Economic evaluation puts a heightened emphasis on getting the "right" measure of effectiveness. Fundamentally, any measure of effectiveness should fully reflect the objectives of the intervention so that a valid comparison can be made between the intervention and the counterfactual. Of course, this is also expected for measures that are applied in impact evaluations. For CE, however, effectiveness must be represented by a single number so that it can be expressed as the denominator in a ratio. This is a significant constraint and may shape the outcome measures selected; so we specify some features of effectiveness measures that make them preferred for CE analysis. Next, we review the main ways to identify effects: experimental, quasi-experimental, and correlational. This review is intended to help the analyst ascertain how suitable each identification strategy is for CE analysis. Finally, we describe multiattribute utility functions, a general method by which educational outcomes can be represented in a single number that reflects the objectives of the decisionmaker. Although utility functions are rarely applied in education research, it is important to develop the analysis to allow for policy preferences to be modelled (Chandra, Jena, & Skinner, 2011).

● 7.1. SPECIFYING EFFECTIVENESS

7.1.1. Examples of Effectiveness Measures

In principle, any measure of effectiveness can be used for CE analysis. Indeed, one advantage of CE analysis is that it is broadly applicable across many areas of education research.

Examples of interventions and their respective effectiveness measures for selected CE analyses are given in Table 7.1. These are U.S. examples; CE studies in developing countries often focus on student achievement or years of schooling as their effectiveness measure (Dhaliwal, Duflo, Glennister, & Tulloch, 2012; McEwan, 2012). As shown in Table 7.1, the range of outcomes available for CE analysis is wide.

As well as the various measures listed in Table 7.1, effectiveness might be counted as the number of reported disciplinary problems, the number of graduates or trainees placed in jobs, or the number of students who complete college. Most CE studies use measures of academic achievement to indicate effectiveness. But studies often use different scales. For ease of comparability, Harris (2009) recommended the use of Cohen's effect size when evaluating interventions using CE analysis, although these effect sizes must be measured in exactly the same way to be comparable across interventions. As discussed next, test scores might be considered the most analytically tractable measures of educational effectiveness, and they are at least a general measure across all students. However, this by no means implies that CE analysis is restricted to such measures. In fact, some tests may

Table 7.1   Examples of Effectiveness Measures for Cost-Effectiveness Analysis

Study	Intervention/Policy	Effectiveness Measure
Levin, Glass, and Meister (1987)	Peer tutoring	Mathematics and reading achievement
Hartman and Fay (1996)	Referral services	Receipt of special education services
Wang et al. (2008)	After-school program (third grade)	Obesity (percentage of body fat)
Yeh (2010)	Teacher board certification	Student achievement
Borman and Hewes (2002)	Success for All	Reading and mathematics scores
Hollands et al. (2014)	Job Corps	High school dropout rate
Bowden and Belfield (2015)	Talent Search program	College access
Hollands et al. (2016)	Wilson Reading System (third grade)	Alphabetics literacy domain

have poor construct validity (e.g., when students score highly on a test but cannot perform the respective competencies; McEwan, 2015). Nevertheless, in principle, any effectiveness measure might be used for CE analysis.

7.1.2. Linking Objectives and Effectiveness

CE analysis is comparative: It involves evaluating one intervention against another or one intervention against the status quo. It is therefore essential that we are comparing apples to apples such that the two interventions are genuine alternatives and can legitimately be ranked or compared based on the selected measure of effectiveness.

For comparability, the measure of effectiveness chosen should reflect as closely as possible the main objective of the alternatives. For example, programs designed to increase reading achievement should select an appropriate reading test as a measure of effectiveness (see Hollands et al., 2016). Dropout prevention programs should be evaluated according to the numbers of potential dropouts that are averted or students who complete each grade. The effectiveness of various physical education programs could be evaluated in terms of the measured improvements that they bring about in the specific physical skills of participants. The measure should therefore be sufficiently comprehensive as to cover all relevant dimensions (e.g., speed and dexterity if both are impacted). This is challenging because many educational interventions have diverse outcomes and do not meet all goals in the same way. For early literacy interventions, for example, effectiveness should capture all facets of literacy, including comprehension, alphabetics, and fluency (National Institute of Child Health and Human Development [NICHD], 2000). For socioemotional learning interventions, effectiveness on any specific dimension might need to incorporate all significant changes in behavior, attitudes, or conduct (Durlak, Weissberg, Dymnicki, Taylor, & Schellinger, 2011).

Programs with different objectives will have entirely different indicators of effectiveness. So they cannot be readily compared within the CE framework (or even within a relative effectiveness framework). We cannot, for example, use CE analysis to compare the CE of a dropout prevention program and a physical education program. Likewise, we cannot strictly compare a literacy program that focuses on alphabetics with one that focuses on comprehension. (An alternative might be to convert the effects into pecuniary terms and apply benefit-cost [BC] analysis as described in Chapters 9 and 10.) CE analysis emphasizes comparability across interventions. As such, it is essential that outcomes from separate evaluations be equivalent. This equivalence is often very hard to obtain: Studies vary in the constructs used in measurement, and even if the construct is similar, the measurement scale may not be. In their review of What Works Clearinghouse–approved studies of literacy programs, Hollands et al. (2016) identified 32 with positive effects. However, early literacy outcomes were grouped under four different domains (alphabetics, fluency, comprehension, and general reading achievement), each of which included multiple subcategories; and few studies used the same scales (e.g., Dynamic Indicators of Basic Early Literacy Skills, or DIBELS).

Effectiveness measures can be intermediate proxies for final outcomes. But these too should be directly related to some program objective (Weiss, Bloom, & Brock, 2014). For many reasons, often as simple as lack of data, evaluators can obtain measures of intermediate outcomes only. For example, Tatto, Nielsen, and Cummings (1991) compared the CE of three Sri Lankan teacher-training programs in raising an intermediate outcome—teacher mastery of subject matter and pedagogy—even as the ultimate goal was improvement in classroom teaching and student learning. Similarly, Hartman and Fay (1996) compared two different methods of referring children to special education in Pennsylvania. The effect was the number of children who received certain kinds of intervention services; the presumption was that these services would ameliorate learning difficulties. Indeed, even many "final" outcomes in education may simply be intermediate ones. For example, academic achievement is often not valued as an end in itself but is valued for its supposed influence on either wages or an increased capacity to participate in a democratic society.

Effectiveness measures should take account of when the effects occur (Harris, 2009). An intervention that is intended to rapidly increase test scores, for example, is preferable to an intervention that does so to the same magnitude but more slowly. Therefore, as with costs, the effects should be discounted back to a present value.

This issue is best illustrated with an example. Imagine that we are conducting CE analysis of three approaches to dropout prevention in high schools that are implemented over a period of 5 years. The measure of effectiveness is the number of dropouts averted in a given year by each program. The programs yield the same number of undiscounted dropouts but at different times: Alternative A yields 100 fewer dropouts in the first year but none in Years 2 through 5. Alternative B yields 20 fewer dropouts each year. Alternative C yields all its 100 fewer dropouts at the end of the fifth year. If effects are not discounted, then the alternatives are judged to be equally effective because they each reduce dropouts by 100. Clearly, in terms of effectiveness Alternative A is the most attractive, and Alternative C is the least attractive. The valid measure of effectiveness is the discounted dropout rate. This is calculated using the present value formula described in earlier chapters. For this example, if the discount rate is 5%,

$$PV_A = \sum_{t-1}^{n} \frac{E_t}{(1+r)^{t-1}} = \frac{100}{(1+0.05)^0} = 100$$

$$PV_B = \sum_{t-1}^{n} \frac{E_t}{(1+r)^{t-1}} = \frac{20}{(1+0.05)^0} + \frac{20}{(1+0.05)^1} +$$

$$\frac{20}{(1+0.05)^2} + \frac{20}{(1+0.05)^3} + \frac{20}{(1+0.05)^4} = 91$$

$$PV_C = \sum_{t-1}^{n} \frac{E_t}{(1+r)^{t-1}} = \frac{100}{(1+0.05)^4} = 82$$

With discounting, Alternative A is 10% more effective relative to Program B, and it is 22% more effective than Program C.

Discount factors for interventions delivered in specific grades and of given durations are reported in Harris (2009, Tables 1 and 2). However, educational CE analyses that discount their effects are rare (for an exception, see Caulkins, Rydell, Everingham, Chisea, & Bushways, 1999; for health literature, where discounting effect is more common, see Weinstein, Torrance, & McGuire, 2009). In general, this is because effects are often measured only at a single point in time (e.g., percentage completing high school) rather than longitudinally or cumulatively. So, evaluators know the percentage of students who did not complete high school when they are aged 18 but not when those students dropped out. Moreover, it is not clear what discount rate to apply. The discount rate for effects need not be the same as for costs. Some health researchers have argued that outcomes should be discounted at a low rate so that policy decisions are not skewed away from preventive interventions (Brouwer, Niessen, Postma, & Rutten, 2005).

Overall, the primary requirement is that measured effectiveness should accurately reflect the objectives of the intervention. This is salient for any impact evaluation. Measures should be valid, that is, bearing a close correspondence to the underlying concept that they are intended to reflect, and they should be reliable, yielding the same results when applied on repeated occasions to the same groups. In principle, any idiosyncratic measure that fully reflects the objectives of the program and offers sufficient comparisons for decisionmaking purposes can be justified for CE analysis.

7.1.3. Single Measures of Effectiveness

As well as matching to objectives, a particular requirement of CE analysis is that the effects of an educational intervention be represented by a single measure. The measure needs to be singular so that it can be readily expressed as the denominator in the CE ratio.

This requirement is reasonable if the alternatives have a single objective. Furthermore, there should be no compelling reason to believe that secondary effects will be produced in other areas—either intentionally or unintentionally. Of course, these assumptions are often unrealistic. Most educational alternatives jointly produce a wide range of outcomes that require numerous measures of effectiveness. For example, we may wish to compare these school investments: lengthening the day in elementary schools and lowering the class size. Lengthening the school day might improve test scores and increase physical activity by students; lowering class size might improve test scores and improve teacher satisfaction. Expressing these effects in a single metric is very challenging. More emphatically, socioemotional learning interventions have been found to influence social skills, attitudes, positive social behavior, and student conduct as well as academic achievement (Durlak et al., 2011; Sklad, Diekstra, De Ritter, Ben, & Gravestein, 2012). To perform CE analysis, it must be valid to represent outcomes for these interventions in a single variable.

The issue of multiple outcomes is important even when the stated objectives of programs have a limited scope. One could imagine three separate programs, each focused on raising the English competencies of recent immigrants. To varying degrees, each program removes children from their standard classroom environments for part of the school day. The fact that children are deprived of some classroom instruction may yield effects (perhaps negative) in other areas, even if the programs succeed in improving English skills. In each of these cases, it behooves the evaluator to measure the important intended and unintended outcomes of each alternative.

Faced with multiple outcomes, the effectiveness measure may be a weighted combination of expected probabilities. For example, an intervention may be delivered to students who want to complete a BA and are deciding on whether to start at community college (see Agan, 2014; Bailey, Jaggars, & Jenkins, 2015). Students can start directly at a four-year college, and their BA degree completion rate can be estimated. Alternatively, students can start at community college; only a proportion of these students will transfer, and a subset of these will ultimately graduate. Their BA completion rate is therefore a product of the transfer and completion probabilities. Hence, we can calculate the expected outcomes of the college-choice intervention as a set of weighted probabilities given the pathways students take through the postsecondary system (Shapiro et al., 2015).

If there is no straightforward way to combine multiple outcomes into a single measure, there are several ways of proceeding. First, the evaluator could conduct a separate CE analysis for each measure of effectiveness. Such an analysis may reveal that a given alternative is to be preferred unambiguously by virtue of its consistently superior CE across many measures. That is, it may yield a given amount of mathematics achievement at a lower cost than other alternatives, and it may also yield a given amount of reading achievement at the lowest cost. In these cases, the evidence clearly supports the use of a particular alternative.

However, it is possible that one alternative is the most cost-effective means of raising mathematics achievement, whereas another is more cost-effective at improving reading. In such an instance, the evaluator could simply present the results of each CE analysis and clearly describe the relevant trade-offs. This approach can also be used if the intervention is differentially effective (e.g., CE results can be presented by sex, race, or socioeconomic status [SES]). In one CE analysis, Levin and colleagues (1987) compared the costs and effects of four interventions: (1) peer tutoring, (2) computer-assisted instruction, (3) class size reduction, and (4) increase in instructional time. The analysis revealed that peer tutoring was the least costly method of obtaining gains in mathematics achievement. While peer tutoring was also the most cost-effective means of raising reading achievement, the analysis showed that computer-assisted instruction assumed the second place. Individual decisionmakers might use these data to make different investment decisions, depending on their priorities.

Alternatively, the evaluator may wish to conduct cost-utility (CU) analysis. In the CU framework, multiple measures of effectiveness—weighted by their importance to parents, administrators, or another audience—are combined into a single summary measure of utility, a decisionmaker's subjective assessment of value. The weights can be estimated subjectively; if so, the evaluator should consult key stakeholders and carefully consider the primary audience for the analysis. Using more rigorous methods, they could also be elicited from key stakeholders using a formal, structured questionnaire. Such an analysis might reveal, for example, that parents in a particular school district place somewhat higher weight on mathematics achievement than other outcomes. An explication of utility functions and the creation of single effectiveness measures (amounts of utility) is given next.

Clearly, the requirement that only a single measure of effectiveness be applied is a significant restriction on the application of CE analysis. (Again, we note here that this requirement does not apply to BC analysis as it uses dollars as its unit of account. As dollars are fungible and additive, any impacts can be included as long as they can be expressed in dollars. See Chapters 9 and 10.) An intervention that has multiple effects cannot always be reduced to a single number. If so, CE analysis is not appropriate.

Yet, there is a danger in evaluating educational interventions using too many outcomes. It is not untypical for evaluations to claim that their intervention will promote a vector of outcomes, to include child health, socioemotional development, approaches to learning, language development, cognition, and general knowledge (e.g., the Parenting for Life Early Childhood Intervention). An evaluation of this comprehensive nature may yield highly valuable information about specific moderators and mechanisms for enhancing child development. However, it may be difficult for a decisionmaker, when presented with many statistical significance tests across the outcomes, to adjudicate between this program and an alternative early childhood intervention. The advantage of Occam's razor is that a simple claim—parenting programs are more cost-effective than professional development for teachers at improving child health—is easier to test, therefore easier to refute or accept, and hence easier to convey to a decisionmaker.

7.1.4. Appraising Effectiveness Measures

Ultimately, we cannot prescribe the best measure of effectiveness (or the number of domains that measure is derived from). The appropriate choice will depend on the particular intervention being evaluated and its specific goals. Nevertheless, there are some attributes that make some effectiveness measures preferred over others.

Ideally, an effectiveness measure should be in a ratio scale and continuous. An example here would be a math test where students can score from 0 to 100 and a score of 80 is considered twice as effective as a score of 40 (and 4 times as effective as a score of 20). In this case, it would not matter whether the intervention increases test scores from 20 to 30 or from 80 to 90; both represent a 10-point gain. Similarly, for community college students, most of whom never complete a degree or certificate, the effectiveness measure might be number of credits accumulated (Bailey et al., 2015). For these students, 24 credits are twice as good as 12 credits and 1 better than 23 credits. In developing countries, years of attainment might be valid: Attending school for 10 years may be regarded as twice as effective as 5 years. Nevertheless, the evaluator might propose that getting each student to complete primary school (6 years of attainment per child) is more important than raising the total stock of attainment (e.g., with half the children with 4 years of attainment and the other half having 8 years).

Although test scores may be useful, they need careful interpretation for use with CE analysis. A thorough discussion of construct validity has been provided by Bloom, Hill, Black, and Lipsey (2008) and Lipsey and colleagues (2012). These authors made several points. First, it is necessary to report not only the posttest gain in achievement from an intervention but also the gain relative to the baseline or counterfactual. An intervention may generate a posttest gain even if scores are below baseline; an alternative intervention may generate a smaller posttest gain but all posttest scores are above baseline. In the former case, all scores are going down; in the latter case, all scores are going up. Second, measured gains in achievement may attenuate dramatically over school grades: from first to second grade, effect size gains in math are typically 1; from 11th to 12th grade, effect size gains in math are almost zero (Lipsey et al., 2012, Table 5). An effect size gain of 0.25 in math is modest for a first grader but enormous for an eleventh grader. Finally, there are many different achievement measures, and the choice of measure will depend on context.

For CE studies, the analyst might prefer to work with grade equivalent (GE) scores (Lipsey et al., 2012, pp. 23–24). These scores indicate the level of a given student's achievement: 5.3 means the student's achievement is equivalent to that of a student who has completed 3 months of fifth grade. For example, a class-size reduction policy that moves each student from an expected 5.3 GE score to a 5.6 GE score has therefore generated 3 months of achievement per student. A decisionmaker might be able to equate—albeit approximately—this metric to a resource measure for a year of schooling. So, if the school spends $12,000 on academic instruction to move each fifth grader 9 months ahead across all subjects, the decisionmaker might be interested in class-size reduction only if it costs less than $4,000.

By contrast with test scores or other continuous scales, binary or discrete indicators of effectiveness may be less clear for policy purposes. For example, with a mentoring intervention to increase the high school graduation rate, many students will receive resources even though they would have graduated anyway; also, many students will receive resources but still never graduate. Both these groups of students will be considered as zero effect if the effectiveness measure is the number of new graduates. Only the new marginal graduates will be counted in the effectiveness measure. Nevertheless, it is likely that the anyway-graduates and never-graduates received some benefits from the program, even as these benefits are not counted. Expressed as odds ratios, binary indicators can be especially hard to interpret. For example, an odds ratio of 1.22—that is, an increase in the odds of high school completion of 22%—will involve a substantial number of new graduates if the baseline completion rate is 70%. But there will be only a few new graduates if the baseline completion rate is 20%.

These issues gain salience because all resources for all students are counted in CE analysis (we discuss an example in Chapter 9). Imagine a high school mentoring program delivered to 100 students with an impact evaluation that shows the high school completion rate increases from 50% to 60%. This yields 10 new graduates. But the intervention has allocated resources to 100 students of which 90 are counted as a zero effect (the 50 students who would have graduated anyway and the 40 who never graduated). A similar logic applies to the second example where effectiveness is measured using the change in the odds. With CE analysis applied to binary outcomes, it matters a lot how well targeted the intervention is and the baseline prevalence of dropping out. If the mentoring program had been delivered only to the 50 students who were expected to drop out, then the cost is approximately half as large (depending on economies of scale). Therefore, the CE results will be significantly different for programs with different baseline prevalences.

In conclusion, if the program objectives warrant it, the evaluator could choose from a wide range of effectiveness measures. Fundamentally, the CE analysis should use as its effectiveness measure the construct that best captures the goals of the intervention.

7.2. METHODS FOR IDENTIFYING EFFECTIVENESS ●

7.2.1. Experiments, Quasi-Experiments, and Correlational Evaluations

Once measures of effectiveness are established, the next task is to determine whether a particular intervention is successful in altering success on these measures. In particular, we need to ascertain whether there is a cause-and-effect relationship between each alternative and the measure of effectiveness. Does reducing class size lead to increased mathematics and reading achievement? Does an after-school program reduce the likelihood of aggressive behavior?

Typically, this involves comparing the measure of effectiveness for a group of individuals who have been "treated" by the alternative with that for a control or comparison group. There is a vast array of evaluation designs or identification strategies for carrying out these comparisons. For our purposes, we distinguish three categories of evaluation designs: (1) experimental, (2) quasi-experimental, and (3) correlational.

The experimental method directly assigns subjects to a control group and one or more treatment groups. Members of the control group do not participate in the educational alternative that is being evaluated; instead, they provide a baseline estimate of what the treatment group *would have* attained in the absence of the treatment. Ultimately, the estimates of effectiveness are based on the difference between the measured outcomes of the treatment and control groups subsequent to the application of the educational program or policy to the treatment group. Subjects are randomly assigned to control and treatment status. Hence, the groups were equivalent at some initial point, and any subsequent difference in outcomes can be causally attributed to the treatment.

Random assignment is a prerequisite of experimental research and is the best way of ensuring equivalence between control and treatment groups. (For a full discussion, see Cook et al. [2002], McEwan [2015], and Smith and Glass [1987]; for the application of experimental methods in health sciences CE analysis, see Greenberg, Rosen, Wacht, Palmer, and Neumann [2010] and Neumann, Greenberg, Ochanski, Stone, and Rosen [2015].) Because randomization provides assurances that the two groups are equivalent on average, prior to the application of the treatment, we can rule out the important threat to validity of group nonequivalence or selection bias. Experiments in education research are also growing in prevalence across a range of educational interventions. A very prominent experiment was on class size (Mosteller, 1995); more recent experiments have tested the effectiveness of guidance programs for college students (Butcher & Visher, 2013), of coaching (Bettinger & Baker, 2014), and of incentive payments in college (Barrow, Schanzenbach, & Claessens, 2015).

The quasi-experimental method relies on plausibly random differences in exposure to an intervention to identify the impact of that intervention. These differences in exposure may be identified using local randomization regression-discontinuity designs, which rely on local randomization of a continuous assignment variable, or instrumental variables designs, which rely on exogenous differences in access to the intervention (see Schlotter, Schwerdt, & Woessman, 2011). Where quasi-experimental methods are not based on random assignment to an intervention, they may still be subject to some selectivity or endogeneity bias (see Heckman & Urzua, 2010; Imbens, 2010). However, evidence from quasi-experimental methods has grown rapidly over recent years (Angrist & Pischke, 2009). Prominent examples include identification of the effects of class size, using exogenous variation of school rules or cohort populations (Angrist & Krueger, 1999; Hoxby, 2000); extra schooling, using exogenous variation in compulsory schooling laws (Oreopoulos, 2006); returns to college based on distance from the local institution (Kane & Rouse, 1995); and the capitalized value of high-quality schooling from additional information (Figlio & Lucas, 2004).

Finally, the correlational method is based on regression analysis controlling for covariates or less restrictive matching estimators (see Imbens & Wooldridge, 2009). When comparing students who receive and do not receive a given "treatment" (e.g., more textbooks or a new curriculum), we make statistical controls for measured characteristics of students (such as a pretest score or SES). If the controls are complete and accurate, then the threat of group nonequivalency is adequately ruled out, but there are often many potential nonobservable influences that make this presumption questionable.

Correlational methods are relatively simple to apply across many educational research topics. Unfortunately, even with matching estimators, it is a fairly tall order to make complete and accurate controls: There are countless unobserved student characteristics that also affect outcomes, such as motivation, family wealth, or ability. If students who received a given treatment tend to possess more or less of these characteristics, then it is quite difficult to separate treatment effects from the preexisting student differences. Statistical procedures can address the threat of group nonequivalence (see Greene, 1997; Wooldridge, 2000), including procedures that specifically model the process of selection into the program or bounding the bias from unobservable characteristics (e.g., Altonji, Elder, & Taber, 2005). But these procedures may not always or completely mitigate bias. Nevertheless, at least since the Coleman Report of 1966 (Coleman et al., 1966), thousands of studies have used nonexperimental data and multiple regression analysis to evaluate educational research interventions.[1] Of particular interest for CE analysis are "production function" studies (Choi, Moon, & Ridder, 2014). These studies attempt to infer causal links between school resources and student outcomes based on observed variation in resources within regression models. Evidence in the United States has been extensively debated since Hanushek (1986, 1997) and Greenwald, Hedges, and Laine (1996), with few firm conclusions (Hanushek, 2003). For a comprehensive review for developing countries, see Glewwe, Hanushek, Humpage, and Ravina (2013).

This description of these methods is deliberately brief. Each category has an enormous body of supporting methodological research to ensure the design is applied correctly. This methodology is beyond the scope of this book (Angrist & Pischke, 2009; McEwan, 2015). Here, our focus is on highlighting the relevant attributes of each evaluation design for an analyst who is contemplating a cost or CE or BC analysis.

7.2.2. Identification Strategies With Cost Analysis

For an economist performing cost analysis, there are several factors to consider. The most obvious is that the appropriate identification strategy for cost analysis is the one that best identifies the effects of the intervention. If the method yields valid results for the outcomes of an intervention, then those results can be combined with cost information to perform CE or BC analysis.

For economic evaluation, there are strong reasons to prefer experimental methods. These reasons are in addition to the stronger "gold standard" claims of causality or internal validity that are typically associated with experimental methods.

First, with experimental research there is typically much more detail on the specifics of the treatment. These details should make it easier for the analyst to estimate the resources required to implement the intervention. As Chapters 3 through 5 indicated, collecting cost

---

[1] To provide one example, there is a long literature comparing the achievement of students who attend private schools with students who attend public schools (Coleman et al., 1966; Lubienski & Lubienski, 2013). Yet, families who send their children to private schools are often of higher SES, so it is necessary to control for this difference. Even with such controls, however, it is feasible that students in private schools are different in some important, but unobserved, ways. Perhaps their families place higher priority on education and so help their children learn at home in subtle and hard-to-observe ways. Using correlational analysis, the effects of private school may therefore be confounded with household resources.

information is far from straightforward in practice—not least because interventions and reforms are often very loosely specified. Having detailed information on the implementation of the intervention is therefore a sizable advantage for CE analysis. This advantage is particularly important when evaluating educational interventions that can be implemented flexibly. For example, literacy reforms such as Reading Recovery or Success for All have many components and levels. Programs such as Read 180 are implemented in diverse ways across sites. Programs such as Reading Partners involve several partner agencies. The actual resources used for these educational interventions are most easily calculated when they are delivered as part of an experimental research project.

A second advantage of the experimental method is that the analyst has direct, parallel information on the control group as well as the treatment group. For CE analysis, this parallel information is critical. The analyst may be able to estimate an effect size gain from a particular reform versus the status quo and may be able to estimate the net costs of the reform. However, it is often difficult to estimate the resources used by the comparison group. For example, an after-school intervention to help students complete high school may cost $4,000 per student to implement, and its effects may be precisely identified by a quasi-experimental study (e.g., where after-school enrollment is instrumented from exogenous variation in program availability in the local area). But it may not be obvious what resources the comparison group receives: Some students may be in other after-school programs, others may be in youth training programs, and others may be employed. This information is not typically collected—most likely because it is not available—when quasi-experimental and correlational methods are applied.

Information on the comparison group is critical for CE analysis (and all economic evaluations). As noted earlier, the recent cost analysis of Success for All establishes that the incremental cost of the program is very low; most schools already allocate resources to students for similar programs (Quint, Zhu, Balu, Rappaport, & DeLaurentis, 2015). The substantive distinction of Success for All is how—rather than how much—resources are allocated for the program. This distinction can best be illustrated with information on the treatment and control groups.

By contrast to the experimental method, it may be more difficult to perform CE analysis with results from quasi-experimental methods. The treatment may be well defined, but the counterfactual is typically not; so the incremental cost of treatment relative to control is hard to calculate. This difficulty is also apparent for correlational studies, although these studies are further compromised if they have weak construct validity.

A third advantage of the experimental method relates to non-compliance and attrition. For cost analysis, it is important to distinguish students who are assigned to receive the treatment but do not (noncompliers) and to identify students who only partially comply with the treatment (attriters). We might expect that noncompliers do not receive any resources and so have zero costs. Therefore, the total cost for the treatment-on-the-treated (TOT) group should be lower than for the intent-to-treat (ITT) group. Similarly, those who only attrite from the treatment will have lower costs than those who complete the program (and presumably have costs that are closer to the control group). Experimental methods usually allow for a clear distinction of these two groups and hence for a more accurate estimate of the costs of the intervention.

These considerations are especially important when examining production function studies, which purport to show the relationship between inputs and educational outputs. Looking across the evidence for developing countries, Glewwe et al. (2013) identified 79 high-quality production function studies. The outcomes of these studies were test scores, and the inputs covered a wide array of potential school resource measures (some of these studies applied experimental methods). The results were summarized using the vote-count method, with each estimation result listed by sign and statistical significance (see Glewwe et al., 2013, Table 2.7). The evidence is strongly plausible for most resource indicators. More resource-intensive provision of books were clearly found to increase student learning, as was classroom furniture (e.g., desks), basic infrastructure (electricity, building structures, and libraries), and basic classroom materials (e.g., blackboards). Similarly, more resources allocated to teachers—as reflected in their education levels and experience, and directly in their pay—were associated with increased learning (Glewwe et al., 2013, Tables 2.8 and 2.9). For the pupil-teacher ratio, results were less conclusive: Across 101 estimates, only 30 were statistically significant and in the expected direction (higher ratios impairing learning outcomes). But it may also be common in some countries to assign weaker students to smaller classes than those who are doing well or rural students to smaller classes because of the dearth of students in their catchment areas. Overall, these results indicate that, in line with theory and common sense, more resources do enhance learning outcomes.

Incorporating this evidence into a CE framework is not straightforward. First, the cost of each input (e.g., the desks or electricity) is unknown and may be very hard to estimate without a direct research inquiry. Second, even if the cost of the input is known, we cannot know whether the school was allocating resources to other inputs. A treatment school with the specific input (e.g., blackboards) may be sacrificing other inputs that are not fully measured (e.g., books) such that the resource levels are different rather than higher in the treatment school. Ultimately, these resource measures are not the same as costs in money terms. The most prominent example is the pupil-teacher ratio. One might think that a school with a low pupil-teacher ratio has relatively more resources. But it may be that the school has fewer management staff or resources for libraries, for example. For production function studies that examine the effect of facilities on educational outcomes, we would need to amortize the value of improvements in facilities (Cellini, Ferreira, & Rothstein, 2010; Duflo, 2001). In general, we must be careful in taking results from production function studies, estimating costs, and then calculating CE ratios because of identification problems.

In summary, for economic evaluation it is especially important that the method used to identify impacts from a treatment can also be used to determine costs—for both the treatment and the counterfactual.

7.2.3. Evidence From Meta-Analysis

Researchers in the social sciences are increasingly using techniques of meta-analysis to arrive at estimates of effectiveness. Often, there are numerous—perhaps hundreds—of individual studies that explore the causal relationship between a particular educational alternative and an outcome such as achievement. Results from individual studies may vary considerably. It is difficult to extract meaningful conclusions from the overall body of findings without resorting to additional analytical techniques. Thus, many researchers use meta-analysis to estimate the "average" effect size of an alternative, which is typically used to support broad conclusions about its effectiveness (see Borenstein, Hedges, Higgins, & Rothstein, 2009; Cooper, 2009).

Meta-analyses have been conducted in many areas of educational research, ranging from the effects of within-class ability grouping to class size reduction (see the review of interventions by Ahn, Ames, & Myers, 2012). Again, we leave aside direct methodology of meta-analysis (Valentine, Cooper, Patall, Tyson, & Robinson, 2010). Instead, we consider how meta-analysis might be used to derive an effectiveness measure for CE analysis.

From our perspective, the pertinent issue is whether meta-analytic summaries can be combined with costs data in order to provide a CE comparison of different educational alternatives. Instead of using a single estimate of effectiveness, is it necessary or preferable for CE analysis to use an estimate derived from a comprehensive meta-analysis?

The incorporation of meta-analytic results into CE analysis warrants a fair amount of caution (Levin, 1988, 1991). Meta-analysis provides an estimate of the average results from many different versions of a single class of interventions (e.g., computer-assisted instruction, ability grouping, or tutoring). However, CE analysis is fundamentally oriented toward providing concrete information to decisionmakers on whether specific programs or policies are desirable to implement. Instead of specifics, a meta-analysis can provide only a general judgment of whether a general variety of policy is effective "on average."

The problem becomes more severe when we attempt to incorporate costs. In prior chapters, we discussed the importance of clearly defining an alternative, providing a detailed account of the ingredients, and carefully estimating the cost of each ingredient. But the effect size from meta-analysis is based on a mixture of many different programs, precluding any conceptual or practical way to identify costs. The effect size does not refer to an implementable program alternative with a set of specific ingredients. Consider a hypothetical meta-analysis of adult tutoring programs in elementary schools. In practice, each of these programs might obtain its tutoring services in a different way. Some might pay on-duty teachers to spend time after school, whereas others might pay local adults the minimum wage to participate. Still others could receive voluntary tutoring services from parents. Faced by such heterogeneity of resource use, there is no obvious way to define the ingredients and costs of a single program.

Moreover, meta-analytic effectiveness estimates are reported after controlling for characteristics of the research evaluation. These characteristics are grouped into categories defined as units; treatment; observing operations; setting; and method (Ahn et al., 2012; Cooper, 2009). Some of these characteristics are almost certainly correlated with the costs of an intervention. For example, the units category may refer to the grades of the students and the scale of the intervention, the treatment category may include information on how long the intervention is implemented for, and the setting may include the locality of the intervention. Each of these domains will influence the costs of the intervention. Controlling for treatment duration is therefore, to some extent, controlling for costs.

Under stringent conditions, it may be acceptable to use meta-analytic results. Overall, meta-analytic results should not be incorporated in CE analyses unless the underlying situations are derived from replication trials of a single intervention and the meta-analytic outcome does not come from a model specification that controls for resources. If the specific studies all refer to different evaluations of precisely the same intervention, then it is more acceptable to ascribe a meaningful policy interpretation to the "average effect." When the intervention is precisely the same, it is more likely that the particular cost ingredients will be similar across studies. For example, a specific intervention—such as a "packaged" reading program—may use a prescribed amount of materials, physical space, time, and human resources, even if it is implemented and evaluated in many different contexts (the messy reality of program implementation, however, provides good reason to be skeptical that this proposition will always hold). Also, meta-analysis can be used as part of a sensitivity analysis to estimate upper and lower bounds for the effects of an intervention.

7.3. UTILITY ANALYSIS ●

Often a single measure of effectiveness does not fully describe a program's outcomes and is not a true reflection of the policymaker's preferences.

One technical solution, as noted previously, is simply to apply each effectiveness measure in a separate CE analysis. If all versions of the analyses yield the same or similar rankings, the multiplicity of outcomes is not salient. If, as is more likely, the analyses yield mixed results, the policymaker still has some information on which to base a resource allocation decision.

A more theoretically grounded solution is to derive a utility function. This function can then embody the relative value to the decisionmaker of increases in diverse educational outcomes. Utility is a shorthand way of describing the relative strength of preference or satisfaction that parents (or students or teachers) have for each outcome within a range of possibilities. It can be applied to any measure of effectiveness. A utility function is intended as a map of the decisionmakers' preferences.

The tricky part is deriving a good estimate of the utility provided by each alternative—that is, to specify a utility function (mathematical representation) that incorporates all outcomes. This task is even more complex if the two outcomes are very different: if, for example, class size reduction improves only achievement in reading and is found to ameliorate externalizing behaviors. To help specify a utility function, researchers have developed techniques in "decision analysis," although these techniques have not been widely applied in education. This section reviews some of the most straightforward approaches. First, we will provide an overview of multiattribute utility theory, which serves as a convenient framework to organize the discussion. This is followed by a review of the methods for estimating utility and a discussion of whose preferences (or utility) should be measured.

Despite the clear relevance of utility theory (and also CU theory) to interventions with multiple outcomes, very few CU analyses have been performed across educational research (Ross, 2008). Of necessity, therefore, our discussion of utility focuses on methodological issues rather than examples of published studies. By contrast, CU analysis is widely practiced in health research, primarily because a consensus on how to measure utility is well established (Neumann, Thorat, Shi, Saret, & Cohen, 2015).

7.3.1. Multiattribute Utility Theory

Multiattribute utility theory is a complicated name for a fairly intuitive idea. An educational program produces outcomes in a multitude of categories: student achievement, student and teacher attitudes, and so on. Within each category, we could imagine a variety of subcategories. For example, student achievement can be divided into mathematics, reading, science, and so on. The literature on utility theory refers to each subcategory or measure of effectiveness as an "attribute." We shall adopt the latter term in the following discussion. Stakeholders may derive utility from—or have a preference for—each of these attributes. Multiattribute utility theory provides a set of techniques for accomplishing two tasks: (1) quantifying the utility derived from individual attributes and (2) combining the utility from each attribute to arrive at an overall measure of utility. The general tool for carrying out these tasks is called the multiattribute utility function.

Imagine that we exhaustively catalogued and evaluated the attributes of a particular educational program. We could use a simple notation to refer to each of these attributes: x_1, x_2, x_3, and so on, through the final attribute, x_m. These attributes are measured in their "natural" units. For example, gains on an achievement test might be expressed in percentage points, the number of test items, or months of learning gain. To perform CE analysis, we will need to express each attribute on a common "utility" scale. That is, we would like to describe the strength of preferences for a given increase in achievement, for an improvement in student attitudes, or for a change in any of the attributes.

We need to estimate a series of single-attribute utility functions: $U_1(x_1)$, $U_2(x_2)$, and $U_3(x_3)$, through $U_m(x_m)$. The preceding notation is an efficient way of saying "the utility produced by the attribute x_1," "the utility produced by the attribute x_2," etc. In the next section, we will specify how to "convert" each attribute to a utility scale.

Once single-attribute utility functions are obtained, the next step is to combine them in an overall measure of utility. The tool for doing so is referred to as the multiattribute utility function. The overall utility from a given alternative (and its m attributes) is expressed as follows:

$$U(x_1, \ldots, x_m) = \sum_{i=1}^{m} w_i U_i(x_i)$$

It is nothing more than a weighted sum of the utilities produced by individual attributes. To make this more concrete, let us assume that the outcomes of a particular alternative are fully described by three attributes:

$$U(x_1, x_2, x_3) = w_1 U_1(x_1) + w_2 U_2(x_2) + w_3 U_3(x_3)$$

Prior to summing the three single-attribute utility functions, each is multiplied by an "importance weight" (w_1, w_2, and w_3). In general, the importance weights across all the attributes should sum to 1 (i.e., $w_1 + w_2 + w_3 = 1$). Each weight should reflect the relative importance of each attribute to the stakeholders. For example, if $w_1 = 0.80$, $w_2 = 0.10$, $w_3 = 0.10$, then the overall utility of stakeholders is primarily determined by attribute x_1 with the other two attributes having lesser (and equal) importance. Below we specify how to elicit importance weights from stakeholders.

This type of multiattribute utility function is "additive": It involves simply adding up the weighted utilities of individual attributes. It makes intuitive sense to most people, and it can be usefully applied in a variety of circumstances. For example, if the attributes are reading, math, and science achievement, researchers might consider these as cognitive gains that can be summed. Nevertheless, the additive utility function is restrictive. It assumes that the preference for each attribute is independent of the preferences for the other attributes. This assumption may not be realistic: Families may care that children make moderate gains in all subjects rather than sizable gains in only one subject.

Before overall utility scores can be obtained, however, there are two remaining steps. First, we need to convert each attribute into a common utility scale that expresses the strength of preference for the attribute. That is, we need to define the functions—$U_1(x_1)$, $U_2(x_2)$, and so on—that describe exactly how additional units of the attributes are associated with utility. Second, we need to establish the weights—w_1, w_2, and so on—that reflect the relative importance of each attribute in overall utility. Toward accomplishing this, the following sections explore a few of the techniques that scholars in the field of decision analysis have devised.

7.3.2. Methods of Assessing Single-Attribute Utility Functions

This section describes several approaches to assessing single-attribute utility functions: proportional scoring, the direct method, and the variable probability method. To better illustrate each approach, we shall employ some hypothetical data on effectiveness. Imagine that we have just evaluated four separate programs for computer-assisted instruction of mathematics. The four alternatives (A, B, C, and D) are each evaluated according to a single attribute: mathematics scores. The test is composed of 25 items, results of which are presented in Table 7.2. In the following sections, we will convert these attribute scores to a utility scale.

Proportional Scoring

The first method, proportional scoring, is simply a linear rescaling of each attribute to a common utility scale. The rescaling can be

Table 7.2   Hypothetical Data From an Evaluation of Four Programs for Computer-Assisted Math Instruction

	Mathematics Scores
Alternative A	4
Alternative B	20
Alternative C	12
Alternative D	16

accomplished via graphical or mathematical means. In Figure 7.1, we provide a graphical representation of proportional scoring. Each mathematics score is plotted on the *x* axis, ranging from the value of the lowest-scoring alternative to that of the highest-scoring alternative. The utility scale, on the *y* axis, ranges from 0 to 100. The low and high values of the utility scale are arbitrary—we could just as easily set the end points at any values. The same utility scale must be shared by each of the attributes that we assess (and eventually combine into a single measure of utility).

As shown in Figure 7.1, the lowest score on mathematics is assigned a utility of 0 and the highest a utility of 100. The straight lines connecting these points imply that increasing mathematics scores lead to constant increases in utility (in this case, a 4-point increase in mathematics scores produces a 25-point increase in utility). Of course, this is an assumption that we are making. We have no direct evidence that people really evince this preference structure. It might be that when reading scores are low, a small increase leads to a substantial utility increase, but when they are higher, the same increase in scores leads to a somewhat smaller gain in utility. This would be represented by a curvilinear, rather than a linear, utility function. Later on, we will allow for this possibility.

Figure 7.1 Assessing Utility Functions With Proportional Scoring

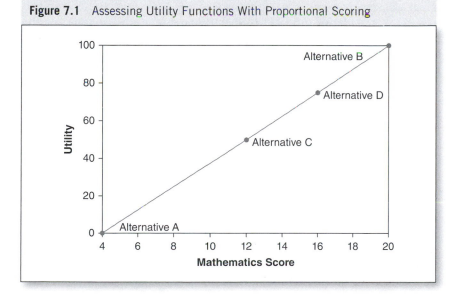

We could derive the same utility scores mathematically, without resorting to graphs. The formula is quite simple:

$$U(x) = \frac{x - \text{Lowest}}{\text{Highest} - \text{Lowest}} \times 100$$

Applying the formula for a reading score of 12 (Alternative C) yields a utility score of 50 (this can be verified by examining Figure 7.1):

$$U(12) = \frac{12 - 4}{20 - 4} \times 100 = 50$$

In a sense, proportional scoring isn't really a "method" because it does not rely on the expressed preferences of stakeholders. It simply assumes that increasing amounts of an attribute are linearly (proportionally) associated with utility.

The Direct Method

Instead of using proportional scoring, we could obtain direct input from individual stakeholders on the utility that they derive from varying amounts of an attribute. The simplest approach for doing so is the direct method. To apply the direct method, one identifies the low and high values on the relevant attribute scale. In this case, the low mathematics score is 4 and the high score is 20. As before, these are arbitrarily assigned low (0) and high (100) values, respectively, on the utility scale. The respondent is then asked to directly rate the preference for middle levels of the attribute, relative to these end points. In our example, the middle levels are the mathematics scores that were obtained by the middle alternatives. For comparison's sake, it would also be helpful to rate other possible scores. We could administer a survey to education professionals or parents asking them to rate scores on a mathematics achievement test. Assume such a process turned up the following results:

$U(4) = 0$ (arbitrary assignment)

$U(8) = 40$ (judgment, relative to arbitrary assignment)

$U(12) = 75$ (judgment, relative to arbitrary assignment)

$U(16) = 95$ (judgment, relative to arbitrary assignment)

$U(20) = 100$ (arbitrary assignment)

The mathematics scores and corresponding utilities are plotted in Figure 7.2. A researcher could use visual means to draw a smooth curve through the points. Alternatively, many researchers use statistical methods to find the curve that provides the best "fit" to the data. In this case, the data suggest a curvilinear relationship between mathematics scores and utility. More specifically, increasing mathematics scores tend to increase utility, but at a decreasing rate. Of course, utility functions can assume many different shapes depending on the survey responses. (The structure of the prior example was borrowed from von Winterfeldt and Edwards [1986]; see also Gray, Clarke, Wolstenholme, and Wordsworth [2011].)

The Variable Probability Method

The variable probability method also calls upon stakeholders to assess their preferences for varying amounts of a given attribute. However, it requires a different sort of thought experiment than the direct method. Imagine that you are able to choose between two different options. On the one hand, you could opt for a gamble in which the "winning" hand leads to the highest attribute score (in this case, a mathematics score of 20) and the "losing" hand produces the lowest (a mathematics score of 4). The probabilities of attaining the highest and lowest scores are, respectively, p and $(1 - p)$. Instead of this risky option,

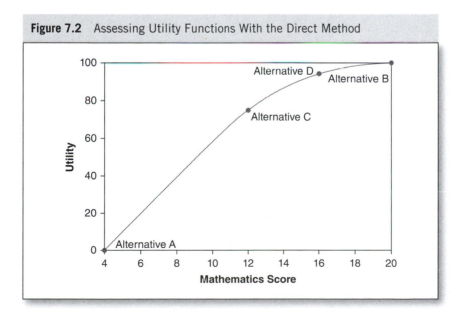

Figure 7.2   Assessing Utility Functions With the Direct Method

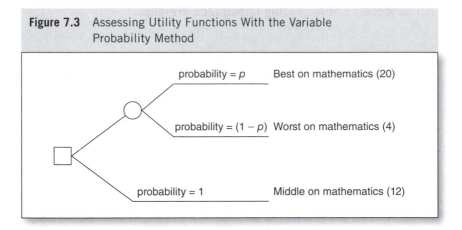

Figure 7.3   Assessing Utility Functions With the Variable Probability Method

you could obtain a given mathematics score with certainty. For the time being, let's fix this middle score at 12. This particular gamble is represented by the decision tree in Figure 7.3.

To assess the utility of the middle score, individuals choose the probability (p) that makes them indifferent between the risky alternative (with a potentially high or low payoff) or the riskless alternative (with a middling payoff). Let us say, for example, that we suggested an initial probability of 0.99. That is, individuals would be faced with the option of receiving the best score with a probability of 0.99 (and, conversely, the worst score with a probability of 0.01) or receiving a middling score with certainty. Many individuals would likely find the risky option to be most attractive.

What if we suggested an initial probability of 0.01 instead of 0.99? In this case, chances are that most individuals would not favor a gamble that offered such a small probability of an attractive payoff. Instead, they might prefer the certainty of obtaining a middle score.

Between 0.99 and 0.01, there is a probability at which individuals would be indifferent between the two options. In the case of Figure 7.3, suppose that a probability of 0.60 leads to indifference for a particular individual. We can then interpret this probability as the utility of a mathematics score of 12 (with the endpoints of the utility scale set at 0 and 1). In order to employ the same utility scale as prior examples, we multiply 0.60 by 100, yielding a utility of 60. The same exercise is repeated for several different mathematics scores. Doing so produces a number of pairs of mathematics scores and their associated utilities. These can be graphed, just as we did in Figures 7.1 and 7.2.

7.3.3. Methods of Assessing Importance Weights

After single-attribute utility functions are defined for each attribute, we require some method for obtaining the relative weight or "importance" of each attribute in overall utility. The two general approaches are the direct method and the variable probability method.

The simplest version of the direct method asks individuals to "allocate" a total of 100 points among attributes, according to their relative importance. Let's say that mathematics scores are considered by individuals to account for about half of overall utility and, consequently, are assigned 50 out of 100 points. Computer literacy is the next most important attribute and is assigned 30 points. Lastly, student satisfaction receives 20 points. Each estimate is divided by 100 in order to obtain a set of three importance weights—0.50, 0.30, and 0.20—that sum to 1. In other variants of the direct method individuals are asked to rank attributes in order of importance.

With the variable probability method, individuals are asked to choose between two options. One is a gamble with two possible outcomes (e.g., the best test score on all attributes with probability p or the worst test score on all attributes with probability $1 - p$). The other option is a certain outcome (e.g., the best test score on just one test). If the probability (p) is 0.99, many individuals would choose the gamble; if the probability is 0.01, the gamble is much less appealing. Between these two values of p, there lies a probability that would cause an individual to be indifferent between the two options. This probability can be interpreted as the importance weight for a particular test. Once importance weights are estimated for all attributes, they should sum to unity.[2]

Thus far, we have addressed several techniques for assessing the utility of individuals. However, we need to specify exactly *whose* preferences should be assessed. There are at least three groups that might be considered: (1) the entire population in a given community; (2) the population that is directly affected by an intervention

---

[2] If they are close (but do not sum to 1), we can normalize them by dividing each individual weight by the sum of the weights. If the sum is not close to 1, this is a signal that the additive utility function does not adequately represent an individual's preferences (Clemen, 1996). The analyst might need to use more complex versions of the utility function that incorporate interactions among the attributes. These were briefly mentioned in a previous section. For further details, the reader is encouraged to consult Clemen (1996) or Keeney and Raiffa (1993).

(such as families with children enrolled in school); and (3) a smaller group of representatives such as teachers, administrators, or school board members. In choosing among these, evaluators should also consider how the results from CU analysis might improve decision-making or change practices. If, for example, the research is motivated to help parents choose between reading strategies, then parental utility is the relevant preference. In keeping with our general approach, the presumption is that CU analysis should attempt to measure the preferences of an entire community.

Preferences can be elicited through survey responses.[3] However, sampling should be performed carefully because it may be hard to judge the degree of variability in preferences. In education research, there is simply little evidence to guide us. Earlier educational CU analysis only elicited the preferences of small groups of administrators or other stakeholders (e.g., Fletcher, Hawley, & Piele, 1990; Lewis, Johnson, Erickson, & Bruininks, 1994). More recently, Ross (2008) found that different groups of professionals had very different weightings and ratings of library services within a local school district. Finally, in a study of reading outcomes, Simon (2011) found that the preferences of reading professionals varied depending on whether the students were average readers or struggling readers. Specifically, these professionals gave greater weight to phonemic awareness outcomes for struggling versus average readers and lesser weight to fluency (Simon, 2011, Table 27). If the preferences vary significantly across groups, the utility measure may not be valid.

7.3.4. Using Utility Measures

Few educational interventions use utility measures as measures of effectiveness (e.g., Ross, 2008; Simon, 2011). A full illustration is given in Example 7.1, where the outcome is special education programs.

---

[3] In some cases, however, it will not be possible to obtain the views of a large sample of community members. Perhaps time is a binding constraint, or the monetary costs of a community survey are judged to be prohibitive. There are two alternatives that might be pursued. First, one can assess the preferences of a representative sample of parents or students who are directly affected by the intervention. Second, one can obtain the views of appropriate representatives of the community, such as school board members or elected officials of civic and community organizations. In other cases, it may be possible for administrators or teachers to determine the utility of the alternatives.

Example 7.1   Cost-Utility Analysis of Special Education Alternatives (Part 1)

The outcomes of special education programs are difficult, if not impossible, to express with a single measure of effectiveness (or attribute). As such, multiattribute utility theory seems especially appropriate. Here, we describe the utility step; in Chapter 8, we link these utility measures to costs to perform cost-utility (CU) analysis.

Darrell Lewis and his colleagues (1994) set out to compare the utility (and costs) produced by three different administrative structures for special education. These alternatives were (a) an independent school district (offering special education services to all students within the locality), (b) an intermediate school district (jointly offering services for students primarily with low-incidence disabilities), and (c) a joint powers special education cooperative (with districts sharing delivery of special education). At issue was which administrative structure would yield the highest utility and at the lowest cost.

The first step is therefore to measure utility. In collaboration with a group of stakeholders—including teachers, administrators, and parents—the evaluators defined the attributes by which the success of alternatives would be judged. These attributes are itemized in the first column of the following table. These are grouped into four categories: (1) student participation in school life, (2) satisfaction with the program, (3) program accomplishments, and (4) program processes.

Estimating the Utility of Special Education Alternatives

	Independent District Alternative		
Interventions	**Importance Weight**	**Unweighted Attribute Utility (0–100)**	**Weighted Attribute Utility**
Student participation in school life			
Access to educational/social experiences	0.09 ×	32.5 =	2.9
Participate in extracurricular/ social activities	0.07 ×	13.3 =	0.9
Participate in mainstream programming	0.09 ×	80.0 =	7.2
Satisfaction with program			
Parents express satisfaction	0.05 ×	84.7 =	4.2
Students express satisfaction	0.05 ×	48.0 =	2.4
Teachers and administrators express satisfaction	0.04 ×	82.7 =	3.3
Public expresses satisfaction	0.05 ×	90.0 =	4.5

(Continued)

(Continued)

Interventions	Independent District Alternative		
	Importance Weight	Unweighted Attribute Utility (0–100)	Weighted Attribute Utility
Accomplishments of program completers			
Demonstrate appropriate social behaviors	0.06 ×	77.5 =	4.7
Live in independent/ semi-independent settings	0.06 ×	54.0 =	3.2
Have social and recreational networks	0.06 ×	89.9 =	5.4
Participate in meaningful vocational settings	0.06 ×	88.5 =	5.3
Complete all years of offered schooling	0.04 ×	100.0 =	4.0
Process of program			
Provides appropriate curriculum components	0.10 ×	74.7 =	7.5
Provides training and support for parents	0.08 ×	59.3 =	4.7
Provides appropriate staff support	0.09 ×	40.0 =	3.6
Sum	1.00		63.9

Source: Adapted from Lewis et al. (1994, Tables 3 and 6).

The same group of stakeholders assigned importance weights to each attribute using the direct method. Individuals ranked all the attributes in order of their importance, with the most important being assigned a value of 100. The rest of the attributes were assigned lesser values, relative to 100, and all these values were normalized to sum to 1. The final importance weights are presented in the second column of the table.

The evaluators then visited school districts and conducted surveys to collect the performance data on each attribute. These attributes were measured on a variety of scales. However, it was necessary to convert each of these to a common utility scale, with the lowest possible utility of each attribute specified as zero and the highest utility as 100. To convert each attribute score, the evaluators used the proportional scoring method. The third column in the table presents the unweighted attribute utilities for one of the three alternatives—independent districts.

The final step is to combine importance weights and unweighted utilities in order to arrive at an overall measure of each alternative's utility. To do so, the evaluators employed the additive multiattribute utility function. Each attribute's utility was multiplied by its respective importance weight (see the fourth column). The weighted utilities were then summed, thereby yielding the overall utility of the alternative. The table shows that the overall utility of the independent district alternative is 63.9. Other calculations, not shown in the table, implied a utility of 70.4 for the intermediate alternative, and 65.2 for the cooperative alternative.

The results suggest that the intermediate alternative is the most attractive: It provides the highest level of utility. However, it is important to combine these results with cost estimates in order to determine which alternative provides a given level of utility at least cost. We report this CU analysis in Chapter 8.

Source: Adapted from Lewis et al. (1994).

One very common, well-accepted utility measure is the quality-adjusted life year (QALY). The QALY takes the value 1 for a year of life in perfect health and is adjusted downward to zero for progressively worse health conditions. Health interventions are frequently evaluated according to their effects on life expectancy. That is, by how many years does a particular medical treatment tend to lengthen one's life? While a useful means of evaluating some interventions, life expectancy does not capture the quality of life or the satisfaction that individuals may derive from additional years of life. Two medical treatments may each add 2 years to an individual's life. Yet, if one of these leaves the individual significantly impaired or incapacitated, then it is clearly less desirable. To estimate the QALYs that are produced by a medical treatment, it is necessary to estimate quality-of-life weights that reflect the satisfaction derived from different health states. These weights can be obtained using a range of methods—for example, the standard gamble or time trade-off method (for a review of these, see Weinstein et al., 2009; Whitehead & Ali, 2010). Increasingly, given its acceptance in health sciences, researchers are using QALYs as a way to value educational interventions. For example, Muennig, Fiscella, Tancredi, and Franks (2010) estimate that a high school graduate will accumulate an additional 2.4 QALYs over his or her lifetime compared with a dropout. Schoeni, Robert, Dow, Miller, and Pamuk (2011) estimated a range of incremental QALYs by education level, also finding large QALY gains for high school graduates over high school dropouts. Educational interventions with a specific focus on child health may therefore rely on an established utility measure.

Finally, despite the lack of explicit utility measures available for education researchers, it is worth noting that many effectiveness measures are based on opinions. For example, college ratings are a mathematical combination of attributes where the weightings are based on survey information, student engagement indices are derived from opinion-based responses of students, and teacher and faculty competence are often based on student evaluations (see respectively Pike, 2004; Spooren, Brockx, & Mortelmans, 2013; Webster, 2001). These measures are artifacts such that they should be justified based on how accurately they reflect the preferences of decisionmakers. In cases where there are no obvious utility measures of effectiveness, analysts might need to perform their own survey as to which outcomes are most valuable and how each outcome should be weighted.

● 7.4. CONCLUSIONS

In this chapter, we have reviewed what makes for a good effectiveness measure for the purposes of CE. The use of impact evaluations for BC analysis is similar but involves a very particular step—turning the effect into a money value. We address this in Chapter 9.

We do not wish to understate the challenges involved in choosing a proper measure of effectiveness and the dangers involved in using a poor measure. It makes little sense to invest time and resources in accurate cost measurements and a rigorous evaluation design if the measure of effectiveness is not suitable. That said, much of our discussion is about what makes for a good effectiveness measure per se, which is—or should be—the focus of all impact evaluations. Of necessity, the effectiveness measure should fully reflect the objectives of the intervention, and it should be expressed as a single number (even as that number may be a composite of several constructs or derived from a utility function). Preferably, the effectiveness measure should be easy to interpret on a continuous scale.

It is also preferable that the measure be estimated using an experimental method. But we note that this preference is not because experimental methods are more reliable and internally valid. Rather, it is because the experimental method allows us to collect much more information on how the intervention is implemented and therefore how much it costs as well as equivalent information for the counterfactual.

With a valid, reliable, and meaningful effectiveness measure, we can combine this with information on costs to calculate the CE ratio. This is the subject of the next chapter.

Discussion Questions

1. What criteria should be applied when choosing an effectiveness measure that is to be applied in CE analysis?

2. What are some potential threats to the validity of a measure of a program's effectiveness? What estimation and measurement methods can be used to overcome these threats, and what are some limitations of these methods?

3. What is meta-analysis? What are some reasons why its applicability to CE analysis might be limited?

Exercises

1. As an analyst for a school district, you review the evidence on programs to increase attainment in high school. You identify the following studies:

Program	Treatment Group Size	Percentage Point Gain Over Control Group in High School Graduation Rate
Talent Search	3,930	10.8
Job Corps	3,940	17.0
JOBSTART	1,028	15.1
New Chance	1,240	9.2
National Guard Youth ChalleNGe Program (NGYCP)	596	19.8

How would you express these results for CE analysis? Which program do you recommend? What other information on effects might be useful?

2. You have been asked to perform CE analysis on a series of middle school math programs, each of which has undergone an experimental evaluation comparing its effects with those of the standard math curriculum on a series of assessments. The following table summarizes the results:

Program	Sample	Measure	Result
Alpha Math	Two classes of sixth-grade math students	Effect size gains on state math assessment	0.1**
Acing Algebra	Four groups of eighth graders in remedial math classes (two years below grade level)	Effect size gains on a program-specific assessment	0.25***
Sigma!	Three groups of sixth-grade math students (performing at grade level)	Effect size gains on standardized math test	0.15*
Primed for Algebra	Three groups of seventh-grade students (one year below grade level)	Effect size gain on a standardized math test	0.08

*Note: *p <= .05, **p<= .01, ***p<= .001*

Which programs would you compare with one another in CE analysis? Which ones would you recommend against comparing in a CE framework? Why? What other factors would you consider in making comparisons?

3. In an experimental test of a financial incentive program for community college students, Barrow, Richburg-Hayes, Rouse, and Brock (2014) estimated the following results (all statistically significant):

	Baseline After Two Semesters	Program Effects
Enrolled in any course (%)	49.6	15.0
Total credits attempted	4.9	1.2
College-level credits earned	2.1	0.9
Total credits earned	2.8	1.1

Which measure is most appropriate for CE analysis?

8

Cost-Effectiveness Analysis

Objectives

1. Combine costs and effects into a single ratio.

2. Interpret cost-effectiveness (CE) ratios.

3. Provide examples of how CE analysis is performed.

4. Review evidence on educational CE.

Cost-effectiveness (CE) analysis is a comparative exercise: It helps evaluate alternative policies to determine which achieves the policymaker's objectives at the lowest cost. Hence, this chapter brings together the cost analysis and evidence on effectiveness into a single metric: the CE ratio. Once estimates of costs and effectiveness are obtained, they can easily be expressed as a ratio for each policy alternative. The ratios can then be ranked to identify the alternatives that provide a given level of effectiveness for the least cost, or the highest effectiveness for a given cost. Though perhaps obvious, some studies neglect to fully explain how such rankings are applied, making it difficult to properly interpret the results and compare policies.

We begin by defining a CE ratio, and we provide a basic example of CE analysis. Next, we report other metrics that might be applied as part of CE analysis. Although mathematically straightforward, the CE ratio requires careful interpretation so that it can improve decisionmaking. The effects of an intervention may be easy to explain per se, and the costs may be explained within their context. The combination of the two is less easy to explain. The CE metric should be understood not as a description of costs or effects but of how the two constructs relate to each other to inform decisionmakers about efficiency (for a discussion within the context of developing countries, see Dhaliwal, Duflo, Glennister, & Tulloch, 2012; McEwan, 2012). Therefore, we discuss in detail how to interpret and explain results from CE analysis. Finally, we review the research evidence on educational CE analysis, focusing on general lessons rather than specific findings. There is an important caveat for this chapter: We assume that the costs and effects are identified using rigorous methods and estimated precisely; how to perform analysis when estimates are uncertain is covered in Chapter 11.

● 8.1. COST-EFFECTIVENESS RATIOS

The CE ratio is the simple expression of costs divided by effects. Cost data should be collected using the ingredients method, as we discussed in Chapter 5. For effectiveness, in theory any measure of educational effectiveness can be applied, but it must be univariate and be identified using a valid research method; these issues were discussed in Chapter 7. Both costs and effects should be expressed in the same units—for example, cost per student and effect per student.

There are two critical and related elements in combining costs and effectiveness appropriately. First, the cost measure must be directly linked to the results on the effectiveness measure. That is, the resources that were costed out—including any induced costs—were in fact those that generated the measured effects. This linkage may not be straightforward if programs are delivered across multiple cohorts and evidence of effectiveness is only available for one group of students for example. Second, the costs of the intervention must be those that are required beyond those required for the "business as usual" as well as its effectiveness results. This is necessary so that the combined ratio can be interpreted properly as an incremental result of both cost and effects.

Given these prerequisites, the mathematics of expressing costs and effectiveness as a ratio is straightforward. To compute a CE ratio

(*CER* in the following equation and subsequent equations), the cost (*C*) of a given alternative or treatment (subscript *T*) is divided by its effectiveness (*E*) relative to an alternative counterfactual (subscript *C*):

$$CER = \frac{C_T - C_C}{E_T - E_C} = \frac{\Delta C}{\Delta E}$$

This ratio is interpreted as the cost required to obtain a single extra unit of effectiveness. For most interventions or programs, a simple version of $CER = C/E$ is typically reported. This is because the effectiveness measure is often identified as a gain or increment (e.g., effect size gain in achievement) relative to the baseline. However, it is important to recognize that, fundamentally, the full version is actually being derived: the ratio is the net increase in costs between the program or treatment *T* and the counterfactual or comparison *C* divided by the gain in effectiveness of the program. As we show next, it is important to be deliberate in calculating this ratio because it requires careful interpretation.

Our general decision rule is to choose the alternative that exhibits the lowest cost per unit of effectiveness. Thus, we should rank order the alternatives, ranging from those with the smallest CE ratios to those with the largest. The alternative that costs the least for a given size of effectiveness is the most cost-effective. In effect, the ratio is the price of an outcome, and it makes sense to pay the lowest price.

To illustrate, we provide a basic example of CE analysis of alternative methods of raising mathematics and reading achievement. In a wide-ranging CE analysis from the 1980s, Levin, Glass, and Meister (1987) set out to compare the relative costs and effects for the elementary grades of four commonly suggested policies to increase mathematics and reading scores relative to regular schooling. (These policy alternatives are still debated, even as their effects and costs may now be quite different from this example.) The alternatives were (1) a longer school day (by 1 hour, half devoted to mathematics and half to reading), (2) computer-assisted instruction (drill and practice of 10 minutes per day), (3) cross-age tutoring (of fifth/sixth graders to students in lower elementary grades), and (4) reduced class size. For each alternative, the annual per-student cost of each alternative was estimated via the ingredients method to correspond with the expected achievement gains in mathematics and reading.

These costs and effects are shown in Table 8.1. The least costly interventions were reductions in class size by five pupils and an increase in the length of the school day. The most costly was the peer

Table 8.1   Costs, Effects, and Cost-Effectiveness Ratios of Four Interventions

Interventions	Mathematics			Reading		
	Cost	Effect	Cost-Effectiveness Ratio	Cost	Effect	Cost-Effectiveness Ratio
Longer school day	$176	0.03	$5,860	$176	0.07	$2,510
Computer-assisted instruction	$343	0.12	$2,860	$343	0.23	$1,490
Cross-age tutoring (peers)	$611	0.97	$630	$611	0.48	$1,270
Reduction of class size from 30 to 25	$181	0.07	$2,590	$181	0.04	$4,540

Sources: Adapted from Levin et al. (1987, Tables 1 and 2). Longer school day: Beginning Teacher Evaluation Study (Glass, 1984). Computer-aided instruction: Drill and practice (Ragosta, Holland, & Jamison, 1982). Cross-age tutoring: National program (Glass, 1984). Class size: Evidence from meta-analysis of 14 experimental evaluations of class size reduction (Glass, 1984).

Notes: 2015 dollars using the Consumer Wage Index for Urban Wage Earners and Clerical Workers (CPI-W). CE ratios rounded.

tutoring program. The effectiveness of each intervention is reported in units of standard deviations (effect sizes) on mathematics and reading tests. Peer tutoring showed the largest effects by far. Class size reduction and a longer school day showed the smallest effects.

The third and sixth columns of Table 8.1 show the results of dividing the costs by effects in order to arrive at CE ratios for each subject. These indicate the annual cost required to obtain one unit of student achievement. For example, to obtain an additional unit of mathematics achievement per year, it would cost about $5,860 a year with a longer school day but only $630 with peer tutoring. In fact, a longer school day is less than half as cost-effective in raising mathematics achievement as computer-assisted instruction or reducing class size. The most cost-effective approach, peer tutoring, requires only one ninth of the resources to obtain the same effect on mathematics achievement. For reading, the interventions also differ in terms of CE. To obtain an additional unit of reading achievement would cost about twice as much for increasing the school day as using peer tutoring ($2,510 versus $1,270). However, for reading achievement, the least cost-effective intervention is class size reduction: A one-unit increase in reading would cost $4,540.

8.2. ALTERNATIVE COST-EFFECTIVENESS METRICS   ●

8.2.1. Cost-Utility Analysis

As established in Chapter 7, it may be appropriate to derive the effectiveness measure from direct estimation of a utility function. Although the utility measure may be an artifact, it has—if created properly—the advantage of accurately measuring the objective of the intervention.

Once utility (U) has been estimated, the cost (C) of each alternative divided by this utility estimate yields the cost-utility (CU) ratio:

$$CUR = \frac{C}{U}$$

$$CUR = \frac{C_T - C_C}{U_T - U_C} = \frac{\Delta C}{\Delta U}$$

The CU ratio is interpreted as the cost of obtaining a single unit of utility from the treatment T versus the comparison group C. As with CE analysis, the CU ratios of each alternative are rank ordered from smallest to largest. The smallest ratios indicate the alternatives that provide a given amount of utility at the lowest cost. The CU ratio is directly analogous to the CE ratio, and the same cautions regarding reporting and interpretation also apply (Detsky & Naglie, 1990). Sensitivity analysis (discussed in Chapter 11) is also performed using the same approaches.

Example 8.1   A Cost-Utility Analysis of Special Education Alternatives (Part 2)

In Example 7.1 in Chapter 7, we described an evaluation by Lewis, Johnson, Erickson, and Bruininks (1994) of three alternatives for the provision of special education alternatives.

Using multiattribute utility theory, the evaluators were able to calculate the overall utility for each alternative. As well, the evaluators estimated the costs of each alternative using an approach similar to that of Chapters 3 through 6 (Lewis et al., 1994). They created a complete list specifying all the activities and services carried out under each alternative. Then, consulting administrative records and school personnel, they identified, measured, and valued all the resources used in all aspects of service delivery. The total cost estimates for each year were divided by enrollments in order to arrive at estimates of the average cost per student per year.

(Continued)

(Continued)

Given the utilities and information on costs, it is straightforward to calculate the cost-utility (CU) ratios. These are shown in the following table:

Cost-Utility Ratios of Special Education Alternatives

	Independent District Alternative	Intermediate Alternative	Cooperative Alternative
Average cost per student per year	$51,060	$26,380	$24,490
Overall utility	63.9	70.4	65.2
Cost-utility ratio	$799	$375	$374

Source: Adapted from Lewis et al. (1994, Table 7).

Note: Adjusted to 2015 dollars.

Dividing costs by utility yields three CU ratios. These ratios can be interpreted as the annual cost per student of obtaining a one-unit increase in overall utility. However, districts must offer special educational services to students. Therefore, these ratios are most appropriately interpreted in terms of their ranks relative to each other—that is, which is the most cost-effective (rather than how much each costs "per unit of utility"). Upon examining the results, it is immediately apparent that the independent district alternative is the least attractive of the three. It is not only more costly than the other alternatives but also results in lower overall utility; its CU ratio is the highest at $799. The other two alternatives have slightly different costs and utilities. However, their CU ratios are almost identical ($375 and $374). In terms of cost-effectiveness, it appears that both alternatives are similarly attractive. When the CU ratios are equal or close, other considerations should be used in making decisions, such as ease of implementation or funding constraints.

Source: Adapted from Lewis et al. (1994).

8.2.2. Effectiveness-Cost Ratios

Some authors opt for a different approach to combining the same evidence on costs and effectiveness. In this case, an effectiveness-cost ratio is obtained by dividing the effectiveness of each alternative by its cost:

$$ECR = \frac{E}{C}$$

$$ECR = \frac{E_T - E_C}{C_T - C_C} = \frac{\Delta E}{\Delta C}$$

This ratio is interpreted as the units of effectiveness that are obtained by incurring a single unit of cost (generally a round dollar amount). For example, the ratio might be expressed as effects per $100,000 of resources. We should choose the alternatives that provide the greatest effectiveness per unit of cost. To do so, we need to rank order the alternatives, ranging from those with the largest effectiveness-cost ratios to those with the smallest. An effectiveness-cost ratio might be helpful if the decisionmaker has a fixed budget and wishes to know how much effectiveness can be "bought" with that budget.

If properly interpreted, there is no difference in the conclusions produced by calculating CE or effectiveness-cost ratios. CE studies in health are quite consistent in presenting CE ratios, a practice that has been endorsed in national guidelines (Gold, Siegel, Russell, & Weinstein, 1996; McGhan et al., 2009; Neumann, Sanders, Russell, Siegel, & Ganiat, 2016). In contrast, education studies have tended to use both of these approaches, so one should exercise care in properly interpreting the results of these studies. To standardize practices and avoid confusion, it is best to report CE ratios.

8.2.3. Expected Value Cost-Effectiveness Ratios

For CE analysis, the effectiveness measure must be univariate. But the measure can still be derived from expected values.

A simple example can be used to illustrate this calculation. The superintendent of a large urban school district recognizes that the high school dropout rate is too high. Within the next year, the district has decided to implement a program to reduce the dropout rate, although a specific plan has yet to be established. There are two main options. During the preceding year, the district had successfully implemented Program A: It prevented 95 students from dropping out and cost $200,000. Hence, there is reasonable confidence that these results can be replicated. Alternatively, a local university is currently promoting an innovative strategy to prevent dropouts (Program B). Cost analysis reveals that the program would cost half that of Program A (at $100,000). However, its effects are uncertain: There is a possibility that Program B will be (1) highly successful, reducing dropouts by 170; (2) partially successful, reducing dropouts by 75; or (3) marginally successful, reducing dropouts by 5. Based on discussions with the program designers and teachers at the school, the superintendent has estimated the probabilities of each of these outcomes occurring at approximately 0.15, 0.60, and 0.25, respectively. How can the superintendent use this information to choose between Programs A and B?

The first step is to summarize the available information in a decision tree (as per Chapter 7). If we were to choose Program A, it would lead to 95 fewer dropouts with a high degree of certainty and a CE ratio of $2,106 (200,000 ÷ 95). In the case of Program B, we calculate the expected value as the sum of the three outcomes weighted by their probabilities of occurring:

$$0.15 \times 170 + 0.60 \times 75 + 0.25 \times 5 = 71.8$$

Given the expected value of 71.8, the CE ratio for Program B is $1,394 (100,000 ÷ 71.8). Program B's CE ratio is smaller than Program A's by more than $700, suggesting that it will require fewer resources per dropout averted. As this example illustrates, using expected values to calculate effectiveness is methodologically straightforward, and an equivalent approach can be applied if there is information on the expected value of costs.

8.2.4. Hybrid Cost-Effectiveness Ratios

On occasion, evaluators may be able to place monetary values on some outcomes but not on all of them. In this case, the evaluator may be in a position to apply a hybrid of CE and benefit-cost (BC) analysis, in which the cost estimate is adjusted for any monetary benefits that might be produced. The numerator is composed of costs minus benefits, and the denominator is the same as what was previously given:

$$CER = \frac{C - B}{E}$$

To provide an illustration, let's imagine that we conducted CE analysis of two after-school tutoring programs designed to increase mathematics achievement. Thus, each alternative was evaluated according to its costs (C) and effectiveness (E) in raising math achievement. Along the way, it was discovered that the after-school programs had the inadvertent outcome of reducing the incidence of vandalism in the neighborhood. This is an important finding, but how should it be incorporated in the analysis? One possibility is to conduct a separate CE analysis, using a second measure of effectiveness (e.g., reduction in the number of crimes reported). Another option is to place a monetary value on the benefits of crime reduction. These benefits can be subtracted from program costs (C − B). The resulting costs—net of selected monetary benefits—are divided by program effectiveness in raising math achievement.

Although valid, this hybrid approach is not typically used. The specification of benefits to subtract may be considered ad hoc. Also, the CE ratio is difficult to interpret: The numerator is a net resource value, not the cost of the program.

8.3. INTERPRETING COST-EFFECTIVENESS RATIOS ●

Although mathematically simple, CE ratios require careful reporting and interpretation if they are to be useful for policymakers. There are a number of issues for understanding CE ratios and placing them in context. We specify these next. First, we begin with a simple application of CE analysis of the Talent Search program.

Talent Search is a multiyear program with the intent of increasing high school completion and access to postsecondary education. Using the ingredients method, the present value cost per student of Talent Search is estimated at $3,900 (weighted by site; Bowden, 2014). For this amount of resources, the expected gain in high school completion is 8.2 percentage points, and the expected gain in postsecondary enrollment is 10.7 percentage points compared with students who did not participate in Talent Search (Constantine, Seftor, Martin, Silva, & Myers, 2006). With this information, we can now perform CE analysis.

For ease of interpretation, it is best to express this effectiveness gain in yields—that is, counts of newly successful students relative to a school without Talent Search. (It is difficult to explain a CE ratio where the costs are divided by the percentage gains in attainment.) In the evaluation, there were 7,146 students, translating into yields of 590 new high school graduates and 768 new college enrollees. Each student (not each newly successful student) required $3,900 of resources over the years of participation, so the total cost at this scale of operation was $27.9 million.

The CE analysis is reported in Table 8.2, with the CE ratios in the bottom row. The ratios can be interpreted as cost per unit of output (or average cost). The cost per new high school graduate is $47,260, and the cost per new college enrollee is $36,310. These are the total amounts of resources required to generate an additional successful student.

Using this simple case study, we explore key issues in understanding these CE ratios. At this stage, we are presuming that the analysis has a sufficient sample size to accurately estimate costs and to detect a statistically significant effect. Here, the focus is on ensuring that the CE results are both reported and interpreted correctly.

Table 8.2   Cost-Effectiveness Ratios for Talent Search

	Compared With High School Failure	
	High School Graduation	College Enrollment
Participants	7,146	7,146
Percentage point gain	8.2	10.7
Yield (successful students) E	590	768
Social cost per participant	$3,900	$3,900
Total cost (millions) C	$27.9	$27.9
Cost-effectiveness ratio ($CER = C/E$)	$47,260	$36,310

Sources: Adapted from Bowden (2014); Bowden and Belfield (2015).

Notes: Adjusted to 2015 dollars. *CER* = cost-effectiveness ratio.

The key issues relate to program scale and how this might influence costs; effects and how valid the selected measures are for understanding CE; and finally, how to interpret the money value reflected in the CE ratio.

First, whenever comparing the CE ratios of several alternatives, the analyst should pay attention to the scale of alternatives. The scale has implications for cost because the cost per participant of the program is unlikely to be the same across different scales of operation. Hopefully, the comparison groups will be of roughly similar scales, although in some cases, they may be of vastly different scales. For example, let us say that a program in a citywide school district will cost $10,000 and reduce high school dropouts by 20 (a CE ratio of $500). A different—and much larger—program will cost $100,000 and reduce dropouts by 160 (a CE ratio of $625). Based on our decision rule, the first program appears to be more cost-effective. Nevertheless, it is also of a much smaller scale. We might choose to implement a larger version of the first program, although we cannot be certain of its CE: The effects might be diluted because of implementation problems, or average costs might be reduced because of economies of scale. For Talent Search, the total number of students in the evaluation was 7,000, but this figure was aggregated from nine sites of varying sizes. Possibly, average cost might be constant as the number of sites increases, but it might not be as the number of participants per site increases. In all cases, the analyst should think carefully about how modifications to the scale of a particular alternative might alter its effectiveness and costs (and, potentially, the CE ranking of alternatives). Preferably, CE ratios should be calculated for programs of similar scale.

Second, we should check the validity of the effectiveness measure. In the case of Talent Search, we recognize that these CE results are based on the count of newly successful students. The value of Talent Search for the participants who still failed to complete high school or failed to enroll in college is counted as zero; similarly, the value of Talent Search for the participants who would have completed high school or enrolled in college regardless of Talent Search is also counted as zero. The resources these participants use are included, but their gain from participation is treated as zero. Is this appropriate? The answer is presumably yes because this effectiveness measure—high school completion—was chosen independently as part of the impact evaluation (see Chapter 7). If it is appropriate to exclude any gains for unsuccessful students from the impact evaluation, it is presumably appropriate to exclude them from the CE analysis (although we can acknowledge that even students who did not reach the effectiveness goals may have benefited from the intervention).

Finally, we should consider how to put these dollar values in context. Is $47,260 a lot of money? Is it worth spending all this money to ensure that an additional student completes high school? Fundamentally, CE analysis cannot answer this question. The answer requires us to determine whether we are willing to pay this amount per completer, and this determination may require BC analysis. Nevertheless, some contextual responses are possible. For example, we might refer to the cost of K–12 schooling as contextual information: In 2015, average expenditure per public school student was approximately $45,000 over the four years of high school (Cornman, 2014). So, Talent Search is equivalent to proposing to spend the same amount again to ensure high school completion. Alternatively, under the performance funding formulae, we might compare this $47,260 figure with the amount of additional funding a school would receive if its high school completion rate increased (or lose if its completion rate fell). If an agency performed a lot of analyses, it might even establish a CE threshold. So, the agency might be willing to fund interventions that could yield new high school graduates as long as the entire resource cost was less than $50,000, for example. This approach is used in some health care rationing contexts (Neumann et al., 2016).

It is worth emphasizing that the CE ratio is a metric to help policymakers understand efficiency in a general way. Cost analysis is used to understand costs; an impact evaluation is used to determine effectiveness. The CE ratio is an efficiency metric. If the CE ratio is $10,000 per one-unit effect size gain, for example, this does not imply either that $10,000 in additional expenditures is necessary or that the given intervention will yield a one-unit gain in effectiveness. Strictly, it means that an intervention with this CE ratio is twice as cost-effective as an intervention with a CE ratio of $20,000.

8.4. EXPLAINING COST-EFFECTIVENESS RATIOS

8.4.1. Asymmetry of Cost-Effectiveness Ratios

The CE ratio is a ratio, so it matters whether the result is derived from negative or positive numbers (and the ratio becomes undefined if effectiveness is zero). Most of the time, the intervention under consideration requires extra resources and might therefore be expected to show some positive impact. But this need not be the case: Some programs may have adverse effects or save on resources. The analyst must therefore check the signs of costs and effects before calculating the ratios.

This caution is illustrated in Table 8.3 for four hypothetical versions of a program that is compared with results for a given control school. Of the four versions, Program A is clearly the most cost-effective: It has lower costs along with positive effects. The CE ratio is –$500: The policymaker is saving money by implementing Program A. Program B is the least preferred program (having high costs and negative effects). Yet Program B has the same CE ratio as Program A. As well, Programs C and D have the same CE ratio (as each other) but have very different implications: Program C is more expensive but more effective, raising the question as to whether the program can be afforded; Program D is less expensive but also less effective, raising the question as to whether

Table 8.3   Cost-Effectiveness Ratios and Negative Numbers

	Incremental Costs	Incremental Effects	Cost-Effectiveness Ratio
Program A	–$1,000	2	–$500
Program B	$1,000	–2	–$500
Program C	$1,000	2	$500
Program D	–$1,000	–2	$500

worse outcomes are acceptable. Hence, the evaluator must check that all the signs are aligned when reporting CE ratios.

Also, Table 8.3 illustrates a more general issue in understanding CE ratios. The results are not continuous or symmetric around zero (Briggs, O'Brien, & Blackhouse, 2002). For example, if Program B_2 costs $1,000 but has incremental effects of –5, it is clearly worse than Program B; but the cost-effectiveness ratio for Program B_2 (at –$200) is lower than for Program B. Consequently, hypothesis testing becomes complicated if the CE ratios have confidence intervals where the numerators and denominators are not the same sign. We address this uncertainty in Chapter 11.

8.4.2. Cost-Effectiveness Planes

One approach to aid interpretation of CE results is to draw a CE plane. As was illustrated in Table 8.3, there are four possible outcomes depending on whether an intervention is more or less costly and more or less effective. We can represent these outcomes as quadrants to create a CE plane.

This plane is shown as Figure 8.1. Interventions can be compared with the status quo of zero effect and zero cost (the origin). Interventions located in Quadrant A are clearly dominant: They are lower cost and more effective. Interventions located in Quadrant B are inferior: They are higher cost and less effective than the comparison. Quadrants C and D illustrate the trade-off: Greater effectiveness requires more resources. The analyst might make the case that interventions in Quadrant D should be rejected under the "do no harm" principle. If so, interventions are preferred insofar as they are the furthest to the northeast in Quadrant C.

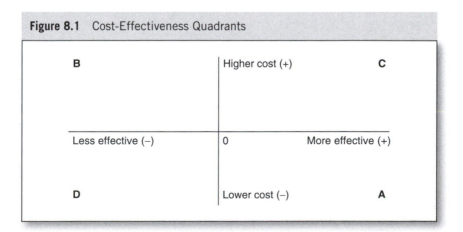

Figure 8.1   Cost-Effectiveness Quadrants

B	Higher cost (+)	C
Less effective (–)	0	More effective (+)
D	Lower cost (–)	A

An example is shown as Figure 8.2, using data for the nine Talent Search sites analyzed by Bowden and Belfield (2015). Each site has its own CE ratio based on the resources used and effectiveness at increasing high school graduation rates (the average across the nine sites is indicated by the marker "All9").

The lines divide the CE space in Figure 8.2 into the quadrants of the plane. All but one of the sites is in Quadrant C, with higher cost but also positive effects relative to the status quo. One site is in Quadrant B and hence is inferior, having positive costs but negative effects.

The advantage of the CE plane is that we can overlay a willingness-to-pay threshold. The threshold is calculated for values of costs and effects that yield a given CE ratio. For example, an intervention costing $1,000 with an effect of 0.5 is equally preferred to an intervention costing $1,100 with an effect of 0.55; for both interventions the CE ratio is $2,000. Hence, we can generalize that any intervention with estimates for costs and effects such that their ratio equals $2,000 is equally preferred. Given a value for the ratio, we can draw a line on the plane through points that will yield this value. In health economics,

Figure 8.2   Cost-Effectiveness Plane: Talent Search (Eight Sites)

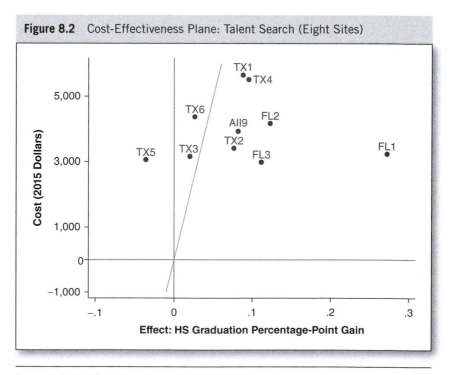

Source: Adapted from Bowden and Belfield (2015).

this value is referred to as the maximum acceptable incremental cost-effectiveness ratio (ICER; see Gray, Clarke, Wolstenholme, & Wordsworth, 2011, p. 12). As discussed previously, CE analysis cannot provide us with the specific value that is preferred; it should be determined from our willingness to pay for educational outcomes.

This threshold is shown as the positively sloped willingness-to-pay line in Figure 8.2. This line is drawn on the assumption that willingness to pay per new high school completer is $100,000; any point on the line has a ratio equal to $100,000. (This number might be derived based on studies that find each new high school completer will earn $100,000 extra over his or her lifetime, for example). This line divides Quadrant C into two areas. Interventions in the area to the left of the threshold are rejected by the policymaker. Although they are effective, their cost is such that they are too expensive relative to our willingness to pay of $100,000; alternatively expressed, given their cost, these interventions are not sufficiently effective to satisfy our willingness-to-pay criterion. Now, only interventions in Quadrant C to the right of the threshold are acceptable: They are sufficiently effective or sufficiently low cost that they are justifiable based on willingness to pay. If we are prepared to have negative effects, the threshold also divides interventions in Quadrant D into those that satisfy our willingness to pay (those to the right of the threshold) and those that do not (those to the left of the threshold). Hence, the willingness-to-pay line attenuates the number of acceptable interventions (recognizing that interventions in Quadrant A were always justifiable).

8.4.3. Incremental Cost-Effectiveness Analysis

Strictly, each CE ratio is calculated for the level of output achieved by that intervention. So, in the example from Table 8.1, the class size reduction cost of $181 relates to achievement gain of 0.07 in mathematics or 0.04 in reading. If we desired magnitudes that were twice these, we would need to extrapolate how much it would cost to yield an achievement gain of double that size for mathematics and reading (0.14 and 0.08) respectively; it might be exactly $362, it might be more, or it might be less.

But, if we are considering "buying" achievement gains, we might want to know what it would cost across the range of achievement levels. Also, if the most cost-effective intervention increases achievement by only a small amount, we might ask whether another—more effective—intervention might also be implemented to increase achievement even more (or if a higher dosage of the preferred intervention might be given). This additional intervention would be implemented on top of the initial intervention. Finally, a policymaker might prefer to evaluate interventions based on their costs, looking to see how much additional achievement can be obtained if more resources are allocated. In effect, the policymaker might want to look at a menu of options with increasing budget constraints but also increasing effectiveness. For instance, a school principal might decide to reduce class sizes, knowing that this will require extra resources but will boost achievement, but then she might ask whether higher-quality teachers should also be recruited, raising costs even more, but also boosting achievement even further. To make the right decision the principal would need to know the changes in costs, the respective changes in achievement, and hence the changes in the CE ratio.

To address these issues, we can modify the approach used by health researchers to calculate ICERs. We illustrate incremental CE using simulated data as per Table 8.4. There are nine interventions (S1–S9), listed in ascending order of cost per student (C) with each intervention intended

Table 8.4   Incremental Cost-Effectiveness Ratios

| Interventions | Cost (C) | Test Score Gain (E) | Incremental Cost-Effectiveness Ratios After Eliminating | |
			Strictly Dominated Interventions	Weakly Dominated Interventions
S9	$2,520	0.112	$22,500	—
S5	$2,680	–0.035	—	—
S3	$2,770	0.021	—	—
S7	$2,820	0.140	$10,720	—
S2	$2,870	0.077	—	—
S8	$3,010	0.176	$9,500	$17,100
S6	$3,840	0.190	$59,290	—
S1	$4,800	0.211	$45,710	$51,140
S4	$4,830	0.096	—	—

Source: Adapted from Bowden and Belfield (2015).

to increase test scores (E). At issue is how to adjudicate among these interventions when our objective is to maximize achievement while recognizing that resources are scarce and that, as we increase spending, we would expect higher achievement.

Viewed independently without regard to any specific increase in achievement, we can calculate CE ratios as C/E relative to the status quo of no intervention. Thus, S8 is the most cost-effective intervention (CER = \$3,010/0.176 = \$17,100). S5 is rejected immediately on the "do no harm" principle, and S6 is then the least cost-effective (CER = \$3,840/0.027 = \$142,220). However, S8 produces a test score gain of only 0.186, and there are two interventions (S6 and S1) that produce larger gains. The policymaker—recognizing an imperative to increase achievement as much as possible—might wish to adjudicate between these interventions as well as S8.

To illustrate, we assume that each intervention can be applied to augment the others—that is, that S9 can be added onto intervention S6 to yield incremental test score gains (for another example, see Boardman, Greenberg, Vining, & Weimer, 2011, pp. 465–467). If so, we can perform the following steps as shown in Columns 3 and 4 of Table 8.4. First, we excise the strictly dominated interventions—that is, ones that are more expensive and less effective than the preceding one. So, S5 is more expensive and less effective than S9, so it is eliminated from consideration. Similarly, S3 is eliminated (now strictly inferior to S9), as is S2 (versus S7), and S4 (versus S7). Having eliminated these strictly inferior interventions, we calculate the ICER—that is, the ratio of each intervention relative to the next lowest cost one. For example, the ICER for intervention S6 equals $(C_{S6} - C_{S8})/(E_{S6} - E_{S8})$. These ICERs are given in the fourth column of Table 8.4. Now, to yield a test score gain of 0.176, S8 should be implemented: With a cost of \$3,010, this yields a CE ratio of \$17,100. Up to this test score gain, the policymaker would be "buying" test score gains at \$17,100 per unit by implementing S8 (but would be paying more using the less effective interventions sequentially). To further raise test scores from 0.176 to 0.211, the CE ratio is \$51,140. Beyond a gain of 0.176, the policymaker would be "buying" test score gains at \$51,140 per unit.

Thus, these ICERs allow the analyst to present a continuum of outcomes to the decisionmaker who, in principle, could select any amount of effectiveness. Again, we emphasize that CE analysis cannot determine whether the policymaker should be willing to pay these amounts for these test score gains. This analysis only provides information on the resource-achievement trade-off, similar to the production-possibility relationship in input-output space.

8.4.4. Cost-Effectiveness Analysis With Induced Costs

So far, the only costs we have considered have been those that are required to implement an intervention. However, as discussed in Chapters 4 and 5, many educational interventions are likely to create induced costs—that is, require resources beyond those needed for implementation. Examples include diagnostic tests in which different test results will have different consequences. For example, college remediation or other placement tests will have consequences for how many and which courses must be taken to gain college credit or to be eligible for a given major. Each induces potential further costs depending upon diagnostic outcomes or which school will accept a student in the case of testing for selective schools. In these cases, the CE ratio should be calculated based on all the resources that generate the effects.

We illustrate this using a simple example from the City Connects program (Bowden et al., 2016). As discussed previously, City Connects helps students by designing an individualized set of services to address their academic, social-emotional, family, and health needs. The cost of the City Connects program is $1,540 per student. However, students then receive the individualized services through community partner organizations (or in after-school programs); these services are extra beyond the services received by students who have not participated in City Connects. These additional services—the induced costs of the program—have been estimated at $3,030 per student.

There is evidence that City Connects is successful at boosting student achievement. Relative to nonparticipants, City Connects students exhibited an effect size gain of 0.39 in English language arts and mathematics (Walsh et al., 2014, Table 7). This gain was measured in eighth grade—that is, after the students received City Connects services and the induced services from community partners. Therefore, both sets of costs should be included in the CE ratio.

As shown in Table 8.5, the CE ratio for City Connects is $11,720. That is, a one-unit increase in eighth-grade achievement requires $11,720 in total resources. However, when induced costs are excluded, the CE ratio is considerably lower, at $3,950. This sizable difference arises because most of the resources associated with City Connects actually derive from the change in resources provided by the community partners. In this example, the induced costs are particularly salient such that the cost to the school per student is considerably less than the total cost of the intervention. As described in detail in Bowden and

Table 8.5   Cost-Effectiveness Analysis With Induced Costs: The City
Connects Program

	Core + Estimated Service Change	Core + No Difference in Service
Effect size gain in eighth grade (E)	0.39	0.39
Core cost of City Connects services	$1,540	$1,540
Induced service cost	$3,030	$0
Total cost (C)	$4,570	$1,540
Cost-effectiveness ratio (CER = C/E)	$11,720	$3,950

Sources: Effectiveness measure: Walsh et al. (2014, Table 7). Costs: Bowden et al. (2016).

Notes: Present value at kindergarten (3.5% discount rate, adjusted to 2013 dollars). CER = cost-effectiveness ratio.

colleagues (2016), however, many interventions may have induced costs that should be incorporated into the CE analysis.

8.5. EVIDENCE ON COST-EFFECTIVE INTERVENTIONS   ●

The range of potential interventions directed toward improving educational outcomes is vast (Chandra, Jena, & Skinner, 2011; Cook et al., 2014; Dhaliwal et al., 2012). There is potential for reform across the entire education production function within schools and colleges (from changing incentives for teachers to massive open online learning courses). There is also significant potential for reforms outside the schoolhouse, including interventions to help families and promote child health. Clearly, policymakers need a method by which to evaluate and compare across these reforms.

CE analysis is growing in practice, partly in response to this need. Hollands et al. (2014) performed CE analysis of seven literacy interventions for students in early grades (see also Ingle & Cramer, 2013). Wang et al. (2008) evaluated how cost-effective an array of after-school programs are at reducing obesity. In a review of a range of separate policies, Yeh (2010) reviewed a range of separate policies and how their CE differs in terms of boosting achievement (for an analysis on the CE of Success for All, see Borman & Hewes, 2002). Even with these studies, however, the growth of CE in educational research is still slow and not always based strictly on the ingredients method. Also, it is growing from a very small base (Clune, 2002; Hummel-Rossi & Ashdown, 2002).

Notably, educational interventions in developing countries are increasingly being evaluated using experimental methods; as discussed in Chapter 7, these methods are particularly amenable to CE analysis. Table 8.6 summarizes evidence on the CE of educational interventions at boosting academic achievement in elementary school (for CE of interventions boosting attendance, see Evans & Popova, 2014, Table 4; see also Dhaliwal et al., 2012; McEwan, 2012; and evidence from the Abdul Latif Jameel Poverty Action Lab [J-PAL] at www.povertyactionlab.org). This evidence, along with the other studies cited in this chapter, illustrates several key conclusions from CE analysis.

First, there are many different interventions that can be compared using CE analysis. Table 8.6, which is by no means exhaustive, includes reforms to teacher incentives, local elections, textbooks, and

Table 8.6 Cost-Effectiveness Ratios: Elementary School Interventions

Country/Intervention	Social Cost (PPP)	Effect Size Gain	Cost-Effectiveness Ratio per One-Unit Effect Size Gain
India:			
Incentives for teacher attendance	$21.04	0.150	$140
Remedial tutoring by contract teacher	$12.81	0.086	$150
Computer-assisted instruction	$89.10	0.013	$6,850
Indonesia:			
Linkage school committee (village)	$0.69	0.069	$10
Election of school committee (village)	$1.95	0.061	$30

Country/Intervention	Social Cost (PPP)	Effect Size Gain	Cost-Effectiveness Ratio per One-Unit Effect Size Gain
Kenya:			
Ability tracking	$1.17	0.176	$10
Teacher performance incentives (group)	$2.00	0.046	$40
Scholarships for high-performing students	$35.65	0.190	$190
Textbooks	$8.36	0.018	$460
Class size reduction	$26.97	0.015	$1,800
Madagascar:			
Information about returns to schooling	$0.43	0.202	<$1
Philippines:			
Libraries, teacher training	$23.07	0.030	$770

Source: Adapted from McEwan (2015, Figure 4).

Notes: PPP = purchasing power parity. Where multiple evaluations of intervention, highest CE ratio selected. CE ratios reported regardless of precision of outcome estimate.

class size reduction. We eschew ranking these interventions because of differences in the scale of each intervention and in educational contexts across the countries. Nevertheless, it is helpful to see the magnitudes of difference in CE; also, as the evidence base grows, our confidence in the ordering of cost-effective interventions should also increase. Second, the most effective interventions are not necessarily the most cost-effective. Some interventions may have very modest effects, but if they are very low cost they can be highly cost-effective. As such, there is no reason why policy recommendations should be based simply on "what works"; it is necessary to know "at what cost." Finally, there are very large differences in CE across interventions. There is no obvious correlation between costs and effects; hence, there is no expectation that the ratio of the two will be narrowly bounded. See Example 8.2.

Example 8.2   Cost-Effectiveness Analysis of Interventions to Improve High School Completion

In recent decades, the U.S. high school graduation rate has been flat: More than 28 million U.S. adults did not complete high school, and these adults are disproportionately from disadvantaged backgrounds. Increasing the high school completion rate is a national priority (Rumberger, 2011). At issue is how to do so using the least amount of resources.

Hollands et al. (2014) investigated which interventions were the most cost-effective. Interventions were selected that met high methodological standards for identifying postive effects (as established by the U.S. Department of Education What Works Clearinghouse). Although most interventions did not have sufficient or available data to rigorously estimate costs, it was possible to calculate CE ratios for five programs: (1) Talent Search, (2) Job Corps, (3) JOBSTART, (4) New Chance, and (5) National Guard Youth ChalleNGe Program (NGYCP). The results are given in the following table.

Cost-Effectiveness Ratios for Programs for High School Completion

	For Students in School	For Youth Who Have Dropped Out of School		For Young Mothers (Dropouts)
	Talent Search	NGYCP	Job Corps	JOBSTART	New Chance
Program scale	3,930	596	3,940	1,028	1,240
Baseline graduation rate	71.8%	67.3%	34.4%	29.3%	49.5%
Percentage point gain from program	10.8	19.8	17.0	15.1	9.2
Yield of new graduates	423	118	670	155	113
Cost per participant	$3,590	$15,370	$24,300	$11,400	$19,420
CE ratio cost per extra graduate	$33,270	$77,630	$142,940	$75,770	$212,160
Yield of extra graduates per $100,000	3.3	1.4	0.8	1.4	0.5

Source: Adapted from Hollands et al. (2014, Table 2).

Note: Adjusted to 2015 dollars. NGYCP = National Guard Youth ChalleNGe Program.

The previously stated programs exhibit substantially different CE ratios, from \$33,270 to \$212,160 per new high school graduate. Sensitivity analysis indicated that the CE ratios varied across sites and contexts. Moreover, as the authors discuss in detail, these overall results need to be put in context. Notably, the interventions were targeted at different groups of high school dropouts. Talent Search is targeted to students who are still in school and are at risk of dropping, New Chance is for young mothers who have already dropped out, and the other three programs are for youth who have already dropped out. Each group faces a different set of obstacles to completing a high school diploma. Program differences are reflected in the baseline graduation rates (from 29% to 72%), the incremental effectiveness, and the cost per participant; each of these factors strongly affects the program CE. Nevertheless, these CE ratios provide useful information to policymakers as to the challenges and resource requirements to boost high school completion rates.

Source: Adapted by Hollands et al. (2014).

In fact, CE results can exhibit heterogeneity across several dimensions. (We distinguish heterogeneity from uncertainty, which is covered in Chapter 11.) Many educational programs are differentially effective (e.g., by sex or race) and vary in implementation; it is therefore likely that they will generate different CE ratios in different contexts.

The importance of analyzing the distribution of effects among students was demonstrated in the CE study by Quinn, Van Mondfrans, and Worthen (1984). The authors compared the effectiveness and costs of two instructional approaches to fifth-grade mathematics instruction in a Utah school district: one was a locally developed program with individualized instruction (Goal-Based Educational Management System Proficiency Mathematics, GEMS Math); the other was a more traditional, text-based approach (Text Math). Students in the GEMS Math classes had higher mathematics achievement scores than those in the traditional classes, after controlling for socioeconomic status (SES). The cost analysis revealed that GEMS Math required more resources than Text Math: The annual cost per pupil of the former was \$770, compared with \$520 for the latter. Initially, the authors calculated a single CE ratio for each program, dividing costs by program effects. These revealed that the GEMS Math cost \$31 per raw score point on the Iowa Test of Basic Skills, while Text Math cost \$36 per point: Therefore, GEMS Math was more cost-effective. Subsequently, the authors calculated several estimates of effectiveness for different socioeconomic groups. In concert with costs, these were used to calculate CE ratios for each level of SES.

These CE ratios are shown in Table 8.7. Based on these results, the GEMS Math curriculum was considerably more cost-effective for low and medium SES students (i.e., the cost per score point for GEMS Math is uniformly lower). On the other hand, the GEMS curriculum was slightly less cost-effective for high-SES students. The results provide useful information to decisionmakers. If a single math program is to be applied to a district with a heterogeneous group of students, it appears GEMS Math is the best option. If implemented in a rather high-SES district, the evidence provides some support for Text Math as the most cost-effective option.

Another source of heterogeneity occurs across sites for a given program. As discussed in Chapter 3 for Read 180 and other programs, the cost to implement a given program can differ significantly across sites. Coupled with differences in effectiveness, CE ratios can differ substantially across sites.

This variation is shown in Table 8.8 for the CE of Talent Search across nine sites in Texas and Florida. For CE ratios for high school completion, sites vary from $11,800 up to $149,800 (and one negative site where the Talent Search program appears to reduce high school completion rates). For CE ratios for college enrollment, sites vary from $9,210 to $183,880. Interpreted as if the policymaker is "buying" completion or college access, the sites offer substantially different value for money. However, there is also heterogeneity across effectiveness measures. Two sites (Florida Site One and Site Three) are the most cost-effective regardless of the effectiveness measure chosen. However, the ranks of the other sites vary depending on whether the policymaker is interested in improving high school completion rates or college enrollment.

Table 8.7   Cost-Effectiveness Ratios for Heterogeneous Groups

Socioeconomic Status	Cost-Effectiveness Ratio Cost per Raw Score Point ITBS	
	Text Math	GEMS Math
High	$22	$27
Medium high	$27	$29
Medium	$36	$31
Medium low	$52	$33
Low	$96	$35

Source: Adapted from Quinn et al. (1984, Table 7).

Note: Adjusted to 2015 dollars.

Table 8.8 Cost-Effectiveness of Talent Search by Site

Site	Cost-Effectiveness Ratio Cost per Extra High School Completer	Rank	Cost-Effectiveness Ratio Cost per Extra College Enrollee	Rank
Texas				
Site One	$62,210	6	$78,620	8
Site Two	$44,210	4	$21,060	3
Site Three	$149,800	7	$43,690	4
Site Four	$58,420	5	$183,880	9
Site Five	–$87,300	9	$62,350	6
Site Six	$161,420	8	$62,260	5
Florida				
Site One	$11,800	1	$9,210	1
Site Two	$33,840	3	$64,790	7
Site Three	$26,530	2	$20,930	2
Average	$47,260		$36,310	

Source: Adapted from Bowden and Belfield (2015).

Notes: Rounded 2015 dollars. The average is weighted by number of students served per site.

8.6. CONCLUSIONS ●

This chapter described how to combine estimates of costs with measures of effectiveness for an educational intervention relative to a counterfactual or the status quo. The basic idea of a CE ratio is straightforward. This ratio is intended to help answer the following question: Given the objectives, what is the least costly way to achieve those objectives? However, the meaning of this ratio and how to explain it to policymakers is not always simple. Hence, in the first instance, it is necessary to deliberatively report costs, effects, and their combination. To further elucidate the results from CE analysis, it may be appropriate to extend the analysis as discussed previously through the use the alternative metrics, the depiction of a CE plane, and the application of incremental CE analysis.

As a final contribution, in this chapter we reviewed some of the available evidence on CE. The evidence is growing, albeit from a small base and not especially rapidly. As such, there is limited guidance for policymakers on what interventions are the most cost-effective at achieving a given set of objectives. There are several reasons for this (see the discussion in Levin, 2001). First, much of the current evidence in education research has not developed in a way that optimizes decisionmaking by allowing interventions to be easily compared against each other. CE analysis—with its emphasis on explicitly comparative methodology—illuminates the challenges in comparing interventions of different scales, for different populations at different time periods. Second, the existing evidence yields CE results that often have very wide ranges and so are not regarded with confidence. This imprecision may arise primarily because of imprecision in estimated costs and impacts rather than their covariance (Evans & Popova, 2014). Finally, many educational researchers appear to reject a basic presumption of CE analysis: that the outcomes of an educational program can be evaluated with a univariate measure (even when that measure is a composite of many separate measures). This rejection is sometimes for good reason, but it raises equally valid questions about the value of impact evaluations generally, independently of CE analysis. Of course, when there are concerns about the validity of research findings, the appropriate response is to check the results and retest and to engage in sensitivity analysis. We outline how this checking and retesting can be done for CE analysis in Chapter 11.

Discussion Questions

1. Describe how you would interpret a CE ratio. Why is it considered a comparative metric?

2. Why is it helpful to draw the CE plane if you have already reported the CE ratio?

3. Different educational alternatives have different educational results among different student groups (e.g., disadvantaged versus advantaged, males versus females). How can CU analysis be used to consider these distributional effects as well as the overall educational results of each alternative?

4. Assume that you derive CE results for a group of alternative interventions for a single school. The school district wants to know if the same CE findings are applicable for the entire school district. How would you go about making this determination?

Exercises

1. A school district is concerned about its shortages of mathematics and science teachers. An advisory group suggests the following alternative solutions to the problem.

    a. Pay salary differentials to attract more mathematics and science teachers.

    b. Ask local industry to contribute teaching time from among their scientists and mathematicians.

    c. Use computer-assisted instruction and online video lectures, in conjunction with college mathematics and science students, to offer instruction.

    Design CE analysis that can evaluate these alternatives and help the district select the one that will be most preferable.

2. A school district is struggling to improve its high school graduation and college completion rates. Two programs are considered as alternatives to add to the regular school day and for students in the summer between eighth and ninth grade. Program A is a highly concentrated one-time program that provides students with a summer course on a college campus that improves their critical thinking skills. The summer program costs $2,400 per student and can serve 1,000 eighth graders. Of the participants, approximately 66% both finish high school and receive their bachelor's degree after finishing college in four years; this is an improvement of 27 percentage points above what would have happened in absence of the intervention. Program B provides summer assistance to students from low-income households. The assistance is on an annual basis throughout the high school and college years and is "just in time" to reflect the students' needs at that point in their academic experience. Program B costs $400 per student per summer and can serve 500 students. Of those students attending this program, 90% finish high school and 60% go on to finish a BA degree from college in four years. These rates equate to an increase in high school graduation by 25 percentage points and in college graduation by 21 percentage points compared with what would have happened in absence of the program.

    a. What is the measure of effectiveness?

    b. How much effectiveness is generated?

c. Does the measure capture most of the program impacts?

d. What is the total cost of each program?

e. What is the effect of discounting costs after Year 1?

f. Which program is more cost-effective?

g. Is the CE ratio the best measure of program impact?

h. Which program would you recommend?

i. Why might your recommendation differ from your answer to (f)?

3. You are considering eight alternative programs for increasing reading test scores. You have measured the costs and the effects, in average effect sizes on the Dynamic Indicators of Basic Early Literacy Skills (DIBELS) assessments. The programs, labeled Programs A through H, have the following costs and test score gains, measured in effect sizes or standard deviation units:

Program	Cost	DIBELS Test Score Gain
A	$1,660	0.087
B	$1,800	0.19
C	$3,130	0.235
D	$1,470	0.077
E	$2,280	0.138
F	$2,800	0.211
G	$3,120	0.229
H	–$2,770	–0.021

a. Which programs are strongly dominated?

b. Calculate the ICERs for the programs.

c. Which programs are weakly dominated?

d. Among the remaining programs, which is preferred? Why?

9

Estimating Benefits

Objectives

1. Present the conceptual underpinnings for estimating benefits.

2. Present methods for estimating the monetary benefits of education.

3. Calculate the present value investment stream benefits of education.

4. Describe benefit-transfer practices.

In order to perform benefit-cost (BC) analysis, we need to translate educational consequences into money values. We refer to these value consequences as benefits expressed in monetary terms. In theory, many outcomes of education can be expressed in dollar values. Does a particular kind of vocational training tend to raise the wages of participating workers? Does early childhood education reduce the likelihood that individuals will eventually commit crimes as adults (thereby reducing the costs of crime)? Do behavioral programs in school reduce bullying (and so reduce teacher time spent on disciplinary matters)? In these and other cases, an integral step in BC analysis is expression of the outcomes of an educational intervention in monetary terms.

The basic economic concept for expressing outcomes in monetary terms is willingness to pay. All resources are scarce and so we ask what society or the individual or the taxpayer is willing to pay for each outcome. If we committed to an antibullying program that reduced the number of bullying cases by 1,000, what would this reduction be worth? In order to compare this outcome with the costs of the program, we need to know how much we value reduced bullying. Similarly, educational interventions improve health status: Young adults who complete a four-year degree are 60% less likely to smoke, 14% less to be obese, and 38% less likely to report depression than those who complete a two-year degree (Rosenbaum, 2012; see also Cutler & Lleras-Muney, 2010). In order to justify spending money on college programs, these health status impacts, which are clearly an important benefit from education, need to be translated into dollars.

Of course, one of the main consequences of education is that it boosts earnings and, as such, the impacts are already in monetary terms. However, for outcomes that are not directly expressed in dollars, we need to find a shadow price—that is, a willingness to pay for that outcome. There are several methods for finding such prices, including the defensive expenditures method and the hedonic method; these methods use changes in behavior to derive willingness to pay for education. Another option is the stated preference approach using contingent valuation surveys based on respondents' views about the value of education (see also Boardman, Greenberg, Vining, & Weimer, 2011, Chapter 15). In this approach, people are asked what they think each educational outcome is worth. Each of these methods has advantages and disadvantages, but together they offer an array of options for putting money values on nonmarket effects. Applying these methods allows us to estimate all the benefits resulting from a particular education program. Once these benefits are monetized, they can be combined with costs to perform the BC analysis.

In this chapter, we describe how to think about benefits in terms of willingness to pay. Next, we discuss how benefits should be specified in terms of shadow prices so that they are valid for use in an economic analysis. Then we review the methods by which we can place actual numbers on the outcomes of education. Finally, we describe how existing shadow prices can be applied across studies.

Throughout this discussion, we assume that the analyst has measured the effects and outcomes appropriately using a rigorous identification strategy. Given valid measures of educational outcomes, in this chapter we investigate what these measures are valued at in dollars. This valuation is a prelude to performing BC analysis, which we do in the next chapter.

9.1. THE CONCEPT OF BENEFITS ●

Some advantages of education lend themselves to being expressed in units of currency, such as higher earnings. Other outcomes are harder to place in monetary terms, such as the increased self-esteem or happiness produced by higher achievement or changes in health status. At least conceptually, however, economists use a similar approach in placing monetary values on all outcomes: We determine the maximum amount that each individual affected by a program would be willing to pay to receive such outcomes. The sum of every individual's maximum willingness to pay provides an estimate of the total benefits.

The notion of willingness to pay is best explained with an example. Suppose that the government funded a literacy program that succeeded in improving the reading ability of a small group of adults. The participants reap a broad range of "benefits" from participating in the program that are probably greater than $1 and less than $1 billion. To narrow the range, we require a means of structuring our thinking about the nature of benefits.

Let us assume that each individual derives increasing amounts of utility (or satisfaction) from two things: (1) income y and (2) literacy l (see Johannesson, 1996). Each participant in the hypothetical program began with a certain amount of each at time zero, which produced an initial level of utility:

$$u = u(y_0, l_0)$$

Upon program completion, the new (and higher) level of literacy is l_1, which leads to an even higher level of utility. To place a monetary value on the literacy gains, we could ask each individual to conduct a simple thought experiment. In the wake of the program—and the literacy gains that it brings about—how much income must individuals give up in order to return to the *initial* level of utility? This requires each individual to attach a specific monetary valuation to the literacy outcomes that they receive. The amount is referred to as that individual's willingness to pay (WTP) for a specific level of literacy (more technical discussions in welfare economics refer to it as the "compensating variation"). The same idea is expressed by the following equality:

$$u(y_0, l_0) = u(y_1 - WTP, l_1)$$

The left-hand side indicates the amount of utility produced by initial levels of literacy and income. Utility on the right-hand side is the same—despite a higher level of literacy—because income is reduced by the amount *WTP*. Again, the amount represents an individual's willingness to pay for added literacy, based on a personal valuation of literacy benefits. By summing the maximum WTP of each individual affected by the program, we arrive at the total program benefits.

Figure 9.1 gives a visual depiction of one individual's willingness to pay for increasing amounts of literacy. It is a demand curve for literacy that traces how the quantity demanded increases as the price declines. Economists refer to it as a utility-compensated demand curve, because the initial level of utility is held constant at all points on the curve. As the quantity of literacy increases—leading to increased utility—a downward adjustment to money income is made "behind the scenes" in order to preserve the initial level of utility.

In our hypothetical example, the true price of literacy is fixed at zero because program participants do not pay a fee. Nevertheless, the curve still provides an estimate of the individual's willingness to pay for different quantities of literacy and, hence, the benefits received. In this case, the program increases the individual's literacy from l_0 to l_1, and the willingness to pay for this outcome is given by the area underneath the demand curve, between l_0 and l_1. The area is equivalent to WTP in the previous equation. As before, the willingness-to-pay estimates for each person affected by the program are summed to arrive at a measure of total program benefits.

The concept of willingness to pay is a powerful one for at least two reasons. First, it does not place undue restrictions on the categories of

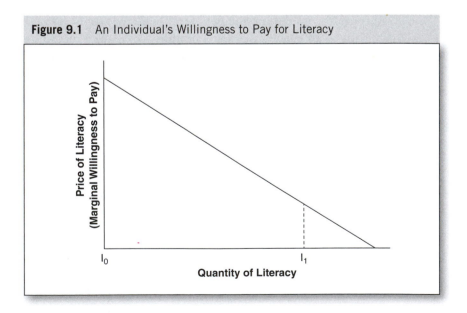

Figure 9.1   An Individual's Willingness to Pay for Literacy

benefits that we might consider. As we shall see, many BC analyses focus narrowly on earnings as the only measure of educational benefits. By neglecting other outcomes, the benefits could be severely understated. Thus, the conceptual framework serves as a constant reminder that we should cast the widest possible net when delineating and measuring program benefits.

Second, the conceptual framework encompasses the benefits received by every individual who is directly or indirectly affected by the program or alternative under consideration—and not just those who are its immediate targets. (Demand curves can be summed across all who express a willingness to pay.) The goal is to obtain a broad estimate of the benefits that accrue to program participants as well as to other members of society (the benefits to those outside the program are often referred to as "externalities" by economists). In this respect, it parallels our discussion of costs in Chapters 3 through 6, where we emphasized the importance of measuring the costs to all groups of stakeholders in society, ranging from program participants to the government.

As one might imagine, the conceptual framework is almost never fully implemented. In an ideal world, we could costlessly obtain accurate information on each individual's maximum willingness to pay for valuable outcomes. In practice, demand curves such as those in Figure 9.1 are not readily available, because of data limitations or simply because many goods and services never pass through markets that would allow prices to be attached to them. Therefore, evaluators rely upon several practical alternatives to obtain estimates of program benefits. The next section describes several of these. When considering these methods and their applications in education, it is always helpful to keep the prior conceptual framework in mind. As one observer noted, "All . . . methods of valuing benefits in monetary terms are to be judged in terms of the closeness with which they approximate [willingness to pay]" (Pauly, 1995, p. 103). Fundamentally, the concept forces us to think: How much scarce resource should we give up for a program that increases literacy by a given amount?

9.2. SPECIFYING BENEFITS •

We now apply this concept of willingness to pay by specifying benefits for use in BC analysis. This is a three-step process: First, we discover the effects of the program (e.g., increased test scores or attainment); second, we calculate a shadow price based on willingness to pay (e.g., the value to the economy of higher test scores or greater levels of attainment); and then to get the benefits, we multiply the size of the effect by the shadow price. So if an intervention increases test scores by 0.5 standard deviations and the shadow price of a test score is $1,000 per standard deviation gain, then the intervention conveys benefits worth $500.

Therefore, the analyst has to think about what effects will occur and how these can be shadow priced. For BC analysis, this is a joint exercise: There is little point in estimating impacts for which there are no shadow prices, and there is little point in performing the analysis if there is no evidence on impacts for the outcomes that have the highest shadow prices. Also, the analyst should consult with key stakeholders and those delivering the program to identify the most important impacts.

In theory, shadow prices can be derived for any impact and from any perspective. The vast majority of studies focus on earnings as the benefit from education, but there are many effects that might also be considered. For instance, a program may increase student engagement, and this increase could be shadow priced in terms of what the college would be willing to pay to have more engaged students. Table 9.1 illustrates some of the effects of more education that may have shadow prices placed on them. As shown, many varied impacts might be shadow priced.

From an economic perspective, impacts are easier to assess with a shadow price if they readily correspond to observed behaviors as opposed to knowledge, attitudes, or opinions (Duckworth & Yeager, 2015). For example, more educated persons are less likely to smoke (Cutler & Lleras-Muney, 2010), presumably because they know more about health conditions (e.g., that smoking causes lung cancer). It is easier to shadow price the difference in behavior (not smoking) than the difference in knowledge motivating the behavior (knowing smoking is bad for one's health). A full discussion of this issue— behaviors and skills over knowledge—is given by Heckman and Kautz (2012), and examples for socioemotional learning interventions are reviewed by Jones, Karoly, Crowley, and Greenberg (2015) and Belfield et al. (2015). Attitudes or opinions can be shadow priced if there is a clear link with willingness to pay, but behavioral changes are easier and more direct.

Researchers should think about impacts and benefits together. They might not readily correspond. An important debate in educational research is about "test score fade-out"—that is, educational interventions that have effects on achievement for only a short period of time. For example, an intervention in fourth grade might

Table 9.1   Illustrative Impacts With Potential for Shadow Pricing

Domain	Illustrative Impacts From Education
Labor market	Earnings, employment, income stability, occupational status, job satisfaction
Personal status	Health, civic engagement, political knowledge, life satisfaction
Informational	Financial literacy, knowledge of health, consumption efficiency
Behaviors	Arrests, criminal activity, incarceration, smoking, drug use, emergency room visits
Time preference	Teenage childbearing, living for today
Time constraints	Rushed feeling, more leisure needed
Fiscal	Welfare receipt

Sources: Baum, Ma, and Payea (2013); Cutler and Lleras-Muney (2010); Haveman and Wolfe (1984); Oreopoulos and Salvanes (2011); Trostel (2010).

increase achievement in sixth grade but have no identifiable effect by eighth grade. In their study of class quality, Chetty et al. (2011) found that an increase in quality at time t increases achievement in time t; it has a negligible effect on achievement at time $t + x$, but it increases earnings at time $t + x + y$ (for a meta-analysis showing general fade-out for interventions to boost IQ, see Protzko, 2015). Thus, class quality conveys benefits much beyond the initial, temporary effect on test scores. A full discussion of how fade-out occurs is beyond our scope (see, e.g., Cascio & Staiger, 2012; Jacob, Lefgren, & Sims, 2010). Nevertheless, for a BC analyst, the issue of fade-out should be understood in terms of behavioral change. Even with fade-out, there may be benefits as long as there has been some associated behavioral change with positive consequences. For example, if test scores are higher only in sixth grade, teachers may have higher job satisfaction (which can be valued as a compensating wage differential), and parents may also value test score gains. These are still benefits, even if they are short-lived. Moreover, behavioral changes might persist in other ways beyond the fade-out period. As found for the Perry Preschool Program, there was cognitive fade-out: An impact of 12 IQ points at age 4 was reduced to zero by age 10 (Barnett & Masse, 2007). However, there was robust and persistent behavioral change among the preschool treatment group. They reported inter alia being one third less likely to have health problems at age 40 and almost half as likely to have had an abortion (Nores, Belfield, Barnett, & Schweinhart, 2006, Table 3), and these behaviors have important resource consequences for the individuals involved and society. From a BC perspective, therefore, it is important to measure impacts that can be translated into benefits.

There can be as many benefits as there are impacts. And because they are all in dollars, we can easily add all the benefits together. However, the impacts or benefits must be independent of each other. For example, a training program might increase trainees' earnings and their health status. But some of the health gains may be because the higher earnings allow the participants to afford better living conditions that improve health. If so, the analyst should shadow price the gains in health but only those gains that are independent of the increased earnings.

This inclusive approach to shadow pricing raises the issue as to how many benefits the analyst should actually count. After all, counting more benefits or benefits over a longer time period will result in an intervention that looks more valuable. Conversely, by looking at only a few benefits or at benefits for a limited time, the analyst will underestimate the value of the educational intervention. Ideally, every impact that has been caused by the intervention should be assigned a shadow price and counted as a benefit for as long as the impact persists. Given the durability of many educational interventions, the impacts might continue for many years.

Certainly, if there are important benefits—even if they are latent for many years—these benefits should be included. Yet, the evaluator might choose to abbreviate the time horizon for analysis. In the interests of parsimony, the analyst might include only those benefits for which there is strong evidence or for which an accurate shadow price exists. Also, to help make comparisons, the analyst might choose only benefits that have been shadow priced in related studies. Indeed, it may be difficult to follow up with students longitudinally over their life course or over the period during which the impacts are influential. If so, the analyst can divide the benefits into those identified by the program evaluator and those that are projected based on the status of the participants at the termination of the research. So, in the case of preschool, there are immediate benefits (free time for parents) and improvements in student behavior and learning. But another benefit—not observable for at least 15 years—might be extra earnings derived from a preschool experience that generates more human capital (Nores et al., 2006; Reynolds, Temple, White, Ou, & Robertson, 2011). This latent earnings gain can be predicted based on linking the additional schooling to established evidence (e.g., on the relationship between education and earnings; Barrow & Malamud, 2015; Rouse, 2007).

There can be negative benefits—that is, program impacts that cause greater resources to be devoted to the treatment group, or side effects. For example, a preschool program may lead participants to enroll for longer in school, and this will mean greater expenditures. The extra resources to provide more schooling should be counted as a negative benefit (in cost-effectiveness analysis, we refer to them as induced costs). Hopefully, this negative benefit leads to a higher positive benefit later on in terms of increased earnings from being in school longer, but either way, it should still be counted.

In general, transfer money flows should not be considered under the class of benefits. Transfers are movements of money that do not involve any opportunity cost or resource use: they are simply flows from one bank account to another. The primary example is welfare payments: These payments are dollars allocated to recipients (e.g., those living below the poverty line) from taxpayers. Studies have found that increased education does reduce welfare reliance (e.g., London, 2006; Waldfogel, Garfinkel, & Kelly, 2007). However, the welfare recipients did not use any resource to obtain these payments; the only direct cost is the administrative cost of providing living expenses through transferring tax revenues to the recipients. From a social perspective, a reduction in transfer payments is therefore not considered as a social benefit from increased education. (Any saving in administrative costs to make the transfer payments should be counted as a benefit.) Looked at from a fiscal perspective or the individual perspective, however, changes in transfer payments may be included as benefits.

Table 9.2 illustrates how benefits are defined according to different perspectives; the example is for job training programs. For program participants, job training leads to earnings gains; these are clearly a benefit to the participants. The participants do receive fewer support services, but as these were a function of the participants' low economic well-being, this is neither a positive nor a negative benefit to the participants. Nevertheless, the participants do now lose some welfare payments because they are no longer eligible; these are negative benefits to those participants. These losses will be offset by any gains in wage subsidies that participants may now be eligible for (we leave aside possible disincentive loss of welfare payments as wages rise).

The analyst is interested in the net benefit from these four categories. From the perspective of other members of society, the resource flows are different. First, earnings gains accrue to the individual (so they are already counted). Second, support service reductions are a benefit or saving to society. Looking at transfers, the impacts for participants are directly offset by the impacts for other members of society. As shown in the Total column in Table 9.2, transfers have no overall effect on the total benefits (again, assuming no productivity disincentive effects).

When calculating benefits, it is critical that all benefits be discounted into present values. The importance of discounting is discussed in the chapters on costs. The logic is the same for benefits, as is the formula that is used. That is, the present value of benefits B_{PV} is the sum of all benefits received at time t over periods $1 \ldots n$ discounted at a rate i:

$$B_{PV} = \sum_{t=1}^{n} \frac{B_t}{(1+i)^{t-1}}$$

Making sure all money amounts are expressed in present values is especially critical for benefits. The advantages of education tend to be persistent and are often lagged such that discounting can substantially change the ultimate figures. As a stylized example, a preschool program for 4-year-olds might have benefits per child worth $200 in third grade (in savings on special education) and then earnings gains worth

Table 9.2 Framework for Benefits for Employment and Training Programs

	Benefits From the Perspective of . . .		
	Program Participants	Other Members of Society	Total
Benefits			
Earnings gains	+	0	+
Reduced support services	0	+	+
Transfers via taxpayers			
Reduced welfare benefits	−	+	0
Wage subsidies	+	−	0
Net benefits	?	?	+

Source: Adapted from Orr (1999, p. 224).

Note: Positive + or negative −.

$1,000 per year at ages 24, 25, and 26. With a discount rate of 3%, the present value of benefits at age four are calculated as follows:

$$B_{PV} = \frac{\$200}{(1+0.03)^4} + \frac{\$1,000}{(1+0.03)^{20}} + \frac{\$1,000}{(1+0.03)^{21}} + \frac{\$1,000}{(1+0.03)^{22}}$$
$$= \$178 + \$554 + \$538 + \$522$$
$$= \$1,791$$

The discounted benefits at age 4 are $1,791. By comparison, the undiscounted value of these benefits is $3,200. Thus, in this example, the present value benefits are less than half the size of the undiscounted benefits.

There is considerable debate as to an appropriate value for the discount rate for benefits (Burgess & Zerbe, 2013; Moore, Boardman, & Vining, 2013). Fundamentally, the rate should reflect the opportunity cost of funds for the investment—that is, where the resources come from to pay for the educational program. So, a state government would face an opportunity cost of capital based on interest rates it would have to pay for investments in education; the federal government would face a different rate, as would private investors and nonprofit agencies. This criterion might suggest interest rates of between 5% and 10% for the United States; in countries where capital markets might function less efficiently, the rate might be between 10% and 20%. However, as education is a social investment with a long time horizon, the appropriate discount rate should be lower than a straightforward market interest rate (see the discussion in Boardman et al., 2011, Chapter 10). Also, to aid interpretation and comparison with other studies, there is a strong case for applying the same discount rates as used by other researchers (Moore, Boardman, Vining, Weimer, & Greenberg, 2004). Hence, our recommendation is to apply a discount rate of between 3% and 5% for U.S. studies and adjust the rate upward for countries with more distorted capital markets (Karoly, 2012, Table 7). As discussed in Chapter 11, checking the robustness of the discount rate is an important sensitivity test for estimating benefits.

Finally, throughout this discussion we have assumed that all dollar gains and losses are equal, so it is legitimate to add them all together. But there may be distributional consequences among different units of analysis, so this assumption might not be valid: The loss of $500 to a low-income family is likely to reduce their well-being considerably more than the gain in well-being derived from a gain of $500 to a high-income individual. Some dollar gains might therefore be given a lower weight than others, depending on who is affected. It is not clear how these weights might be determined, however: Boardman et al. (2011, Chapter 19) suggested weights based on the progressivity of the tax code. But there is a danger that arbitrary or idiosyncratic weights will make it difficult for decisionmakers to understand the benefits. Therefore, we recommend addressing this assumption explicitly when making a policy decision (as discussed in Chapters 11 and 13).

9.3. VALUING EDUCATIONAL BENEFITS THROUGH EARNINGS

One of the important goals of educational investments is the benefit from boosting future earnings as reflected in earnings data. Indeed, there is a whole research industry estimating the earnings gains from educational interventions, reforms, and policies. However, in order for this evidence to be useful for BC analysis, the measured earnings gain has to meet the specifications described in the previous section. So, the measure has to be discounted back to the start of the policy reform, and ideally, it has to be calculated for the entire duration over which effects persist and be based upon valid methods of causal inference. Even more importantly for BC analysis, the earnings gain has to be expressed in a way that can be related to the costs of the intervention.

For the purposes of BC analysis, the benefits of education need to be modeled in terms of the full earnings gain. For example, the benefit of completing a college degree over not enrolling in college is the lifetime difference in earnings between these two attainments, expressed as a present value at the time when the choice between the two conditions must be made. As noted previously, we are assuming that the earnings gap has been causally identified; a detailed explanation of how to do this is given in Barrow and Malamud (2015) and Altonji, Blom, and Meghir (2012).

With large-scale labor market surveys, it is possible to calculate lifetime earnings profiles for many different educational conditions. Table 9.3 presents nine estimates of the earnings benefits of completing a four-year BA degree relative to high school completion. These estimates use the lifetime earnings profile method to calculate the present value earnings gains at age 18, which for most students is the primary decision point for enrolling in college. These estimates can be interpreted as actual shadow prices for application or for transfer to studies where the outcome measured is four-year degree completion. (Later in this chapter, we discuss how to perform this "benefit transfer.") One immediate conclusion is that the returns on a four-year degree for

Table 9.3   Lifetime Present Value Earnings Gain From College

Study	Earnings Gains for BA Degrees Over High School Graduation Present Value at Age 18	Source
Agan (2014)*	$243,700	NLSY79
Tamborini, Kim, and Sakamoto (2015)	$266,100	SIPP, IRS
Kim, Tamborini, and Sakamoto (2015)	$321,100	SIPP, IRS
Mitchell (2014)	$354,300	SIPP 2008
Barrow and Malamud (2015)*	$434,900	CPS 2013
Avery and Turner (2012)*	$462,000	CPS2009
Webber (2014)*	$492,400	NLSY79, ACS
Herschbein and Kearney (2014)	$610,000	ACS 2009-12
Barrow and Rouse (2005)*	$629,400	CPS 2004
Average (N = 9)	**$423,800**	

Notes: SIPP = Survey of Income and Program Participation; IRS = Internal Revenue Service tax files; CPS = Current Population Survey; ACS = American Community Survey. Discount rate of 3% (except Webber, 2014, at 3.5%). Males only in Mitchell (2014). Median earnings (except Barrow & Malamud, 2015; Barrow & Rouse, 2005). *Indicates costs of college subtracted from present value. Adjusted to 2015 dollars.

recent cohorts of U.S. college students are very high (not accounting for labor market distortions; see Haveman & Weimer, 2015). At age 18, a student who decides to attend and complete a four-year degree is expected to earn $423,800 more over his or her lifetime. Second, there is variation in the estimated shadow price, with estimates ranging from $243,700 to $629,400. Given these examples, we might apply the conservative principle to benefits and apply the lower bound shadow price. Finally, knowing these benefits—and in this case, their large size—helps us understand the context for analysis. An intervention to boost degree completion need only be modestly effective in order to have very large benefits. Even very high cost interventions might potentially pass a BC test if they increase college completion. (Of course, if in the future labor markets change so that college skills are in less demand, then the analyst should apply a lower shadow price.)

Given the focus of education policy on test score accountability, one might expect to find many shadow prices of society's willingness to pay for increases in test scores. Certainly, most evidence thus far has found that high school math skills have a positive effect on earnings. Reviewing four studies, Hanushek (2006) estimated an earnings premium from a one-standard-deviation increase in math test scores of 12% (see also Gaertner, Kim, DesJardins, & McClarty, 2014; Goodman, 2012). However, compared with attainment, far fewer published shadow prices of gains in achievement are available as gains in the present value of lifetime earnings. (There are many reasons for this dearth of evidence. One is that test score gains are correlated with attainment—in order to finish, high school students have to satisfy a math requirement, for example. Another is the issue of fade-out, discussed previously, and that achievement gains are harder to get at higher grades.)

So far, we have emphasized the full lifetime profile method of describing all the earnings gains. The alternative to the full method is to use a production function approach. This approach identifies the links between school resources and longer-term outcomes such as success in the labor market. For example, do students who attend elementary and secondary schools with higher per-pupil expenditures eventually receive higher earnings in the labor market? Although not all authors have explicitly done so, the results of these studies might be incorporated in BC analysis where benefits from increased earnings are compared against the increased per-pupil spending.

In a widely cited study, Card and Krueger (1992) found a positive association between school resources such as teacher-pupil ratios and teacher salaries and later student earnings. In a later review article, the same authors concluded that "a 10% increase in school spending is associated with a 1% to 2% increase in annual earnings for students later in their lives" (Card & Krueger, 1996, p. 133). Subsequent empirical studies and reviews cast some doubt on these conclusions (Betts, 1996; Heckman, Layne-Farrar, & Todd, 1996; but see McHenry, 2011). Much of the disagreement stemmed from the uncertainty that is inherent in correlational methods and aggregation by states (but for rigorous impacts of school finance reforms on educational outcomes, see Jackson, Johnson, & Persico, 2016).

More recently, studies have investigated exogenous variations in educational opportunities to identify gains in earnings. Some of these studies are able to exploit idiosyncratic changes in educational policies or access to education. For example, in Germany in 1966–1967, some students were exempt from school for 13 weeks (out of the regular 37-week school year) as part of a reorganization of the school calendar.

Following these students over time, Pischke (2007) found no effect on earnings of having had a shortened school year. Another fertile research area is how changes in compulsory schooling laws have affected earnings; although early studies found strong gains from extra schooling, these may be sensitive to model specification (see, e.g., Stephens & Yang, 2014). Finally, there has been an increase in studies that look at how teacher quality affects earnings (Chetty, Friedman, & Rockoff, 2014) as well as growing interest in the returns on college quality and selectivity (Dale & Krueger, 2011).

However, these quasi-experimental results must be applied cautiously in a BC framework. Studies usually examine benefits at a single point in time (e.g., at age 26); this makes it difficult or impossible to model the full-time flow of benefits as present values. More importantly, these studies need to be accompanied by a rigorous investigation of costs—for example, to increase the school leaving age or to recruit higher-quality teachers. If not, even if the benefits are precise, it is likely that the costs will be very imprecise. It is not straightforward to estimate the cost of increasing the school leaving age or the managerial and administrative costs of recruiting higher-quality teachers (and dismissing low-quality teachers). Also, in cases where the earnings gains are reported as percentage gaps in earnings, it is hard to combine these numbers with costs in the BC framework. Under some restrictive assumptions, the earnings gains from an educational intervention may be interpreted as a rate of return. We discuss this particular approach—and the use of each shadow price for BC analysis—in the next chapter.

9.4. VALUING EDUCATIONAL BENEFITS THROUGH SHADOW PRICING

Earnings are by no means the only (or even the most important) component of benefits from educational interventions. There are a wide range of additional benefits that education may confer upon individuals or society, although these will vary according to the educational alternative that is being considered. Individuals could derive an increased ability to enjoy literature and the arts, an improved sense of self-worth, or any number of intangible and hard-to-measure benefits.

These impacts can occur at both the individual and societal level. For example, what are the values of lower rates of smoking and obesity for the individual? What is society's willingness to pay for lower crime rates that might be induced by effective after-school programs? Within schools, what value might teachers place on an orderly classroom with few disruptions? To answer these questions within a BC framework, we need to put dollar values on each impact. Yet, many of these impacts are not bought and sold in markets, so we have little hope of directly observing the willingness to pay for them. Instead, we apply shadow pricing techniques to approximate willingness to pay.

There are two main classes of shadow pricing. One is the observed behavior or revealed preference approach; here, willingness to pay is derived from the economic decisions that individuals make. Within this class, there are several methods for estimating willingness to pay. An important general assumption of these methods to valuing benefits is that individuals are rational and well informed about the consequences of their decisions. The other class, referred to as the contingent valuation approach, employs direct surveys of individuals to elicit their willingness to pay for outcomes. Contingent valuation studies are distinguished by the survey methods and instruments used. For these approaches, individuals need to understand what is being asked and correctly convey their preferences to the analyst. Next, we discuss the methodology of each shadow pricing alternative, distinguishing between how shadow prices are calculated and actual dollar estimates of those that already exist as part of the education research base.

9.4.1. Defensive Expenditure Method

The defensive expenditure method is based on the logic that something can be valued by how much society or an individual pays to avoid its opposite. For example, to avoid disruptions in the classroom, the school might hire a teacher's aide; the wages paid to the aide are how much the school values the avoidance of disruption or more precisely the disruption the aide prevents. The method can be generalized to other domains. For example, welfare payments represent the value society places on alleviating poverty; health expenditures are how much society values improvements in health.

The general approach to monetizing behaviors with these consequences is to calculate the average expenditure on such behaviors. Often budgetary data is relied on, although expenditures may be measured directly. Indeed, many of the consequences of education are felt through changes in resource use within the public sector. For example, a school intervention to enhance socioemotional skills will reduce pressure on school budgets for counseling and—by enhancing school climate—improve job conditions for teachers (Durlak, Weissberg, Dymnicki, Taylor, & Schellinger, 2011). So, if an educational intervention reduces the counseling caseload by 10%, the monetary value is equal to one tenth of whatever the school typically spends on counseling.[1] Similarly, educational interventions that improve youth health status will have consequences for public health systems. Often, educational interventions have consequent impacts on later education. For example, the defensive expenditure method can be used to value school quality insofar as improved K–12 schooling reduces the need for remediation in college. More generally, educational interventions have implications for youth and adult behavior outside the school. In turn, all these behaviors influence government spending. The value to the taxpayer of education programs that reduce welfare caseloads can be proxied by government spending saved on welfare (Waldfogel et al., 2007); the same logic can apply to criminal activity (Cohen & Piquero, 2009).

The defensive expenditure method can be widely applied. For example, Foster, Jones, and the Conduct Problems Prevention Research Group (2005) estimated that the annual service costs for each student with conduct disorder is $6,820 annually, and Miller and Hendrie (2008) estimated burdens from substance abuse by school-aged youth. A common approach is to assemble all the defensive expenditures across the life course per educational status. So, Cohen, Piquero, and Jennings (2010) estimated economic burdens per at-risk youth, including high school dropouts. In a detailed examination, Trostel (2010) estimated how differences in education level affect tax contributions (i.e., income, payroll, property and sales taxes) as well as receipt of food stamps, public assistance, and other government supports (e.g., housing subsidies). From a taxpayer perspective, the effect on government budgets serves as an indication of the willingness to pay to avert them.

The defensive expenditure approach has some deficiencies. First, it is difficult to calculate all the resources used to avert the undesirable outcomes. An analyst might suppose that the amount a school spends on special educational services is their willingness to pay to avert placing a student in special education: If a student is no longer in special education, the school will not have to spend that money (see Barnett, 1996; Reynolds et al., 2011). But schools are not the only agency affected by special educational placement: Family expenditures will also change (e.g., on tutoring services or school liaisons), and family behavior will also change (e.g., with extra time on educational development). Also, there may not be any observable changes in actual expenditures:

---

[1] This approach is similar to the cost-of-illness approach that is common in the health literature (Gold, Siegel, Russell, & Weinstein, 1996). It is also similar to the defensive approach used in environmental BC analysis (Boardman et al., 2011).

If a school's funding is already allocated, a reduced need for special education is likely to mean that resources are reallocated to other educational services within the school. For the averted expenditure method to work well, all resources devoted to averting the undesirable outcome need to be included.

Second, defensive expenditures may not fully offset the undesirable outcome. In the example of classroom disruption, the school may pay for a teacher's aide. That aide may reduce the level of disruption but probably will not eliminate it. Faced with disruptive students, the school might seek to reduce disruption to an acceptable level but not fully eliminate disruption. As such, the payment to the aide is capturing willingness to pay for only a reduction in disruption. Also, this method assumes the school has immediately reacted to disruption by hiring the aide; it may be that the disruption persists for some time before any defensive expenditures are made.

Together, these deficiencies suggest that the defensive expenditure method will generate lower bound estimates of willingness to pay. It will understate the resources used to offset the consequences of low levels of education.

9.4.2. Hedonic Method

One way to value education is to identify how much people are willing to pay for assets that have educational quality capitalized within them. This approach is called the hedonic approach. It is conventionally applied to measure the value of school quality as it is capitalized into the value of home prices.[2]

Although we do not directly observe willingness to pay for public schools, we may be able to observe it indirectly in home purchase decisions. It is common in the United States for public school attendance to be defined by a zone of residence or catchment area. It is also common that home purchasers will consider the characteristics of local public schools when deciding to move to an area (indeed, real estate agents frequently boast of school quality in home advertisements). So, it is unlikely that a family with children will be indifferent between two identical homes if one has access to much better public schools (Figlio & Lucas, 2004). The difference in purchase price between the

---

[2] A related application of the hedonic approach is to estimate the willingness to pay for a microrisk reduction in the chance of sudden death (or value of mortality risk [VMR]), previously referred to as the value of a statistical life. For this application, the VMR is capitalized into the wages that are paid for jobs that have a higher fatality risk (Viscusi, 2015; for international estimates, see Viscusi & Aldy, 2003).

homes can be interpreted as the implicit price of school quality, and it indicates the family's willingness to pay.

The predominant method of estimating the implicit price is the "hedonic price function." Researchers obtain data on home prices and other variables and estimate a multiple regression of the following form:

$$\text{Home price} = f \text{ (home characteristics, neighborhood characteristics, school characteristics)}$$

The intent of the analysis is to hold constant all the relevant determinants of home prices so that we may observe how home prices are directly affected by additional quantities of one or more school characteristics (e.g., test scores, per-pupil expenditures, and class size). If home prices are higher in areas where test scores are higher, the premium in price represents the willingness to pay for school quality by local residents. Because it is a community-wide measure, this hedonic method captures willingness to pay of all local persons and not just the individual who receives the education. All the persons in that community are paying a premium to be close to a good school (even if they do not enroll their children). It might therefore better approximate the entire social value of education.

Although this is an intuitive way to measure the value of school quality, calculating the precise association requires several restrictive assumptions (Nguyen-Hoang & Yinger, 2011). Families' demand for school quality must correspond directly with their incomes, and there must be a variety of choices of school quality (so families can "buy" their preferred amount). All households are homeowners, and only residents purchasing homes in the area can benefit from local schools. Finally, households are sufficiently mobile to move when school quality diverges from their preferred amount. Of course, the value of living in a particular neighborhood does not just reflect the quality of the local schools: Other local amenities—such as proximity to parks or shopping centers—matter too. To identify the net effect of school quality, these factors must be controlled for, as must all the other relevant determinants of home prices. If the researcher fails to control for yard size, for example, and it happens that homes in better school districts also have larger yards, then estimates of the effects of school quality will be biased upward.

The evidence on the capitalization of school quality into house prices is now substantial (Black & Machin, 2011; Nguyen-Hoang & Yinger, 2011). A variety of data sets, methods, and local contexts have been investigated to calculate the value of school quality. Of course, measuring school quality itself is not straightforward, and studies have examined measures of input prices (e.g., teacher salaries), outputs (e.g., standardized test scores), and other factors (e.g., investments in school facilities). Nevertheless, the results are broadly consistent in establishing a positive link between community valuations of higher school quality and house prices. See Example 9.1.

Example 9.1   How Much Is It Worth to Attend a Good Public School?

A substantial amount of literature now exists on how to value schools using local property prices (Black & Machin, 2011). For the United States, Nguyen-Hoang and Yinger (2011) cataloged 35 studies since 1999. These studies predominantly assume a log-linear relationship between house prices and the measure of school quality, and almost all control for housing characteristics directly. Otherwise, they vary significantly in other dimensions. Studies have investigated house prices across a range of local markets to address variations in school quality and housing stock. To adjust for neighborhood effects, studies directly include neighborhood characteristics, apply fixed effects estimators, or use instrumental variables (based on district zoning). To account for local tax rates, studies apply effective or nominal tax rates. Finally, there are many possible proxies for school quality: Studies have utilized test scores (per school/district) in levels and test score gains, per-pupil expenditures, and student-teacher ratios.

Consistently, these studies have found that test score advantages are capitalized into the value of the local housing stock. Overall, this effect may be economically meaningful in that "house values rise by 1–4% for a one-standard deviation increase in student test scores" (Nguyen-Hoang & Yinger, 2011, p. 46). Local residents are willing to pay for improved outcomes from school. However, the evidence is less conclusive that school input quality is reflected in house prices.

Potentially, these valuations can be adapted to serve as the monetary benefits from increased school quality in BC analysis. Also, they might serve as validation checks for estimates of benefits using alternative methods. Thus far, however, application of the hedonic method as part of BC analysis is limited.

9.4.3. Identifying Willingness to Pay From Trade-Offs

The general idea behind these revealed preference methods is that willingness to pay for education is based on related behaviors that trade off resources for outcomes that might otherwise be generated by more education. For instance, if we know that an extra year of education increases job satisfaction by 2 points and $1,000 of extra income increases job satisfaction by 1 point, then a worker should be willing to pay $2,000 for the extra year of education. We refer to this general approach as the trade-off method (see Haveman & Wolfe, 1984).

This approach can be applied in a variety of ways that are related to or derived from the defensive expenditure and hedonic methods. For example, an educational intervention to increase test scores can be valued based on how much extra teachers have to be paid to work in schools with lower test scores (Goldhaber, Destler, & Player, 2010). An innovative approach to valuation by Rohlfs and Zilora (2014) examined how a money value can be placed on smaller classes based on the lower attrition rate of children who were treated with smaller classes as part of the Tennessee STAR experiment (i.e., families with children in smaller classes stayed in their schools and did not transfer to other schools). This approach, using exogenous changes in behavior to measure willingness to pay, is growing. In particular, researchers can trade off changes in test scores or teacher ratings with a range of direct expenditures on education-related behaviors to estimate willingness to pay.

9.4.4. Contingent Valuation Method

A general alternative to revealed preference methods is contingent valuation: This method derives money values of benefits from individuals' statements about their willingness to pay. The contingent valuation approach is complex and requires many assumptions; it is also rarely applied in education evaluations. But it may be the only option if benefits cannot be observed from individual behaviors. For example, it is very difficult to observe families' valuations of educational services to the severely disabled. Also, the value of building a new college cannot easily be estimated directly from individuals' preferences about education if no college has previously served the community. In both these examples, there are important benefits that should not be ignored, even though they are difficult to monetize.

There are many approaches to contingent valuation, although they share several characteristics (Boardman et al., 2011, Chapter 15). First, the researcher defines an appropriate sample of individuals to survey about their willingness to pay and applies a questionnaire or survey instrument of some kind. Second, this information is used to calculate willingness-to-pay estimates for each individual and particularly for the median individual. Third, the individual responses are used to estimate the benefits for the entire population of individuals that is affected by the policy or program.

The critical element of contingent valuation is the survey design. This has become increasingly intricate and sophisticated.[3] One approach—contingent ranking—embeds constraints or trade-offs into the survey. Respondents are asked to rank specific feasible combinations of the good being valued and monetary payments. For example, respondents might be asked about their preferences for high investments in public education with high taxes versus low investments in public education with low taxes. Another approach is the referendum method: Using iterative bidding, respondents are asked whether they would be willing to pay a specified amount for a particular good. If they answer affirmatively, the question is repeated with the amounts gradually increased until the respondent answers negatively. Getting respondents to change their minds forces them to reconsider their willingness to pay. An example referendum question to elicit the society's willingness to pay for truancy reduction might be this: "Last year, a new after-school program supported by your community successfully prevented one in every ten truancies from occurring at your local high school. *Would you be willing to pay [INSERT $ AMOUNT] per year to continue this program?"* By varying the dollar amount and relating this to the probabilities of acceptance, it is possible to calculate the median willingness to pay for the truancy prevention program.

Few contingent valuation studies have been undertaken for education research. An early example for preschool services for students with disabilities was undertaken by Escobar, Barnett, and Keith (1988), who found substantial differences in willingness to pay for services by disability type. Using a referendum design survey, Persson and Svensson (2013) estimated willingness to pay for bullying prevention programs in schools in Sweden.[4] More recently, Blomquist, Coomes, Jepsen, Koford, and Troske (2014) conducted a contingent valuation

---

[3] Initially, individuals were asked open-ended questions about their maximum willingness to pay for whatever good is being valued. However, respondents typically gave answers that were subject to hypothetical bias—that is, it was unclear whether individuals appreciated the real-world consequences of their responses and so if their behaviors would genuinely correspond to their answers.

[4] Contingent valuation approaches are used to derive quality-adjusted life years (QALYs). However, health researchers and the health policy community are reluctant to express QALYs in dollar terms. The current consensus value per QALY of $50,000 has been described as an "arbitrary but convenient round number" (Neumann, Thorat, Shi, Saret, & Cohen, 2015).

survey of willingness to pay for expanding community college provision and validated the survey findings against labor market studies of earnings gains from college. See Example 9.2.

Example 9.2 Using Contingent Valuation to Measure the Benefits of Community College

Blomquist et al. (2014) applied the contingent valuation method to measure the benefits from the community college system in Kentucky. The primary benefit from having a community college system is reflected in the gain in productivity of its students; this private benefit can be measured via gains in earnings. However, there are also local externalities: These benefits may be mediated through the students, or they may reflect the value of the system as a resource for the local area (e.g., through agglomeration externalities). These local externalities are harder to measure directly but should be added to the private gains to yield the aggregate social benefits.

Blomquist et al. (2014) administered a survey to 1,023 Kentucky residents to elicit their willingness to pay for expanding the Kentucky Community and Technical College System (KCTCS). Respondents' knowledge of and experience with the KCTCS was established, along with a reminder that allocating resources to one public program has opportunity costs for other public services. Respondents were informed that a referendum on expanding KCTCS would require a one-time increase in taxes. Willingness to pay was then derived from this: "Would you vote for the referendum to expand KCTCS by 10% here and now if you were required to pay a one time $TAX [varying from $25–$400] out of your own household budget?" (Blomquist et al., 2014, p. 7).

Adjusting the responses to the referendum question for prior characteristics and weighted to represent the state's population, the estimated social value of a 10% expansion in KCTCS is $106 million [90% CI of $79–$132m]. Separately, the researchers calculated the private gains—through increased earnings net of taxes—at $48 million. These gains, along with other private gains (e.g., to personal health) of $19 million, should be subtracted from the total social value to yield the local externalities. Therefore, the value of these externalities is estimated at $39 million, which is 58% as large as the total private gain from KCTCS. Interestingly, this result is close to the very approximate estimate published more than 30 years before by Haveman and Wolfe (1984).

There are many challenges in deriving estimates of the social value of community college through contingent valuation. Responses may be sensitive to the questioning, and analysis may be sensitive to a series of assumptions as to what these responses mean. Nevertheless, the analysis by Blomquist et al. (2014) shows how these social values might be approximated and how results from contingent valuation surveys can be an important validity check on estimates using other methods.

Source: Adapted from Blomquist et al. (2014).

The fundamental criticism of contingent valuation is that respondents' answers are unreliable and are subject to many significant biases (Hausman, 2012). The first is that of hypothetical bias: If individuals do not face any consequences from their responses, they may give answers that do not correspond to actual behavior. Other biases are also significant. Individuals may have varied understanding of what good or service they are being asked to value, and it is challenging in surveys to properly and sufficiently convey the exact nature of the good (ignorance bias). For education, some respondents may be generally in favor of more investment and interpret any question about a specific intervention as an opportunity to express their views about the need for more funding in general (embedding bias). As well, individuals may act "strategically" in providing answers and misreport their true willingness to pay. For example, they may fear that they will be required to pay for the service and thus understate their willingness to pay. Or they may overstate their willingness if they feel that such an answer will influence the provision of the good, without affecting what they must pay (strategic bias). Some respondents may not wish to give a response (noncommitment bias). As an additional complication, respondents may give different answers depending on whether the researcher is trying to ascertain willingness to pay for a benefit or willingness to accept a loss (see, e.g., Kahneman & Tversky, 1984). That is, respondents may report very high benefits if a college is threatened with closure but very low benefits from opening a new college in an underserved area. Finally, responses are likely to vary according to how the proposal is funded, whether through lump-sum grants, annual taxes or subsidies, or student fees.

Solutions to address these many biases rely on emphasizing consequentialism and realism—that is, respondents should be given enough information and should answer under the presumption that their responses will be influential and may affect the provision of the good. Nevertheless, it is a challenge to make consequences feel "real" for respondents unless they have some stake in the results of the survey.

Despite these many challenges, the contingent valuation method should not be discarded entirely (but see Hausman, 2012). Certainly, great care must be taken in the design of survey instruments, application of the method, and validity of results from one study for other contexts. For some inquiries, contingent valuation may be the only way to ascertain valuation of some education provision (and might be considered against the alternative of no attempt to identify economic value). As well, the method may be used as a validity check on estimation of benefits using alternative methods. In light of these issues, though, it is perhaps unsurprising that the method of contingent valuation is rarely applied in education.

9.5. APPLYING BENEFITS IN BENEFIT-COST ANALYSIS   ●

Shadow prices are like regular prices. We can explain them using economic theory, and we can just apply an established value (e.g., $1,000 per effect size gain in achievement). Above, we have cited selected studies that have put an actual value on, for example, high school graduation, school quality, test scores, and the location of a new college. Given that these shadow prices already exist, it may be appropriate for the analyst to adopt an existing price and plug this price in as a measure of benefits in her own study.

In practical terms, this adoption has some advantages. For example, imagine a mentoring program that has been found to reduce the high school dropout rate by 10%. In order to accurately shadow price the failure to complete high school, the researcher would need to estimate a series of shadow prices for each independent, causally induced delinquent behavior over the life course—potentially using several shadow pricing techniques and making sure the benefits are not double counted and of course making sure that the impact measures and benefit measures cohere (Belfield & Levin, 2009). Faced with this task, it seems much easier to apply the estimate of society's willingness to pay for high school graduates of $480,000 calculated by Cohen and Piquero (2009, Table 12, present value at age 18 discount rate 2% in 2015 dollars; see also Cohen et al., 2010). This application is much more convenient, and there are formal reasons for using existing shadow prices as well. It adds credibility in that the shadow prices have already been peer-reviewed and so reflect a significant effort by the calculators of the shadow prices. And it helps decisionmakers in that results are more likely to be harmonized and hence can be compared; sensitivity testing is also more straightforward.

However, the researcher should not just plug in any price. An important benefit transfer step must be performed. This is an explicit step in which the researcher justifies the use of an existing shadow price to calculate benefits in her study. In making this transfer, the researcher must establish that the shadow price is valid for her purposes.

This benefit transfer step requires knowledge of the context of the initial study and its relation to the analyst's own study and a formal comparison between the two. For example, the high school dropout figure from Cohen and Piquero (2009) cited previously is a national average figure. If the analyst's mentoring program is only for low-income first-generation students in rural states, the national figure will need to be adjusted for demographic differences. If the new graduates are more disadvantaged than the typical graduate, the shadow price per dropout averted (or new graduate accrued) will need to be adjusted downward for application to the mentoring program. Conversely, if the labor market returns have increased since 2009, the shadow price per high school graduate will need to be adjusted upward. As the national shadow price includes extra tax revenues as a benefit of high school completion, any differences in the tax system should be accounted for. Hence, the older the existing shadow price, the less likely it is to be relevant for new studies. Some adaptations may be difficult to make. This national shadow price is discounted by the authors at 2%; if the discount rate for the mentoring program is different (say 5%), there may be no direct way to transfer the values from one study to the next.

The important issue here is that shadow prices must be formally transferred through correcting or comparing assumptions from one study to the next. They cannot simply be plugged in from study to study. The process of transfer will involve some judgment as to how equivalent the existing shadow price is to the analyst's own population of interest. This judgment should consider factors such as the correspondence of the populations and the similarity of the education systems and labor markets as well as changes over time.

9.6. CONCLUSIONS

Education can have many influences on individuals and societies and many—but not all of these influences—can be expressed in monetary terms. Clearly, if education makes individuals more productive, then they will have higher earnings, a benefit that is already expressed in dollars. For other benefits, we need to apply shadow pricing techniques. Although there are concerns about these techniques in practice, there are enough techniques such that we can often estimate shadow prices and place them within a plausible range. Even if there is no clear behavioral change, we can use contingent valuation surveys to identify willingness to pay for the outcomes of educational programs. As well, there is a growing methodological and empirical literature that yields actual values for some educational outcomes as well as other behavioral changes caused by more education. We can illustrate only some of these extant shadow prices; more are being produced annually. Typically, they show that education has a substantial and profound effect on economic well-being—that is, society's willingness to pay for educational outcomes is potentially very high. Through a formal benefit transfer modeling, these values can be used in other studies that identify similar outcomes.

Once we have calculated the benefits of changes in education, we can then combine these with the costs of education within a formal BC analysis. This is the subject of the next chapter.

Discussion Questions

1. What is the theoretical basis for estimating the value, in monetary terms, of educational outcomes for which there are no markets?

2. What are some ways that the hedonic pricing method can be applied to valuing educational outcomes?

3. Why might the defensive expenditures method of benefits valuation be an underestimate of social willingness to pay for educational programs that reduce college remediation?

4. What are some challenges in implementing a stated preference, or contingent valuation, method of estimating benefits?

Exercises

1. According to Nguyen-Hoang and Yinger (2011), "house values rise by 1–4% for a one-standard deviation increase in student test scores" (p. 46). Estimate the economic value of increasing student test scores across a district with 100,000 residents.

2. Perform the following steps to obtain an estimate of the returns on high school graduation versus high school dropout in the United States:

    a. Construct age-earnings profiles of high school dropouts versus high school graduates for a particular race and gender subgroup, using mean earnings from the Current Population Survey from the U.S. Census Bureau (available at www.census.gov) and interpolating from age bands to individual years, from ages 16 to 65.

    b. Apply a discount rate to obtain the present value of high school graduation at age 12.

c. What sensitivity analyses would you want to perform on this estimate? What do you see as the limitations of this approach, and what additional data would you like in order to obtain a more precise or accurate estimate of the returns on high school graduation?

3. The state of Idaho is considering a large investment in making welfare recipients economically independent. Three programs have been recommended to the state. One group has argued that job development with living wages must be the centerpiece. A second has pushed for high school equivalency completion and job training. A third has claimed that counseling and child care are the keys. The state wants to know the benefits of each of these separately and in various combinations. How would you formulate and carry out the study to estimate benefits?

10

Benefit-Cost Analysis

Objectives

1. Define the three metrics: (1) net present value (NPV), (2) benefit-cost (BC) ratio, and (3) internal rate of return (IRR).

2. Describe the general challenges in calculating these three metrics.

3. Consider how to interpret these metrics.

4. Review evidence on BC analysis across educational research.

B C analysis allows us to determine if an educational investment is socially efficient. This determination is made when the monetized benefits—resources accrued as a result of the investment— exceed the costs, which are all the resources used to implement the investment. The method for calculating the costs of an intervention was described in detail in Chapters 4 through 6, and the methods for estimating the benefits were covered in Chapter 9 (and prefigured in Chapter 7). We assume here that costs and benefits have been correctly measured and that they correspond to one another. This chapter serves as the capstone for application of the ingredients method and shadow pricing techniques. Here, we bring the costs and benefits together to derive an economic metric that is informative for decisionmakers who are interested in the efficiency of educational investments.

We begin by describing the economic metrics—the NPV, BC ratio, and IRR. The metrics presented are mathematically straightforward. But this simplicity belies the challenges in interpreting them and placing them in context. We devote the following section to discussing some of these challenges. Finally, we provide an illustrative review of evidence generated from BC analyses. This review is not intended to summarize the range of literature or adjudicate between educational investments. It is intended to illustrate the main areas of BC analysis in education.

This chapter may appear to be the culmination of all the research inquiry into costs and benefits. In fact, there are still several more important steps to follow. These relate to checking the robustness of the results and interpreting the results for policymakers. These steps are documented in Chapters 11 and 12. The material covered here is a necessary precursor to following these steps.

● 10.1. COMBINING BENEFITS AND COSTS INTO ECONOMIC METRICS

In this section, we discuss three economic metrics: (1) NPV, (2) the BC ratio, and (3) the IRR. We illustrate each of these metrics using a stylized example of an adult literacy program. The stylized dollar flows are shown in Table 10.1.

The literacy program helps adults adapt to the labor market and obtain more highly paid jobs. Using the ingredients method, it is determined that the 1-year program costs $300 per participant. After completion, the participants earn $150 extra per year compared with what they would have earned without the program; this gain lasts for 4 years. Having accurately collected this information, creating the

Table 10.1 Stylized Example: Literacy Program for Benefit-Cost Analysis

	Undiscounted Costs	Undiscounted Benefits
Year 1	$300	0
Year 2	0	$150
Year 3	0	$150
Year 4	0	$150
Year 5	0	$150

economic metrics is mathematically simple, although each one requires careful interpretation.

10.1.1. Net Present Value

The primary economic metric for BC analysis of educational interventions is the NPV. The NPV is the discounted value of the benefits minus the discounted value of the costs. To discount, we apply the formulae from Chapters 5 and 9 respectively:

$$B_{PV} = \sum_{t=1}^{n} \frac{B_t}{(1+i)^{t-1}} \text{ and } C_{PV} = \sum_{t=1}^{n} \frac{C_t}{(1+i)^{t-1}}$$

Where B_t and C_t are the benefits and costs, t is the year in a series ranging from 1 to n, and i is the discount rate. Hence, the NPV of a project is straightforwardly calculated as follows:

$$NPV = B_{PV} - C_{PV}$$

Interventions with higher NPV amounts are preferred, and there is a strong presumption to reject any interventions with NPV amounts less than zero.

We can apply this to the simple example that was described in Table 10.1. Assuming a discount rate of 3%, the discounted sum of benefits in our example is given by the following:

$$B_{PV} = \frac{150}{(1+0.03)^1} + \frac{150}{(1+0.03)^2} + \frac{150}{(1+0.03)^3} + \frac{150}{(1+0.03)^4}$$

$$B_{PV} = 146 + 141 + 137 + 133$$

$$B_{PV} = \$557$$

As all the costs are incurred immediately, the discounted costs are as follows:

$$C_{PV} = \frac{300}{(1+0.03)^0} = \$300$$

Therefore, the NPV is calculated straightforwardly as this:

$$NPV = \$557 - \$300 = \$257$$

Given the NPV is clearly above zero, we can conclude that investment in this literacy program yields a positive stream of resources if we discount the future at a rate of 3%. Prima facie, the program is a good investment. Certainly, if there is an alternative program that costs about the same ($300) and has an NPV of only $100, for example, then this literacy program is clearly preferred.

However, we need to interpret this result carefully. The extra earnings count as social benefits, but they flow to the participant directly. The investor (such as the local government) will not recoup these extra earnings. If we had adopted a narrower perspective, the NPV and actual dollar amounts would correspond more closely (e.g., if we had counted only the taxpayer benefits and the taxpayer costs). Also, this NPV = $257 amount should be compared with NPV figures for similarly sized projects. A program that costs $100 with discounted benefits of $357 has the same NPV but it may be preferred as less risky. As well, the NPV should be compared with programs of similar duration. For example, we can imagine an intervention that costs the same ($300) and yields the same discounted benefits ($557), but these benefits come from one lump-sum undiscounted gain (of $867) in 10 years' time. In this case, the literacy program is almost certainly preferred. It is less risky, and it has an option value in that the NPV is received within 5 years such that we can reinvest over the remaining 5 years before the second intervention yields its returns.

The NPV metric has the advantage of being the most straightforward to report and interpret. The school invests $300, and there are benefits in extra earnings of $557, yielding a surplus (akin to a profit) of $257. However, it is often difficult to compare NPVs because the scale of the program makes such a difference to the final number. A $20 million program—with even very modest benefits—will almost certainly yield a higher NPV than a $2 million program. It is possible to express the NPV per participant. But then it may be unclear what total amount of resources is required, and it may give the impression that the NPV is constant as the number of students expands. The simplicity of the NPV is therefore traded off against the difficulty of comparing benefits and costs across programs in ways decisionmakers can use.

10.1.2. Benefit-Cost Ratio

The BC ratio is a simple adaptation from the NPV metric. Instead of taking the difference between present value benefits and costs, we divide benefits by costs:

$$BCR = \frac{B_{PV}}{C_{PV}}$$

A BC ratio greater than 1 is one where the benefits exceed the costs. Interventions with higher BC ratios are preferred, and there is a strong presumption that interventions with BC ratios less than 1 (i.e., where costs exceed benefits) should be rejected.

For our stylized literacy program in Table 10.1, the BC ratio is as follows:

$$BCR = \frac{557}{300} = 1.86$$

This ratio is clearly greater than one and therefore indicates that the program is a good investment with a discount rate of 3%. As a shorthand explanation, the BC ratio is often interpreted as "for every dollar invested in this literacy program, there will be a return of $1.86." As with the NPV, however, we caution that this interpretation does not imply that the program yields the same NPV for each marginal dollar invested.

Here, we can see why we emphasize the term *negative benefits* rather than induced costs when performing BC analysis. Imagine a college access program with a cost of $2 million, benefits of $4 million in extra earnings, but also with $1 million spent on newly induced college enrollment. If the extra college enrollment is counted as a negative benefit, the BC ratio is 3/2 = 1.5. However, if the extra college enrollment is counted as an induced cost, the BC ratio is 4/3 = 1.33. As there may be many negative benefits that necessitate discounting, the former way of calculating the ratio is preferred.

The advantage of the BC ratio is that it can be easily applied in comparisons of investments as if it is a return on investment. For example, a program with a BC ratio of 4 offers a higher return than a program with a BC ratio of 2. Looking across a set of different interventions, the decisionmaker might rank BC ratios and choose those that are the highest. This approach is valid in some contexts—for example, when the programs are of similar scale, riskiness, and duration—but not always. Moreover, the BC ratio may offer a simplistic interpretation: The shorthand explanation might lead decisionmakers to think that they can invest in the program in any dollar amount, whereas measured benefits in this case are tied to implementing the program at a particular scale, in this case the $300 level.

10.1.3. Internal Rate of Return

A third economic metric is the IRR. This is the rate of interest that equates the present value of benefits to the present value of costs.

Formally, the IRR is defined as the discount rate (i) that causes the NPV or net benefits to equal zero:

$$NPV = \sum_{t=1}^{n} \frac{B_t}{(1+i)^{t-1}} - \sum_{t=1}^{n} \frac{C_t}{(1+i)^{t-1}} = 0$$

Or, equivalently, this:

$$NB = \sum_{t=1}^{n} \frac{B_t - C_t}{(1+i)} = B_{PV} - C_{PV} = 0$$

The IRR for an educational investment can be compared with the interest rate on investments of comparable size and duration. So, if the funding agency can invest in programs that yield returns of 10%, any educational intervention with an IRR above 10% would represent a good investment; any intervention with an IRR below 10% would be presumed to be rejected.

In our stylized literacy program example as per Table 10.1, the IRR turns out to be approximately 0.349 (or 34.9%). The discounted costs of the program are $300, so we need to find the discount rate that will make the discounted sum of benefits equal to $300. We can identify this IRR by calculating the discounted sum of benefits when $i = 0.349$, which can be obtained iteratively or by using automated software algorithms (e.g., Excel or many electronic spreadsheets):

$$B = \frac{150}{(1 + 0.349)^1} + \frac{150}{(1 + 0.349)^2} + \frac{150}{(1 + 0.349)^3} + \frac{150}{(1 + 0.349)^4}$$
$$= 111 + 82 + 61 + 45 = \$300$$

This IRR at 34.9% is considered attractive. There is no mathematical threshold for interpreting the IRR (other than that it should be positive). However, given that most government agencies work with interest rates below 10%, a figure of 34.9% appears to be very high.

There are advantages to using the IRR as an economic metric for evaluating educational programs. Inherently, calculating the IRR does not set out an assumed discount rate. As the value for the discount rate can make a big difference to the NPV, this freedom may be useful. Of course, it is still necessary to compare the IRR with another threshold interest rate for decisionmaking purposes for comparing the profitability of the investment. So this freedom is not fully liberating.

Intuitively, the IRR may be appealing because it can be readily placed in context. Most investors would regard somewhere between

5% and 10% as a reasonable interest rate on their investments. (Private individuals tend to discount at much higher rates—for example, 20%; see Warner and Pleeter [2001]—but a reasonable social interest rate should be below that of private investors.) So any IRR above 10% would suggest that the program represents a good investment. However, the IRR is quite sensitive to changes in the stream of benefits and costs and so must be interpreted cautiously. For example, the IRR for the literacy program given its current flows is 34.9%, which is a very high rate. If we learn that in fact the undiscounted costs were 10% higher ($330) and the undiscounted benefits in each year were 10% lower ($135), this does not mean that the IRR falls by 10% or even by 20%. Instead, the new IRR becomes 23.1%, a reduction of one third from its initial value. If the stream is longer, this sensitivity is magnified: If the original undiscounted benefits are spread over 12 years instead of 4, the IRR falls to 13%.

Also, the IRR does not provide any indication of the project scale. Thus, we could estimate identical IRRs for two separate projects, indicating that they are equally desirable, even when the NPV of one project is larger. An IRR of 34.9% is attractive to a policymaker for a project of $1 million, but it is especially attractive for an investment of $100 million. Finally, it is sometimes difficult to calculate a unique value for the IRR. This does not occur in instances like our numerical example in which all the costs occur at the beginning of the project and benefits come later. This stream closely parallels most projects, but it need not. If costs and benefits are dispersed unevenly throughout the project cycle, it is sometimes possible to calculate more than one IRR.

Finally, we distinguish the IRR from the idea of the social return on investment (SROI). This term is often used loosely to refer to the returns an enterprise obtains on its philanthropic investments (for a definition, see Millar & Hall, 2013). In theory, the enterprise should conduct BC analysis to derive the IRR. However, the enterprise may be interested in its own independent impact along certain unique dimensions. For example, a private company might contribute $1 million to a mentoring program for at-risk youth; this contribution triggers matched funding of $1 million by the local government. If an evaluation establishes that delinquent behaviors fell by 10%, this reduction in delinquency can be valued by its shadow price. The private company might calculate the value of all reduced delinquency and compare that with its $1 million contribution rather than the total resource cost of $2 million: The private company regards the matched funding as leveraged funding, which its initial contribution has created. (In other examples, the benefits might be defined more narrowly than they would for a full social

BC analysis.) This SROI is therefore not strictly based upon a full social perspective. As such, it is not an IRR.

10.1.4. Break-Even Analysis

A final metric can be derived using break-even analysis. In this case, the analysis is constrained such that the present value benefits equal the present value costs within a given period of time (sometimes referred to as the payback period). So, costs are calculated over the entire project length, but the benefits are counted only over the time period until they sum to the value of the costs. The analyst then reports the time period as the break-even point for the intervention. Formally, we are identifying the value for n in the following equation:

$$NPV = \sum_{t=1}^{n} \frac{B_t}{(1+i)^{t-1}} - \sum_{t-1}^{n} \frac{C_t}{(1+i)^{t-1}} = B_{PV} - C_{PV} = 0$$

For the stylized example, the break-even point is partway through the third year (assuming a discount rate of 3%). After 2 years, the discounted benefits are $279, which is just below the $300 cost. After 3 years, the benefits exceed the costs.

Clearly, this is a shorthand metric for an economic evaluation: It simply indicates how long the investor must wait before recouping the investment. The advantage is that it is very simple to explain in terms of, for example, "after three years, the benefits will cover the costs." This might be helpful to a policymaker with a limited time horizon. It also might be useful in the context of uncertain policy contexts and outcomes; in some contexts, projecting forward 10 or 20 years may seem to require a tremendous leap of faith.

However, this metric is simplistic. It does not provide information on the complete value of the investment: Lagged but high-return education programs will look less valuable than programs with an immediate payback. The metric invites comparisons—based on the shortness of the break-even time period—which may not be legitimate. Early education programs, in particular, will have later break-even points than youth or college programs but may have higher NPVs because of higher lifetime efficacy. Finally, this break-even metric may be misleading if benefits are spread across groups. For most educational investments, the benefits accrue to society or the broader community and not to any specific individual or government agency. Thus, a preschool program run by the state will accumulate benefits to the participants, local taxpayers, and the broader community. The total social returns may be equal to the costs after 5 years, but the separate groups do not receive all the returns. Adopting a narrow perspective, some investments may yield returns that are never recouped in actual money terms.

10.2. PERFORMING BENEFIT-COST ANALYSIS ●

The main challenges in performing BC analysis are measuring costs, calculating benefits, and making sure it is legitimate to combine them—the mathematics of the metrics is straightforward. Indeed, given that they are directly linked, it makes sense for the analyst to report all three metrics where possible. This obviates the need to consider which one is the most relevant. It also provides more information. Regardless of the number of metrics reported, the analyst should explain the results from BC analysis in a way that allows the reader to interpret the results, to place them in a policy context, and—essentially—to make better decisions.

As a summary for our stylized example in Table 10.1, we can say that the present value benefits are $557 compared with costs of $300; this is a BC ratio of 1.86 and yields an IRR of 34.9%. The break-even point for this investment is in the third year, post-intervention. Each metric conveys useful information, and we note that an IRR of 34.9% might "sound" better than $1.86 returned for each $1 invested. Nevertheless, in this case, the results prompt the same conclusion: The program is efficient from this social perspective. See Example 10.1 for the results for the HighScope Perry Preschool Program.

Example 10.1   Benefit-Cost Results for the HighScope Perry Preschool Program

Here, we bring together the evidence on costs and benefits of the HighScope Perry Preschool Program (see the table after this paragraph). The costs were calculated using the ingredients method (see details in Example 5.1 in Chapter 5). The benefits were derived from surveys of the subjects at ages 27 and 40, many years later, to compare outcomes by random assignment to the program relative to a control group. Benefits were valued by shadow prices using a range of methods (see details in Chapter 9). The costs and benefits are expressed relative to the status of a child who did not participate in the program.

(Continued)

(Continued)

Benefit-Cost Analysis: HighScope Perry Preschool Program

	Present Value at Program Start From the Perspective of:		
	Participants	General Public	Total (Society)
Program Costs (C)	–	$20,947	$20,947
Measured benefits up to age 40 (child care, K–12 education, adult education, college, earnings, crime, welfare)	$14,944	$105,060	$120,004
Projected benefits after age 40 (earnings, crime, welfare)	$18,233	$44,859	$63,092
Total Benefits (B)	$33,177	$149,919	$183,096
Net Present Value (B – C)	$33,177	$128,972	$162,149
Benefit-Cost Ratio (B/C)	n/a	7.2	8.7
Internal Rate of Return (IRR)*			8.1%

Source: Adapted from Barnett (1996); Nores, Belfield, Barnett, and Schweinhart (2006).

Notes: *IRR from reanalysis by Heckman, Moon, Pinto, Savelyev, and Yavitz (2010). 2015 dollars rounded. Discount rate 3%. Annual cost adjusted for years of participation.

The results for the economic metrics are given in the table. For participants, there are no costs; the net present value (NPV) is therefore the sum of the benefits at $33,177. This is the gain in economic well-being for participants accrued over their lifetime but expressed as a lump sum at age 4. For the general public, the program cost is $20,947. This amount is what the program is expected to cost in 2015 dollars, but it is not adjusted for possible changes in ingredients based on changes in either relative prices or technologies. The benefits for the general public—again, expressed as a lump sum at the same time the costs are incurred—are $149,919. The NPV is therefore $128,972, and the benefit-cost (BC) ratio is 7.2. From the social perspective, the costs are $20,947, and the benefits are the sum of the benefits to participants and the general public at $183,096. The NPV is therefore $162,149, and the BC ratio is 8.7. Finally, from a reanalysis by Heckman and colleagues (2010) using alternative models of benefits spread over 36 years, the IRR for society is 8.1%.

Overall, the BC analysis of the HighScope Perry Preschool Program indicates that the program is efficient from all perspectives and most likely yields returns that exceed alternative uses of investment funds.

We emphasize that reporting the results of BC analysis is not a substitute for decisionmaking—that is, a formal "reasoned determination" based on the evidence and other considerations. As we discuss in Chapter 11, policymakers should not simply rank interventions based on their net benefits and choose the one with the highest net benefits. Here, we note a number of important issues that might undermine our ability to compare programs according to their NPVs, BC ratios, or IRRs.

To begin, it is essential to perform BC analysis from the appropriate perspective and for affected populations. The default perspective is that of an entire society—counting all resources—but alternative perspectives for subpopulations or constituencies are often informative. Just as the ingredients spreadsheet can be divided according to funding agency, the stream of benefits and hence NPV results can also be divided according to funding agency. Taxpayers, in particular, may be interested in the amount of public funding versus the amount of public benefits from each educational investment (e.g., Trostel, 2010). Shaffer (2011) recommended performing multiple account BC analyses—that is, analyses that take a particular perspective within an overall BC analysis and identify the winners and losers (beneficiaries and payers or students and taxpayers). For health evaluations, Neumann, Sanders, Russell, Siegel, and Ganiat (2016) stated that results should always be reported from both a societal and a payer perspective. Certainly, results will vary considerably depending on the perspective adopted, so it is important the perspective adopted be clearly stated and justified by the analyst.

Also, it may be informative to assess the distribution of benefits across different groups in society. Groups can be defined quite broadly. Among program participants, for example, we may wish to separately calculate benefits by income level, gender, or race, in order to assess whether one group obtains a larger share of benefits. As with costs, it is common that benefits received by one group are not the same as benefits received by another group. The BC ratios may therefore be very different across subgroups. But heterogeneous results should not be overly interpreted: Policymakers should not infer that when, for instance, NPVs are higher for boys than girls, the analyst is recommending greater investments in boys. There are important issues related to equity and equality that should determine investments across different groups. This is another reason why it is important to separate out the BC result from policy decisions.

There are many factors associated with research study design that might influence BC analysis across different interventions. For example, interventions may start at different ages (preschool through to college). They may count a different array of benefits (including some crime or health status impacts, for example) and look over a different time horizon. Studies may also apply a different set of shadow prices or apply different benefit transfer procedures. Finally, interventions may cost very different amounts such that some interventions may not be financially viable in all contexts. For example, the Abecedarian preschool program is more than 4 times as expensive as the HighScope Perry Preschool Program to implement (Barnett & Masse, 2007, Table 2). As the interventions vary across more dimensions, comparisons become even less tenable (see the discussion in Harris, 2009).

One critical element of most research designs is the ability to test for statistical significance. In most empirical research, the underlying framework is one of hypothesis testing: By convention, the determination to reject the null hypothesis is based on the significance level of the p value, which is usually 1%, 5%, or 10% (but for a critique of statistical significance, see Wasserstein & Lazar, 2016). In contrast, BC analysis is not motivated by hypothesis testing but instead by guiding decisionmakers. Therefore, statistical significance is less important, and it need not be influential in selecting benefits for inclusion in BC analysis. As declared by Farrow and Zerbe (2013, p. 370), "Statistical significance levels for program and policy effect size are not relevant to BCA [benefit-cost analysis]. Regardless of the associated level of significance, all estimated effects should be included in the BCA model with the appropriate standard error." In other words, the researcher should include the average of each estimated effect in the baseline BC analysis and then report results for the variance as part of the sensitivity testing. Insofar as BC analysis involves hypothesis testing, the hypothesis is that the NPV is greater than zero. This is clearly different from testing if each impact is statistically significant. We recognize that this practice—considering statistical significance irrelevant—may not be agreed upon or followed in all research studies. The analyst must therefore be clear when combining benefits and costs what assumptions are made about statistical significance.

These issues are best discussed with examples. In the next section, we provide examples of BC analyses that have been performed to illustrate the main results and reporting conventions. For these examples, we focus on the baseline results. In Chapter 11, we provide a detailed discussion of uncertainty, sensitivity testing, and distributional analysis. In that chapter, we discuss more thoroughly how the results might vary depending on the assumptions.

10.3. EXAMPLES OF BENEFIT-COST ANALYSIS   ●

10.3.1. Investments in Preschool

By far the most attention in BC analysis of educational interventions has focused on preschool and early childhood education. Early studies applied experimental methods, which can more readily accommodate BC methods, and the strong results from these studies stimulated broader interest in the returns on early education. Summaries of the evidence on the benefits and costs of early education programs are given in Barnett and Masse (2007); Bartik, Gormley, and Adelstein (2012); Duncan and Magnuson (2013); Institute of Medicine and National Research Council (2014); and Karoly (2012).

One prominent program is the Chicago Child-Parent Center program (Reynolds, Temple, White, Ou, & Robertson, 2011). This program provides support for children from age 3 to third grade, including reading and math instruction, a parenting program, outreach to help enrollment, and health/nutrition services (Reynolds, Temple, Robertson, & Mann, 2002, p. 272). The preschool program was delivered through preschool centers that were located to serve children in low-income neighborhoods who had limited access to alternative early education services.

In Table 10.2, we report the BC results for the preschool component of the Chicago Child-Parent Center program (Reynolds et al., 2011). The comparison group received business-as-usual services available in the local area or no comparable services. Following the published evidence, we report the results per child rather than in total; on average, each center served 100 to 150 children, so from a policy perspective these per-child numbers might be multiplied by 100 to 150 to indicate the amount of total funding needed per operating unit.

The program was extremely valuable for the families: Benefits by age 26 were valued at $10,080 with an estimated $26,520 in benefits from earnings and other behaviors. As there was no cost to the families, the NPV is $36,600. Of key interest are the BC results for the general public and for society (the sum of individuals and the general public). Expressed at the initial time of the program (when the child is age 3), the discounted cost of the program is $10,060. Looking across the measured benefits up to age 26, the general public accrues benefits of $37,020; projecting forward, additional benefits of $33,700 are expected. The NPV is therefore $60,660, and the BC ratio is 7.1—that is, the program yields general public benefits that are 7 times the costs of the program. From the social perspective—that is, including the benefits to

Table 10.2   Benefit-Cost Analysis of the Chicago Child-Parent Center Program

	Present Value at Age 3 From the Perspective of:		
	Participants	General Public	Total (Society)
Program Costs (C)	–	$10,060	$10,060
Estimated Benefits at age 26 (B1)			
Child care, child abuse and neglect, K–12 education, juvenile crime (net of college)	$10,080	$37,020	$47,100
Projected Benefits (B2)			
Earnings, adult crime, health	$26,520	$33,700	$60,210
Total Benefits (B = B1 + B2)	$36,600	$70,720	$107,310
Net Present Value (B – C)	$36,600	$60,660	$97,250
Benefit-Cost Ratio (B/C)	n/a	7.1	10.8

Source: Adapted from Reynolds et al. (2011, Table 4).

Notes: 2015 dollars rounded to nearest 10. Discount rate 3%. Preschool program.

participants and the general public net of transfers between the two groups—the NPV is $97,250 per child and the BC ratio is 10.8. Finally, from detailed tabulations in Reynolds et al. (2011, Table 4), the program's break-even point is before the end of high school (age 18). For society as a whole, this investment appears to provide a very high yield.

Example 10.2   Rate of Return Studies

In many examples of educational benefit-cost (BC) analysis, the internal rate of return (IRR) is not calculated, and analysts rely on the net present value (NPV) and the BC ratio. However, the IRR is used almost exclusively in estimating the benefits and costs of obtaining additional years of schooling.

In many low-income countries, a large portion of the young population does not attend school, even at the primary level. Governments are forced to make difficult decisions about which levels of education—primary, secondary, or higher—should be the recipients of scarce investment funds. To allocate these resources across levels of education, one could attempt to compare the costs and the benefits of each of the three alternatives. The investment that yields the highest net benefits—or BC ratio or IRR—would produce relatively greater benefits for a given cost. In fact, hundreds of studies have done exactly that, albeit with somewhat restricted definitions of what constitutes benefits and costs. For an extensive review of this literature, see Psacharopoulos and Patrinos (2004).

Figure 10.1 illustrates a basic schematic that is followed in estimating the benefits and costs of education (for further details on the method, see Barrow & Malamud, 2015; Carnoy, 1995). The researcher first obtains data on individual earnings, usually from a census or household survey. Using these data, the researcher constructs an "age-earnings profile" for each level of education, which traces out the average lifetime earnings of individuals who have attained a given level of education. This approach for estimating benefits is discussed in Chapter 9. The figure depicts hypothetical age-earnings profiles for two levels of education: (1) secondary and (2) postsecondary. The secondary profile begins at age 18, following graduation from secondary school; the postsecondary education profile begins at 22, after graduation from university. Both end at the retirement age of 65, when individuals cease working.

The benefits of higher education are calculated as the difference at each age between what individuals earn as higher-education graduates and what they might have earned as secondary graduates. The costs of higher education are divided into two components. The first is the cost of income forgone while receiving a university degree—an opportunity cost of studying instead of working. The second includes all the direct costs of studying, such as books, tuition, and so forth (represented by the shaded area).

In this simple framework, the IRR for a university education is calculated by finding the discount rate that equalizes the discounted sum of benefits

Figure 10.1   A Schematic for Calculating Rates of Return

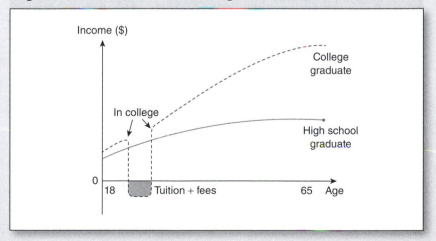

(Continued)

(Continued)

and the discounted sum of costs. Often, a shortcut is applied, using education premia from cross-sectional earnings equations. The general consensus from this approach, mostly based on studies spanning back over 30 years, is that the average IRR from a university education is somewhat lower than that of primary education (see Psacharopoulos, 1994, Table 1; Psacharopoulos & Patrinos, 2004). In a simplistic way, this suggests that primary education is a better candidate for scarce investment funds than higher education.

Despite the relative ease of conducting these studies, there are also many critiques of the method (Glewwe, 1999; McEwan, 1999). First, the method assumes that the sole benefit of education is higher earnings, despite suggestive evidence of many other benefits. Second, it focuses exclusively on the rate of return on a greater *quantity* of education, when decisionmakers may be more interested in the return on the *quality* of education. Third, many authors assume that the only cost of education is forgone income when it is well known that the direct costs of education may be substantial. Fourth, the age-earnings profiles are usually constructed with data from a single cross section, rather than longitudinal data that track a group of workers over their careers. Implicitly, this assumes that the earnings of a 65-year-old today, adjusted for price levels, are a good approximation of what a 25-year-old will earn in 40 years. Finally, it assumes that the earnings of a current high school graduate are a good approximation of what current university graduates *would have* earned without a degree.

10.3.2. Investments in Youth

Educational interventions to enhance youth development and economic well-being can also be evaluated using BC analysis. There is a case that early investments have the highest payoff (NPV); this is represented graphically as the Heckman curve (www.heckmanequation.org) and is summarized by the idea of "prevention being more efficient than remediation." But there are good reasons why investments in youth might be a priority. The time between costs and benefits is shorter: Most educational benefits are from higher earnings, and youth are closer to the labor market (obviously) than preschoolers. Also, youth behavior has more behavioral consequences, not just in the labor market but also with respect to crime, health status (e.g., through substance abuse), and other social acts (e.g., teenage pregnancy). Thus, there are potentially more benefits during youth. Finally, investments in youth might be targeted more accurately. An educational intervention such as class size reduction in kindergarten might have considerable benefits (Chetty et al., 2011), but it is typically applied to all students within a given classroom and is therefore expensive per at-risk child. By high school, there is more evidence on which subset of students need remedial or developmental supports; resources are therefore required for fewer students. Ultimately, of course, whether investments in youth or preschool pay off is an empirical question.

Youth programs do appear to have many benefits that exceed costs. Indeed, programs that are targeted at at-risk youth, often high school dropouts, can be very high yield especially if they reduce involvement in the criminal justice system (for YouthBuild, see Cohen & Piquero, 2015; for Job Corps, see McConnell & Glazerman, 2001). A detailed BC analysis of the National Guard Youth ChalleNGe Program (NGYCP) was performed by Perez-Arce, Constant, Loughran, and Karoly (2012). NGYCP is an intensive program for high school dropouts aged 16 to 18. In a residential program initially for 22 weeks, National Guard participants receive discipline training, academic instruction, and fitness programs. The following year entails the next phase, comprising more education, training, and employment counseling services. Outcomes were modeled as earnings gains mediated through changes in educational attainment, plus changes in welfare receipt and criminal activity (service to the community was also counted as a benefit). The analysis was novel in that it included an estimate of the marginal excess tax burden (METB) and the opportunity cost of time for the participants (for a cost-effectiveness [CE] analysis of NGYCP, see Hollands et al., 2014). Expressed as present values at age 17 using a 3% discount rate, the cost per admittee was $16,825, and the present value benefit was $44,674 (2015 dollars). This yields an NPV of $27,848, a BC ratio of 2.66, and an IRR of 6.4%. Recognizing that the measured benefits were not exactly the same, these values are comparable to some early childhood investments (see Karoly, 2012, Table 2; Temple & Reynolds, 2015).

10.3.3. Benefit-Cost Analysis in Developing Countries

Increasingly, educational interventions in developing or low-income countries are being evaluated using BC analysis (Dhaliwal, Duflo, Glennister, & Tulloch, 2012; McEwan, 2012). Given the variation in education systems, it is difficult to generalize from this literature. Also, these interventions are often a bundled set of services that includes an education component and other investments and program services. One prominent program in low-income countries, the Graduation Program, is an intensive, multicomponent program involving health education and technical skills training along with asset transfer, consumption support, and home visits (see Banerjee et al., 2015). The influence of just the educational services on outcomes is hard to isolate. Moreover, the benefits are specified—and valued in shadow prices—in diverse ways, over different time horizons, and in very different economic contexts.

One general conclusion is that investments in education for girls have an extremely high payoff (World Development Report, 2011). Typically, girls' schooling has been very limited, yet their role in the household and with respect to fertility and child-rearing is so important that the social benefits of education are high. There are also significant benefits mediated through the effect of education on health. This is illustrated in BC analysis of expanding primary school enrollments for girls in Tanzania by Brent (2009). The expansion—a projected 1% increase in enrollments—is valued in terms of reduced rates of HIV/AIDS infections. The shadow price of HIV/AIDS is derived from the value of human capital in the labor market. Even applying a conservative specification of benefits, expansions of primary schooling yield social benefits with a BC ratio of 1.3 to 2.9 times the present value costs of education provision.

10.3.4. Programs to Increase Wages for Welfare Recipients

There is sizable evidence on the benefits and costs of training programs. Much of this evidence applies experimental methods to identify the returns to program participants (see Redcross, Deitch, & Farell, 2010).

One of the largest examples was the experimental evaluation of the Job Training Partnership Act (JTPA) between 1987 and 1992. More than 20,000 potential job training participants were randomly assigned to either receive training or serve as a control group. BC analyses of JTPA and other training programs looked at the costs of the program and compared these with the benefits in terms of earnings and employment subsidies net of lost welfare payments for participants (see the framework in Chapter 9 adapted from Orr, 1999). For JTPA, a comparison across treatment and control groups showed the impact of training was earnings gains of 19% to 21% overall, although these gains were concentrated in the adult sample and varied across the quantiles of trainees' earnings (see Abadie et al., 2002, Tables II and III; Orr, 1999; and Orr et al., 1996). Other benefits were generated because individuals required fewer government-provided services (e.g., public assistance and criminal justice involvement) as a result of their job training. These benefits were received by taxpayers and other members of society. Interestingly, not only did the benefits of JTPA vary across groups, but the program costs did also: From a social perspective, the benefits for adult men were $2,700 and the costs $1,640; for male youth, the benefits were –$1,940 and the costs were $3,910 (Bloom et al., 1997, Table 8, adjusted to 2015 dollars).

We might expect welfare participants would respond to education programs to improve their labor market prospects. Greenberg, Deitch, and Hamilton (2009) summarized results of BC analyses from 10 welfare-to-work programs that relied on educational investments. Five were "education-first" programs: Participants were provided with educational supports to help them obtain credentials (e.g., GEDs) and so become more successful in the labor market. The other five were "mixed-initial-activity" programs: Participants were assigned to either educational supports or job search assistance depending on need. The education-first programs typically failed the BC test (Greenberg et al., 2009, Table 5.1). From the individual trainees' perspectives, three of the five programs had negative benefits (with zero costs). From the government perspective, four programs had negative present values (with BC ratios of less than 1). Finally, from the social perspective, all five education-first programs had negative present values and BC ratios less than 1. As a contrast, mixed-initial-activity programs showed more positive BC results (Greenberg et al., 2009, Table 6.1). Only one program site yielded losses from each of the participant, government, or social perspectives. From the social perspective, the BC ratio ranged from 0.7 to 3.79.

Overall, welfare-to-work programs that rely primarily on educational supports appear to have a negative return with costs greater than their benefits. When targeted based on need or income at baseline, the returns are positive but not always. Thus, it is not always the case that educational investments have positive NPVs. Of course, we have not accounted for any justification of investments for these populations on equity grounds.

10.4. CONCLUSIONS   ●

In this chapter, we have presented the basic structure of BC analysis and how to present the results using three economic metrics. This presentation reflects the fact that BC analysis is a numerical method. Although there are different ways to estimate costs and shadow price benefits, costs and benefits are combined in a specific way. With respect to costs, it is expected that all resources are valued even if a school or district does not directly pay any money for their use. For benefits, the analyst applies quantitative measures of educational outcomes and models of these for as long as they persist. The consequence of these prescriptions is that the metrics for comparing policies are simple and easy to understand; thus, the appropriate conclusions can be drawn. The disadvantage is that some aspects cannot be incorporated into the BC analysis: Any outcomes that cannot be shadow priced, for example, are excluded; issues of fairness are not addressed.

Regardless, the number of BC studies in education is growing, in part because of the increase in random assignment methods for evaluating effectiveness (and the use of earnings as measures of benefits).[1] There is also interest from government departments, state legislatures, and nonprofit agencies in identifying high-return social programs (for an inventory of BC studies for Washington State, see Lee et al., 2012; for a broader discussion, see Revesz & Livermore, 2008). Yet, there are still many fields in education policy to which BC analysis has not been widely applied—for example, value-added modeling, continuing education programs, education for select groups such as ex-offenders or veterans, and parental education programs. Presently, BC analysis is a long way from being a default approach to economic evaluation.

Thus far, the evidence suggests that—in many but not all cases— the NPV from educational investments is positive. Large labor market effects, as well as broad and persistent effects on behavior, translate into large benefits when programs are effective. Indeed, some educational programs may be efficient even if they do not improve the educational standing of the participants; for example, Papay and Johnson (2012) described a program that helps teachers improve their practice but that primarily yields cost savings. Ultimately, though, education is an investment for future benefits and so we cannot be certain that each investment will yield a positive NPV. Also, even if the expected NPV is positive, it may be that the estimate cannot be precisely bounded above zero. In the next chapter, we consider how to address this uncertainty.

---

[1] For an investigation of the IRR for the Japanese ronin examination process, see Ono (2007). For a baseline calculation of the IRR for underperforming teenagers in Israel, see Lavy and Schlosser (2005). For a BC of financial incentives in community colleges, see Barrow, Schanzenbach, and Claessens (2015). For a BC analysis that reduces child maltreatment, see Maher, Corwin, Hodnett, and Faulk (2012).

Discussion Questions

1. How would you interpret each of the following metrics: NPV, BC ratio, and IRR? Under what circumstances would you use each metric, and why?

2. What types of educational interventions lend themselves best to BC analyses? Why?

3. Under what conditions might BC analysis be preferable to CE analysis for evaluating educational interventions?

4. Why might a decisionmaker reject an educational evaluation with a positive NPV?

Exercises

1. The Chicago Child-Parent Center program serves approximately 3,000 3- to 5-year-olds from low-income families in more than 20 centers across Chicago. Students receive 3 hours of instruction per day, 5 days per week during the school year and for 6 weeks over the summer. The program featured structured math and reading activities led by certified teachers and aides in small classes, with a substantial parent component and supplemental health and nutrition services. Reynolds et al. (2002) estimated the per-student costs, present value at age 3 with a 3% discount rate, at $8,510, adjusted to 2007 dollars. Adapted from Reynolds et al. (2011), selected benefits of the program are estimated as follows:

	Present Value Benefits/Savings (2007 Dollars)
Child care for families	$4,387
Child abuse/neglect public services	$7,330
Grade retention school services	$880
Special education school services	$5,317
Earnings in adulthood	$28,844

(Continued)

(Continued)

	Present Value Benefits/Savings (2007 Dollars)
Criminal activity expenditures	$42,462
Health expenditures	$3,294
College tuition	−$294
Total benefits	$92,220

    a.   Calculate the social NPV and BC ratio for the program.

    b.   Divide the benefits into private benefits and fiscal benefits. What is the private NPV and BC ratio and the fiscal NPV and BC ratio?

    c.   Under what circumstances would distributional weights change your recommendation on implementing the program?

2. The HighScope Perry Preschool Program was a high-quality preschool education program for 3- and 4-year-old African American children living in poverty and at high risk of low academic performance. The program involved an active learning curriculum and weekly 1.5-hour home visits to each mother and child, designed to involve the mother in the educational process and help implement the preschool curriculum at home. To test the benefits of the program, 123 students were randomly assigned to either the control group or the preschool treatment group. These 123 students were followed up at ages 19, 27, and 40. The present value cost of the program at age 4 was $15,000 (in 2000 dollars). Adapted from Nores et al. (2006), selected results were as follows:

	HighScope Perry Preschool Group	Control Group
Earnings at age 27 (2000 dollars)	$13,328	$11,186
Earnings at age 40 (2000 dollars)	$24,466	$19,699
Felony total count ages 19 to 27	0.12	0.26
Felony total count ages 28 to 40	0.05	0.07
Misdemeanor total count ages 19 to 27	0.12	0.22

	HighScope Perry Preschool Group	Control Group
Misdemeanor total count ages 28 to 40	0.17	0.25
Months on welfare entire ages 19 to 27	4.74	4.71
Months on welfare entire ages 28 to 40	2.15	2.02
HS graduate by age 19	67%	46%

Perform a social BC analysis of this program. You may find the following helpful: shadow prices for social willingness to pay for crimes of $47,000 per felony, $7,200 per misdemeanor (McCollister, French, & Fang, 2010), and welfare payments of $400 per month.

3. A school district is looking to boost high school graduation and college completion rates. It has a choice of two summer programs for students between eighth and ninth grade. Without the programs, the district has a high school graduation rate of 40% and a college completion rate of 20%. Program A is delivered to 1,000 students and costs $2,400 per student; for these students, the high school and college completion rate is 66%. Program B is delivered to 500 students and costs $400 for each year per student but only when the student is enrolled in either school or college; for these students, the high school graduation rate is 90%, and the college completion rate is 60%. As an economist, you calculate the lifetime earnings of high school dropouts at $300,000, of high school graduates at $400,000, and of college graduates at $600,000 (present values at age 20 using a 3% discount rate). Assume there are only these three possible educational states. Perform BC analysis of the two programs relative to the status quo.

11

Accounting for Uncertainty

Objectives

1. Classify different types of uncertainty.

2. Describe methods for sensitivity testing of economic evaluations.

3. Specify methods for estimating confidence intervals for economic evaluations.

4. Discuss implications of sensitivity for interpreting results.

Thus far, we have discussed how to calculate the best estimate of costs, cost-effectiveness (CE) or benefit-cost (BC) metrics. However, we have emphasized that in each case these estimates are uncertain and that this uncertainty needs to be addressed explicitly through sensitivity testing. We examine uncertainty in this chapter.

Broadly, the types of uncertainty common across empirical research apply in economic evaluation. However, there are some differences because economic evaluations introduce additional sources of variation: As well as uncertainty of impacts, there is also uncertainty over costs and over shadow prices. In addition, the uncertainty is transformed when we take the ratio of costs and effects or costs and benefits. As there are more possible sources of uncertainty, sensitivity testing becomes more complex but also more necessary. In fact, Vining and Weimer (2010) asserted that one type of sensitivity testing—Monte Carlo simulation—"should be the standard basis for assessing net benefits in social policy" (p. 17). We focus on this method next.

In this chapter, we consider the multiple forms of uncertainty and demonstrate the main ways in which such uncertainty and sensitivity can be addressed. We begin by discussing types of uncertainty. We then describe the general forms of sensitivity analyses applicable for economic evaluations. We then provide more detail for cost, CE and BC analyses respectively, illustrating our analysis with examples from prominent studies. As discussed in Chapter 7, considerable research energy is devoted to identifying impacts and their uncertainty as reflected in the standard errors of any point estimate. Here, we focus on uncertainty of costs, benefits (shadow prices), and the economic metrics (CE and BC ratios, net present values [NPVs], and internal rates of return [IRRs]).

Most sensitivity tests are numerical. But we recognize the role of judgment in CE and BC analyses. There is a formal method, and there are "right" and "wrong" (methodologically valid and invalid) ways to perform CE and BC analyses (see Farrow & Zerbe, 2013). There are also standards and principles to guide analysis. But both assumptions and judgments are frequently applied to derive CE and BC analyses results. It is important to establish that these assumptions and judgments have not predetermined the results.

● 11.1. TYPES OF UNCERTAINTY AND SENSITIVITY

For economic evaluation, we distinguish two broad types of uncertainty: (1) parameter uncertainty and (2) structural uncertainty (Briggs et al., 2012; Gray, Clarke, Wolstenholme, & Wordsworth, 2011).

Parameter uncertainty refers to the fact that estimates of all parameters will vary, and this variation is reflected in the respective standard errors or other measures of parameter variance. These standard errors may be wide or narrow; the wider they are, the less precisely the analyst can estimate the BC results. Most discussion of parameter uncertainty focuses on estimates of impacts and testing across confidence intervals (see the discussion in Chapter 7). However, shadow prices may also be uncertain and, as we emphasized in Chapters 2 through 5, cost ingredients and prices may also be uncertain.

Structural uncertainty refers more broadly to how a model is specified (Jain, Grabner, & Onukwugha, 2011). This form of uncertainty includes econometric issues such as regression model specification (e.g., ordinary least squares versus propensity score matching). But it also includes the many different ways in which the model used in the analysis might capture the mechanisms that generate outcomes (a classic example of how different models identify crime deterrents is by Leamer, 1983). For example, a preschool program may be economically valuable because it has a positive NPV. If this result is because preschool induces families to select higher-quality elementary schooling, then these additional elementary school resources need to be counted. If instead preschool is advantageous because it reduces the need for special educational services, then the resources saved on these services should be included in the BC analysis. To fully investigate structural uncertainty, it is essential to have a well-specified theory of change. There are many assumptions and modeling decisions that the analyst might consider to see how sensitive the results are.

Structural uncertainty and parameter uncertainty are distinct. For example, a college mentoring program might yield earnings gains one or two decades after program completion. But if these can be precisely estimated, parameter uncertainty will be trivial. It may be that most of the gains accrue within the first decade and that discounting further reduces any benefits in the second decade to a trivial amount. If so, then the BC ratios for these two durations would be very similar, and we would conclude that the BC analysis is not sensitive to the time horizon beyond one decade—that is, there is no structural uncertainty with respect to the time horizon.

Potentially there are many structural uncertainties. The analyst might not know if the mentoring program operates through changes in major choice or labor market participation, for instance, or whether the mentoring program reduces the time spent working while enrolled (and so reduces earnings in the short term). Parameter uncertainty is typically represented using standard errors and confidence intervals. Structural uncertainty is represented by alternative explanations of the theory of change. Again, early education provides a notable example. The HighScope Perry Preschool Program had large effects on criminal activity; by contrast, the Abecedarian preschool program had little effect on criminality. This difference in the "early education to crime" mechanism is one of the main reasons the BC results differ between the two preschool programs (Barnett & Masse, 2007).

In addition to these types of uncertainty, it is also helpful to consider variability and heterogeneity. Variability refers to the random chance that affects each measure of cost or outcome and is captured by the respective standard deviations. Of course, all variables have a distribution (i.e., they exhibit variability). But the distributions for costs and for CE and BC ratios may require particular attention: They are ratios of variables such that the distribution of the ratio is not obvious; also, as discussed in Chapter 8, the interpretation changes depending on whether the denominators are negative or positive. Reporting this sensitivity is important. See Example 11.1 for the Talent Search program.

Example 11.1   Sensitivity Testing: Talent Search

Talent Search is a middle and high school program with the goal to provide more equitable opportunities for students from low-income households to attend college. Importantly, Talent Search providers have considerable flexibility in what services to provide, how they provide them, and for how long. In a recent evaluation, information on costs and effects was collected across nine sites in two states (Bowden & Belfield, 2015). Thus, there were opportunities to perform sensitivity tests in various different ways. A selection of these are shown in the following table. The intent is to examine the robustness of the baseline cost-effectiveness (CE) ratio of 2.4 (first row of the table).

Sensitivity Testing for Cost-Effectiveness Ratios

	Yield of New High School Graduates	Cost per New High School Graduate	Cost-Effectiveness Ratio per $100,000
Best estimate (pooled across 9 sites)	590	$44,650	2.4
A. Sampling:			
Texas sample	214	$88,750	1.2
Florida sample	376	$19,600	5.6
B. Statistical significance criteria:			
Sites: stat. sig. positive effects; all costs	489	$53,810	2.0
Sites: stat. sig. positive effects; associated costs	489	$26,440	4.1

	Yield of New High School Graduates	Cost per New High School Graduate	Cost-Effectiveness Ratio per $100,000
Sites: mean positive effect; all costs	620	$42,470	2.6
Sites: mean positive effect; associated costs	620	$38,380	2.8
C. Treatment dosage:			
PV cost with 3 years of treatment	590	$25,360	4.3
PV cost with 1 year of treatment	590	$7,960	13.7
D. Outliers:			
Least cost-effective site only	−30	−$83,550	−1.3
Most cost-effective site only	192	$11,260	9.7
Excl. most and least effective	427	$50,590	2.2
Excl. most and least cost	409	$46,770	2.3

Source: Adapted from Bowden and Belfield (2015).

Notes: PV = present value. PV amounts in 2015 dollars (nearest 10).

Within the confines of the study design, the sensitivity tests are grouped according to their purpose. The first panel examines sensitivity due to sampling error. We note that the sampling frame did not incorporate variations in costs, so the potential for sampling error for CE ratios might be high. As shown, the CE ratios varied significantly between states. The second panel looks at how assumptions about statistical significance can influence the CE ratios. Not all sites obtained effects that were statistically significant; looking only at sites that are statistically significant increases the CE ratio to 4.1. Next, the researchers considered how sensitive the results are to treatment dosage; the interpretation here is that students need only receive 1 or 3 years of services to get the full impact (not the six estimated in the baseline). Finally, the researchers attempt to bound the distribution of CE ratios by drawing from within the possible distribution of costs and effects. In its worse case, Talent Search is not all cost-effective. However, trimming the analysis does not change the CE ratios substantially.

As shown here, there are many different ways to perform sensitivity testing for a given education program. We emphasize that the analyst should choose tests with an explicit purpose in mind rather than simply to amass CE ratios for their own sake.

Heterogeneity refers to the fact that outcomes will likely differ across groups of students. For example, students who are struggling to learn will need longer sessions of a given reading program than students who are reading at grade level; this will lead to higher costs. Also, the trajectory of child development is such that interventions in early grades—such as reducing class sizes or hiring more experienced teachers—might not be expected to have the same effect across all grades (Lipsey et al., 2012). Similarly, educational programs in urban areas might not work as effectively in rural schools, and the shadow prices might also differ across localities (e.g., if wages differ; see Moretti, 2013). Given the importance of context for educational interventions and policies, heterogeneity is likely to be pervasive for both estimation and testing of results. Hence, the analyst might wish to perform extensive subgroup sensitivity testing to examine heterogeneity.

In practice, the two types of uncertainty, along with issues related to variability and heterogeneity, are often mixed together and addressed via a general approach of sensitivity testing. In fact, although it is helpful to distinguish each type of uncertainty, it is important to remember the purpose of sensitivity testing: to see if the results—and therefore the decisions—are robust to any alternative versions of the evaluation. The goal of the analyst is to test if Intervention A is substantively more cost-effective than Intervention B. It is not the same as a test that the cost of Intervention A is statistically significantly different from that of Intervention B. The aim is to help the decisionmaker choose the most cost-effective intervention. The goal is equivalent for BC analysis. The BC analyst is testing the hypothesis that the NPV of Intervention A is positive and exceeds that of Intervention B. This test is distinct from a test that each benefit is statistically significantly different from zero (or that the incremental cost is zero). The goal is to improve decisionmaking, and so all important forms of uncertainty—even those that cannot be quantified—should be included in sensitivity testing to see if a decision would change.

● 11.2. GENERAL SENSITIVITY TESTING

Before describing specific procedures for calculating uncertainty for each type of analysis, we consider more general approaches to testing for sensitivity (see also Boardman, Greenberg, Vining, & Weimer, 2011, Chapter 7).

For each model, the analyst should test for general parameter sensitivity. That is, we should check that alternative but plausible values for each parameter do not substantially alter the magnitude of the results or the conclusions drawn from those results. The choice of parameter will vary across interventions. However, most educational interventions are labor-intensive. The critical price of an ingredient is therefore the salary of the teacher or education professional. It is therefore worthwhile to see how cost estimates would be affected by assuming the top of a teacher salary range rather than the average. For K–12 interventions, class or group size may be an important parameter affecting cost estimates. The costs of interventions with individualized instruction (e.g., Reading Recovery) may be sensitive to assumptions about the length of instructional time needed per child. As another example, a critical benefit from the Perry Preschool Program was the lower rate of criminal activity by the treatment group. Given society's high willingness to pay for lower crime, the program can be justified—in the sense that the NPV is positive—purely as a crime prevention strategy (Nores, Belfield, Barnett, & Schweinhart, 2006). Hence, it is important to see how the results would differ if an alternative shadow price for crime reduction was applied. It is also important to test for sensitivity of the discount rate: crime impacts occur many years after preschool. As each parameter is varied, all other parameters and modeling assumptions should be held constant so that the sensitivity of the results to that parameter can be directly established.

This approach is the most commonly used form of sensitivity testing, and many parameters might potentially be varied in CE or BC analysis. The choice of parameters for further investigation should be motivated by several criteria: which parameter is the "largest," which parameter is the most influential, which parameter has the most variance, and which parameter is the most controversial. Importantly, substitute values for key parameters should be drawn from alternative sources of evidence. They should not be arbitrarily assigned. This drawing may have an additional virtue in promoting consistency across studies. For example, the Perry Preschool Program currently has followed up on participants over a 35-year time horizon, and the Chicago Child-Parent Center program has followed up over 20 years. In sensitivity testing, it may be appropriate to constrain the parameter values so they are harmonized—for example, over a common time horizon (Karoly, 2012). This would allow for more accessible comparisons (see Barnett & Masse, 2007).

For most BC analysis, one of the likely candidates for parameter sensitivity testing is the discount rate. A major justification for education policies is that they are investments in future productivity, so this justification will depend on how much the future is valued relative to the present. To illustrate, we can imagine a kindergarten program that yields labor market benefits immediately after high school graduation (i.e., 12 years later). If the discount rate is 3%, these benefits will be worth 2.2 times more than if the discount rate is 10%. As a matter of convention, the BC analysis should be tested for different discount rates.

An alternative approach is to estimate the highest and lowest ratios that might be plausibly obtained (based on the available evidence). This form of sensitivity testing might encompass either parameter or model uncertainty. For example, a worst-case scenario might be that a college scholarship would have to be funded from a private loan; this would imply a high discount rate. Alternatively, a worst-case scenario might be that an educational program only improves cognitive scores and has no mediating effect on noncognitive performance such that consequent behaviors that improve workplace productivity and earnings cannot be attributed to the program.

This approach is less frequently applied than the others. Often, the worst-case scenario is that the program has zero impact, in which case the CE and BC ratios collapse to infinity. In the case of Talent Search, for example, the worst case is that the program is harmful (as well as costly; see Example 11.1). Plus, an important principle of CE and BC analyses is that estimates should be conservative. Some "worst casing" should therefore already be incorporated into the baseline estimates. On the other side, the best-case scenario may be far too optimistic and lack credibility for policymakers.

Break-even sensitivity tests may be useful. Of course, as explained in Chapter 10, the calculation of the IRR (the discount rate where benefits equal costs) is the primary example of break-even analysis. (See Example 11.2, which is later in this chapter, for sensitivity testing of the IRR.) (The break-even construct is harder to conceptualize for CE analysis: It might correspond to a position where each program was "buying" outcomes at the same price or to an external willingness-to-pay threshold.) The intent is to choose values such that the benefits and costs converge and then to contrast the evidence-based baseline model with the break-even values. Beyond the discount rate, the choice of how to vary parameters to make the analysis break even may be quite arbitrary. For example, one might infer that a BC ratio of 4 implies break-even if the program is assumed to be four times as expensive as expected. As one of the main benefits of education is the higher earnings that accrue from human capital, one approach is to see how little effect a college degree would have to have on earnings for it still to pay off.

Finally, the analyst should consider context sensitivity. In order for BC analyses of social programs to yield high returns, there should be some behavioral change over time. If it is not possible to follow this behavioral change over its full course, then the analyst must make predictions or extrapolations. Although these predictions should be model-based, some contextual influences should be considered. First, there may be changes in the school environment that, in turn, affect shadow prices. For example, a program to reduce special education placement may generate high benefits if these students are placed in independent centers; if, however, there is a trend toward mainstreaming special education students, the shadow prices will change. Second, there may be changes to government programs and the tax code. For example, the Patient Protection and Affordable Care Act of 2010 has enrolled many more people into health insurance plans, some of which are subsidized. As of 2010, therefore, educational programs that improved health status became more valuable from the fiscal perspective: Federal and state governments were now providing more subsidized health care and so gained if use of health care services was averted. Finally, the labor market changes over time. A program to boost earnings may have a very different impact if the graduates enter the labor market during a recession or a period of strong economic growth (Oreopoulos, von Wachter, & Heisz, 2012).

These contextual influences might not be included in the quantitative economic evaluation. Instead, they may be included as general issues regarding sensitivity. For instance, given that the long-run labor market trend has been one of increasing returns to schooling (Goldin & Katz, 2008), the analyst might note this in a discussion of the sensitivity of results from current or historic evaluations. Most studies are small-scale and so do not need to consider general equilibrium effects. However, these may be important for large-scale policies—for example, where large numbers of new students enroll in college and then drive up average cost or where large numbers of graduates enter the labor market and drive down wages.

Clearly, there are a lot of sensitivity tests that might be performed. To decide which ones to perform, it is important to refer back to the decisionmaking process and the needs of users of a given CE or BC analysis. So, if a particular sensitivity test does not help decisionmakers, it is probably unnecessary. If the BC ratio is substantially greater than one even under worst-case scenarios, sensitivity testing need not be extensive. One way to help decisionmakers is to increase confidence in the estimated CE results. Another way is to identify the conditions under which a CE decision (or set of rankings) might be overturned or where the NPV might change from positive to negative. A third way is to use sensitivity analysis to indicate whether more information is needed in order to make a decision. Levin and Garcia (2013) performed extensive sensitivity tests of the benefits and costs of the Accelerated Study in Associate Programs (ASAP) at community colleges in New York. ASAP has a BC ratio exceeding one; for sensitivity testing, Levin and Garcia (2013) considered how comprehensive the benefits are, what positive and negative externalities are generated, and the importance of student mobility away from the local tax jurisdiction.

Finally, when choosing sensitivity tests, comparability is an important consideration. When CE and BC analyses apply different assumptions, it becomes very difficult to compare the results for decisionmaking. Therefore, sensitivity testing might be motivated so as to allow the research to be compared with other related studies. For example, the discount rate might be chosen so as to be harmonized with other studies. For BC analysis, the catalog of benefits may be selected to correspond with prior research (as recommended by Karoly, 2012).

● 11.3. SENSITIVITY TESTING OF COST ESTIMATES

For cost analysis, there are several approaches to checking for robustness. Ideally, if we have a valid sampling frame and sufficient sample size, we can simply estimate standard errors for costs using standard formulae as one would estimate the standard error of an impact estimate. We would then represent uncertainty with the range of confidence intervals. This uncertainty could be estimated for both the quantities and prices of ingredients. Notably, although we have provided a number of techniques for estimating costs, there are several challenges in understanding uncertainty with respect to cost estimates (Weimer, 2015).

The first challenge is when there simply is no reliable standard on which to base a cost estimate. That is, the intervention may require an input for which there is no information on costs. For example, the project may require the preparation of a manual to instruct teachers. What will the manual cost? The best way to address this type of problem is to try to divide the manual itself into sub-ingredients for producing it. In so doing, it will be possible to focus on the process and the ingredients for creating the manual, and the prices of each of these ingredients can be estimated with greater precision than the more abstract task of estimating the overall cost of a manual. Also, after specifying the manual's requirements, it is possible to get the cost of similar manuals in the market.

A more difficult example is that of estimating the cost of ingredients that are not readily available at the time that an intervention is being planned. A project that uses future technology will face this type of problem. For example, although the cost of computer hardware may not pose a problem for cost estimation, the school district may need to develop its own instructional software. Such development is not always predictable in terms of the time and other resources that will be required to design it and make it operational. In this case, it is best to obtain several independent opinions from experts on the probable costs.

One of the most challenging issues that might face an evaluator occurs when the program itself has not been implemented or even clearly defined. The discussion thus far has assumed that a well-defined educational program exists and that the evaluator is familiar with its operations. When this is not the case, the level of uncertainty is magnified. A common instance is site-level variation in costs: Sites adopt interventions often without exact prescriptions on what inputs to use and how much to pay for each ingredient. Often they must rely on internal resources to reorganize their operations to deliver a new curriculum or school reform. And both organizational capacity and leadership can affect the process of implementation. Unsurprisingly, therefore, sites often vary in how much of a given resource they deploy. Examples of substantial variation in cost per site were described earlier for Read 180 and for Talent Search (Bowden & Belfield, 2015; Levin, Catlin, & Elson, 2007). If the "program" is ill-defined or changes greatly from one site to another, then the evaluator is hard-pressed to catalog the specific ingredients used and attach values to them. In such cases, it is difficult to carry out and interpret the results of cost analysis, and site-specific sensitivity testing is therefore an important way to check the robustness of the results.

A variety of cost estimates can arise when there is no previous experience on what a particular ingredient may cost. The uncertainty of a new technology is obvious, but the problem can arise even when estimating personnel or facilities costs. For example, a proposal to hire science and mathematics teachers at their market salaries to overcome shortages in the schools would be immediately beset by the challenge of knowing what salary level would be required to attract adequate numbers of such personnel into teaching. A proposal to build a new facility might face uncertainty about some of the structural requirements, a dilemma that can be resolved only after extensive and costly testing of the subsoil. Perhaps the most prominent example is online learning, the average cost of which depends critically on economies of scale. In these cases, it is important to take into consideration a range of cost estimates.

As well as these practical challenges, there are significant statistical challenges. One is that the distribution of costs across the population or sites may be unknown, and it is unlikely to approximate a normal distribution. In most cases, costs do not fall below zero (unless the program substitutes for a more expensive program) such that the distribution of costs will be significantly left-censored. In educational research, where costs are measured at the classroom, school, or program level, sample sizes may not be large enough to easily determine the distribution of costs. If the distribution of costs is not normal, then it may be appropriate to consider an alternative central tendency measure such as the median or mode. However, these alternatives typically need to be retransformed so that the actual dollar differences between programs can be reported. To estimate the total cost difference between one program and another, the analyst cannot multiply the mode by the number of participants. As well, it might be misleading to think of costs as a continuous variable: If a program requires $5,000 to properly implement, a site that spends $3,000 is likely to be just as ineffective as a site that spends $2,000. This has implications for hypothesis testing of cost differences between treatment and control groups.

A second challenge is that a sampling frame for cost estimates may be hard to devise; this makes it difficult to estimate (or in some cases conceive of) a distribution for estimated costs. Programs are often delivered at the classroom, site, or district level. Thus, educational costs are often aggregated such that only the total costs of the program are meaningful (with average costs simply total cost divided by the number of participants). For example, the cost of the Chicago Child-Parent Center program was $1.8 million across 4,100 students; no distribution of estimates of this total cost figure can be calculated. We might obtain a distribution of costs at the level of each preschool center, although the validity of this variable depends on how much organization, management, and governance is at the aggregate program level.

If the sample of cost data is not large enough to generate meaningful standard errors (or the sampling frame may not be appropriate), we may consider using bootstrapping techniques (see Mooney & Duval, 1993). Bootstrapping involves randomly drawing n observations with replacement from the sample of unit-level cost data.

The analyst then calculates the mean of those n observations. This random draw is performed 500 or 1,000 times and those means are then averaged. The random draws also yield a distribution of costs so that a confidence interval may be derived. Unfortunately, most cost data does not come in unit-level form of sufficient sample size or from a sampling frame, which is representative of the variation in costs. For example, although there may be 400 student observations in an intervention that involves randomly assigning students to smaller classes, this might mean only 20 classroom-level cost observations. If the reform is districtwide, the sample might include thousands of students and only one district-level aggregated cost. Thus, it is unclear how feasible—or useful—it is to apply bootstrapping to cost estimates in educational research.

In light of these issues, simple approaches to sensitivity testing of cost estimates are typically applied. These approaches are testing for parameter uncertainty (e.g., for the most important ingredient) and reporting of best-case and worst-case scenarios.

11.4. SENSITIVITY TESTING OF COST-EFFECTIVENESS

Sensitivity testing for CE analysis is potentially more complex. With CE analysis, there are three variables to model in order to estimate confidence intervals: (1) cost, (2) effect, and (3) the ratio of cost over effect. As noted previously, distributions of costs (and possibly of effects) are hard to determine; the fact that they have to be expressed as a ratio adds further complications. Even if both costs and effects are normally distributed, the ratio need not itself be normally distributed. CE ratios cannot be considered as continuous variables: As effectiveness tends toward zero, the CE ratio tends toward infinity (Briggs, O'Brien, & Blackhouse, 2002). Also, the interpretation of the CE ratio depends on whether it is the product of negative or positive numbers. This challenge was noted in Chapter 9: A program with negative incremental costs and positive effects will have a negative CE ratio even as it dominates other programs. Thus, hypothesis testing will be flawed unless the distribution of CE ratios has numerators and denominators of all the same sign.

In light of these issues, simple approaches to sensitivity testing of CE ratios are usually applied. One approach is to see how sensitive the CE ratios are to alternative assumptions about costs or effects sequentially. So, new CE ratios can be calculated for different cost estimates depending on assumptions about, for example, teacher salaries or instructional time. Separately, new CE ratios can be calculated for alternative estimates of effects (typically derived from alternative model specifications). This approach was shown in Example 11.1.

A second approach attempts to put boundaries on the expected CE ratio. To begin, the analyst reports expected costs divided by expected effects (incremental over the comparison group). Next, the analyst reports a lower bound: costs plus the standard error of costs divided by effects minus the standard error of effects. This boundary corresponds to high costs and low effects. Similarly, the analyst reports an upper bound: costs minus the standard error of costs divided by effects plus the standard error of effects. This boundary corresponds to low costs and high effects. The analyst would then report these ranges of CE ratios and note if they overlap across interventions. These results will give some indication of how the CE ratios might vary. However, these are not confidence intervals: They do not reflect a distribution of the CE ratios per se.

To derive confidence intervals for CE ratios, there are two approaches. One is the bootstrapping method discussed in the previous section but applied to the CE ratios. The other is to use Fieller's theorem to directly calculate the confidence intervals. As explained in detail in the context of health sciences research by Briggs et al. (2002), Fieller's theorem requires information on the ranges of costs and effects of both the intervention and the comparison groups as well as the covariance of incremental costs and effects. Other than by Bowden and Belfield (2015), the theorem has not been applied in education research to calculate confidence intervals for CE ratios. As discussed previously, it is unlikely that the analysis has a sufficient sample size and power to detect a statistically significant difference among CE ratios. Typically power calculations are based on the study's ability to identify effectiveness with statistical significance. Power calculations to identify CE are rarely considered, and there is no reason why the necessary sample size would be equivalent for effectiveness and CE tests (for discussion in the context of health sciences, see Briggs et al., 2002; Glick, 2011).

● 11.5. SENSITIVITY TESTING OF BENEFIT-COST ANALYSIS

Many of the general sensitivity tests discussed previously can also be applied for BC analysis. Tests for parameter uncertainty should focus on key components of the BC calculation (such as the discount rate and important shadow prices). Also, worst-case scenarios can be calculated to see if the NPV becomes negative.

Some of the challenges for sensitivity analysis of CE may also apply to BC analysis. The distribution of benefits may be difficult to estimate. Benefits are the product of impacts times shadow prices: If the distributions of impacts and prices are normally distributed, the product might follow a normal distribution (if the analyst considers all impacts regardless of statistical significance). However, benefits are unlikely to fall below zero (unless the program substantively disadvantages participants) and so, as with costs, the distribution of benefits will be heavily left-censored.

Therefore, following Vining and Weimer (2010), the primary form of sensitivity testing for BC analysis is Monte Carlo simulation. This method uses information on the values of the distribution to derive a range of NPV estimates.

Example 11.2   Sensitivity Testing: HighScope Perry Preschool Program

Extensive benefit-cost (BC) analysis—including sensitivity testing—has been performed on early education programs (see Chapters 9 and 10 for results). Karoly (2012, Table 7) listed the recommended sensitivity tests for these analyses across early childhood interventions. This list includes investigation of parameter uncertainty with respect to alternative discount rates (up to 10%) and alternative shadow prices (in particular for victims' willingness to pay to avoid crime). It also refers to structural uncertainty with respect to how to project future consequences of early education.

An extensive sensitivity testing of the HighScope Perry Preschool Program has been performed by Heckman, Moon, Pinto, Savelyev, and Yavitz (2010). As described in earlier examples, this program was an early childhood intervention to help disadvantaged children in Ypsilanti, Michigan, in the 1960s. Children were randomly assigned to the program or a control group. The Perry Preschool Program is ripe for sensitivity testing: Because these children have been followed up periodically since the 1960s, there are many possible outcomes over a long duration, and many of these outcomes do not have clearly established shadow prices.

As shown in earlier examples, BC analyses have established that the program yields benefits that easily exceed its costs. Expressed as an internal rate of return (IRR) on the program as a social investment (i.e., the rate of return at which the discounted benefits equal the discounted costs), a baseline estimate for the Perry Preschool Program is 8.1%. In their sensitivity analysis, Heckman and colleagues (2010) examined both forms of uncertainty regarding this finding.

(Continued)

(Continued)

To address parameter uncertainty relative to the baseline estimate, the authors applied a higher shadow price for lost life, used national costs/prices, applied crime-specific shadow prices, and used an alternative data set to project earnings growth over time. To address structural uncertainty, the authors excluded hard-core criminals from the sample, used an alternative form of imputation for earnings, and extrapolated the model only up to age 40. Heckman and colleagues (2010) also constrained their analysis so that it could be directly compared with earlier BC analysis (see Nores et al., 2006).

HighScope Perry Preschool Program Sensitivity Testing

	Internal Rate of Return
Baseline	8.1%
Sensitivity Testing: Parameter Uncertainty	
a. Higher shadow price for lost life	9.2%
b. National costs/prices	8.0%
c. Crime-specific criminal justice system shadow prices	8.0%
d. Uses CPS data for earnings instead of PSID	8.5%
Sensitivity Testing: Structural Uncertainty	
a. Excludes hard-core criminals from sample	9.7%
b. Uses piecewise linear regressions for imputation instead of kernel matching	7.6%
c. Extrapolates only to age 40 instead of age 65	7.5%

Source: Heckman et al. (2010, Tables 5–7).

The results of this sensitivity testing are shown in the table. Overall, the returns on the program appear to be stable and robust with respect to both parameter and structural uncertainty. If we assume that the value of lost life was underestimated, the IRR rises by 1.1 percentage points. Even if we assume that the effects of the program have completely faded out by age 40, the IRR is reduced by only 0.6 percentage points. For each test, the IRR remains above most plausible estimates of the social discount rate. In light of this sensitivity testing and its finding that the benefits consistently exceeded the costs, decisionmakers should be strongly confident that the Perry Preschool Program was an efficient investment.

To gain a better understanding of the distribution of NPVs, their range can be simulated using Monte Carlo techniques. The first step is to report the baseline estimate of the NPV using the expected value of costs and benefits. Next, each variable is assigned a distribution; ideally, this distribution should be the observed distribution, but it may be reasonable to use random draws from an upper and lower bound. Then, a single value for each variable is drawn, given its distribution, and the NPV is then recalculated using these values. This step is then repeated (simulated) 500 or 1,000 times. The result will be a mean estimate of the NPV (from the 500 or 1,000 observations); that mean should be very close to the baseline estimate. More importantly, the result will be a simulated distribution of NPVs. This distribution can be used to depict the range of possible outcomes.

Monte Carlo analysis is useful when impacts cannot be estimated precisely and when variables interact with each other. In BC analysis, even if an impact is not statistically significant, the economic value of that impact is included in the benefits side of the ledger.[1] In fact, this is the reason why impacts that are not statistically significant are included. Of course, when they are included, the lower- and upper-bound confidence intervals for that benefit will include zero; their inclusion is so that the distribution of NPVs is based on full information. These numbers will then be reported in the sensitivity analysis for the NPV.

Also, if variables interact with each other, it may be difficult to trace through the implications of uncertainty for each parameter. In this case, Monte Carlo simulation is especially useful and can provide a more detailed picture of the distribution of possible NPVs. For example, we can imagine a training program where the effects on trainees' wages are mean gains of 0.1 (10%) with a standard deviation of 0.05, and the trainees' additional hours of work per week have a mean of 5 and standard deviation of 2. If the baseline wage is $10 per hour and baseline hours worked are 30, the mean benefit is 30 × ($10 × 0.1) + 5 × ($10 × 1.1) = $85. However, we can also calculate different estimates of expected benefits if we assume the values for the effects on wages and hours are drawn from the distributions of (0.1, 0.05) and (5, 2) respectively. Making 1,000 draws will yield 1,000 estimates of expected benefits, each of which can be compared with the costs of the program

---

[1] This may be surprising to many readers—namely that findings that are not statistically significant are not dismissed. However, it reflects the fundamental difference between statistical significance and economic significance that distinguishes an impact evaluation from a BC analysis. See Chapter 10.

and so yield 1,000 NPVs. The distribution of these 1,000 NPVs can then be reported to indicate how likely it is that the program will have a positive NPV. For example, with a normally distributed wage gain (0.1, 0.05) there is a 2% possibility of zero wage gain for trainees. Unless hours of work were increased significantly, an intervention with a zero wage gain will not have a positive NPV.

● 11.6. DISTRIBUTIONAL ISSUES

As a final way to think about sensitivity we consider distributional issues. Thus far, we have assumed that dollars are equally valued across all those involved in the intervention. For CE analysis, a $500 tuition fee incurred by a low-income family is equivalent to a $500 charge to a high-income family. In the case of BC analysis, for example, an incremental $1,000 of benefits are assumed to be worth the same whether the student is earning $10,000 per annum or $100,000 per annum. This assumption is open to challenge: Different groups may place differing values on money. Most likely, low-income groups have a higher marginal utility of money such that income gains for them are more valuable than income gains for high-income groups.[2]

In other words, it might matter who receives the benefits and who pays the costs and not just whether the benefits exceed the costs. This is a fundamental issue of model sensitivity in that we are questioning whether the unit of account (money) is appropriate. Here, we present a technical solution to address distributional considerations that might be included in a sensitivity analysis.

First, we would need to designate groups for which we might value costs or benefits differently. Among program participants, for example, we may wish to calculate money values separately by income level, gender, or race, in order to assess whether one group obtains a larger share of benefits. (In some cases, this is precluded by an already limited sample of individuals in an evaluation. In the Perry Preschool Program, for example, the sample was relatively small and already limited to low-income, minority children.) We can also calculate benefits separately for

---

[2] Relatedly, we have assumed that effectiveness is equally valuable to all students and stakeholders. Yet, it is unlikely that policymakers would view effect size reading gains for illiterate students as equivalent to effect size reading gains for highly literate students or that an additional year of attainment is equivalent for a student who drops out of school in 8th grade versus one who drops out in 12th grade. Potentially, this issue could be addressed by deriving a utility function.

program participants and for other members of society (the "taxpayers"). As with costs, it is common that benefits received by one group are not the same as benefits received by another group.

Once dollar amounts are separately estimated for each group, there are three ways to proceed. The first and least attractive option is to simply ignore the distribution of benefits across groups and present the sum of total benefits, even though this limits our understanding of the program. Second, we can separately calculate and present the benefits (and costs) that are received by each group (as per the cost spreadsheet example, except by group rather than funder or agency). Individuals who read the evaluation can use this information to form their own opinions about whether the distribution of benefits should figure in judgments about the program's desirability. Third, we can multiply each group's benefits by a set of distributional weights before they are summed in an overall measure of benefits, thereby placing greater (or lesser) emphasis on the benefits received or costs borne by certain groups. (Even when doing so, however, it is important to also present the unweighted, baseline estimates.)

Imagine that we are assessing a program for 100 children, half of whom are low-income and half of whom are middle-income. The program costs $5,000 per child, paid for by the federal government, for a total cost of $0.5 million. The discounted sum of benefits is found to be $10,000 per low-income child and $15,000 per high-income child. The total benefit is therefore an unweighted sum of $1.25 million, assuming that we do not treat one group's benefits as more important than the other's. However, we may decide that benefits accruing to low-income children are twice as important as those received by middle-income children. If so, the total benefits are now $1.75 million—that is, equals $(2 \times 10,000 \times 50) + (1 \times 15,000 \times 50)$. Accounting for distributional considerations, the BC ratio is now 3.5. An alternative is to report net benefits separately by group. Per low-income child, the net benefits are $15,000 (= $2 \times \$10,000 - \$5,000$). For middle-income children, the net benefits are $10,000 (= \$15,000 - \$5,000$).

These solutions explicitly recognize the priority given to investments in low-income children. However, there are two drawbacks. The first is that the results are no longer in actual dollar amounts. In our example, it is not the case that low-income children will obtain benefits of $20,000 instead of $10,000. Second, and more importantly, it is not at all clear how to choose the weights for distributional analysis. In the example, our choice of weights was quite arbitrary, and although most policymakers might favor interventions to low-income groups, it is not easy to specify the extent of favorability.

One source might be the tax code, the progressivity of which presumably reflects—to some extent—society's views about the marginal utility of income at different income levels.

11.7. CONCLUSIONS

There are many sources of uncertainty in CE and BC analyses, and it is essential to address these either by sensitivity testing or by directly reporting confidence intervals. In so doing, economic evaluations will be catching up with impact evaluations, which exhaustively estimate bias and precision of model coefficients.

Ideally, all types of uncertainty should be explicitly considered in any CE or BC analysis. However, in practice the analyst should select the most important tests with respect to changes in the model. This selection should depend on the purpose of the sensitivity testing. It may be that the intent is to increase credibility that the NPV is greater than zero; or to identify conditions under which the NPV is less than zero; or more generally to establish which parameters or model assumptions are driving the results. Indirectly, sensitivity testing may help the analyst identify what evidence or information is needed in the future to make a more informed decision. For example, if the impact on IQ of an early childhood program fades out, the analyst might focus attention on behavioral change in elementary school. If a college access program helps students attend higher-quality colleges, the analyst might focus on the relative earnings gains from college selectivity. In the case of educational BC analysis, one important consideration is the long-run trend in education gradients. Since the 1980s, the income-education gradient and the health-education gradient have been growing steeper: Income and health increasingly depend on one's education level (Goldin & Katz, 2008). An important consideration for sensitivity analysis is whether this trend in gradients will continue or even accelerate. If it does, current estimates of the benefits of education are most likely to be understated. Finally, general sensitivity analysis can also highlight heterogeneity—a feature that is common in educational settings. For example, one might question whether economic returns from programs for highly disadvantaged youth in urban settings will be a useful guide to the expected returns if such programs are delivered to high-income families in suburban settings.

Sensitivity testing is an essential element of economic evaluation. Even if the results of a sensitivity analysis are not reported in exhaustive detail, they serve as a powerful reminder to the analyst that uncertainty may alter the fundamental conclusions of the evaluation. In turn, this reminder must be conveyed to the analyst's audiences.

Discussion Questions

1. For what types of ingredients might costs be most uncertain? Give specific illustrations.

2. You are performing BC analysis of physical education programs aimed at improving children's health status. What are some sources of uncertainty in benefit estimates, and how would you account for each? How would you do a sensitivity analysis for your estimates?

3. What is the difference between heterogeneity and uncertainty?

4. Why is it important to consider the distribution of costs and benefits in Monte Carlo analysis?

Exercises

1. As part of an individualized after-school program, a randomly selected sample of 10 students has received one-on-one mentoring. The costs vary on an individual basis, in part because of student need and mentor availability. You have estimated the student-level costs of the program for students in the control and treatment groups as follows:

Control		Treatment	
Student	Cost	Student	Cost
1	3,642	11	7,674
2	12,122	12	7,707
3	5,786	13	6,531
4	7,900	14	18,329
5	13,883	15	5,949
6	13,345	16	6,030

(Continued)

(Continued)

Control		Treatment	
Student	Cost	Student	Cost
7	5,327	17	6,136
8	4,005	18	6,292
9	6,014	19	13,826
10	9,322	20	7,568

a. Calculate the mean and standard deviation costs for the treatment and control groups.

b. Calculate the mean difference between the two groups and the standard error of the mean difference.

c. Using simulation methods in a spreadsheet or statistical software package, run a bootstrap simulation whereby you randomly draw 10 treatment and 10 control students, with replacement, calculate the mean of each group and difference in means, and repeat the simulation 1,000 times.

d. Based on your constructed sample of 1,000 mean differences, calculate summary statistics for the distribution of mean differences, including the mean, median, standard deviation, 2.5th percentile, 97.5th percentile, minimum, and maximum.

2. You have performed BC analysis of a smoking cessation and prevention program delivered at 20 colleges. You estimate the average per student cost at $1,200 and an average reduction of four cigarettes smoked per person. You also estimate that society is willing to pay $250 per reduced cigarette smoked. However, you also observe wide site-level variability in effects. Costs range from $800 to $1,500, the standard deviation of cigarette reduction is 2, and the value of a reduction in cigarettes smoked ranges from $150 to $350 per cigarette.

a. What is the baseline NPV?

b. Perform a Monte Carlo sensitivity analysis of the distribution of effects.

c. How would you explain the results of the Monte Carlo analysis to decisionmakers? What additional information does it provide beyond the baseline results?

3. You conduct CE analysis of a reading program whereby students are randomly assigned to a treatment or business-as-usual condition at each site. You calculate the costs of the traditional reading program versus the new curriculum, as well as effects for each group, as follows:

Control Group		Treatment Group	
Cost (C)	Effect (E)	Cost (C)	Effect (E)
$1,123	0.064	$2,517	0.112
$1,123	0.109	$2,683	0.035
$1,124	0.012	$2,771	0.021
$1,178	0.084	$2,820	0.273
$1,321	0.003	$2,868	0.077
$1,333	0.023	$3,651	0.123
$1,444	0.011	$3,844	0.027
$1,456	0.054	$4,799	0.091
$1,654	0.017	$4,829	0.096

a. Calculate the mean costs and effects for the treatment and control groups, as well as the mean differences in costs and effects and the CE ratio.

b. How would you estimate the precision of the CE results in deciding between the control group and the treatment group?

12

Checklist for Economic Evaluations

Objectives

1. Provide a quality checklist for economic evaluations.

2. Identify the main ways in which economic evaluations might not meet the checklist standards.

3. Consider the value of a checklist.

A t this point, the reader may find it useful to have a checklist of criteria for appraising the quality of an economic evaluation in education. We set out our preferred checklist (see Box 12.1). The criteria are drawn from the methodological discussions of previous chapters and can be applied to cost-effectiveness (CE) or benefit-cost (BC) analyses.

We note that there are some unsettled methodological issues: Studies may apply alternative assumptions without one being necessarily incorrect. As well, no cost study will be free of imperfections. The main concerns are how serious they are and if they distort the findings substantially. Sometimes, the methodological failings of a study are due to errors or omissions by the authors. More often, they are due to unavoidable constraints such as limited data or time available to authors. We are not encouraging readers to immediately discard a study if it fails to meet each of the following criteria. But the careful reader should attempt to understand the limitations of each study and ask whether its results can still be utilized. In the best studies, the authors assist in identifying the strengths and weaknesses of their study's methodology, data, and conclusions. In doing so, they establish caveats to its interpretation. In the worst studies, there are outright errors or insufficient detail to completely understand what the authors did; in these cases, it is best to set aside the study. As a guide, we review the items on the checklist that are most likely to be problematic. This review should help illustrate the value of using a checklist to appraise economic evaluations. Finally, we note some basic principles which analysts should be mindful of both when performing economic evaluations and when appraising them.

● 12.1. A CHECKLIST FOR APPRAISING ECONOMIC EVALUATIONS

The checklist is itemized as a series of questions that cover each of the stages in economic evaluation. See Box 12.1 for our preferred checklist. An alternative checklist—most relevant for BC analyses of early childhood interventions—is given in detail in Karoly (2012); a reporting checklist for CE analyses for health interventions is itemized in Neumann, Sanders, Russell, Siegel, and Ganiat (2016). For BC analysis, this checklist is similar to the standards itemized in detail by Zerbe, Davis, Garland, and Scott (2013, pp. 369–373).

Box 12.1 *Template Checklist for Appraising Economic Evaluations*

A. Establishing the decision framework

A.1. Does the study carefully define a problem?

A.2. Does the study delineate the alternatives under consideration?

A.3. Do the alternatives correspond with their corresponding theories of change?

A.4. Do the alternatives represent the most feasible options for decisionmakers?

A.5. Is the audience and perspective clearly specified and justified?

A.6. What is the analytical technique designated to choose among the alternatives (cost-effectiveness [CE], cost-utility [CU], or benefit-cost [BC])? Is this form of analysis justified in relation to the theory of change?

A.7. Is the time horizon for the evaluation specified?

B. Calculating costs

B.1. Is the sampling frame for cost analysis reported?

B.2. Are all ingredients for each alternative described in detail, along with their sources?

B.3. Are ingredient quantities and prices considered separately in the calculation of cost?

B.4. Is the study clear on whether expected/national costs or site-specific/local costs are being calculated?

B.5. Are costs expressed in constant dollars and discounted into present values?

B.6. Are total costs and average costs for the intervention reported? Are these costs incremental to an alternative intervention or business as usual? Is the denominator for the average cost per student or school listed and justified?

B.7. Are induced costs estimated?

B.8. Is there an analysis of the distribution of cost burdens among constituencies?

B.9. Is the cost analysis differentiated for different scales of the alternatives?

B.10. Does the cost analysis correspond to an effectiveness estimate? Are limitations of the correspondence between costs and effects discussed?

C. Evaluating effects, utility, or benefits

C.1. Is the measure of effectiveness appropriate? Does it neglect important outcomes of the alternative that should be taken into consideration?

(Continued)

(Continued)

C.2. When multiple effects are combined, is the CU method clearly described?

C.3. Are the measures of effectiveness identified using rigorous methods?

C.4. What methods are used to translate impacts into benefits? Are these methods valid?

C.5. Are all benefits—positive and negative—counted over the life of the intervention?

C.6. Are benefits expressed as present values to correspond with costs?

C.7. Is there an adequate analysis of distributional effects and benefits of the alternatives across different groups?

D. Combining costs and outcomes

D.1. Is the information on costs and effects used to calculate CE ratios? Are these results used correctly to rank alternatives? Does this analysis appropriately include limitations presented in the presentation of costs and effects?

D.2. In the case of a CU study, are CU ratios calculated and interpreted?

D.3. Are costs and benefits used to calculate BC ratios, net present values (NPVs), and internal rates of return (IRRs)? Is the perspective for each metric clearly stated?

D.4. Are economic metrics reported precisely or with ranges or confidence intervals?

D.5. Is a sensitivity analysis included? Is the choice of sensitivity analysis appropriate?

E. Explaining the results

E.1. Are the results explained in a way that decisionmakers can understand and apply them?

E.2. Are the differences in estimates among alternatives large enough that you would have confidence in using them as a basis for decisions?

E.3. How generalizable are the results to other decision contexts?

Each of the items in this checklist refers to a systematic attempt to appraise a report and to ascertain its strengths and weaknesses. As structured, this template checklist is a series of questions that require proper answers. The specific questions are divided into five general categories. The first category refers to the overall decision context in which the study is situated. The decision framework and the alternatives under scrutiny should be described explicitly in order to understand the nature of the decision problem and the alternatives that were considered in addressing it (see Chapter 2). The second category refers to the procedures for estimating and analyzing costs (extensively discussed in Chapters 3 through 6). The third category addresses the conceptualization, measurement, and analysis of effects, benefits, or utility (these topics were discussed in Chapters 7 and 9 respectively). The fourth category includes questions on the calculation of all relevant economic metrics (as in Chapters 8 and 10) as well as sensitivity testing (Chapter 11). Once alternatives are ranked with some degree of confidence, the fifth category addresses the generalizability (or external validity) of results (these issues are discussed throughout and in detail in the following chapter).

12.2. APPRAISING ECONOMIC EVALUATIONS ●

The first, and most important, step in appraising an economic evaluation is to apply the previously given checklist (or a similar one as proposed by other authors). This application should reveal to the reader the rigor and quality of the economic evaluation. Yet, we recognize that our proposed checklist is a series of questions rather than an itemized list that can be ticked off *yes* or *no*. As such, we cannot look at a study and say that it has met, for example, 70% of the criteria and it is therefore a strong study (or stronger than a study that meets 60% of the criteria).

For several reasons, we argue for a more interpretative version of a checklist. First, it is usually difficult to appraise a study in binary yes or no terms. Although a study that does not include any sensitivity testing is likely to be deemed deficient, most research studies make some attempt to address each of the relevant items on a checklist and so should receive a partial *yes* (or *no*). Second, when reviewing a study, the reader soon appreciates that the analyst has had to make some specific assumptions and decisions, and the validity of these assumptions and decisions cannot be appraised either in binary terms or independently of each other. Individually, an assumption may seem reasonable, but if each assumption is weighted toward a particular conclusion, the final results may be significantly biased. Finally, the goal of this appraisal is to understand the value of each study for decisionmaking purposes, rather than to score it against a set of criteria. For example, if a BC study of a preschool program reports an IRR to the taxpayer of 20%, the appraisal should look at why such large benefits were produced (rather than note that the study does not report the IRR from a social perspective that would almost certainly be higher). Hence, our proposed checklist is intended as a way by which readers can better—and more systematically—understand each economic evaluation.

Based on experience as both practitioners and reviewers of economic evaluations across education research, we do not believe there is a perfect study that would satisfy any checklist. The complexity of interventions in education settings—and the constraints placed on research—mean that every study will have some deficiencies. Hence, when appraising studies, it is helpful to consider where research practice is less than ideal and to what extent any imperfections undermine the value of each study (as discussed in Levin & Belfield, 2015).

First, there are steps in the research that are likely to be more difficult than others. When calculating costs, it may be hard for the analyst to devise a sampling frame from which to select units for empirical study. *Ex ante*, it may not be obvious which sites are going to be high cost or low cost or where the information on costs can be collected from. These challenges mean that the analyst should, where possible, attempt to collect cost information contemporaneously with the implementation of the intervention and from as many sites as possible. Studies that include more up-to-date information on costs are more likely to be accurate and should therefore be regarded more favorably.

When looking at effects and impacts, the analyst may face a problem: The research evidence reports evidence on multiple outcomes, some of which overlap statistically, and so are highly collinear, and that are often measured at different time points. For CE analysis, the challenge is to choose one single outcome that reflects the goal of the intervention, recognizing that this choice will fundamentally influence the research inquiry. For BC analysis, the challenge is to determine which impacts are independently valuable—and so should be added together—versus those impacts that are different measures of the same behavior.

On the benefits side, the analyst may find it difficult to identify shadow prices that correspond to all impacts. This challenge is hardest when impacts are not easily expressed as behaviors but instead are measured with attitudinal scales (e.g., engaged in school) or at aggregated levels (e.g., school climate). In these cases, the analyst may be forced to create her own shadow prices. Studies that can rely on well-established, independent values for shadow prices are likely to be more credible. To provide further structure for the analysis, the analyst might identify impacts for which there are valid shadow prices, impacts for which there is potential for shadow pricing, and impacts for which shadow pricing proves very difficult (e.g., due process; see Bowden, Shand, Belfield, Wang, & Levin, 2016).

Second, there are parts of the research that are more open to discretion and judgment by the analyst. We identify several areas where analysts will have to make decisions for which there may be limited external evidence. One important decision is the timeline for analysis—that is, when to measure effects and benefits. Our answer in Chapter 9 was that all benefits should be measured—and for as long as they are impactful. But we recognize that the analyst might not have any independent way to operationalize this timeline and might feel obliged to project benefits forward far into the future and consequently count the maximum possible benefits. Another important consideration is which costs to count. All studies will count operating costs, but some may arbitrarily decide that start-up costs or design costs should be excluded because they are incurred only one time. Finally, at the completion of the evaluation the analyst will have calculated a series of economic metrics (CE ratios or BC ratios, etc.). Hopefully, these metrics provide clear guidance: One intervention is more cost-effective than the alternatives, or the NPV of the intervention is positive. But the analyst may still be expected to determine the substantive meaning of these results: How big should the difference in CE ratios be in order to state that one reading intervention is "more cost-effective" than another? Or how large should the NPV be in order to claim that an intervention is a good investment? There is no accepted, independent standard to which the analyst can refer in order to make these determinations.

Finally, there are aspects of the research that are most troubling to reviewers. First, we note that reviewers are usually troubled by research practices that allow for considerable discretion and judgment by the researcher. This caution is understandable, but it should not be used to fully reject a study and its corresponding policy. If there is no scientific or objective way to decide on a policy, that does not mean that the policy should be rejected. Rather, it means that the evidence we have in favor of the policy is not definitive or certain. However, being definite or certain is too high a threshold for making policy: The evaluator need only establish that the preponderance of evidence and analysis point toward a particular option.

One of the aspects of economic evaluation that appears most troubling to reviewers is the choice of outcomes used in the analysis. Interestingly, this concern has little to do with economics per se. As argued previously, the economic evaluation utilizes the outcomes chosen by education researchers that they have deemed most valid. So, if reading experts believe that comprehension is the most valuable reading skill, CE analysis should examine the most efficient ways to boost comprehension and use a scale that accurately measures gains in comprehension. It is within the purview of the reading expert to specify this outcome measure. Nevertheless, many economic evaluations— particularly CE analyses—have been criticized for their choice of outcome measure. Thus, the analyst should be aware that the choice of outcome matters emphatically.

The other main concern that reviewers have is that any program-induced gains may not be as valuable as the analyst's shadow prices might suggest. For example, a program for high school dropouts might be effective at increasing the graduation rate. However, these new, marginal graduates are typically considered to be "not the same" as the average graduate—that is, their skill levels are lower. Again, we note that this concern is primarily an issue relating to outcomes: With this program's results, we are implicitly redefining the graduation rate to a lower threshold that includes these marginal graduates. For BC analysis, this caution might be relatively easy to deal with: The analyst can simply adjust the shadow prices of benefits to reflect society's willingness to pay for these new graduates. For example, the analyst might equate these new graduates to the pool of graduates from the lowest quartile of ability and derive a shadow price accordingly (Belfield & Levin, 2007). However, it may be difficult to assign a shadow price to incremental outcomes that are of relatively lower "quality."

Overall, these difficulties, discretionary decisions, and cautions reinforce the need for readers to perform a rigorous appraisal of each study. However, that appraisal must be nuanced rather than prescriptive and, recognizing that the goal is to help decisionmakers, it should not be overly critical in rejecting studies outright (see the excellent discussion by Vining & Weimer, 2010).

12.3. CONCLUSIONS ●

This checklist is an instrumental device to see if a reported CE or BC analysis satisfies a set of prescribed criteria. As with all research, there will be some elements of the activity that might be improved (and some that do not fit easily into the checklist). These elements will be clearer after the checklist has been applied. Also, where possible, research should be harmonized with or comparable to existing studies. This is especially important for economic evaluations that are intended to help decisionmakers: A checklist can help to standardize research practices and so improve decisionmaking.

More generally, economic evaluations are situated within a broader framework of research inquiry with a set of principles that analysts should adhere to. This framework stands outside the checklist approach and cannot be easily applied. Therefore, it is important to consider if the analysis accords with basic principles of research.

Following Zerbe and colleagues (2013, pp. 368–369), we can think of principles as overarching aspects that affect all parts of the analysis. For CE and BC analyses, several stand out. One important principle is transparency: The analysis should be performed in such a way that readers can understand how the calculations were made and conclusions drawn. For example, the analyst should report each important shadow price in both undiscounted and present values. A second principle is conservativeness: Assumptions should be made that are not biased toward a particular conclusion. Indeed, analysts should adopt assumptions that might falsify their conclusions. So, if the investment appears to have a positive NPV, the analyst might make assumptions about benefits that are more conservative to see how the results might change.

Finally, an important but often overlooked principle is proportionality. This principle refers to the amount of effort put into the analysis: Effort should be invested in research inquiries that will meaningfully increase the precision of the estimates or affect the conclusions drawn. As described by Zerbe et al. (2013, p. 369), proportionality is the amount of effort committed relative to how much that effort influences the conclusions a decisionmaker might draw from the analysis. So, if a high school mentoring program is consistently found to have a positive NPV, a reevaluation using higher shadow price values for benefits would not be worthwhile. Also, research that exhaustively estimated benefits but then eyeballed or guesstimated costs would not uphold the proportionality principle. Cost estimation requires the same attempt at methodological rigor as that of estimating effectiveness.

Discussion Questions

1. What is the purpose of using a checklist like the one provided in this chapter?

2. What items would you add to the checklist, if any, based on specific contextual elements of your intended research?

3. Which items in the checklist do you think are hardest to satisfy?

Exercises

1. Take a specific CE or BC study. Use the checklist to assess that study.

13

Economic Evaluations for Education Policy

Objectives

1. Describe the potential applications of economic evaluations.

2. Describe steps to expand application of economic evaluations.

3. Review the links between economic evaluations and decisionmaking.

4. Consider ways to prioritize educational investments.

I n this final chapter, we discuss how to move from research to policy, from empirical inquiry to a "reasoned determination" of how to allocate scarce resources to improve educational systems.

We begin by distinguishing between instrumental and conceptual applications of economic evaluations. Although the goal of each empirical study is to test a specific hypothesis, the results of that test can have broader implications. For instance, benefit-cost (BC) analysis of the Abecedarian preschool program yields a numerical net present value (NPV), but it also fosters the concept that, broadly, early childhood investments are "good policy." Ideally, each economic evaluation should have this dual application. Next, we discuss the methodological obstacles that constrain the use of cost-effectiveness (CE) and BC analysis. Most of these are general obstacles relevant for all social sciences, so we continue the discussion by looking at how economic evaluations should be linked to the needs of decisionmakers. This reflects the underlying motivation for these evaluations—that they help policymakers decide how to spend educational dollars. To allocate these scarce dollars, policymakers need a way to prioritize investments; we review the basic idea of prioritization through league tables but caution against a literal interpretation of rankings. Finally, we conclude the chapter by speculating on the future of economic evaluations in education and how they might be adapted.

This last chapter attempts to put economic ideas and methods in their appropriate place within the context of policy evaluation. By better understanding that place, we can see more clearly the role of economic evaluation and we can enhance the quality of such evaluations so they are better suited to that role. By improving research practice, the intent is that educational policymaking is also improved.

13.1. APPLYING ECONOMIC ANALYSIS

The general uses of cost evaluations can be divided into two broad categories (Rossi, Lipsey, & Freeman, 2004). First, they may be put to direct, or instrumental, use. This is most often the case when a cost study has been commissioned—perhaps by a school district or state office of education—usually with the express intent of providing input into a decision. The decisionmaker is usually the primary audience that was referred to in Chapter 2, though a secondary audience may also take advantage of a study to directly inform a decision.

Second, cost evaluations may be used in a conceptual manner. In conceptual use, a cost evaluation does not directly influence a decision to adopt or eliminate a program; rather, it informs the thinking of key stakeholders about educational issues. For example, BC analysis of a specific program for early childhood education may have little effect on the immediate support received from local policymakers. However, the results could have a far-reaching impact—if widely disseminated— on the general importance with which politicians and parents view early childhood education.

There have been few investigations of how—and how appropriately— cost, CE, and BC analyses are being used by educational decisionmakers. Some evidence has been influential. For example, the national evaluation of the Job Training Partnership Act (JTPA), briefly described in earlier chapters, probably had direct effects on federal funding decisions in the 1980s (Orr, 1999; Orr et al., 1996). As well, many states have vocational rehabilitation (VR) agencies for people with disabilities; in the 1990s, Lewis, Johnson, Chen, and Erickson (1992) noted that "almost all state VR agencies employ some form of BC analysis and its related ratios for reporting to legislatures and policymakers on likely efficiency effects" (p. 267; for a recent example of return-on-investment studies for VR, see Bua-lam and Bias, 2011). For the state of Washington, the Washington State Institute for Public Policy (WSIPP) has been influential in conducting BC analyses, including some for educational investment, for the state legislature (www.wsipp.wa.gov). See Example 13.1.

Example 13.1   Benefit-Cost Analyses for K–12 Education in Washington State

The Washington State Institute for Public Policy (WSIPP) conducts benefit-cost (BC) analyses across a range of social investments (crime, health, and mental health), including educational programs. These BC analyses are explicitly intended to assist the state legislature in the formation and implementation of new policies. Since its creation in 1983, WSIPP has performed many analyses of K–12 education programs and interventions. The institute has developed a standardized method for calculating impacts and for specifying and shadow pricing the benefits of each educational intervention. Thus, it is possible to arbitrate between them based on either the net present value (NPV) or BC ratio metric.

Benefit-Cost Analyses for K–12 Interventions in Washington State

Order by Net Present Value	K–12 Interventions	Total Benefits	Costs	Net Present Value	Benefit-Cost Ratio
1	Becoming a Man (BAM) with high-dosage tutoring	$37,292	$4,461	$32,831	8.36
2	State and district early childhood education programs	$37,036	$7,130	$29,906	5.19
3	Consultant teachers: Literacy Collaborative	$26,388	$740	$25,647	35.64
4	Head Start	$27,175	$8,783	$18,392	3.09

(Continued)

(Continued)

Order by Net Present Value	K–12 Interventions	Total Benefits	Costs	Net Present Value	Benefit-Cost Ratio
5	Tutoring: By peers	$16,041	$113	$15,928	142.28
/					
45	Full-day kindergarten	–$304	$2,714	–$3,018	–0.11
46	Check-in behavior interventions	–$2,020	$1,329	–$3,349	–1.52
47	Educator prof. development: Using data to guide instruction	–$3,370	$18	–$3,388	–186.59
48	Even Start	–$4,889	$4,251	–$9,140	–1.15
49	Early Head Start	–$2,124	$10,937	–$13,061	–0.19

Source: Retrieved from http://wsipp.wa.gov/BenefitCost?topicId=4, January 28 2016.

Notes: Top five and bottom five across 49 K–12 interventions ordered by NPV. All benefits included. Benefits are per participant. Adjusted to 2015 dollars.

For illustration, this table shows the first five K–12 interventions ordered by NPV, as well as the last 5 (out of the 49 analyses currently performed).

This table provides a substantial amount of information for policymakers, at least instrumentally. There are large differences between the most and least efficient interventions. This suggests there is scope for resource reallocation that would enhance economic well-being across the state. In fact, most of the inefficient interventions have negative benefits leading to NPVs that are strongly negative. By contrast, some interventions are extremely high-yield, despite being very low cost. The extreme example here is peer tutoring, where the BC ratio is 142.

However, it is notable that, at the conceptual level, there is less clear guidance. State and district early childhood programs have a clearly positive NPV, as does Head Start; this suggests early interventions pay off. Yet, Even Start and Early Head Start—early interventions predicated on similar models of child development—have strongly negative NPVs.

Overall, the WSIPP approach shows how—given adequate time and resources and a very specific mandate from decisionmakers—educational interventions can be evaluated on efficiency grounds. Even so, we emphasize that these results are specific for Washington State and are based on the specific cost methods, shadow prices, and general assumptions applied by WSIPP analysts. Readers should be cognizant of how this perspective drives the costing method, the cost numbers, and the estimated benefits reported in WSIPP evaluations.

Perhaps more common than such direct uses are the conceptual uses of economic evaluations. During several decades, developing-country researchers devoted great energy to comparing the costs and benefits of various levels of education, including primary, secondary, and higher (see Example 10.2). Influential reviews of the accumulated literature (e.g., Psacharopoulos, 1994; Psacharopoulos & Patrinos, 2004) showed that rates of return were generally higher for primary education. This, in turn, influenced the lending priorities of the World Bank and other international agencies such that primary education supplanted higher education as the focus of much development aid.

In the United States, the economic analyses of the HighScope Perry Preschool Program appear to have been put to "conceptual" use. While the evaluations dealt with a small-scale version of a single program, they nonetheless played a role in modifying overall perceptions of the benefits and costs of early childhood education. As a result, they may have affected investments in larger initiatives such as Head Start. Evidence on the program has also driven a research agenda on how early education influences child development (https://heckmanequation.org; nieer.org) and so facilitates a more efficient use of resources.

13.2. EXPANDING THE USE OF ECONOMIC EVALUATION ●

There are several factors that restrict and limit the use of cost, CE, and BC analyses. An obvious constraint is that not many such studies are available; there are not many studies in education (compared, e.g., with the thousands of studies in the CEA Registry, www.cearegistry.org). Therefore, there are few replication studies of each particular intervention. The focus of education research is very much on "what works?" (not "what works at what cost?"). Even in a comprehensive review of evidence on educational inputs for education in developing countries, Glewwe, Hanushek, Humpage, and Ravina (2013) concluded, "Nothing has been said along the way about the costs of any programs. Clearly, effective policy needs to consider both the benefit side and the cost side, particularly in developing countries where resource constraints are binding at low levels. However, very few of the existing evaluations have provided solid information about costs of programs and policies." Thus, even for many interventions that might be effective, it is impossible to determine if they are cost-effective. Also, another significant proportion of education research is on "how does it work?" (rather than "what resources are needed to make it work?").

As discussed clearly by Ludwig, Kling, and Mullainathan (2011) and Keele, Tingley, and Yamamoto (2015), education researchers should be interested in policy mechanisms that determine effectiveness alongside evaluations of effectiveness: If it works, the next stage should be to determine why it works. These "what" and "how" approaches leave little space for economic evaluation.

Hence, the primary way to expand the use of economic evaluation is to actually perform economic evaluations. As an intermediate way, analysts should perform components of economic evaluations, including, for example, more shadow prices that can be applied through benefit transfer (Vining & Weimer, 2010). But there are other factors that should also be taken into account.

First, the quality of studies may sometimes be less than ideal. In a review of more than 1,300 relevant academic papers in education on CE, Clune (2002) divided them on a quality scale as follows: 56% rhetorical, 27% minimal, 15% substantial, and 2% plausible. As a revealing guide to the quality of this research, Clune's (2002) definition of *substantial* was an "attempt to count data on cost and effectiveness, even with serious flaws" (p. 56). *Rhetorical* was defined as "cost-effectiveness claims with no data on either costs or effects" (Clune, 2002, p. 56). Although the quality of studies has improved significantly over the past decade, it has started from a low base. Sometimes studies are inordinately careful to identify impacts but make very broad (sometimes unverified) assumptions about costs.[1]

There are many areas where economic evaluations can fall short (Levin & Belfield, 2015). We note the main ones here. First, the overall

---

[1] Unfortunately, there are quite a few such studies. Fredriksson, Ockert, and Oosterbeck (2013) applied rigorous methods to identify earnings gains from reducing class size, but the BC analysis is as follows: "Assume average class size during upper primary school is reduced from 25 to 20. This increases the number of teachers from 4 per 100 pupils to 5 per 100 pupils, thereby increasing the per pupil wage costs by 1% of teachers' average wage during three years. There are also costs involved with overhead and extra classrooms; say that this adds one-third to the extra costs of teachers" (Fredriksson et al., 2013, pp. 277–278). Some studies use shortcuts to estimate CE. For example, Banerjee et al. (2015) presumed low costs for the Balsakhi Program in Mumbai, India. This presumption is based on the very low wages paid to each *balsakhi* (young woman) and that this was the main ingredient of the program (pp. 1262–1263). And in evaluating the Action Lecture program in Paris, France, Massoni and Vergnaud (2012) do not estimate costs directly. Instead, they estimate how resources from class size reduction policies might be redistributed to the *Action Lecture* program for nursery students. This reallocation allows them to calculate comparative CE ratios. Ingle and Cramer (2013) estimated costs using the ingredients method but used a correlation coefficient as the metric for CE. For examples of very "terse" cost reporting for educational interventions, see the examples provided in Evans and Popova (2014, Table 7).

decision framework of the study may be poorly specified, or key alternatives may have been omitted from consideration. Second, costs could be measured in a flawed or incomplete manner. Indeed, this problem can assume a number of forms: Key ingredients, such as the time commitments of stakeholders or the fringe benefits that accompany wages, may be omitted; ingredients may be improperly valued (e.g., by failing to amortize capital); and, of course, the ingredients method itself may be misapplied (through either the use of budgetary data or shortcuts in analysis). Third, effects may be measured incorrectly and shadow prices calculated imprecisely. Finally, the combination of costs and effects or benefits may be integrated improperly.

Certainly, these shortcomings are not restricted to economic evaluations in education (for a review of failures in practice across various policy topics, see Belfield, 2015). A general failure by regulators to accurately estimate costs was well documented by Harrington, Morgenstern, and Nelson (2000). On energy policy, Ansar, Flyvbjerg, Budzier, and Lunn (2014) found substantial errors in *ex ante* cost estimates of 250 hydroelectric power dams built over the last four decades. In health sciences, Udvarhelyi, Colditz, Rai, and Epstein (1992) found significant fault in their review of 77 CE and BC studies; Neumann, Greenberg, Olchanski, Stone, and Rosen (2005) documented improvements in analyses since this review, although they note some persistent omissions from best practice.[2] Finally, reviews of government agency efforts to conduct CE and BC analyses highlight many substantial deficiencies in the practice of research and evaluation (Hahn & Tetlock, 2008; Schwartz, 2010). Overall, policymakers need better—as well as more—information for more effective decisionmaking.

---

[2] Specifically, only one in five studies explicitly stated the perspective of the study. In cases where costs and benefits occurred over a longer time horizon than 1 year, half of the studies failed to discount properly. Similarly, about half the articles failed to calculate and report summary measures such as CE or BC ratios. Lastly, around two thirds of the studies failed to conduct sensitivity analyses in order to evaluate the overall robustness of findings. Another review by Gerard (1992) focused on 51 cost-utility (CU) studies in health that used quality-adjusted life years (QALYs) as their utility measure. Only about 70% of studies were judged to have included a "comprehensive" set of ingredients in calculating their cost estimates; for others, it was rarely possible to evaluate this because studies omitted key information. Only 63% of studies provided a clear description of the procedures used to value ingredients, and only 61% clearly described the sources of their cost data. Where discounting should have been employed, 15% of studies failed to do so. Only 37% of studies conducted "extensive" sensitivity analysis. A review of health-related cost studies conducted in Australia was similarly pessimistic: Of 33 studies, "only 55% gave an adequate description of how the costs were measured. . . . Certain costs such as capital and overheads were often omitted completely and inappropriately" (Salkeld, Davey, & Arnolda, 1995, p. 117).

Second, comparing across economic evaluations is fraught because few studies are harmonized to follow the same methods and same assumptions. This lack of harmony is especially problematic for an evaluative practice that is motivated by the ideal of comparisons across policies based on opportunity cost. Ideally, the comparisons should be across alternative interventions that address the same goals and serve similar populations with regard to efficiency in the use of social resources. The method of accounting for costs and desirable outcomes and their measures must be similar and for comparable populations. For CE, effect sizes among interventions dedicated to such broad goals as dropout prevention or early childhood literacy cannot be compared unless the outcome measures are the same and they are evaluated across equivalent populations. Simply taking effect sizes under a broad category of educational endeavor and comparing them is inappropriate. Even the most sophisticated research designs with equivalent groups must be limited to comparisons for the populations and measures of outcome that are represented (see the discussion of reading measures in Hollands et al., 2013). Moreover, as discussed in Chapter 10, meta-analytic techniques are not easily adapted for economic evaluations. More standardization—even if just for shadow prices—would aid comparability.

A third issue is the relevance of even an excellent study to a different setting. The question of generalizability from one sample or setting to another pervades the field of evaluation and social science research in general. A study that can be adequately generalized to another population or context is said to possess "external validity." Unfortunately, there is no easy recipe for determining external validity; judgments are best made on a case-by-case basis, depending on both the cost study and the setting to which it might be applied. There are three varieties of external validity to consider, relating to the population, the environment, and the operations (see Smith & Glass, 1987, or most evaluation textbooks for a complete discussion of external validity).

Population external validity occurs when the results of a particular cost study can be generalized to a different or broader group of individuals. Frequently, the data on effectiveness or costs are estimated from a small sample of individuals. If the sample was drawn at random from a well-defined population (e.g., elementary students in the state of Washington or secondary students in Argentina), then study results might be generalized to that population. This population is referred to as the "accessible" population. Quite often, however, the researcher or decisionmaker would like to apply results from such a cost study to a different population, referred to as the "target" population. For example, a researcher may wish to apply results from a random sample of Argentinian secondary students to others in a neighboring country. Or a researcher may have data on a nonrandom sample of second graders in New York City, chosen because their parents volunteered them for a study. Nonetheless, the researcher would like to make broader statements about second graders in Los Angeles. In these cases, we should ensure that individuals in the sample resemble individuals in the target population as closely as possible—in gender, age, socioeconomic status (SES), ability, or other important characteristics. Short of conducting a new study, however, there is no way of guaranteeing that results can be applied from one group of individuals to another.

Environmental external validity exists when the environment of a study is comparable to other settings in which the cost study might be applied. In many cases, the environments will be quite different. For example, many studies of effectiveness are carried out in a well-managed demonstration setting, which would not carry over to a large-scale implementation of the intervention. We could imagine an experimental study in which second graders are given a particular kind of instruction in a laboratory classroom under pristine conditions. When placed in the less-controlled environment of a public school, the same instructional method may not produce identical results. As well, in cost studies, it is particularly important to consider the economic environment. The prices of key educational ingredients, such as teacher salaries, textbooks, and even parent time, could vary drastically from one setting to another (Rice, 1997). Thus, even if the alternatives under consideration are equally effective in two settings, a different set of costs could alter the CE rankings of alternatives.

Finally, there is the issue of operations external validity. To apply the results of a study, we must be sure that the educational "treatment" is faithfully replicated in the new setting—an issue of program implementation. In some cases, this might be relatively straightforward, such as reducing a class size from 30 students to 25. In education, this is usually the exception rather than the rule. We often refer blithely to interventions such as "textbooks" or "teacher training." However, the form and content of these interventions can change drastically from one setting to another. In many cases, these changes are probably necessary, in order to adapt interventions to a new context or language. But the process of change makes it difficult to assume that the effects or costs of a study alternative will be duplicated by the modified alternative. A related aspect of operations external validity is the measure of effectiveness used to gauge success or failure. For example, we often say that an alternative is effective in raising mathematics achievement. But often, that mathematics test has been customized for its particular setting, perhaps because it is meant to reflect elements of a particular curriculum. The alternative could prove to be less effective if applied in a setting where effectiveness is gauged by other means.

In sum, a cost study is generalizable to another setting when the study setting and the new one reflect similar populations, environments, and operations. However, one should be wary of factors that are not similar (and not observed) between the two situations and their consequences for generalizability. There is no method of guaranteeing generalizability beyond the good judgment and experience of individuals. The best remedy is to carefully examine the environment of the study and the environment to which the study might apply in order to ensure that they are roughly similar. In the case of cost data, it may be possible to collect new costs, which can be combined with the existing evidence on effectiveness.

Overall, these research imperatives are quite general: There should be more and better quality economic evaluations that are harmonized and that can be more easily generalized (for recommendations specifically for BC analyses of social policies, see Vining & Weimer, 2010, p. 2). Another, more direct, way for economic evaluations to be more useful is to link them to the needs of decisionmakers.

● 13.3. DECISIONMAKING AND ECONOMIC EVALUATION

Explicit attention should be paid to providing economic evaluations that are linked to the needs of decisionmakers. Conventionally, such evaluations have been reported using a social perspective—that is, taking into account all of the resources required to implement the intervention. This convention follows a long tradition of welfare economics and the adoption of the social perspective for BC analyses. However, for some decisionmakers, this social perspective may not be the most relevant. Indeed, it is likely that more CE and BC studies will need to adopt a specific agency perspective. For example, schools may be interested only in the costs that they must pay for, omitting any burden on other parties. Some interventions, particularly those involving peer tutoring, may look more cost-effective simply on the grounds that the "labor" (by the peer students) is cheap. CE and BC analyses should be performed in ways that provide the most use for decisionmakers, although a social perspective is valuable for informing the public on the full costs and optimal scale.

We have argued that when CE analysis and other cost analyses are integrated into evaluations, the evaluation exercise is more likely to yield the types of information that are crucial to decisions than when costs are ignored. This does not mean that even the best economic evaluations can be used mechanically to make decisions. Perhaps the most important principle is that of viewing such studies as sources of information rather than as sources of decisions.

As helpful as evaluation studies can be in providing information on alternatives, they are often incomplete. All evaluations reduce complex organizational and social dynamics to a manageable set of relations for analysis. Although every effort should be made to consider the principal issues, there may be other factors that can be taken into account only as one reviews the results of cost evaluations. For example, there may exist institutional or organizational factors that make one alternative easier to implement than another. Implementation of a new intervention is hardly a mechanical task, and many alternatives that show promise at the drawing-board stage are relegated to failure at the implementation stage because of the simplistic assumptions underlying them (Berman & McLaughlin, 1975). Those alternatives that are presently being used or are similar to present approaches are more likely to provide the predicted results than those that represent a radical departure from existing practices. Clearly, this information must be taken into account in considering the implications of cost evaluations. Certainly, if one alternative seems slightly more cost-effective than another but will require massive changes in organizational structure, there is a strong case to select the slightly less cost-effective approach that is more easily implementable. See Example 13.2.

Example 13.2 Making Decisions With Cost-Effectiveness Findings

The constituents of a school district are concerned about the number of high school dropouts. After interviewing former students, it is concluded dropping out is affected by poor academic performance, involvement in the juvenile justice system, and family responsibilities. Accordingly, three alternative programs are formulated to reduce dropouts. Alternative A concentrates on upgrading dropouts' academic skills with a program of financial incentives based on

(Continued)

(Continued)

improved school behaviors. Alternative B focuses on an intensive counseling program to address both academic and nonacademic problems. Alternative C focuses on additional academic assistance through peer tutoring as well as placement in part-time jobs.

After evaluation, the school district identifies as dropout-prone those students with test scores in the bottom 30% of the population, those who behave disruptively, and those with poor attendance records. The school district randomly assigns 300 tenth-grade students who are characterized as dropout-prone into four groups of 75. The first group is a control group that will not receive any special treatment. Each of the other three groups will be the focus of one of the three program interventions to reduce dropouts. On the basis of a 1-year intervention, data are collected for all four groups. The control group has the highest proportion of dropouts, as expected. The difference between the number of students who dropped out of each treatment group and the number who were expected to drop out is used to assess the effects of each program.

The following table shows the costs for reducing dropouts for the three alternative programs. Of the 75 students in the control group, 35 had dropped out by the end of the year. Among the other groups, there were fewer dropouts. Using the control group as the baseline, it appears that 17 students were saved from dropping out by Program A, 15 students were saved by Program B, and 10 students were prevented from dropping out by Program C. Costs for each program were fairly similar, but the "cost per dropout prevented" showed that Program C was the most costly, while Programs A and B were rather close in costs per dropout prevented.

Costs, Effects, and Cost-Effectiveness of Dropout Prevention Programs

Alternative	Incremental Cost of Alternative	Dropouts Prevented	Cost per Dropout Prevented	Teacher Attitudes
A	$12,750	17	$750	resistant
B	$12,375	15	$825	enthusiastic
C	$13,500	10	$1,350	neutral

Because Programs A and B were so close in the cost per dropout prevented, other information was sought to inform the decision. One crucial influence on the implementation of a program is teacher attitudes. Accordingly, teachers were surveyed regarding their attitudes toward the three alternatives. First, teachers were given a description of each program and what would be required of them. Second, they were asked to rank the programs and give the reasons for their rankings. Third, they were asked to provide any information they thought should be considered in making a program decision.

On the basis of this survey, it was concluded that teachers would be resistant to the adoption of Program A, enthusiastic about Program B, and neutral about Program C.

When this information was combined with the cost per prevented dropout, the decisionmakers concluded that Program B should be implemented. Although Program A was less costly for each success, a higher risk was attached to its full implementation by the apparent resistance of teachers to financial incentives. Since the teachers were enthusiastic about Program B, it was assumed that they would cooperate to implement it. Hence, the additional information convinced the decisionmakers to adopt a slightly less cost-effective program (and provided further confirmation that Alternative B would be preferable to Alternative C).

For almost any educational objective, such as improvement of academic achievement in a specific subject, there are usually many alternatives—better personnel selection and training, new instructional strategies, use of technologies, class size reduction, and curriculum innovations. Yet, the analysis must reflect the needs of the decision-maker. For example, it is purposeless to devise a study on the economic returns to a college counseling program versus a preschool program; the counselor is not going to suddenly decide to transform the college program so that it serves kindergarten children.

Unavoidably, many comparisons have to be narrowly described. For example, Glewwe (1999) compared the relative costs and effects of three interventions aimed at raising mathematics and reading achievement in Ghana. The three interventions included (1) repairing classrooms with leaky roofs, (2) providing classrooms with blackboards, and (3) providing more textbooks to students. In Botswana, a study by Fuller, Hua, and Snyder (1994) compared the CE of three interventions designed to raise mathematics achievement; these included (1) reducing class size, (2) providing additional teacher in-service training, and (3) incorporating supplementary mathematics readers. In making recommendations about the most cost-effective investments, the authors of each study are limited to the range of well-defined alternatives. Nevertheless, in each of the examples presented previously, it is certainly possible that other interventions exist, beyond present consideration, that are more cost-effective than these. Within the scope of a single cost study, there is no way to determine this. Given how most evaluations are structured, it is difficult to choose beyond these three options presented here.

The important point is that there are always considerations that cannot be fully incorporated into the evaluations. At the decision stage, however, these considerations should be explicated and brought into play in using the information generated by the economic evaluations. By establishing an evaluation that circumscribes certain issues, it is then easier to appraise the issues that cannot be included in the evaluation. For example, citizens may have a view about what level of resources should be given to young children based on what they think is "fair." The fact that many early investments in children are efficient makes being fair easy: There is no trade-off in the sense that resources would be sacrificed to help preschoolers; the resources will return in the form of future benefits.

The fundamental test of the utility of CE analysis is whether or not it influences decisions in a useful and constructive manner. Although researchers may wish to perform research unaffected by the constraints of decisionmaking, it is important to acknowledge such constraints and incorporate them into the research design. Such incorporation might involve recognizing that schools do not typically have the resources to implement large-scale reforms, that comparing a very low cost reform with an expensive one is uninformative, and that decisionmakers have prior beliefs about what should be implemented. It is also important to consider how cost-saving or effectiveness-enhancing information can be persuasive in overcoming political bottlenecks. In this respect, the presentation and demonstration of CE and BC analyses findings should be considered for their accessibility and understanding to those who might influence educational policy such as citizens and the media.

13.4. PRIORITIZING EDUCATIONAL INVESTMENTS

By now, it should be evident that CE analysis is always a comparative undertaking. So, we estimate the costs and effectiveness of two or more interventions and choose that which exhibits the lowest cost per unit of effectiveness. Similarly, BC analysis—by reducing the evaluation to a single metric of NPV—can, in theory, be applied across every educational intervention. We calculate the NPV and choose the intervention that has the highest NPV.

Stylized in this way, deciding on educational investments is like investing in the stock market: The goal is to choose the investment with the highest return (or the most cost-effective intervention). In this case, the district superintendent, state education official, or CEO of a nonprofit enterprise is the decisionmaker who is maximizing his or her own investment portfolio. The investor selects all programs and interventions that have returns above the marginal cost of borrowing. Logically, the investor would ideally have a list of all possible educational investments, ranked from highest to lowest. This suggests the development of a "league table" that conveys these rankings.

League tables combine the results of many different CE or CU analyses. They can also be used for BC studies, although this is less frequent (see Karoly, 2012, Table 2). Over the past two decades, league tables were a common feature of CE studies in the health fields (see the discussion by Drummond, O'Brien, Stoddart, & Torrance, 1997; Morrall, 1986). As well, the World Bank commissioned a large number of studies in developing country health systems that were used to produce a wide-ranging league table (Jamison, Mosley, Measham, & Bobadilla, 1993; World Bank, 1993). Explicitly, health interventions were expressed in terms of disease control priorities, with CE playing an important role (Jamison et al., 1993).

However, creating league tables is not the same as using league tables. So far, the use of league tables has been somewhat limited. For developing countries, health investments have been influenced by the disease control priorities evidence (www.dcp-3.org). But in the United States, the use of league tables has been stalled. The largest inventory, the CEA Registry, posts some illustrative league tables on its website. But these are not a guide for investors: The reported CE ratios demonstrate the range of results (including interventions that are cheaper and more effective and those that are more expensive and less effective).[3]

League tables are much less common in education, perhaps because of the relative scarcity of CE studies. Fletcher, Hawley, and Piele (1990) produced a table that summarized the results of several CE studies of computer-assisted instruction. Another early example that

---

[3] The health care field witnessed several attempts—some more successful than others—to put CE analysis to a direct use in the decisionmaking process (see Neumann, Sanders, Russell, Siegel, & Ganiat, 2016, Chapter 2). Oregon attempted to construct a CU "league table" in order to prioritize the medical benefits that would be available to recipients of Medicaid (Eddy, 1991; Sloan & Conover, 1995). A panel of experts and consumer representatives was convened in order to prioritize hundreds of medical interventions; high-priority items exhibited the lowest costs per unit of utility (based on QALYs). Following the completion of the list, the rankings were subjected to much public debate and subsequent modification. Consequently, the initial CU results "were ultimately abandoned in favor of a hybrid process in which cost was not a major factor in determining the final rankings" (Sloan & Conover, 1995, p. 219). More recently, the mandate of the Patient-Centered Outcomes Research Institute (PCORI), funded through the Patient Protection and Affordable Care Act of 2010, explicitly proscribes CE for research guidance (www.pcori.org/sites/default/files/PCORI_Authorizing_Legislation.pdf).

summarized a number of educational CE studies in developing countries was performed by Lockheed and Hanushek (1988). Most recently, the Abdul Latif Jameel Poverty Action Lab (J-PAL) has performed a series of CE analyses that might allow for prioritization of investments (Iqbal, Duflo, Glennerster, & Tulloch, 2013). See Example 13.3.

Example 13.3   Cost-Effectiveness Prioritization to Reduce Poverty

The Abdul Latif Jameel Poverty Action Lab (J-PAL) conducts research to reduce poverty across the globe. Evaluations of reforms to the education sector are one component of this strategy.

In evaluating cost-effectiveness (CE), J-PAL focuses on two outcome measures: test scores and additional years of participation in the school system. Given the contexts in which J-PAL performs these evaluations, these outcome measures can be affected by an array of educational, health-related, or social infrastructure projects. For example, in Kenya, free primary school uniforms have an effectiveness-cost ratio of 0.71 in terms of additional years of participation per $100. That is, for $100 worth of spending on uniforms, each student is expected to stay in school for 0.71 more years. Given the expected value of school, this appears to be a worthwhile investment.

J-PAL identifies positive impacts on years of schooling from a range of policies. In South Asia, these include building village schools (EC ratio of 1.51); iron fortification and deworming in pre-school (EC ratio of 2.73); and fellowship schools (0.34). In Latin America, providing information about the returns on education to boys appears cost-effective (EC ratio of 0.24). As this evidence accumulates, it may be possible to prioritize investments that will increase schooling in countries with high levels of poverty.

Source: www.povertyactionlab.org.

Despite their intuitive appeal, there are many reasons to be cautious about the role of league tables. As noted previously, there are a number of reasons why economic metrics that prima facie look comparable are in fact quite different (see also Drummond, Torrance, & Mason, 1993). In particular, studies calculate their economic metrics in a distinctive way, and this in turn will affect their ranking. First, each study must choose a discount rate, and if studies use different discount rates, then their CE estimates may differ and interpretations may be skewed. Second, CU studies require the use of utility weights, and there are numerous methods for estimating these weights, all of which might turn up varying answers (reflecting the different views of audiences and problems with interpersonal comparisons of utility). Third, studies vary in terms of what cost ingredients are considered and in the care that is taken in placing values on ingredients. Finally, each intervention in CE analysis is compared with a baseline, such as the "status quo" or an existing program. Even though baselines might vary widely across studies and contexts, the CE comparisons in league tables implicitly presume a common baseline. Creating a league table is an exercise in generalizability that may not be valid among different populations, contexts, operations, and time periods. Decisionmakers should not base policy on league tables where each investment is evaluated idiosyncratically.

There may be broader reasons to be skeptical of league tables. Further concerns arise if CE studies from several countries are compared (Drummond et al., 1993; Levin, 1995). In many health interventions—such as a particular vaccination or drug—estimates of effectiveness might be generally applied across countries. In education, however, it may be difficult to reasonably extrapolate the estimates of effectiveness from one context to another. For example, "teacher training" or "textbooks" are particular kinds of interventions, but they obviously vary widely in their objectives and content across countries. Thus, evidence of textbooks' CE in one country may not tell us a great deal about how effective textbooks will be elsewhere. Even roughly similar interventions may be less effective in some contexts due to the culturally specific nature of educational production (Fuller & Clarke, 1994). In particular, ingredients prices may vary. The relative prices of cost ingredients—such as teacher salaries for teachers of a given quality or building materials—often differ across countries or even across time periods in the same country. These differing prices could alter their relative CE. For example, if teacher salaries are particularly low in one country, then it might prove more cost-effective to invest in interventions that are labor-intensive (such as class size reduction). The opposite is true where teacher salaries are quite high. Second, costs must be converted into standard currency units. Frequently utilized nominal exchange rates may yield different answers than alternative exchange rates based on purchasing power parity.

Another concern is temporal. Most educational interventions are irreversible (they cannot be resold to other students), and their economic evaluations are produced ex post. We might know, for instance, that computer-assisted learning worked well in the 1990s and had a high BC ratio: Computers in the 1990s (i.e., before the Internet) helped students learn. The relevance of this information more than two decades later is very questionable. Rankings in league tables will likely change depending on the relative pace of technical change.

Also, league tables may not be read and interpreted in the simplistic way described previously. First, often the rankings do not correspond to the perspective of any decisionmaker. So, investments in preschool may have the highest return overall, but the benefits are split between the participating family, the federal government, the state, and the local community. Each decisionmaker would need his or her own set of rankings. Second, the reader of a league table cannot tell if interventions are independent. If the first-ranked intervention is preschool and the second-ranked is reduced class size in kindergarten, then investing in the former might reduce the ranking of the latter. Third, it is not obvious that the decisionmaker should just go down the list. When picking stocks, investors typically prefer a balanced portfolio to reduce risk. In actuality, citizens might exhibit more balanced preferences. An interesting study from health economics illustrates this: When surveyed about how to spend $1 million to save lives, respondents clearly preferred saving 34 lives by treating two diseases (30 saved for one disease and 4 from the other) over saving 50 lives by treating only one disease (Chandra, Jena, & Skinner, 2011, Table 1). In the context of education policy, decisionmakers might prefer to spread their investments through preschool, K–12 education, and the postsecondary system. Flat funding of each year grade might also be justified on equity grounds.

Operationally, decisionmakers might not be able to respond to the implied priorities of a league table. As noted previously, faced with a table where early education interventions outrank college programs, the policymaker is unlikely to declare that the college should enroll preschoolers. Even if the policymaker was this bold, the cost of transitioning from a college to a preschool center may be prohibitive (and league tables rarely capture these transition costs).

Hence, even if league tables accurately reflect the *ex ante* returns to educational investments, there are still considerable obstacles in using them to determine policy. The idea is logical, the metaphor of the stock market is helpful, and inevitably some form of prioritization or rationing must occur. See Example 13.1. But the rankings implied by league tables should not be interpreted strictly as a way of determining which educational investments to make.

13.5. USING ECONOMIC EVALUATIONS ●
TO IMPROVE EDUCATION RESEARCH

As presented throughout this book, there are inherent reasons in favor of more economic evaluations of educational investments. In addition, we believe that economic evaluations can help enhance the quality of education research more generally. Specifically, we identify several different ways through which economic evaluations—in conjunction with impact evaluations—can lead to improved educational research.

First, cost analysis requires information about both the treatment and the control (comparison) group and hence forces identification of treatment contrast. By definition, the control group is not getting what the treatment group receives. But that does not mean that the control group is getting fewer resources than the treatment group. One example is from Quint et al. (2015): although Success for All is a resource-intensive school reform, it costs only a small amount more than the interventions students would otherwise receive via regular schooling. Consequently, Success for All supports would need to be only modestly more effective in order to justify the investment. In some cases, comparisons are misleading because one intervention clearly receives a lot more resource than another: In its current configuration, the What Works Clearinghouse, appears to compare interventions of very different resource intensities (e.g., a 2-week program is contrasted with a 10-week program; see Levin & Belfield, 2015). Either way, by requiring that incremental costs be calculated, economic evaluation highlights treatment contrast.

Second, economic evaluations can help to clarify the outcomes to study. With BC analysis, there is guidance on what constitutes an important outcome (see the section on specifying benefits in Chapter 9). So, the analyst is encouraged to identify as many outcomes as possible, and these outcomes should be independent of each other. Also, because of discounting, the analyst must pay attention to the timing of these benefits. The analyst should estimate more accurately those impacts with relatively high shadow prices. For CE analysis, the outcomes must be prescribed and represented in a single number. Although this might appear to be highly restrictive, it might serve as a creative self-imposed constraint, forcing the analyst to identify the determinative outcome of an intervention (Elster, 2000). Moreover, in situations where there are multiple outcomes that cannot be mathematically aggregated, policy-makers must still make decisions, and these decisions must implicitly reflect some weighting of the outcomes.

Third, economic evaluation can assist investigations into program fidelity. Educational interventions often take place in contexts where resources and organizational practices are inflexible. So, schools often operate with fixed budgets such that implementing a new intervention reduces resources for other educational services. If class size is reduced in third grade, for example, this has implications for fourth grade. Hence, schools and colleges cannot always adjust their input use so as to be able to implement an intervention faithfully. Research suggests that what appears to be the same educational intervention can be implemented in dramatically different ways at different sites (Durlak & DuPre, 2008). Through a detailed examination of resource use, the analyst can determine whether an intervention has been implemented according to its design (see the example of Read 180 by Levin, Catlin, & Elson, 2007).

Finally, economic evaluations can provide information complementary to the power of the test and statistical significance tests used in impact evaluations. Standard hypothesis testing emphasizes statistical significance testing and the minimum detectable effect size—that is, the smallest true effect that has a "good chance" of being statistically significant (Bloom et al., 1997). By contrast, BC studies are testing an alternative metric—that is, whether the NPV is positive. In studies where the impacts of statistical significance are uncertain or imprecisely identified, this alternative metric may be useful. For example, point estimates of separate findings from recent evaluations of the Millennium Villages Project have been disputed at length (Malenga & Molyneux, 2012). Comparatively little attention has been paid to whether these disputes affect the NPV or policy decision. From a BC perspective, each separate estimate is only of interest insofar as it changes the sign and interpretation of the NPV. Instead of more precisely identifying a single causal estimate, the analyst can place this effect within the context of an economic evaluation of an array of benefits that sum to create the NPV of the investment. Another example, based on an educational intervention that diagnoses support services for inner-city youth—City Connects—is described by Bowden, Shand, Belfield, Wang, and Levin (2016). A prospective evaluation might determine how much (or how little) change in support services would be needed in order for the intervention to break even.

Overall, there is an important role for economic evaluations to complement and enhance impact evaluations.

13.6. THE FUTURE OF ECONOMIC ●
EVALUATION OF EDUCATION

Originally, BC analysis was developed for large-scale infrastructure projects such as dams or bridges. Only in recent decades has its application extended from environmental impact assessments to social policy (see the discussion in Farrow & Zerbe, 2013; Vining & Weimer, 2010; Weimer, 2015). Similarly, CE analysis flourishes best in fields such as health where outcomes are easily quantifiable and often unidimensional. As such, it is not surprising to see some discrepancies and methodological mutations when these evaluative techniques are applied to educational research.

Nevertheless, we believe there are several trends that should make economic evaluations of this type more commonplace in the future. First, fiscal pressures will continue to place pressure on education systems to allocate resources more efficiently and to demonstrate that they are doing so. Policy reforms such as performance funding or accountability metrics should motivate educational analysts to look for efficiency gains.

Second, the economic rationale for social investments is the presence of externalities or market failure; and there is growing appreciation that externalities are important and that government has a role to play in ameliorating market failure. For example, the U.S. federal government commits substantial funds to the loanable funds market for college; in part, this is motivated by the failure of this market to reach a socially efficient level of investment in college. More emphatically, investments in early education have been recognized as an important way to reduce the negative externalities arising from children whose early development is suboptimal. Home visiting and parenting programs—as well as nudges to college students—can be seen as correcting information failure. By justifying educational interventions in terms of market failure, there is a straightforward efficiency argument.

Third, education is increasingly being considered as a palliative for general economic or social challenges. Conventionally, educational investments are promoted as a way to enhance economic well-being through higher earnings. But they have also been advocated as crime prevention policies, or as public health solutions, or as a way to ameliorate social inequality (Putnam, 2015; Stiglitz, 2012). As the influence of educational interventions expands, a more comprehensive approach—such as BC analysis—will be needed to ascertain the optimal level of investment.

Fundamentally, economic evaluations will develop and expand in the future insofar as they improve the quality of decisionmaking by education professionals and policymakers (Posner, 2000). Hopefully, the material discussed in this book gives grounds for expecting such improvements.

● 13.7. A FINAL WORD

This volume was designed for a wide audience with differing proficiencies in evaluation and economics and with differing expectations for their use of such analysis. In theory, economic evaluation is simple: Estimate C over E or B minus C. In practice, there are many challenges to performing this estimation. Yet, the goal of this type of economic evaluation is to reach this level of simplicity while still being useful. That is, the goal is to make a clear statement—the BC ratio of National Guard Youth ChalleNGe Program (NGYCP) is 2.66 or the internal rate of return (IRR) to the HighScope Perry Preschool Program is 8.1%—that is credible and helpful for decisionmakers. With this statement, while taking all other factors into account, decisionmakers should be able to make a "reasoned determination" as to which educational investments are socially efficient in the broadest sense.

Discussion Questions

1. Assume that you undertake a CE study of alternative ways of improving the mathematics proficiencies of high school students in your state. Your report will be sent to school administrators in all the school districts. What advice would you give them in considering how to apply the results of your report to their districts?

2. You are a district superintendent who has come across a CE "league table" that summarizes the results of many studies that assessed interventions to improve reading achievement. Computer-assisted instruction appears to have the lowest CE ratios. Is this a compelling enough reason to devote more resources to this intervention?

3. How does economic evaluation help education researchers?

Appendix A

Answers to Even-Numbered Exercises

a. Benefit-cost (BC) analysis: One could compare the earnings of high school graduates in vocational and general education curricula. For each alternative, an estimate would be made of costs and of estimated future earnings based on employment experiences and wages for recent graduates. Since the vocational curriculum is typically more costly than the others, the benefits would have to be higher as well to justify expansion of vocational enrollments.

b. Cost-utility (CU) analysis: The results cannot be evaluated in monetary terms and the measures of effectiveness for different courses would differ. The administration can nominate groups of courses that are nonmandatory and susceptible to cuts. These can be evaluated for their enrollments, teaching effectiveness, value to students, and so on through student, parent, and administrator ratings. Using a weighting scheme, these values can be converted to utility scales. These ratings can be related to costs to create CU values. Those with the highest CU ratios would be cut first until the desired reduction was reached.

c. Benefit-cost (BC) analysis: A single program is being weighed to determine if it is worthwhile in the sense that its benefits exceed its costs. The costs of the program would be the new faculty, staff, and facilities that would be required. The benefits might be viewed as the additional tuition and instructional grants that could be obtained. In this case, the new program would be undertaken if costs were less than benefits and if the BC ratio were lower than for other alternatives that might also be considered.

d. Cost-feasibility (CF) analysis: To ascertain what the costs of the new policy would be, this can be compared with available resources.

e. Cost-effectiveness (CE) analysis: All of these alternatives can be evaluated on the basis of their contribution to student writing. Accordingly, a common measure of effectiveness can be used for the evaluation.

f. Cost-utility (CU) analysis: This is a community college version of Answer 2b.

g. Cost-effectiveness (CE) analysis: Since both alternatives can be evaluated on a common measure of effectiveness, we can compare the costs of each intervention with the respective gains in math competencies to see which program yields the highest gain in math per dollar spent.

● CHAPTER 3. QUESTION 2

a. $10,000: This is the cost of the program that does not vary with number of students served.

b. $100q: This is the cost of the program that varies with the number of students served, $100 per student.

c. $\dfrac{C}{q} = \dfrac{10,000 + 100q}{q}$: The average cost per participant is the total cost divided by the number of students served.

d. $\dfrac{\partial C}{\partial q} = \$100$: The marginal cost of the program is the cost of serving an additional student. Therefore, it is estimated as the derivative of the cost function.

e. The fixed cost of a program is important to consider when thinking about cost-feasibility (CF) and implementation. Schools operating with historical budgeting may incur high fixed costs and then have insufficient funds to cover operating costs. Also, a high fixed cost can be spread out over a large number of students such that average cost declines. However, if the program is targeting a small group of individuals, the fixed costs can increase the average cost of the program significantly. The variable cost of a program is the part of the total cost of the program that varies with the number of students served. Therefore, it can be used to analyze how cost will vary as the number of students served changes and is important to consider, for example, when scaling up. The average cost per participant is an important measure to characterize the cost of the program as it includes average fixed and variable costs per participant. Finally, the marginal cost can also give us important information when expanding the program; it tells us the cost of offering the program to an additional student.

CHAPTER 4. QUESTION 2 ●

a. The ingredients include the facility, parent volunteers, tutors, materials, resources for training (including both the trainer and facilities to host the training), and professional staff to implement the program. Try to describe each of these in more detail on the basis of some hypothetical set of requirements. For example, the facility would include one regular classroom with its share of energy requirements, maintenance, furnishings, and insurance. Also, the teacher trainer would need a certain amount of experience and qualifications to provider the training. You should also consider the opportunity cost of the peers' time.

b. The ingredients would include the coaches and other personnel, equipment and uniforms, space to practice, insurance, transportation requirements for travel to competitions, and so on. One key issue is how many games each team will include in the schedule. Another is the health insurance or medical costs of hosting sporting events. Try to provide more detail.

c. The ingredients the school district would need to consider include personnel such as administrators, teachers, audiologists, health personnel, facilities, equipment, materials and supplies, and so on. One key issue is the scale of the program and what the staff-to-student ratios will be. Another issue—for cost-feasibility (CF) analysis—is whether the district will have sufficient funding to provide this new program. Also, the cost analysis should be related to the resources mandated through each student's Individualized Education Program (IEP). Try to provide more detail.

d. The ingredients include materials and equipment and personnel such as construction workers, architects, and engineers. If the teachers are already included in the costs of the elementary school, these are not additional to the construction of the new center. A key issue is how to amortize the costs of the preschool center over cohorts of students. Try to provide more detail.

CHAPTER 5. QUESTION 2

The general formula is this:

$$\sum_{t=1}^{T} \frac{C_t}{(1+r)^{t-1}}$$

The results plugging in 0.03 and 0.07 for r, respectively, are as follows:

Year	Costs	$r = 0.03$	$r = 0.07$
Year 1	$11,000	$11,000	$11,000
Year 2	$13,000	$12,621	$12,150
Year 3	$18,500	$17,438	$16,159
Year 4	$10,800	$9,884	$8,816
Year 5	$27,000	$23,989	$20,598
Total		$74,932	$68,722

Note that this approach uses discrete time discounting, once per year, and assumes the costs for the first year are borne immediately and thus not discounted. You may obtain slightly different results if you use different assumptions. The average of the present value at these two discount rates is ((74,932 + $68,722)/2) = $71,827. The present value for the average of the two discount rates ($r = 0.05$) is $71,703. Although these values are similar, they are not the same. This happens because the PV formula is not a linear operator.

CHAPTER 6. QUESTION 2

Answers may vary. Your worksheet should include ingredients that might be relevant for the program and information on the quantity, unit, and price of each ingredient. Here is a suggested answer:

Ingredients Table		
	Ingredients	Unit prices
Students	4,200	
Sites	10	

	Ingredients	Unit prices
Class size	15	
Teachers	280	$40,000
Principal	10	$60,000
Other staff	5	$30,000
Deputy principal	10	$50,000
Facilities per site (sq. ft.)	10,000	$90
Instructional materials (books, toys, games)	4,200	$100
Other equipment (per center)	10	$8,000
Transport (per child)	756,000	$10
Food services (per child)	756,000	$5
Health services (per child)	756,000	$8
School district monitors (per child per year)	4,200	$75
Parent time (20 hours per child)	84,000	$8

Notes: Prices include fringe benefits. 180 days per school year. Prices are national prices from Bureau of Labor Statistics website and other price databases. Prices are in 1998 dollars.

Cost Spreadsheet

Ingredients	Cost to Preschool Centers	Cost to Other Agencies	Cost to Clients (Students/ Parents)	Total Cost
Personnel:				
Instructional staff	$11,200,000	$-	$-	$11,200,000
Administration	$1,250,000	$-	$-	$1,250,000
Facilities:				
Rental cost	$9,000,000	$-	$-	$9,000,000
Depreciation	$-	$-	$-	$-

(Continued)

(Continued)

Ingredients	Cost to Preschool Centers	Cost to Other Agencies	Cost to Clients (Students/ Parents)	Total Cost
Materials and equipment:				
Instructional materials	$420,000	$-	$-	$420,000
Other equipment	$80,000	$-	$-	$80,000
Other inputs:				
Transportation and food services	$11,340,000	$-	$-	$11,340,000
Health services	$6,048,000	$-	$-	$6,048,000
Required inputs from others:				
School district support	$-	$315,000	$-	$315,000
Parent program participation	$-	$-	$672,000	$672,000
Total ingredients cost	$39,338,000	$315,000	$672,000	$40,325,000
User fees	$-	$-	$-	$-
Cash subsidies	$-	$-	$-	$-
Net costs	$39,338,000	$315,000	$672,000	$40,325,000
Net cost in 2015 dollars (49% inflation)	$58,613,620	$469,350	$1,001,280	$60,084,250
Cost per child	$14,247	$114	$243	$14,605

CHAPTER 6. QUESTION 4

For both services of breakfast (in class or in the cafeteria), there are going to be costs for the food itself. These costs should be equivalent (i.e., there is no change in the breakfast menu). But the food costs might be different if some foods cannot be delivered in a classroom. The main difference in costs is the delivery of food. We might expect costs to be lower in the cafeteria because of specialization in food delivery (including waste management) and because cafeteria staff are paid lower wages than teachers (who are more involved in breakfast in the classroom).

An important consideration is total cost: More students will receive breakfast in the classroom; breakfast in the cafeteria is typically served to students who arrive early at school.

CHAPTER 7. QUESTION 2   ●

First, cost-effectiveness (CE) analysis requires that interventions be evaluated on the same outcomes: Sigma! and Primed for Algebra appear to use the same measure for outcomes; to also consider Alpha Math and Acing Algebra, we would need to know the equivalence with state math assessments to program-specific assessments. Second, CE analysis is more valid if the scales of the interventions are the same: We would need to know the sizes of the groups. As well, we would need to know the duration of each intervention. Third, CE analysis is more valid when the populations are similar. Considerations should include interventions that serve similar populations (e.g., Alpha Math and Sigma! both serve sixth-grade students on grade level). Finally, you may wish to exclude from consideration results for which effects are not statistically significant for the purposes of a CE analysis.

CHAPTER 8. QUESTION 2   ●

a. Given the goal of the programs, the main measure of effectiveness is an increase in BA graduates.

b. Program A generates 660 graduates and 270 additional BA graduates, and Program B generates 300 graduates and 105 additional BA graduates.

c. No. The programs differ significantly in how many students complete high school, so that may be considered as an outcome. Alternatively, the two outcomes could be put together in a single measure: years of attainment per program participant. Another measure of effectiveness of the program is the increase in high school graduates.

d. The total present value cost of Program A is $2,400,000. The total cost of Program B is more complicated: It depends on how many students complete the full program and the rate of attrition (because these students will not cost anything). Assuming 50 students exit after 11th grade and 150 more students exit after the third year of college (a conservative assumption), the present value costs of Program B are $1.19 million (5% discount rate).

e. The effect of discounting costs to present value is to reduce the total cost of Program B to reflect the fact that much if its costs occur in the future.

f. To determine cost-effectiveness (CE), we report results in a table:

Students	1,000	500
Total costs	$2,400,000	$1,191,322
Effects (yield of new BA graduates)	270	105
Cost-effectiveness ratio	**$8,889**	**$11,346**

The cost per new BA graduate is lower with Program A at $8,889 (than for Program B at $11,346). This program is therefore more cost-effective.

g. Not necessarily. The CE ratio expressed as cost per new BA graduate is best for comparing programs that target similar outcomes at similar scale; it may not be the best measure of program impacts if educators want to increase the high school graduation rate. Alternatively, the analyst may prefer to perform benefit-cost (BC) analysis to incorporate the differential changes in the high school graduation rate.

h. The more cost-effective program is preferred.

i. The preference for the most cost-effective program assumes there are no countermanding funding constraints, political issues, or equity considerations. However, Program A is high-risk in that all the resources are incurred before any impacts are realized; if the program is ineffective, all resources are already spent. If Program B turns out to be ineffective, costs will be lower.

CHAPTER 9. QUESTION 2 ●

a. Using 2015 data from the U.S. Census Bureau, undiscounted earnings profiles for both males and females combined are as follows:

Age	Dropout	High School Graduate
18 to 24 years	$9,863	$18,255
25 to 29 years	$20,829	$32,519
30 to 34 years	$27,877	$36,145
35 to 39 years	$25,983	$39,710
40 to 44 years	$32,060	$40,636
45 to 49 years	$31,519	$40,619
50 to 54 years	$29,956	$43,785
55 to 59 years	$35,736	$40,772
60 to 64 years	$29,504	$39,391

Assuming zero earnings between ages 16 and 17 as well as linear rates of wage growth and decline, lifetime total earnings for dropouts are $1.26 million and for graduates are $1.73 million.

b. Discounting each dollar earnings amount back to age 12, the formula $PV = FV/(1 + r)^n$ is used. Discounted, present value total earnings for dropouts are $514,000 and for graduates are $727,000 (3% discount rate).

c. Answers will vary based upon the demographic subgroup selected as well as the assumptions applied, including the discount rate used, the earnings of those ages 16 to 17, and nonwage outcomes included. Sensitivity analysis can include varying the discount rate, including or excluding nonwage employment factors such as part-time vs. full-time employment, labor force participation, and working conditions as well as including or excluding additional private and fiscal benefits such as reduction in welfare receipt, reduced crime, or improved health. Also, for a causal interpretation, the analyst should adjust for unobservable differences by education level that also influence earnings.

● CHAPTER 10. QUESTION 2

Answers will vary based on assumptions used regarding horizon for analysis, interpolation, and discount rates. Here is a template answer:

Express all numbers in 2010 dollars at age 4.

Assume all differences are modeled until age 40. (We could project forward beyond age 40 if we believe the earnings gains for the treatment group persist.)

Assume a social discount rate of 3%.

Assume earnings start at age 18 and grow at a rate of 2% per year from age 18 up to age 27 and linearly between ages 28 and 40.

Assume felony counts and misdemeanors are equally distributed across years. So 0.12 felonies between ages 19 and 27 imply 0.0133 felonies per year. Transform the willingness to pay for crimes into present values at age 4.

Assume welfare payments are transfers between taxpayers and recipients; therefore, the amount of welfare does not count as a benefit but the administration of welfare does count. Administration costs are 15% of total welfare payments.

Ignore the differences in high school graduation. Shadow pricing educational differences would be double counting unless there are benefits from high school graduation that are not reflected in earnings, criminal activity, or welfare receipt.

With these assumptions, we estimate the following:

	Treatment	Control	Difference
PV earnings	$165,449	$136,579	$28,870
PV crime burden	$3,520	$6,731	$3,210
PV welfare burden	$1,071	$1,045	$(25)
Program costs	$15,000	$0	$15,000
Total benefits			$32,055
Net present value			$17,055
Benefit-cost ratio			2.14
Internal rate of return			6%

For sensitivity testing for the net present value (NPV), we should vary the discount rate upward.

For sensitivity testing for the conclusion, we should vary the willingness to pay for crimes, the time horizon (whether to go beyond age 40), and the assumption that the control group received no services. For further research, we would want to look at early benefits (e.g., reductions in special education during the school years) as these should have high present values.

CHAPTER 11. QUESTION 2 ●

a. Assuming that the willingness to pay per reduced cigarette and the average cost per student of the program are already discounted, the net present value (NPV) per student is $B - C = (250 \times 4) - 1,200 = -\$200$.

b. Results may vary as they are based on random draws from the data. The results will also depend on the distributional assumptions made for the parameters of the estimation.

Assume the cost per student is drawn randomly from between $800 and $1,500, the willingness to pay per reduction is drawn randomly from $150 to $350, and the impact is drawn from a normal distribution with mean 4 and standard deviation 2. Perform 1,000 simulations. If so, the distribution of NPVs ($B - C$) should be close to the following:

	Cost per student	Effectiveness	Willingness to pay	Benefits	NPV ($B - C$)
Mean	$1,150	4	$247	**$995**	($155)
SD	$203	2	$56	$533	$423
Minimum	$800	-2	$150	($470)	($1,734)
Maximum	$1,500	10	$350	$3,289	$2,192

Note that the mean answers from the simulations vary from the expected result because the costs and willingness to pay are not drawn from normal distributions. Note also that the NPV minimum and maximum are drawn from the 1,000 simulations.

c. The Monte Carlo sensitivity analysis provides additional information on possible variation of the estimates obtained from the mean. A useful metric is the probability that the NPV is negative or the proportion of cases where the NPV is less than some financing constraint.

From the previously given simulations, 61% of all draws produced a negative NPV.

Appendix B

CostOut *Tool*

PURPOSE OF *COSTOUT* ●

With the support of the Institute of Education Sciences, the Center for Benefit-Cost Studies of Education (CBCSE) at Teachers College, Columbia University, has developed a tool to facilitate cost and cost-effectiveness (CE) analysis for researchers. Like other software packages designed to support researchers, the tool does not obviate the need for thoughtful planning and expertise in research design, data collection, and analysis. Rather, it provides a basic framework that guides and assists researchers in matching ingredients with associated prices, simplifies and automates necessary calculations, and helps researchers make assumptions and analytical choices in a transparent and consistent manner. This tool is available for no charge at https://www.cbcse costtoolkit.org.

HOW *COSTOUT* AIDS ANALYSIS ●

CostOut can assist in calculating the costs of a single program or of multiple programs and can also perform comparative CE analysis across programs. The tool requires you to make decisions about what type of analysis you would like to perform and provide data on a program's sample of participants; its ingredients; and, if applicable, its effectiveness. With the information you provide, the tool helps guide you through organizing and analyzing your data, selecting appropriate prices for your ingredients, and automatically making adjustments to prices to make them consistent and comparable within a program and across programs within a project. By default, the tool uses national average prices, gathered by a research team at CBCSE from nationally representative surveys such as the Current Population Survey by the U.S. Census Bureau in the CBCSE Database of Educational Resource Prices. If there are ingredients unique to your intervention, if you are performing an economic evaluation outside the domain of education, or if you would like to use local prices as opposed to national average prices, you can add your own prices to the tool's MyPrices Database. For local prices, the tool can also make adjustments to national average prices to reflect local markets using regional price parities (Atten, Figueroa, & Martin, 2012).

In addition to helping you select appropriate prices for ingredients, the tool also automates the process of making adjustments for discounting, inflation, geographic location (if applicable), and annualization. Most parameters are set globally within a program or project so as to ensure consistency and comparability, whereas others (such as timeframe for annualization) are set at the ingredient level to allow for flexibility. The tool can also assist in making assumptions regarding units of ingredients or prices, such as the percentage of time an ingredient is used for an intervention or the number of hours in a school year for dividing an annual salary into an hourly wage, so as to make those assumptions transparent and consistent. Automating these calculations and assumptions also has the advantage of reducing error arising from hand calculations.

Once all data have been entered, the tool can automatically generate a set of summary statistics, including estimated total cost, average cost per student, and a cost-effectiveness (CE) ratio. These costs can then be distributed across multiple constituencies based on who funds or provides each ingredient, marking a clear delineation between cost and financing but still allowing for analysis of distributional consequences of a program or policy. In a similar vein, the tool also allows users to document transfers, subsidies, and user fees, which do not alter the social cost in an economic sense (no additional resources are expended) but do shift the burden of payment among constituencies. Finally, *CostOut* can automatically produce a range of comparative reports and graphs that summarize and visualize differences between programs in costs and CE. These include a breakdown of costs by whether they are fixed or variable, cost by category of ingredient, and a CE plane that plots CE ratios with effectiveness on the x-axis and costs on the y-axis.

What *CostOut* Does and Does Not Do

CostOut will provide you with a platform to help you organize your ingredients data, help you select appropriate prices, make the process of making assumptions and adjustments both automatic and transparent, simplify and automate calculations, and allow for easy sensitivity analysis by duplicating a project and changing parameter values. The tool will not calculate effectiveness, tell you what ingredients a program entails, or make decisions about the design of your analysis; in other words, it is imperative that researchers still are familiar with the ingredients method for economic evaluation and thoughtfully approach the research design, data collection, and analysis activities with an eye toward the research questions they are trying to answer and whether the analyses they are conducting and data they are collecting provide valid answers to those questions.

FOR MORE INFORMATION   ●

We encourage you to peruse further resources available at the *CostOut* website, including a full manual, a set of video tutorials, additional informational resources, and example projects built into the tool, for more information. We also encourage you to review cost and CE analyses that have been completed with the assistance of *CostOut*, including a CE analysis of early literacy programs and a benefit-cost (BC) analysis of a comprehensive student support intervention, at www.cbcse.org.

References

Agan, A. Y. (2014). *Disaggregating the returns to college* [Working paper]. Princeton University, Princeton, NJ. Retrieved from https://docs.google .com/viewer?url=https://sites.google.com/site/amandayagan/Agan_ CollegePaths.pdf?attredirects=0

Ahn, S., Ames, A. J., & Myers, N. D. (2012). A review of meta-analyses in education: Methodological strengths and weaknesses. *Review of Educational Research, 82,* 436–476.

Allgood, S., & Snow, A. (1998). The marginal cost of raising tax revenue and redistributing income. *Journal of Political Economy, 106*(6), 1246–1273.

Altonji, J. G., Blom, E., & Meghir, C. (2012). Human capital investments: High school curriculum, college major, and careers. *Annual Review of Economics, 4*(1), 185–223.

Altonji, J. G., Elder, T. E., & Taber, C. R. (2005). Selection on observed and unobserved variables: Assessing the effectiveness of Catholic schools. *Journal of Political Economy, 113*(1), 151–184.

Angrist, J. D., & Krueger, K. (1999). Empirical strategies in labor economics. In O. Ashenfelter & D. Card (Eds.), *The handbook of labor economics* (Vol. III, Part B). Amsterdam, The Netherlands: Elsevier.

Angrist, J. D., & Pischke, J. S. (2009). *Mostly harmless econometrics: An empiricist's companion.* Princeton, NJ: Princeton University Press.

Ansar, A., Flyvbjerg, B., Budzier, A., & Lunn, D. (2014). Should we build more large dams? The actual costs of hydropower megaproject development. *Energy Policy, 69,* 43–56.

Atten, B. H., Figueroa, E. B., & Martin, T. M. (2012). *Regional price parities for states and metropolitan areas, 2006–2010.* Retrieved from http://www.bea .gov/scb/pdf/2012/08%20August/0812_regional_price_parities.pdf

Autor, D. H. (2014). Skills, education, and the rise of earnings inequality among the "other 99 percent." *Science, 344,* 843–851.

Avery, C., & Turner, S. (2012). Student loans: Do college students borrow too much—or not enough? *Journal of Economic Perspectives, 26,* 165–192.

Bailey, T., Jaggars, S., & Jenkins, D. (2015). *Redesigning America's community colleges: A clearer path to student success.* Cambridge, MA: Harvard University Press.

Banerjee, A., Duflo, E., Goldberg, N., Karlan, D., Osei, R., Parienté, W., . . . Udry, C. (2015). A multifaceted program causes lasting progress for the very poor: Evidence from six countries. *Science, 348,* 772–789.

Barnett, W. S. (1996). *Lives in the balance: Age-27 benefit-cost analysis for the High/Scope Perry Preschool Program.* Ypsilanti, MI: High/Scope Press.

Barnett, W. S., Carolan, M. E., Squires, J. H., Clarke Brown, K., & Horowitz, M. (2015). *The state of preschool 2014: State preschool yearbook.* New Brunswick, NJ: National Institute for Early Education Research.

Barnett, W. S., & Masse, L. N. (2007). Comparative benefit-cost analysis of the Abecedarian program and its policy implications. *Economics of Education Review, 26*(1), 113–125.

Barrow, L., & Malamud, O. (2015). Is college a worthwhile investment? *Annual Review of Economics, 7,* 519–555.

Barrow, L., Richburg-Hayes, L., Rouse, C. E., & Brock, T. (2014). Paying for performance: The education impacts of a community college scholarship program for low-income adults. *Journal of Labor Economics, 32*(3), 563–599.

Barrow, L., & Rouse, C. E. (2005). Do return to schooling differ by race and ethnicity? *American Economic Review, 95*(2), 83–87.

Barrow, L., Schanzenbach, D. W., & Claessens, A. (2015). The impact of Chicago's small high school initiative. *Journal of Urban Economics, 87,* 100–113.

Bartik, T. J., Gormley, W., & Adelstein, S. (2012). Earnings benefits of Tulsa's pre-K program for different income groups. *Economics of Education Review, 31*(6), 1143–1161.

Baum, S., Ma, J., & Payea, K. (2013). *Education Pays 2013.* Retrieved from https://trends.collegeboard.org/sites/default/files/education-pays-2013-full-report.pdf

Belfield, C. R. (2015). How can cost-benefit analysis help create public value? In J. M. Bryson, B. C. Crosby, & L. Bloomberg (Eds.), *Public value and public administration.* Washington, DC: Georgetown University Press.

Belfield, C. R., Bowden, A. B., Klapp, A., Levin, H. M., Shand, R., & Zander, S. (2015). The economic value of social and emotional learning. *Journal of Benefit-Cost Analysis, 6*(3), 508–544.

Belfield, C. R., Crosta, P., & Jenkins, D. J. (2014). Can community colleges afford to improve completion? Measuring the cost and efficiency consequences of reform. *Educational Evaluation and Policy Analysis, 36*(3), 327–345.

Belfield, C. R., & Levin, H. M. (2007). *The price we pay: The economic and social cost of inadequate education.* Washington, DC: Brookings Institution.

Belfield, C. R., & Levin, H. M. (2009). *The economic burden of juvenile crime: A case study for California* [Working paper]. Center for Benefit-Cost Studies of Education, Teachers College, Columbia University, New York, NY.

Berman, P., & McLaughlin, M. (1975). *The finding in review* (Federal Programs Supporting Educational Change, Vol. 4; R-1589/4-HEW). Santa Monica, CA: RAND.

Bettinger, E. P., & Baker, R. B. (2014). The effects of student coaching: An evaluation of a randomized experiment in student advising. *Educational Evaluation and Policy Analysis, 36*(1), 3–19.

Bettinger, E. P., Long, B. T., Oreopoulos, P., & Sanbonmatsu, L. (2012). The role of application assistance and information in college decisions: Results from the H&R Block FAFSA experiment. *Quarterly Journal of Economics, 127*(3), 1205–1242.

Betts, J. R. (1996). Is there a link between school inputs and learning? Fresh scrutiny of an old literature. In G. Burtless (Ed.), *Does money matter? The effect of school resources on student achievement and adult success* (pp. 141–191). Washington, DC: Brookings Institution.

Black, S. E., & Machin, S. (2011). Housing valuations of school performance. In E. A. Hanushek, S. Machin, & L. Woessmann (Eds.), *Handbook of the economics of education* (Vol. 3, pp. 485–519). Amsterdam, The Netherlands: Elsevier.

Blau, D., & Mocan, H. N. (2006). The supply of quality in child care centers. *The Review of Economics and Statistics, 84*, 483–496.

Blomquist, G. C., Coomes, P. A., Jepsen, C., Koford, B. C., & Troske, K. R. (2014). Estimating the social value of higher education: Willingness to pay for community and technical colleges. *Journal of Benefit-Cost Analysis, 5*(1), 3–41.

Blonigen, B. A., Harbaugh, W. T., Singell, L. D., Horner, R. H., Irvin, L. K., & Smolkowski, K. S. (2008). Application of economic analysis to school-wide positive behavior support (SWPBS) programs. *Journal of Positive Behavior Interventions, 10*(1), 5–19.

Bloom, H. S., Hill, C. J., Black, A. R., & Lipsey, M. W. (2008). Performance trajectories and performance gaps as achievement effect-size benchmarks for educational interventions. *Journal of Research on Educational Effectiveness, 1*(4), 289–328.

Bloom, H. S., Orr, L. L., Bell, S. H., Cave, G., Doolittle, F., Lin, W., & Bos, J. M. (1997). The benefits and costs of JTPA Title II-A Programs: Key findings from the National Job Training Partnership Act Study. *Journal of Human Resources, 32*(3), 549–576.

Boardman, A. E., Greenberg, D. H., Vining, A. R., & Weimer, D. L. (2011). *Cost-benefit analysis: Concepts and practice* (4th ed.). Upper Saddle River, NJ: Pearson Education.

Borenstein, M., Hedges, L. V., Higgins, J. P. T., & Rothstein, H. R. (2009). *Introduction to meta-analysis*. West Sussex, UK: Wiley.

Borman, G. D., & Hewes, G. M. (2002). The long-term effects and cost-effectiveness of success for all. *Educational Evaluation and Policy Analysis, 24*(4), 243–266.

Bowden, A. B. (2014). *Estimating the cost-effectiveness of a national program that impacts high school graduation and postsecondary enrollment*. New York, NY: Academic Commons. Retrieved from http://dx.doi.org/10.7916/D8K 935PK

Bowden, A. B., & Belfield, C. R. (2015). Evaluating TRIO: A benefit-cost analysis and cost-effectiveness analysis of Talent Search. *Journal of Benefit-Cost Analysis, 6*(3), 572–602.

Bowden, A. B., Shand, R., Belfield, C. R., Wang, A., & Levin, H. M. (2016). Evaluating educational interventions that induce service receipt: A case study application of city connects. *American Journal of Evaluation*. Advance online publication. doi:10.1177/1098214016664983

Bowen, W. G., Chingos, M. M., Lack, K. A., & Nygren, T. I. (2014). Interactive learning online at public universities: Evidence from a six-campus randomized trial. *Journal of Policy Analysis and Management, 33*(1), 94–111.

Bray, M. (1987). *Are small schools the answer? Cost-effectiveness strategies for rural school provision*. London, England: Commonwealth Secretariat.

Brent, R. J. (2009). A cost-benefit analysis of female primary education as a means of reducing HIV/AIDS in Tanzania. *Applied Economics, 41*(14), 1731–1743.

Brewer, D. J., Krop, C., Gill, B. P., & Reichardt, R. (1999). Estimating the costs of national class size reductions under different policy alternatives. *Educational Evaluation and Policy Analysis, 21*(2), 179–192.

Briggs, A. H., O'Brien, B. J., & Blackhouse, G. (2002). Thinking outside the box: Recent advances in the analysis and presentation of uncertainty in cost-effectiveness studies. *Annual Review of Public Health, 23*, 377–401.

Briggs, A. H., Weinstein, M. C., Fenwick, E. A. L., Karnon, J., Sculpher, M. J., & Paltiel, A. D. (2012). Model parameter estimation and uncertainty analysis: A report of the ISPOR-SMDM Modeling Good Research Practices Task Force Working Group–6. *Medical Decision Making, 32*(5), 722–732.

Brouwer, W. B. F., Niessen, L. W., Postma, M. J., & Rutten, F. F. H. (2005). Need for differential discounting of costs and health effects in cost effectiveness analyses. *BMJ: British Medical Journal, 331*(7514), 446–448.

Bryk, A. S. (Ed.). (1983). *Stakeholder-base evaluation* (New Directions for Program Evaluation, Vol. 17). San Francisco, CA: Jossey-Bass.

Bua-lam, P., & Bias, T. K. (2011). Economic impacts of West Virginia Division of Rehabilitation Services on significant disabilities: Realistic return-on-investment models for state-federal VR programs. *Journal of Rehabilitation, 77*(3), 25.

Burgess, D. F., & Zerbe, R. O. (2013). The most appropriate discount rate. *Journal of Benefit-Cost Analysis, 4*(3), 391–400.

Burwick, A., Zaveri, H., Shang, L., Boller, K., Daro, D., & Strong, D. A. (2014). *Costs of early childhood home visiting: An analysis of programs implemented in the Supporting Evidence-Based Home Visiting to Prevent Child Maltreatment Initiative*. Washington, DC: Mathematica Policy Research. Retrieved from http://www.chapinhall.org/sites/default/files/documents/Costs%20 of%20EC%20Home%20Visiting.Final%20Report.January%2030%20 2014.2.pdf

Butcher, K. F., & Visher, M. G. (2013). The impact of a classroom-basd guidance program on student performance in community college math classes. *Educational Evaluation and Policy Analysis, 35*(3), 298–323.

Card, D., & Krueger, A. B. (1992). Does school quality matter? Returns to education and the characteristics of public schools in the United States. *Journal of Political Economy, 100*, 1–40.

Card, D., & Krueger, A. B. (1996). Labor market effects of school quality: Theory and evidence. In G. Burtless (Ed.), *Does money matter? The effect of school resources on student achievement and adult success* (pp. 141–191). Washington, DC: Brookings Institution.

Carnoy, M. (1995). Rates of return to education. In M. Carnoy (Ed.), *International encyclopedia of economics of education* (2nd ed., pp. 364–369). Oxford, England: Pergamon.

Cascio, E. U., & Staiger, D. O. (2012). *Knowledge, tests, and fadeout in educational interventions* (NBER Working Paper No. 18038). Retrieved from National Bureau of Economic Research website: http://www.nber.org/papers/w18038

Castleman, B. L., Page, L. C., & Schooley, K. (2014). The forgotten summer: Does the offer of college counseling after high school mitigate summer melt among college-intending, low-income high school graduates? *Journal of Policy Analysis and Management, 33*(2), 320–344.

Caulkins, J. P., Rydell, C. P., Everingham, S., Chisea, J., & Bushways, S. (1999). *An ounce of prevention a pound of uncertainty: Cost-effectiveness of school-based drug prevention programs.* Santa Monica, CA: RAND.

Cellini, S. R., Ferreira, F., & Rothstein, J. (2010). The value of school facility investments: Evidence from a dynamic regression discontinuity design. *Quarterly Journal of Economics, 125*(1), 215–261.

Chambers, J. (1980). The development of a cost of education index. *Journal of Education Finance, 5*(3), 262–281.

Chandra, A., Jena, A. B., & Skinner, J. S. (2011). The pragmatist's guide to comparative effectiveness research. *Journal of Economic Perspectives, 25*(2), 27–46.

Chetty, R., Friedman, J. N., Hilger, N., Saez, E., Schanzenbach, D. W., & Yagan, D. (2011). How does your kindergarten classroom affect your earnings? Evidence from Project STAR. *Quarterly Journal of Economics, 126*(4), 1593–1660.

Chetty, R., Friedman, J. N., & Rockoff, J. E. (2014). Measuring the impacts of teachers II: Teacher value-added and student outcomes in adulthood. *American Economic Review, 104*(9), 2633–2679.

Chingos, M. M. (2012). The impact of a universal class-size reduction policy: Evidence from Florida's statewide mandate. *Economics of Education Review, 31*(5), 543–562.

Choi, E. J., Moon, H. R., & Ridder, G. (2014). Estimation of an education production function under random assignment with selection. *American Economic Review, 104*(5), 206–211.

Clemen, R. T. (1996). *Making hard decisions: An introduction to decision analysis* (2nd ed.). Belmont, CA: Duxbury Press.

Clune, W. H. (2002). Method strength and policy usefulness of cost-effectiveness research. In H. M. Levin & P. McEwan (Eds.), *Cost-effectiveness and educational policy* (pp. 55–68). Larchmont, NY: Eye on Education.

Cohen, M. A., & Piquero, A. R. (2009). New evidence on the monetary value of saving a high risk youth. *Journal of Quantitative Criminology, 25*(1), 25–49.

Cohen, M. A., & Piquero, A. R. (2015). Benefits and costs of a targeted intervention program for youthful offenders: The youthbuild USA offender project. *Journal of Benefit-Cost Analysis, 6*, 603–627.

Cohen, M. A., Piquero, A. R., & Jennings, W. G. (2010). Estimating the costs of bad outcomes for at-risk youth and the benefits of early childhood interventions to reduce them. *Criminal Justice Policy Review, 21*(4), 391–434.

Colegrave, A. D., & Giles, M. (2008). School cost functions: A meta-regression analysis. *Economics of Education Review, 27*(6), 688–696.

Coleman, J. S., Campbell, E. Q., Hobson, C. J., McPartland, J., Mood, A. M., Weinfeld, F. D., & York, R. L. (1966). *Equality of educational opportunity* (National Center for Educational Statistics Report No. OE-38001). Washington, DC: Government Printing Office.

Constantine, J. M., Seftor, N. S., Martin, E. S., Silva, T., & Myers, D. (2006). *Study of the effect of the Talent Search program on secondary and postsecondary outcomes in Florida, Indiana and Texas: Final report from Phase II of the national evaluation.* Washington, DC: U.S. Department of Education Office of Planning, Evaluation and Policy Development, Policy and Program Studies Service.

Cook, P., Dodge, K., Farkas, G., Fryer, R., Guryan, J., Ludwig, J., . . . Steinberg, L. (2014). *The (surprising) efficacy of academic and behavioral interventions with disadvantaged youth in the United States: Results from a randomized experiment in Chicago* (NBER Working Paper No. 19862). Retrieved from National Bureau of Economic Research website: http://www.nber.org/papers/w19862

Cooper, H. (2009). *Research synthesis and meta-analysis: A step-by-step approach.* Thousand Oaks, CA: Sage.

Cornman, S. Q. (2014). *Revenues and expenditures for public elementary and secondary education: School Year 2011–12 (Fiscal Year 2012)* (NCES 2014-301). Washington, DC: National Center for Education Statistics.

Crowley, D. M., Jones, D. E., Greenberg, M. T., Feinberg, M. E., & Spoth, R. L. (2012). Resource consumption of a diffusion model for prevention programs: The PROSPER Delivery System. *Journal of Adolescent Health, 50*(3), 256–263.

Cutler, D. M., & Lleras-Muney, A. (2010). Understanding differences in health behaviors by education. *Journal of Health Economics, 29*, 1–28. doi:10.1016/j.jhealeco.2009.10.003

Dale, S., & Krueger, A. B. (2011). *Estimating the return to college selectivity over the career using administrative earnings data* (NBER Working Paper No. 17159). Retrieved from National Bureau of Economic Research website: http://www.nber.org/papers/w17159

Deming, D. J., Goldin, C., Katz, L. F., & Yuchtman, N. (2015). Can online learning bend the higher education cost curve? *American Economic Review, 105*(5), 496–501.

Desrochers, D. M., & Hurlburt, S. (2016). *Spending and results: What does the money buy? A Delta data update: 2003–2013.* Washington, DC: Delta Cost Project. Retrieved from http://www.deltacostproject.org/resources/pdf/Delta-Cost-Trends-Outcomes.pdf

Detsky, A. S., & Naglie, I. G. (1990). A clinician's guide to cost-effectiveness analysis. *Annals of Internal Medicine, 113*(2), 147–154.

Dhaliwal, I., Duflo, E., Glennister, R., & Tulloch, C. (2012). *Comparative cost-effectiveness analysis to inform policy in developing countries.* Cambridge, MA: Abdul Latif Jameel Poverty Action Lab, MIT.

Dorfman, R. (1967). *Price and markets.* Englewood Cliffs, NJ: Prentice Hall.

Drummond, M., Brixner, D., Gold, M., Kind, P., McGuire, A., & Nord, E. (2009). Toward a consensus on the QALY. *Value in Health, 12,* S31–S35.

Drummond, M., O'Brien, B., Stoddart, G. L., & Torrance, G. W. (1997). *Methods for the economic evaluation of health care programmes* (2nd ed.). Oxford, England: Oxford University Press.

Drummond, M., Torrance, G., & Mason, J. (1993). Cost-effectiveness league tables: More harm than good? *Social Science and Medicine, 37*(1), 33–40.

Duckworth, A. L., & Yeager, S. (2015). Measurement matters: Assessing qualities other than cognitive ability for educational purposes. *Educational Researcher, 44*(4), 237–251.

Duflo, E. (2001). Schooling and labor market consequences of school construction in Indonesia: Evidence from an unusual policy experiment. *American Economic Review, 91*(4), 795–813.

Duncan, G. J., & Magnuson, K. (2013). Investing in preschool programs. *Journal of Economic Perspectives, 27*(2), 109–132.

Durlak, J., & DuPre, E. P. (2008). Implementation matters: A review of research on the influence of implementation on program outcomes and the factors affecting implementation. *American Journal of Community Psychology, 41*(3–4), 327–350.

Durlak, J. A., Weissberg, R. P., Dymnicki, A. B., Taylor, R. D., & Schellinger, K. B. (2011). The impact of enhancing students' social and emotional learning: A meta-analysis of school-based universal interventions. *Child Development, 82,* 405–432.

Eberts, R. W. (2007). Teachers unions and student performance: Help or hindrance? *Future of Children, 17*(1), 175–200.

Eddy, D. M. (1991). Oregon's methods: Did cost-effectiveness analysis fail? *Journal of the American Medical Association, 226*(15), 2135–2141.

Elster, J. (2000). *Ulysses unbound: Studies in rationality, precommitment, and constraints.* Cambridge, England: Cambridge University Press.

Escobar, C. M., Barnett, W. S., & Keith, J. E. (1988). A contingent valuation approach to measuring the benefits of preschool education. *Education Valuation and Policy Analysis, 10*(1), 13–22.

Evans, D. K., & Popova, A. (2014). *Cost-effectiveness measurement in development: Accounting for local costs and noisy impacts* (World Bank Policy Research Working Paper No. 7027). Retrieved from SSRN website: http://ssrn.com/abstract=2495174

Farrow, R. S., & Zerbe, R. O. (Eds.). (2013). *Principles and standards for benefit-cost analysis.* Cheltenham, England: Edward Elgar Publishing.

Figlio, D. N., & Lucas, M. E. (2004). What's in a grade? School report cards and the housing market. *American Economic Review, 94*(3), 591–604.

Fletcher, J. D., Hawley, D. E., & Piele, P. K. (1990). Costs, effects and utility of microcomputer assisted instruction in the classroom. *American Educational Research Journal, 27*(4), 783–806.

Foster, E. M., Jones, D. E., & the Conduct Problems Prevention Research Group. (2005). The high costs of aggression: Public expenditures resulting from conduct disorder. *American Journal of Public Health, 95*(10), 1767–1772.

Foster, E. M., Porter M. M., Ayers, T. S., Kaplan, D. L., & Sandler, I. (2007). Estimating the costs of preventive interventions. *Evaluation Review, 31*(3), 261–268.

Fredriksson, P., Ockert, B., & Oosterbeek, H. (2013). Long-term effects of class size. *Quarterly Journal of Economics, 48*, 249–285.

Freudenberg, N., & Ruglis, J. (2007). Reframing school dropout as a public health issue. *Preventing Chronic Disease, 4*, 4. Retrieved from www.cdc .gov/pcd/issues/2007/oct/07_0063.htm

Fryer, R. (2013). Teacher incentives and student achievement: Evidence from New York City public schools. *Journal of Labor Economics, 31*(2), 373–427.

Fuller, B., & Clarke, P. (1994). Raising school effects while ignoring culture? Local conditionals and the influence of classroom tools, rules and pedagogy. *Review of Educational Research, 64*(1), 119–157.

Fuller, B., Hua, H., & Snyder, C. W. (1994). When girls learn more than boys: The influence of time in school and pedagogy in Botswana. *Comparative Education Review, 38*(3), 347–376.

Gaertner, M. N., Kim, J., DesJardins, S. L., & McClarty, K. L. (2014). Preparing students for college and careers: The causal role of algebra II. *Research in Higher Education, 55*(2), 143–165.

Gelber, A., & Isen, A. (2013). Children's schooling and parents' behavior: Evidence from the Head Start Impact Study. *Journal of Public Economics, 101*, 25–38.

Gerard, K. (1992). Cost-utility in practice: A policy maker's guide to the state of the art. *Health Policy, 21*, 249–279.

Gillen, A., & Robe, J. (2011). *Stop misusing higher education-specific price indices.* Center for College Affordability and Productivity. Retrieved from http:// files.eric.ed.gov/fulltext/ED536149.pdf

Glass, G. V. (1984). *The effectiveness of four educational interventions* (Project Report No. 84-A19). Stanford, CA: Stanford University, Institute for Research on Educational Finance and Governance.

Glewwe, P. (1999). *The economics of school quality investments in developing countries: An empirical study of Ghana.* London, England: St. Martins's.

Glewwe, P. W., Hanushek, E. A., Humpage, S., & Ravina, R. (2013). School resources and educational outcomes in developing countries: A review of the literature from 1990 to 2010. In P. W. Glewwe (Ed.), *Education policy in developing countries.* Chicago, IL: University of Chicago Press.

Glick, H. A. (2011). Sample size and power for cost-effectiveness analysis (Part 1). *PharmacoEconomics, 29*(3), 189–198.

Gold, M. R., Siegel, J. E., Russell, L. B., & Weinstein, M. C. (1996). *Cost-effectiveness in health and medicine.* New York, NY: Oxford University Press.

Goldhaber, D., Destler, K., & Player, D. (2010). Teacher labor markets and the perils of using hedonics to estimate compensating wage differentials. *Economics of Education Review, 29*(1), 1–17.

Goldin, C., & Katz, L. F. (2008). *The race between education and technology.* Cambridge, MA: Belknap Press of Harvard University.

Goodman, J. (2012). *The labor of division: Returns to compulsory math coursework* (Faculty Research Working Paper Series No. RWP12-032). Cambridge, MA: Kennedy School, Harvard University.

Gray, A. M., Clarke, P. M., Wolstenholme, J. L., & Wordsworth, S. (2011). *Applied methods of cost-effectiveness analysis in health care.* Oxford, England: Oxford University Press.

Greenberg, D., Deitch, V., & Hamilton, G. (2009). A synthesis of random assignment benefit-cost studies of welfare-to-work programs. *Journal of Benefit-Cost Analysis, 1*(3).

Greenberg, D., Rosen, A. B., Wacht, O., Palmer, J., & Neumann, P. J. (2010). A bibliometric review of cost-effectiveness analyses in the economic and medical literature: 1976–2006. *Medical Decision Making, 30*(3), 320–327.

Greene, W. H. (1997). *Econometric analysis* (3rd ed.). Upper Saddle River, NJ: Prentice Hall.

Greenwald, R., Hedges, L., & Laine, R. D. (1996). The effect of school resources on student achievement. *Review of Educational Research, 66*(3), 361–396.

Grissmer, D. (1999). Class size effects: Assessing the evidence, its policy implications, and future research agenda. *Education Evaluation and Policy Analysis, 21*(2), 231–248.

Gronberg, T. J., Jansen, D. W., & Taylor, L. L. (2011). The adequacy of educational cost functions: Lessons from Texas. *Peabody Journal of Education, 86*(1), 3–27.

Grossman, J., & Tierney, J. P. (1998). Does mentoring work? An impact study of the Big Brothers Big Sisters program. *Evaluation Review, 22*(3), 403–426.

Hahn, R. W., & Tetlock, P. C. (2008). Has economic analysis improved regulatory decisions? *Journal of Economic Perspectives, 22,* 67–84.

Hanushek, E. A. (1986). The economics of schooling: Production and efficiency in public schools. *Journal of Economic Literature, 24*(3), 1141–1177.

Hanushek, E. A. (1997). Assessing the effect of school resources on student performance: An update. *Education Evaluation and Policy Analysis, 19*(2), 141–164.

Hanushek, E. A. (2003). The failure of input-based schooling policies. *Economic Journal, 113*(485), F64–F98.

Hanushek, E. A. (2006). Alternative school policies and the benefits of general cognitive skills. *Economics of Education Review, 25,* 447–462.

Harbison, R. W., & Hanushek, E. A. (1992). *Educational performance of the poor: Lessons from rural northeastern Brazil.* Oxford, England: Oxford University Press.

Harrington, W., Morgenstern, R. D., & Nelson, P. (2000). On the accuracy of regulatory cost estimates. *Journal of Policy Analysis and Management, 19*(7), 297–322.

Harris, D. N. (2009). Toward policy-relevant benchmarks for interpreting effect sizes combining effects with costs. *Educational Evaluation and Policy Analysis, 31*(1), 3–29.

Hartman, W. T., & Fay, T. A. (1996). Cost-effectiveness of instructional support teams in Pennsylvania. *Journal of Education Finance, 21*(4), 555–580.

Hausman, J. (2012). Contingent valuation: From dubious to hopeless. *Journal of Economic Perspectives, 26*(4), 43–56.

Haveman, R. H., & Weimer, D. L. (2015). Public policy induced changes in employment: Valuation issues for benefit-cost analysis. *Journal of Benefit-Cost Analysis, 6*(1), 112–153.

Haveman, R. H., & Wolfe, B. L. (1984). Schooling and economic well-being: The role of nonmarket effects. *Journal of Human Resources, 19*(3), 377–407.

Heckman, J. J., & Kautz, T. (2012). Hard evidence on soft skills. *Labour Economics, 19*(4), 451–464.

Heckman, J. J., Layne-Farrar, A., & Todd, P. (1996). Does measured school quality really matter? An examination of the earnings-quality relationship. In G. Burtless (Ed.), *Does money matter? The effect of school resources on student achievement and adult success* (pp. 141–191). Washington, DC: Brookings Institution.

Heckman, J. J., Moon, S. H., Pinto, R., Savelyev, P. A., & Yavitz, A. (2010). The rate of return to the HighScope Perry Preschool Program. *Journal of Public Economics, 94*(1–2), 114–128.

Heckman, J. J., & Urzua, S. (2010). Comparing IV with structural models: What simple IV can and cannot identify. *Journal of Econometrics, 156*(1), 27–37.

Herschbein, B., & Kearney, M. (2014). *Major decisions: What graduates earn over their lifetime.* Hamilton Project Report. Retrieved from http://hamilton project.org/papers/major_decisions_what_graduates_earn_over_their_ lifetimes

Hollands, F. M., Kieffer, M. J., Shand, R., Pan, Y., Cheng, H., & Levin, H. M. (2016). Cost-effectiveness analysis of early reading programs: A demonstration with recommendations for future research. *Journal of Research on Educational Effectiveness, 9*(1), 30–53.

Hollands, F., Levin, H. M., Belfield, C. R., Bowden, A. B., Cheng, H., Shand, R., . . . Hanisch-Cerda, B. (2014). Cost-effectiveness analysis of interventions that improve high school completion. *Educational Evaluation and Policy Analysis, 36*, 307–326.

Hollands, F. M., Pan, Y., Shand, R., Cheng, H., Levin, H. M., Belfield, C. R., . . . Hanisch-Cerda, B. (2013). *Improving early literacy: Cost-effectiveness analysis of effective reading programs.* New York, NY: Center for Benefit-Cost Studies of Education, Teachers College, Columbia University. Retrieved from http://cbcse.org/wordpress/wp-content/uploads/2013/05/2013-Hollands-Improving-early-literacy1.pdf

Hoxby, C. M. (2000). The effects of class size on student achievement: New evidence from population variation. *Quarterly Journal of Economics, 115*(4), 1239–1285.

Hsieh, C. T., & Urquiola, M. (2006). The effects of generalized school choice on achievement and stratification: Evidence from Chile's voucher program. *Journal of Public Economics, 90*(8–9), 1477–1503.

Hummel-Rossi, B., & Ashdown, J. (2002). The state of cost-benefit and cost-effectiveness analyses in education. *Review of Educational Research, 72*(1), 1–30.

Imbens, G. W. (2010). Better late than nothing: Some comments on Deaton (2009) and Heckman and Urzua (2009). *Journal of Economic Literature, 48*(2), 399–423.

Imbens, G. W., & Wooldridge, J. M. (2009). Recent development in the econometrics of program evaluation. *Journal of Economic Literature, 47*(1), 5–86.

Ingle, W. K., & Cramer, T. (2013). *A cost effectiveness analysis of third grade reading diagnostic tools.* Retrieved from https://aefpweb.org/sites/default/files/webform/CE analysis_reading assessments.pdf

Institute of Medicine and National Research Council. (2014). *Considerations in applying benefit-cost analysis to preventive interventions for children, youth, and families: Workshop summary.* Washington, DC: The National Academies Press.

Iqbal, D., Duflo, E., Glennerster, R., & Tulloch, C. (2013). Comparative cost-effectiveness analysis to inform policy in developing countries: A general framework with applications for education. In P. W. Glewwe (Ed.), *Education policy in developing countries.* Chicago, IL: University of Chicago Press.

Jackson, C. K., Johnson, R. C., & Persico, C. (2016). The effects of school spending on educational and economic outcomes: Evidence from school finance reforms. *Quarterly Journal of Economics, 131*(1), 157–218.

Jackson, K. (2014). Teacher quality at the high-school level: The importance of accounting for tracks. *Journal of Labor Economics, 32*(4), 128–145.

Jacob, B. A. (2007). The challenges of staffing urban schools with effective teachers. *The Future of Children, 17*(1), 129–153.

Jacob, B. A., Lefgren, L., & Sims, D. P. (2010). The persistence of teacher-induced learning. *Journal of Human Resources, 45*(4), 915–943.

Jacob, R., Armstrong, C., Bowden, A. B., & Pan, Y. (2016). Leveraging volunteers: An experimental evaluation of a tutoring program for struggling readers. *Journal of Research on Educational Effectiveness, 9*, S1.

Jain, R., Grabner, M., & Onukwugha, E. (2011). Sensitivity analysis in cost-effectiveness studies from guidelines to practice. *Pharmacoeconomics, 29*(4), 297–314.

Jamison, D. T., Mosley, W. H., Measham, A. R., & Bobadilla, J. L. (Eds.). (1993). *Disease control priorities in developing countries.* Oxford, UK: Oxford University Press.

Johannesson, M. (1996). *Theory and methods of economic evaluation of health care.* Dordretch, The Netherlands: Kluwer Academic.

Jones, D. E., Karoly, L. A., Crowley, D. M., & Greenberg, M. T. (2015). Considering valuation of noncognitive skills in benefit-cost analysis of programs for children. *Journal of Benefit-Cost Analysis, 6*(3), 471–507.

Kahneman, D., & Tversky, A. (1984). Choices, values and frames. *American Psychologist, 39,* 341–350.

Kane, T. J., & Rouse, C. E. (1995). Labor-market returns to two- and four-year college. *American Economic Review, 85,* 600–614.

Karoly, L. (2012). Toward standardization of benefit-cost analysis of early childhood interventions. *Journal of Benefit-Cost Analysis, 3*(1), 1–45.

Keele, L., Tingley, D., & Yamamoto, T. (2015). Identifying mechanisms behind policy interventions via causal mediation analysis. *Journal of Policy Analysis and Management, 34,* 937–963. doi:10.1002/pam.21853

Keeney, R. L., & Raiffa, H. (1993). *Decisions with multiple objectives.* New York, NY: Wiley.

Kim, C., Tamborini, C. R., & Sakamoto, A. (2015). Field of study in college and lifetime earnings in the United States. *Sociology of Education, 88*(4).

Krueger, A. B. (1999). Experimental estimates of education production functions. *The Quarterly Journal of Economics, 114*(2), 497–532.

Kumbhakar, S. C., & Lovell, C. A. (2000). *Stochastic frontier analysis.* Cambridge, England: Cambridge University Press.

Lavy, V., & Schlosser, A. (2005). Targeted remedial education for underperforming teenagers: Costs and benefits. *Journal of Labor Economics, 23*(4), 839–874.

Leachman, M., Albares, N., Masterson, K., & Wallace, M. (2016). *Most states have cut school funding, and some continue cutting.* Washington, DC: Center on Budget and Policy Priorities. Retrieved from http://www.cbpp.org/sites/default/files/atoms/files/12-10-15sfp.pdf

Leamer, E. E. (1983). Let's take the con out of econometrics. *The American Economic Review, 73*(1), 31–43.

Lee, S., Aos, S., Drake, E., Pennucci, A., Miller, M., Anderson, L., & Burley, M. (2012). *Return on investment: Evidence-based options to improve state-wide outcomes.* Olympia: Washington State Institute for Public Policy.

Lee, V. E., & Smith, J. B. (1997). High school size: Which works best and for whom? *Education Evaluation and Policy Analysis, 19*(3), 205–227.

Leithwood, K., & Jantzi, D. (2009). A review of empirical evidence about school size effects: A policy perspective. *Review of Educational Research, 79*(1), 464–490.

Levin, H. M. (1975). Cost-effectiveness analysis in evaluation research. In M. Guttentag & E. L. Struening (Eds.), *Handbook of evaluation research* (Vol. 2, Chap. 5). Beverly Hills, CA: Sage.

Levin, H. M. (1983). *Cost-effectiveness analysis.* Beverly Hills, CA: Sage.

Levin, H. M. (1988). Cost-effectiveness and educational policy. *Education Evaluation and Policy Analysis, 10*(1), 51–69.

Levin, H. M. (1991). Cost-effectiveness at quarter century. In M. W. McLaughlin & D. C. Phillips (Eds.), *Evaluation and education at quarter century* (pp. 188–209). Chicago, IL: University of Chicago Press.

Levin, H. M. (1995). Cost-effectiveness analysis. In M. Carnoy (Ed.), *International encyclopedia of economics of education* (2nd ed., pp. 381–386). Oxford, England: Pergamon.

Levin, H. M. (2001). Waiting for Godot: Cost-effectiveness analysis in education. In R. J. Light (Ed.), *Evaluation findings that surprise* (Vol. 90, pp. 55–68). San Francisco, CA: Jossey-Bass.

Levin, H. M., & Belfield, C. (2015). Guiding the development and use of cost-effectiveness analysis in education. *Journal of Research on Educational Effectiveness, 8*(3), 400–418.

Levin, H. M., Belfield, C., Hollands, F., Bowden, A. B., Cheng, H., Shand, R., . . . Hanisch-Cerda, B. (2012). *Cost-effectiveness analysis of interventions that improve high school completion.* New York, NY: Center for Benefit-Cost Studies of Education, Teachers College, Columbia University. Retrieved from http://cbcse.org/wordpress/wp-content/uploads/2012/10/IES HighSchoolCompletion.pdf

Levin, H. M., Catlin, D., & Elson, A. (2007). Costs of implementing adolescent literacy programs. In D. Deshler, A. S. Palincsar, G. Biancarosa, & M. Nair (Eds.), *Informed choices for struggling adolescent readers: A research-based guide to instruction programs and practices* (Chapter 4). New York, NY: Carnegie Corporation.

Levin, H. M., & Garcia, E. (2013). *Benefit-cost analysis of Accelerated Study in Associate Programs (ASAP) of the City University of New York (CUNY).* New York, NY: Teachers College, Columbia University.

Levin, H. M., Glass, G. V., & Meister, G. (1987). Cost-effectiveness of computer-assisted instruction. *Evaluation Review, 11*(1), 50–72.

Levin, H. M., & McEwan, P. J. (2001). *Cost-effectiveness analysis: Methods and applications.* Thousand Oaks, CA: Sage.

Levin, H. M., & Woo, L. (1981). An evaluation of the costs of computer-assisted instruction. *Economics of Education Review, 1*(1), 1–25.

Lewis, D. R., Johnson, D. R., Chen T. H., & Erickson, R. N. (1992). The use and reporting of benefit cost analyses by state vocational rehabilitation agencies. *Evaluation Review, 16*(3), 266–287.

Lewis, D. R., Johnson, D. R., Erickson, R. N., & Bruininks, R. H. (1994). Multiattribute evaluation of program alternatives within special education. *Journal of Disability Policy Studies, 5*(1), 77–112.

Lipscomb, J., Weinstein, M. C., & Torrance, G. W. (1996). Time preference. In M. R. Gold, J. E. Siegel, L. B. Russell, & M. C. Weinstein (Eds.) *Cost-effectiveness in health and medicine* (pp. 214–246). New York, NY: Oxford University Press.

Lipsey, M. W., Puzio, K., Yun, C., Hebert, M. A., Steinka-Fry, K., Cole, M. W., . . . Busick, M. D. (2012). *Translating the statistical representation of the effects of education interventions into more readily interpretable forms* (NCSER 2013-3000). Washington, DC: National Center for Special Education Research, Institute of Education Sciences, U.S. Department of Education.

Lockheed, M. E., & Hanushek, E. A. (1988). Improving educational efficiency in developing countries: What do we know? *Compare, 18*(1), 21–38.

London, R. A. (2006). The role of postsecondary education in welfare recipients' paths to self-sufficiency. *Journal of Higher Education, 77,* 472–496.

Long, K., Brown, J. L., Jones, S. M., Aber, J. L., & Yates, B. T. (2015). Cost analysis of a school-based social and emotional learning and literacy intervention. *Journal of Benefit-Cost Analysis, 6*(3), 545–571.

Lubienski, C. A., & Lubienski, S. T. (2013). *The public school advantage: Why public schools outperform private schools.* Chicago, IL: University of Chicago Press.

Ludwig, J., Kling, J. R., & Mullainathan, S. (2011). Mechanism experiments and policy evaluations. *Journal of Economic Perspectives, 25*(3), 17–38.

Maher E. J., Corwin, T. W., Hodnett, R., & Faulk, K. (2012). A cost-savings analysis of a statewide parenting education program in child welfare. *Research on Social Work Practice, 22*(6), 615–625.

Malenga, G., & Molyneux, M. (2012). The Millenium Villages project. *The Lancet, 379*(9832), 2131–2133.

Mankiw, G. (2011). *Principles of microeconomics.* Mason, OH: Southwestern.

Massoni, S., & Vergnaud, J. C. (2012). How to improve pupils' literacy? A cost-effectiveness analysis of a French educational project. *Economics of Education Review, 31*(1), 84–91.

Maxwell, N. L., & Rubin, V. (2000). *High school career academies: A pathway to educational reform in urban school districts?* Kalamazoo, MI: W. E. Upjohn Institute.

McCollister, K. E., French, M. T., & Fang, H. (2010). The cost of crime to society: New crime-specific estimates for policy and program evaluation. *Drug and Alcohol Dependence, 108*(1), 98–109.

McConnell, S., & Glazerman, S. (2001). *National Job Corps study: The benefits and costs of Job Corps.* Washington, DC: Mathematica Policy Research. Retrieved from http://files.eric.ed.gov/fulltext/ED457357.pdf

McEwan, P. (2015). Improving learning in primary schools of developing countries: A meta-analysis of randomized experiments. *Review of Educational Research, 85*(3), 353–394.

McEwan, P. J. (1999). Private costs and the rate of return to primary education. *Applied Economics Letters, 6*(11), 759–760.

McEwan, P. J. (2012). Cost-effectiveness analysis of education and health interventions in developing countries. *Journal of Development Effectiveness, 4*(2), 189–213.

McEwan, P. J. (2015). Quantitative research methods in education finance and policy. In H. F. Ladd & M. E. Goertz (Eds.), *Handbook of research in education finance and policy* (2nd ed., pp. 87–104). New York, NY: Routledge.

McGhan, W. F., Al, M., Doshi, J. A., Kamae, I., Marx, S. E., & Rindress, D. (2009). The ISPOR good practices for quality improvement of cost-effectiveness research task force report. *Value in Health, 12*(8), 1086–1099.

McHenry, P. (2011). The effect of school inputs on labor market returns that account for selective migration. *Economics of Education Review, 30*(1), 39–54.

Millar, R., & Hall, K. (2013). Social return on investment (SROI) and performance measurement. *Public Management Review, 6,* 923–941.

Miller, S., & Connolly, P. (2012). A randomized controlled trial evaluation of Time to Read, a volunteer tutoring program for 8- to 9-year-olds. *Educational Evaluation and Policy Analysis, 35,* 23–27.

Miller, T., & Hendrie, D. (2008). *Substance abuse prevention dollars and cents: A cost-benefit analysis* (DHHS Pub. No. [SMA] 07-4298). Rockville, MD: Center for Substance Abuse Prevention, Substance Abuse and Mental Health Services Administration.

Mitchell, J. (2014). *Educational attainment and earnings inequality among US-born men: A lifetime perspective.* Urban Institute Report. Retrieved from http://www.urban.org/sites/default/files/alfresco/publication-pdfs/413092-Educational-Attainment-and-Earnings-Inequality-among-US-Born-Men.PDF

Mooney, C. Z., & Duval, R. D. (1993). *Bootstrapping: A nonparametric approach to statistical inference.* Thousand Oaks, CA: Sage.

Moore, M. A., Boardman, A. E., & Vining, A. R. (2013). More appropriate discounting: The rate of social time preference and the value of the social discount rate. *Journal of Benefit-Cost Analysis, 4*(1), 1–16.

Moore, M. A., Boardman, A. E., Vining, A. R., Weimer, D. L., & Greenberg, D. H. (2004). Just give me a number! Practical values for the social discount rate. *Journal of Policy Analysis and Management, 23,* 789–812.

Moretti, E. (2013). Real wage inequality. *American Economic Journal: Applied Economics, 5*(1), 65–103.

Morrall, J. F. (1986). A review of the record. *Regulation, 10*(2), 25–35.

Mosteller, F. (1995). The Tennessee study of class size in the early school grades. *The Future of Children, 5*(2), 113–127.

Muckelbauer, R., Libuda, L., Clausen, K., Toschke, A. M., Reinehr, T., & Kersting, M. (2009). Promotion and provision of drinking water in schools for overweight prevention: Randomized, controlled cluster trial. *Pediatrics, 123*(4), e661–e667.

Muennig, P., Fiscella, K., Tancredi, D., & Franks, P. (2010). The relative health burden of selected social and behavioral risk factors in the United States: Implications for policy. *American Journal of Public Health, 100,* 1758–1764.

Murnane, R. J., & Willett, J. B. (2010). *Methods matter: Improving causal inference in educational and social science research.* New York, NY: Oxford University Press.

National Institute of Child Health and Human Development. (2000). *Report of the National Reading Panel: Teaching children to read: An evidence-based assessment of the scientific research literature on reading and its implications for reading instruction* (NIH Publication No. 00-4769). Washington, DC: Government Printing Office.

Neumann, P. J., Greenberg, D., Olchanski, N. V., Stone, P. W., & Rosen, A. B. (2005). Growth and quality of the cost–utility literature, 1976–2001. *Value in Health, 8*(1), 3–9.

Neumann, P. J., Sanders, G. D., Russell, L. E., Siegel, J. E., & Ganiat, T. G. (2016). *Cost-effectiveness in health and medicine* (2nd ed.). Oxford, England: Oxford University Press.

Neumann, P. J., Thorat, T., Shi, J., Saret, C. J., & Cohen, J. T. (2015). The changing face of the cost-utility literature, 1990–2012. *Value in Health, 18*(2), 271–277.

Newcomer, K. E., Hatry, H. P., & Wholey, J. S. (2015). *Handbook of practical program evaluation (essential texts for nonprofit and public leadership and management)* (4th ed.). San Francisco, CA: Wiley.

Nguyen-Hoang, P., & Yinger, J. (2011). The capitalization of school quality into house values: A review. *Journal of Housing Economics, 20*(1), 30–48.

Nores, M., Belfield, C. R., Barnett, W. S., & Schweinhart, L. (2006). Updating the economic impacts of the High/Scope Perry Preschool program. *Educational Evaluation and Policy Analysis, 27*, 245–261.

Ono, H. (2007). Does examination hell pay off? A cost–benefit analysis of "ronin" and college education in Japan. *Economics of Education Review, 26*(3), 271–284.

Oreopoulos, P. (2006). Estimating average and local average treatment effects of education when compulsory schooling laws really matter. *The American Economic Review, 96*(1), 152–175.

Oreopoulos, P., & Salvanes, K. G. (2011). Priceless: The nonpecuniary benefits of schooling. *The Journal of Economic Perspectives, 25*(1), 159–184.

Oreopoulos, P., von Wachter, T., & Heisz, A. (2012). The short- and long-term career effects of graduating in a recession. *American Economic Journal: Applied Economics, 4*, 1–29.

Organisation for Economic Co-operation and Development. (2014). *Education at a Glance 2014: OECD Indicators. OECD Publishing.* Retrieved from https://www.oecd.org/edu/Education-at-a-Glance-2014.pdf

Orr, L. L. (1999). *Social experiments.* Thousand Oaks, CA: Sage.

Orr, L. L., Bloom, H. S., Bell, S. H., Doolittle, F., Lin, W., & Cave, G. (1996). *Does job training for the disadvantaged work? Evidence form the national JTPA Study.* Washington, DC: Urban Institute.

Papay, J. P., & Johnson, S. M. (2012). Is PAR a good investment? Understanding the costs and benefits of teacher peer assistance and review programs. *Educational Policy, 26*(5), 696–729.

Pauly, M. V. (1995). Valuing health care benefits in money terms. In F. A. Sloan (Ed.), *Valuing health care: Costs, benefits and effectiveness of pharmaceuticals and other medical technologies* (pp. 99–124). Cambridge, England: Cambridge University Press.

Perez-Arce, F., Constant, L., Loughran, D. S., & Karoly, L. A. (2012). *A cost-benefit analysis of the national guard youth ChalleNGe program.* RAND Research Monograph, TR1193. Santa Monica, CA: RAND.

Persson, M., & Svensson, M. (2013). The willingness to pay to reduce school bullying. *Economics of Education Review, 35*, 1–11.

Pike, G. R. (2004). Measuring quality: A comparison of *US News* rankings and NSSE benchmarks. *Research in Higher Education, 45*(2), 193–208.

Pischke, J. S. (2007). The impact of length of the school year on student performance and earnings: Evidence from the German short school years. *The Economic Journal, 117*(523), 1216–1242.

Posner, R. A. (2000). Cost-benefit analysis: Definition, justification, and comment on conference papers. *The Journal of Legal Studies, 29*(S2), 1153–1177.

Protzko, J. (2015). The environment in raising early intelligence: A meta-analysis of the fadeout effect. *Intelligence, 53,* 202–210.

Psacharopoulos, G. (1994). Returns to investment in education: A global update. *World Development, 22*(9), 1325–1343.

Psacharopoulos, G., & Patrinos, H. A. (2004). Returns to investment in education: A further update. *Education Economics, 12*(2), 111–134.

Putnam, R. D. (2015). *Our kids: The American dream in crisis.* New York, NY: Simon & Schuster.

Quinn, B., Van Mondfrans, A., & Worthen, B. R. (1984). Cost-effectiveness of two math programs as moderated by pupil SES. *Educational Evaluation and Policy Analysis, 6*(1), 39–52.

Quint, J., Bloom, H. S., Black, A. R., Stephens, L., & Akey, T. M. (2005). *The challenge of scaling up educational reform: Findings and lessons from First Things First* (Final Report. MDRC). Retrieved from http://www.mdrc.org/sites/default/files/full_531.pdf

Quint, J., Zhu, P., Balu, R., Rappaport, S., & DeLaurentis, M. (with Alterman, E., Botles, C., & Pramik, E.). (2015). *Scaling up the Success for All model of school reform: Final report from the Investing in Innovation (i3) evaluation.* Retrieved from http://www.mdrc.org/sites/default/files/SFA_2015_FR.pdf

Ragosta, M., Holland, P. W., & Jamison, D. T. (1982).*Computer-assisted instruction and compensatory education: The ETS/LAUSD study* (Final Report, Project Report No. 19). Princeton, NJ: Education Testing Service.

Redcross, C., Deitch, V., & Farell, M. (2010). *Benefit-cost findings for three programs in the Employment Retention and Advancement (ERA) Project.* New York, NY: MDRC. Retrieved from www.mdrc.org

Revesz, R., & Livermore, M. (2008). *Retaking rationality: How cost-benefit analysis can better protect the environment and our health.* New York, NY: Oxford University Press.

Reynolds, A. J., Ou, S. R., & Topitzes, J. W. (2004). Paths of effects of early childhood intervention on educational attainment and delinquency: A confirmatory analysis of the Chicago Child-Parent Centers. *Child Development, 75*(5), 1299–1328.

Reynolds, A. J., Temple, J. A., Robertson, D. L., & Mann, E. A. (2002). Age 21 cost-benefit analysis of the Title I Chicago Child-Parent Centers. *Educational Evaluation and Policy Analysis, 24*(4), 267–303.

Reynolds, A. J., Temple, J. A., White, B. A., Ou, S. R., & Robertson, D. L. (2011). Age 26 cost-benefit analysis of the Child-Parent Center early education program. *Child Development, 82*(1), 379–404.

Rice, J. K. (1997). Cost analysis in education: Paradox and possibility. *Education Evaluation and Policy Analysis, 19*(4), 309–317.

Rodriguez, O., Bowden, B., Belfield, C., & Scott-Clayton, J. (2014). *Testing for remediation in community colleges: What does it cost?* (Paper No. 73). Community College Research Center, Teachers College, Columbia University. Retrieved from http://ccrc.tc.columbia.edu/publications/remedial-placement-testing-resources.html

Rohlfs, C., & Zilora, M. (2014). Estimating parents' valuations of class size reductions using attrition in the Tennessee STAR experiment. *The BE Journal of Economic Analysis & Policy, 14*(3), 755–790.

Rosenbaum, J. (2012). Degrees of health disparities: Health status disparities between young adults with high school diplomas, sub-baccalaureate degrees, and baccalaureate degrees. *Health Services and Outcomes Research Methodology, 12*(2–3), 156–168.

Ross, J. A. (2008). Cost-utility analysis in educational needs assessment. *Evaluation and Program Planning, 31,* 356–367.

Ross, J. A., Barkaoui, K., & Scott, G. (2007). Evaluations that consider the cost of educational programs: The contribution of high-quality studies. *American Journal of Evaluation, 28*(4), 477–492.

Rossi, P. H., Lipsey, M. W., & Freeman, H. E. (2004). *Evaluation: A systematic approach* (7th ed.). Thousand Oaks, CA: Sage.

Rouse, C. (2007). The earnings benefits from education. In C. R. Belfield & H. M. Levin (Eds.), *The price we pay: The social and economic costs to the nation of inadequate education.* Washington, DC: Brookings Institution.

Rumberger, R. W. (2011). *Dropping out: Why students drop out of high school and what can be done about it.* Cambridge, MA: Harvard University Press.

Salkeld, G., Davey, P., & Arnolda, G. (1995). A critical review of health-related economic evaluations in Australia: Implications for health policy. *Health Policy, 31*(2), 111–125.

Schlotter, M., Schwerdt, G., & Woessman, L. (2011). Econometric methods for causal evaluation of education policies and practices: A non-technical guide. *Education Economics, 19*(2), 109–137.

Schoeni, R. F., Dow, W. H., Miller, W. D., & Pamuk, E. R. (2011). The economic value of improving the health of disadvantaged Americans. *American Journal of Preventive Medicine, 40*(1), S67–S72.

Schwartz, A. E., Leardo, M. A., Aneja, S., & Elbel, B. (2016). Effect of a school-based water intervention on child body mass index and obesity. *JAMA Pediatrics, 170*(3), 220–226.

Schwartz, J. A. (2010). *52 experiments with regulatory review: The political and economic inputs into state rulemakings.* New York, NY: The Institute for Policy Integrity, New York University School of Law.

Scott-Clayton, J., Crosta, P., & Belfield, C. R. (2014). Improving the targeting of treatment: Evidence from college remediation. *Educational Evaluation and Policy Analysis, 36*(3), 371–394.

Scriven, M. (1974). Evaluation perspectives and procedures. In J. W. Popham (Ed.), *Evaluation in education: Current applications.* Berkeley, CA: McCutchan.

Shaffer, M. (2010). *Multiple account benefit-cost analysis: A practical guide for the systematic evaluation of project and policy alternatives.* Toronto, Canada: University of Toronto Press.

Shapiro, D., Dundar, A., Wakhungu, P. K., Yuan, X., Nathan, A., & Hwang, Y. (2015). *Completing college: A national view of student attainment rates—Fall 2009 cohort* (Signature Report No. 10). Herndon, VA: National Student Clearinghouse Research Center.

Simon, J. (2011). *A cost-effectiveness analysis of early literacy interventions* (Doctoral dissertation, Columbia University).

Sklad, M., Diekstra, R., De Ritter, M., Ben, J., & Gravestein, C. (2012). Effectiveness of school-based universal social, emotional, and behavioral programs: Do they enhance students' development in the area of skill, behavior, and adjustment? *Psychology in the Schools, 49,* 892–910.

Sloan, F. A., & Conover, C. J. (1995). The use of cost-effectiveness/cost-benefit analysis in actual decision making: Current status and prospects. In F. A. Sloan (Ed.), *Valuing health care: Costs, benefits and effectiveness of pharmaceuticals and other medical technologies* (pp. 207–232). Cambridge, England: Cambridge University Press.

Smith, M. L., & Glass, G. V. (1987). *Research and evaluation in education and the social sciences.* Englewood Cliffs, NJ: Prentice Hall.

Spooren, P., Brockx, B., & Mortelmans, D. (2013). On the validity of student evaluation of teaching: The state of the art. *Review of Educational Research, 83*(4), 598–642.

State Higher Education Executive Officers Association. (2009). *State Higher Education Finance, FY2008* [Monograph]. Retrieved June 12, 2011, from http://www.sheeo.org/finance/shef_fy08.pdf

Stephens, M., Jr., & Yang, D. Y. (2014). Compulsory education and the benefits of schooling. *American Economic Review, 104*(6), 1777–1792.

Stern, D., Dayton, C., Paik, I. W., & Weisberg, A. (1989). Benefits and costs of dropout prevention in a high school program combining academic and vocational education: Third-year results from replications of the California Peninsula Academies. *Education Evaluation and Policy Analysis, 11*(4), 405–416.

Stiglitz, J. (2012). *The price of inequality: How today's divided society endangers our future.* New York, NY: W. W. Norton.

Tamborini, C. R., Kim, C., & Sakamoto, A. (2015). Education and lifetime earnings in the United States. *Demography, 52,* 1382–1407.

Tatto, M. T., Nielsen, D., & Cummings, W. (1991). *Comparing the effects and costs of different approaches for educating primary school teachers: The case of Sri Lanka* (BRIDGES Research Report Series No. 10). Cambridge, MA: Harvard University Press.

Taylor, L., & Fowler, W. J. (2006). *A comparable wage approach to geographic cost adjustment.* Education Finance Statistical Center, United States Department of Education. Retrieved from https://nces.ed.gov/pubs2006/2006321.pdf

Temple, J. A., & Reynolds, A. J. (2015). Using benefit-cost analysis to scale up early childhood programs through pay-for-success financing. *Journal of Benefit-Cost Analysis, 6*(03), 628–653.

Trostel, P. A. (2010). The fiscal impacts of college attainment. *Research in Higher Education, 51*(3), 220–247.

Udvarhelyi, I. S., Colditz, G. A., Rai, A., & Epstein, A. M. (1992). Cost-effectiveness and cost-benefit analyses in the medical literature: Are methods being used correctly? *Annals of Internal Medicine, 116*, 238–244.

Valentine, J. C., Cooper, H., Patall, E. A., Tyson, D., & Robinson, J. C. (2010). A method for evaluating research syntheses: The quality, conclusions, and consensus of 12 syntheses of the effects of after-school programs. *Research Synthesis Methods, 1*(1), 20–38.

Vining, A., & Weimer, D. L. (2010). An assessment of important issues concerning the application of benefit-cost analysis to social policy. *Journal of Benefit-Cost Analysis, 1*(1), 1–40.

Viscusi, W. K. (2015). Pricing lives for corporate risk decisions. *Vanderbilt Law Review, 68*(4), 1117–1162.

Viscusi, W. K., & Aldy, J. E. (2003). The value of a statistical life: A critical review of market estimates throughout the world. *Journal of Risk and Uncertainty, 27*(1), 5–76.

von Winterfeldt, D., & Edwards, W. (1986). *Decision analysis and behavioral research.* Cambridge, England: Cambridge University Press.

Waldfogel, J., Garfinkel, I., & Kelly, B. (2007). Welfare and the costs of public assistance. In C. R. Belfield & H. M. Levin (Eds.), *The price we pay: Economic and social consequences of inadequate education* (pp. 160–174). Washington, DC: Brookings Institution.

Walsh, M. E., Madaus, G. F., Raczek, A. E., Dearing, E., Foley, C., An, C., . . . Beaton, A. (2014). A new model for student support in high-poverty urban elementary schools: Effects on elementary and middle school academic outcomes. *American Educational Research Journal, 51*(4), 704–737.

Wang, L. Y., Gutin, B., Barbeau, P., Moore, J. B., Hanes, J., Johnson, M. H., . . . Yin, Z. (2008). Cost-effectiveness of a school-based obesity prevention program. *Journal of School Health, 78*(12), 619–624.

Warner, J. T., & Pleeter, S. (2001). The personal discount rate: Evidence from military downsizing programs. *American Economic Review, 91*(1), 33–53.

Wasserstein, R. L., & Lazar, N. A. (2016). The ASA's statement on p-values: Context, process, and purpose. *The American Statistician.* doi:10.1080/0003 1305.2016.1154108

Webber, D. A. (2014). The lifetime earnings premia of different majors: Correcting for selection based on cognitive, noncognitive, and unobserved factors. *Labour Economics, 28*, 14–23.

Webster, T. J. (2001). A principal component analysis of the *US News & World Report* tier rankings of colleges and universities. *Economics of Education Review, 20*(3), 235–244.

Weimer, D. L. (2015). The thin reed: Accommodating weak evidence for critical parameters in cost-benefit analysis. *Risk Analysis, 35*(6), 1101–1113.

Weinstein, M. C., Torrance, G., & McGuire, A. (2009). QALYs: The basics. *Value in Health, 12*(s1), S5–S9.

Weiss, M. J., Bloom, H. S., & Brock, T. (2014). A conceptual framework for studying the sources of variation in program effects. *Journal of Policy Analysis and Management, 33,* 778–808.

Whitehead, S. J., & Ali, S. (2010). Health outcomes in economic evaluation: The QALY and utilities. *British Medical Bulletin, 96*(1), 5–21.

Wooldridge, J. M. (2000). *Introductory econometrics: A modern approach.* Florence, KY: Southwestern College Publishing.

World Bank. (1993). *World development report 1993: Investing in health.* New York, NY: Oxford University Press.

World Development Report. (2011). *Gender equality for all.* Washington, DC: World Bank.

Yeh, S. S. (2010). The cost-effectiveness of NBPTS teacher certification. *Evaluation Review, 34*(3), 220–241.

Zerbe, R. O., Davis, T. B., Garland, N., & Scott, T. (2013). Conclusion: Principles and standards for benefit-cost analysis. In S. Farrow & R. O. Zerbe (Eds.), *Principles and standards for benefit-cost analysis* (pp. 364–445). Northampton, MA: Edward Elgar Publishing.

Index